The Mind of Aristotle:
A Study in Philosophical Growth

PHOENIX

Journal of the Classical Association of Canada
Revue de la Société canadienne des études classiques
Supplementary Volume xxv
Tome supplémentaire xxv

JOHN M. RIST

The Mind of Aristotle: A Study in Philosophical Growth

UNIVERSITY OF TORONTO PRESS
Toronto Buffalo London

Toronto Buffalo London
Printed in Canada
ISBN 0-8020-2692-3

Printed on acid-free paper

Canadian Cataloguing in Publication Data

Rist, John M.
The mind of Aristotle

(Phoenix. Supplementary volume; 25 = Phoenix.
Tome supplémentaire, ISSN 0079-1784; 25)
Bibliography: p.
Includes index.
ISBN 0-8020-2692-3

1. Aristotle. I. Title. II. Series: Phoenix.
Supplementary volume (Toronto, Ont.); 25.

B485.R5 1989 185 C89-094260-9

This book has been published with
the help of a grant from
the Canadian Federation for the Humanities,
using funds provided by the Social Sciences and
Humanities Research Council of Canada.

IN MEMORIAM A.L. PECK
AND OTHER MASTERS

CONTENTS

PREFACE

In 1923 Werner Jaeger published in Berlin his *Aristoteles: Grundlegung einer Geschichte seiner Entwicklung*, of which an English translation by Richard Robinson (*Aristotle: Fundamentals of the History of His Development*) appeared from Oxford in 1934. Though not without forerunners, above all the article on Aristotle in the *Encyclopedia Britannica* of 1910, the book revolutionized Aristotelian studies, not because Jaeger's claims about the development of Aristotle's thought were demonstrated, but because he made it hard to avoid the problem that a man who lived among philosophers and as a philosopher for forty years, a man who justly earned the title 'Il maestro di color che sanno,' is most unlikely to have had the same thoughts at age seventeen as at age fifty-seven. But Jaeger's failure to establish the details of Aristotle's philosophical development, and the comparative failure of many others who followed him, have encouraged in more recent years something of a reaction and a return to a unitary notion of Aristotelian thought, to the older picture of Aristotle as a man born with a golden system in his mind. Or if not that, then the other extreme: we concentrate on the details of specific arguments in Aristotle almost to the exclusion of Jaeger's proper concern to understand these arguments in terms of the living and growing man. For the history of philosophy is not a mere study of formal 'doctrines' or of arguments taken in isolation; it is also an observation of the painful birth of new ideas and a reflection on the development of living philosophers trying to think.

In this book I have presented in chapter 1 what I believe to be an approximately correct account of the growth of Aristotle as a thinker. Necessarily this has involved me with certain questions of biography. I have written chapter 1, however, without notes, but with some indication of where fuller discussion can be found on subsequent pages. I attempt in the remaining chapters (which are to some extent cumulative, the later developing and expanding on the earlier) to justify by supporting philological and philosophical studies most of the claims I have made in chapter 1. But I wished to write an opening chapter as a narrative which might be read without constant reference to scholarly 'literature'; what I have written in chapter 1 could, I suppose, be reprinted separately or just torn out of a complete volume. I should add that in attempting a chronology of Aristotle's writings I have been concerned primarily to establish the dates of composition of the texts we have; naturally what I can say about when Aristotle began to think about certain topics is much more circumscribed, much more a matter for mere speculation. At the end of my discussions, I have provided a summary, in table form, of my chronological conclusions. Readers should refer to this table at appropriate points during their examination of the text.

Throughout this study there remains a tension between philological and philosophical questions. Philological questions demand attention when they help establish a chronological sequence of Aristotelian writings with a minimum of philosophical assumption about the 'obvious' replacement of 'worse' theories by those which are 'superior.' But the purpose of these philological enquiries is to understand the growth of Aristotle's thought, for if we understand the genesis of that thought, we can progress in our understanding of the nature it eventually assumes. But the reader will need patience: the claim of the book is that the philology helps us understand the philosophy, so that there will be a good deal of philological material which will require sorting out before the philosophical value of its implications can be assessed. I have tried, where possible, to keep the two types of material separate both between chapters and within chapters themselves. Hence, for example, chapter 4 will be a good deal less philosophical than chapter 9 or 14, and within chapter 8 philosophical questions will be almost, but not entirely, lacking in the first three sections. But although I have attempted to keep the two types of question apart, and not to allow the reader to lose sight of the fact that the final cause of the philology is the philosophy of Aristotle, I have probably not entirely succeeded.

At various times during the gestation of my thoughts about Aristotle, I had to make specific decisions about methodology: primarily whether to use stylometry, whether to take seriously the cross-references in Aristotle's texts as a guide to the dates of composition, and what to do about the ancient lists of Aristotle's works. In fact I had no difficulty in deciding against any further attempt at stylometric analysis, despite the recent use of such techniques by a number of scholars, especially by Anthony Kenny in his analysis of Aristotle's ethical writings. Apart from mere conservatism – for stylometry is still used comparatively little in Aristotelian studies – my reason was simple. Since it is very likely that the text of many Aristotelian works was comparatively fluid during many years of their author's life, but the stylistic details of this fluidity cannot be recovered, no 'base style' for any particular period of Aristotle's thought can be established. In this situation, the stylometrist cannot avoid the charge of treating as homogeneous chunks of Greek a set of sentences in our texts which may have assumed their present form over unspecifiable periods of time. Data of this kind are necessarily unsuitable for stylometric analysis.

I am aware, as I have noted, that in *The Aristotelian Ethics* (Oxford 1978) Kenny has taken the opposite tack, but I do not think that his conclusions about the *Ethics* (whether right or wrong) depend upon it. I have, in fact, assumed that Kenny has shown in the non-stylometric parts of his book that the 'common books' of the *Ethics* (*Eudemian Ethics* 4–6 = *Nicomachean Ethics* 5–7) were originally composed for the *Eudemian* version. I do not think that Kenny has shown by stylometry – partly for the reason I have mentioned – or by more philosophical means that the *Nicomachean Ethics* as a whole is earlier than the *Eudemian* version. I have, however, assumed, and not repeated, many of Kenny's arguments about the 'common books,' though I offer a certain amount of additional evidence which supports this part of Kenny's thesis.

The second methodological decision I had to make concerned possible use of the lists of Aristotle's writings which seem to derive from catalogues of holdings in the library of Ptolemaic Alexandria. In recent years these lists have been studied extensively, particularly by Düring and Moraux. But despite such excellent work, we still do not know enough about the library catalogues, or, except anecdotally, about how the books reached the library in the first place. The gap between the composition of the texts and their appearance in Alexandria is still too big to be bridged. Few reliable inferences can be made from the lists of texts in Alexandria to the books and notes Aristotle left when he died, let alone when he was actually writing. Hence, though I have occasionally alluded to possible editorial work in Alexandria (as well as by Theophrastus in Athens), I have not dared to make much use of the Alexandrian lists of Aristotelian writings.

There is a further and not unrelated consideration. I have assumed (as do most scholars) that Aristotle's early writings were intended for fairly wide circulation, and that the rest are 'lecture-notes,' or could have been used as such. The writings of this class are more or less homogeneous in the comparative unpretentiousness of their Greek, though some, such as much of the *De Anima*, are considerably polished, and others, like the *Historia Animalium*, are more like reference works. And although Aristotle may have *used* his notes differently in Assos and Macedon and Athens, he seems to have *organized* them in more or less similar and predictable ways. That may seem odd, but it is what the texts themselves show.

To my procedure as outlined above, however, two further objections may be made. First it may be said that the cross-references and the lecture-note style may indicate that what can be reconstructed on my assumptions is not the original order of composition, but the order of material presented by Aristotle in a series of lecture-courses given at Athens after 334 BC. This objection, of course, will only tell against my chronology in the case of those works which can be assumed to have existed, at least in substantial subsections, before 334. In particular, since these are the texts in which cross-references are the most significant, it will be aimed at my history of the *Topics*, the *Rhetoric*, and the biological writings. But in none of these cases have I relied on the cross-references alone; I have also argued from what seem to be clear developments in Aristotle's thought on specific topics (such as about *pneuma*, or the nature of pleasure, or *energeia*), or from references to Platonic texts which indicate not only what Aristotle might have done in reorganizing material after his return to Athens in 334, but what he must have done in originally composing it. Nor have I neglected Aristotle's own reports about his philosophical intentions or the concrete historical references in the texts which in some cases can provide a good deal of evidence about the composition of the extant versions of Aristotelian material. These versions are hereafter referred to as ours (e.g., our *Metaphysics*) to distinguish them from earlier drafts. Thus two further specific points should be made: I have not used cross-references to explain away possible lines of philosophical development (even the temptation to do this hardly ever arose), for what has impressed me has been the harmony between chronology dependent on cross-references and intelligible and supportable philosophical development. In the second case I *have* taken account, in my treatment of our *Physics*, *Politics*, and *Rhetoric*, for example, of possible revising activity by Aristotle in 334 and thereafter.

There is a second objection to my attempt to discover the origins of Aristotelian material, not unrelated to the problem of Aristotelian revisions of his earlier texts. We know from traditions which probably go back to Strabo, and are represented by further comments in Plutarch and Porphyry, that manuscripts of Aristotle were re-edited and arranged by subject-matter in the first century BC by Andronicus of Rhodes. Our own texts of Aristotle's 'lecture-notes' presumably derive from this recension. But what sort of 'arrangement' of material did Andronicus produce? If parallels can be drawn with the work of Thrasyllus in sorting the Platonic writings into sets of four, our present 'tetralogies,' or with the editorial work of Porphyry in sorting out the *Enneads* of Plotinus (of which Porphyry knew the chronological order) into a new sequence based on broad distinctions of subject-matter, we might expect that Andronicus too generally worked on the macro-level: that is, his main activity was not putting together bits and pieces and labelling them 'Topics' or 'De Anima,' though he may have done a little of that, but consisted primarily in sorting out logical writings (our so-called *Organon*) from writings to be generally labelled 'Physics' or 'Metaphysics.' Porphyry knew of Andronicus's work, and claimed to be following the same pattern in editing Plotinus, and his work was almost exclusively at the macro-level: that is, he put our *Ennead* 6.1 next to our *Ennead* 6.2. He did not, it seems, add to the contents of *Ennead* 6.1 by attaching it to other Plotinian material on the same subject, thus producing a bigger '*Ennead*. 6.1.'

If the methods of Andronicus were similar to those of Thrasyllus and Porphyry (or to the macro-organizer of the mass of material composed by the Stoic Chrysippus), then Andronicus is probably responsible for at most only small additions in our versions of complete works: he may, for example, have added the tenth book to the *Historia Animalium*, or he may have inserted material into the *Parva Naturalia*, perhaps failing to understand the nature of the small psychological works written by Aristotle *after* he had done the major studies of the topic which we find in our *De Anima*; but he is most unlikely to have arranged the *Nicomachean Ethics* or the *Politics* in the form they now have by a process of assembling odd bits of material on ethical or political subjects. The boldest suggestion I should therefore wish to make, though tentatively, about his work at the 'micro-level' would be that he is responsible for the present bizarre order of our books of the *Metaphysics*. I shall argue in the course of the present study that the order of our *Metaphysics* represents neither the original order of composition nor an intelligible order of exposition. Perhaps the hand of Andronicus may be detected in the production of parts of such an otherwise inexplicable sequence. But in general it seems that we can try our hand at reconstruction of Aristotelian chronology without being too disturbed by anxieties about the editorial activities of Andronicus.

If I may return at last to the cross-references in Aristotle's text, I can finally say, therefore, that I have followed the prima facie reasonable course of assuming in general that a reference in work B to work A shows that A was composed before B (or at least this part of B). It turns out that this working hypothesis makes developmental sense in almost every case, and it fails to generate conflicts with other evidence available for use in research into Aristotelian chronology. It is only on very rare occasions when I revert to the suggestion that a cross-reference is in fact a chronologically uninformative or even misleading addition, that is, that it is a later insertion in an earlier work.

In a very few cases, such as the *Metaphysics*, Aristotle's apparent working-methods may introduce yet another problem. Did he ever intend a book quite like our *Metaphysics*, that is, a complete whole? No a priori answer can be given, and Aristotle may indeed have composed some parts originally as independent studies. But if investigation seems to indicate that an Aristotelian work could indeed be used as a complete book (with beginning, middle, and end), then I assume such to have been at some point his clear intention. In some cases, furthermore, I try to indicate when that intention becomes clear. How the notes moved from the lecture-room, the seminar, or the private discussion to the more public domain is uncertain, but, as the tradition has it, in some cases at least the hand of Theophrastus may be detected.

The bibliography on Aristotle is vast, and of course I have not read it all. (Connoisseurs should turn, for starters, to *Aristotle: A Bibliography*, by J. Barnes, M. Schofield, and R. Sorabji [Study Aids volume 7, Sub-faculty of Philosophy, Oxford 1980].) The bibliography on Aristotle is also ongoing, but, as Aristotle says, one has to stop somewhere, and I have listed few items after 1986. Nor have I even been able to remember, and hence to cite all the studies to which I am indebted for individual pieces of interpretation, and, though I hope that I have not allowed major alternative readings to pass entirely unnoticed, I have often been more dogmatic than I should have wished. But the book is long enough as it is, and this is the chief reason why my treatment of certain matters comparatively peripheral to a study of Aristotle's overall philosophical development – such as *catharsis* and *hamartia* in the *Poetics* – may seem somewhat cavalier, even if correct.

Of the older writers on Aristotle I have learned most from Brentano, whose work in the history of philosophy, as in philosophy itself, still seems almost wilfully slighted in the English-speaking world. On questions of Aristotle's biography I have benefited especially from I. Düring's *Aristotle in the Ancient Biographical Tradition* (Göteborg 1957), E. Berti's *La filosofia del primo Aristotele* (Padova 1962) and J.P. Lynch's *Aristotle's School* (Berkeley/Los Angeles, London 1972). In such matters I have dissented – and always with hesitation – from only a few of the judgments of W.K.C. Guthrie in volume 6 of his *History of Greek Philosophy* (Cambridge 1981).

My general policy, in using abbreviations to refer to ancient authors, has been to follow the conventions employed in *LSJ* (Liddell, Scott, Jones, *Greek Lexicon*[9]). There are two major exceptions: for the *Nicomachean Ethics*, I have adapted the more current *NE* (rather than the *EN* of *LSJ*); and similarly I have preferred the normal *Met.* for *LSJ*'s *Metaph.* (for the *Metaphysics*).

This book has been published with the help of a grant from the Canadian Federation for the Humanities, using funds provided by the Social Sciences and Humanities Research Council of Canada. I am most grateful to Joan Bulger and Lorraine Ourom for helping it towards publication at various stages. Many scholars and friends have improved it by their scrutiny of what I had written, and in conversations. I should like in particular to thank the following, in addition to various learned and unknown readers: Anna Rist (whose queries about my judgments and impatience about my assumptions are always the most provocative and impelling), John Cleary, Lloyd Gerson, the late Joan Kung, Father Joseph Owens, Richard Sorabji, and Brad Inwood, with whom I have 'kicked the stuff around' endlessly to my (and I hope his) profit and enjoyment. The revised product was copy-edited by Kathy Gaca with meticulous care and attention both to clarity and consistency.

By inviting me to speak at a conference at the University of Sydney in 1984, Godfrey Tanner compelled me to take the problem of *pneuma* in Aristotle more seriously, and to remember that the late Dr A.L. Peck had assured me when I was an undergraduate that, if I could begin to understand *pneuma*, I should begin to understand Aristotle. This has proved to be correct in all sorts of unexpected ways, and in recognition of Arthur Peck's wisdom and kindness I should like to dedicate this book to his memory.

The Mind of Aristotle

1

Aristotle's Life and Works

Aristotle's father Nicomachus was a doctor, and his mother Phaestis belonged to an Asclepiad, or traditionally medical family. Nicomachus's family, though originating from the Ionian island of Andros, owned property in the small northern Greek town of Stagira where in 384 BC Aristotle was born. Phaestis had an ancestral property at Chalcis in Euboea. But Aristotle became an orphan at a fairly early age and was brought up by his guardian Proxenus of Atarneus, of whom we know little. Proxenus was later to marry Aristotle's younger sister Arimneste, and, to judge from his will, Aristotle's memories of him were happy. There was also a younger brother Arimnestus who died without issue, presumably as a young man.

Apparently Aristotle's earliest years were spent at Stagira and in Pella where his father was physician to King Amyntas II of Macedon. Nicomachus was probably dead by the time of Amyntas's own death and the ensuing struggles for the succession which ended with the ascendancy of the king's youngest son Philip. If Aristotle received any training at all in his father's medical skills, it can hardly have been extensive, and it may have been because of the turbulence in Macedonia that his guardian Proxenus sent him so early – while still a minor – to finish his education with Plato and his associates in the Academy at Athens. The date was 367, and Aristotle was seventeen years old. He left his friends behind in Macedonia, perhaps including the young Philip himself and others near the centre of power. With such men – sympathizers with Amyntas and his sons – Aristotle would retain his connections to the end of his life or theirs.

When Aristotle arrived in Athens in 367, Plato was away in Sicily, trying, at the instigation of his friend Dion, to convert Dionysius II, the new ruler of Syracuse, to philosophy. But there were others to attract Aristotle's attention: Eudoxus, the mathematician and astronomer from Cyzicus, perhaps the most illustrious of them, was to be recalled with great affection by Aristotle when writing the *Nicomachean Ethics* near the end of his life. Speusippus, Plato's nephew, was now forty years old. His ascetic and Pythagoreanizing tendencies and his strong emphasis on the importance of mathematics in philosophy were probably already visible. Then there was the more erratic Heraclides from Pontus, and a younger man from Aristotle's part of the world, Xenocrates of Chalcedon, twelve years older than Aristotle himself and seemingly his closest associate in these early days. None of these was a teacher of Plato's 'philosophy'; all were admirers of Plato and his moral goals: namely the education of a new generation of Greeks who should be neither oligarch nor democrat, but honest leaders of Greek society, men whose minds had been disciplined by their mathematical and philosophical studies to think and act in freedom from the demons of ambition and greed. With such ideals in their minds, the leading men of the Academy hoped to promote an education which, as Plato put it in the *Republic*, was to be both practical and theoretical.

Plato's great 'metaphysical' dialogues (*Symposium*, *Phaedo*, *Republic*, and *Phaedrus*) had been completed some years before. Their challenging call to a new education which was to replace both the traditional readings of the poets, especially Homer, and the slick Sophistic alternatives – as Plato believed them to be – had been heard and taken seriously. Now the thinkers of the school were both pursuing their own philosophical concerns and subjecting Plato's metaphysical claims to serious and detailed scrutiny. Their energies turned to the classification of the furniture of the world, for Plato himself in the *Phaedrus* had hailed 'collection and division' as the technique par excellence of the dialectician; and also to the resolution of problems about the mechanics of Plato's theory of Forms, such as Plato himself was soon to discuss in the *Parmenides*. Such questions would now often be called problems of logic, but as a formal discipline logic had not yet been recognized, and the boundaries between logic and metaphysics had not yet been drawn.

Shortly before Aristotle's arrival Plato had completed his dialogue *Theaetetus*, a discussion of the nature of knowledge (and its relation to perception) dedicated to the memory of a young mathematician and member of the Academy recently killed in battle at Corinth. In this dialogue, specifically if briefly, Plato directed his critical eye to the philosophy of the Eleatic school, to the followers of Parmenides and Zeno. He himself owed much to the Eleatics, whose radical rejection of the claims of the senses as guides to knowledge had greatly influenced the development of his own metaphysics. But already in *Republic* 5 he had come to think that Parmenides had gone too far, and by the 360s he was convinced that the

Eleatic version of distrust of the senses, their consequent emphasis on the mind as the sole source of our understanding of the world, together with their recognizably questionable logic, could not fail to make the visible cosmos unintelligible. Plato's associates, especially Eudoxus, were interested in the workings of the visible cosmos – and perhaps Parmenides' arguments themselves could now be *proven* fallacious. Yet at the same time, in the Academy, Plato's own metaphysics, particularly his account of the relation between the world of Forms and the 'particulars' around us, was under fire. Eudoxus tried to 'save' Plato's positions, but his solutions – involving an explanation of the presence of Forms in things as if they were *in re* universals – were unpalatable to Plato himself. As for Speusippus, he had probably never accepted Plato's 'special' theory of Forms, only his 'general' theory that there is 'somewhere' a supra-sensible world – which for Speusippus was the world of mathematical objects. 'Platonism' in mathematics, if not yet born, was at least conceived and developing (59 below). It was an exciting time for the young Aristotle to come to Athens, a time of greater intellectual ferment than there had been since the heady days of the foundation of the Academy itself.

Plato was away for about three years – and he was to make a further visit to Sicily a few years later. Soon after his return in 364 he composed (or perhaps completed) the notoriously difficult *Parmenides*, in which Aristotle himself is given a minor supporting role. Parmenides wants an interlocutor who will give him as little trouble as possible, and 'Aristotle' is chosen: a characteristic piece of Platonic irony at the expense of the young philosopher, whom, so it is said, Plato was to acclaim a great reader and the mind of the school. Interesting too is the fact that whatever its metaphysical implications, the *Parmenides* is among other things a 'logical' dialogue, and it seems that Aristotle may have started giving courses on logic during this period. But his interests were wider: he began to concern himself with rhetoric and the theory of literature, perhaps under the influence of a friend who was also a pupil of Isocrates, a certain Theodectes of Chios, himself known as an orator and writer of tragedy. He was to figure, almost alone of fourth-century tragedians, in Aristotle's *Poetics*, a work written many years later, perhaps at about the time of Theodectes' premature death (334 BC).

But the relations of the Academy with the 'school' of Isocrates were not free from storms. Plato disagreed radically with Isocrates' educational programme, and is decidedly ambiguous about him in the *Phaedrus*: he was a man whose potential was not matched by his performance, and as a successor of the fifth-century Sophists he overestimated the importance of rhetoric as an educational instrument. But Aristotle did not simply take over Plato's stance. His criticism of Isocrates, in his first published work, the

Gryllus of about 361, seems to have been mixed with a serious examination of the claims of rhetoric. Written in honour of Xenophon's son, who had been killed in 362 in a cavalry skirmish near Mantinea – or at least taking its starting-point from such an encomium – the *Gryllus* marks Aristotle's first appearance on a wider stage than that of the intramural debates of the Academy, and seems to have elicited a reply in four books from Cephisodorus, another pupil of Isocrates. We cannot be sure of what Aristotle said, or how polemically he said it – though allegations of mud-slinging have come down to us. It seems, however, that the *Gryllus* was at least influenced by Plato's *Gorgias* in its critical attitude to the practice of rhetoric, and since Isocrates himself was apparently one of the many to write encomia on Gryllus (allegedly to flatter his father Xenophon), Aristotle's piece was perhaps an attack on the master of the rhetoricians – or could be construed as such. Such would account too for Cephisodorus's reply.

The *Gryllus* was, it seems, a dialogue, influenced by the *Gorgias*, and in the Platonic style. Over the next few years the young Aristotle was to write a number of dialogues, which obtained the seal of approval of many, including Cicero, for the elegance of their style. (Cicero also tells us that Aristotle often figured as the main speaker.) Some bore the same name as writings of Plato; they included a *Symposium* (on whether the wise man should get drunk), a *Sophist*, a *Statesman*. Others, like the *Gryllus* itself and the more famous *Eudemus*, inspired by the death of a friend, discussed Platonic themes. In the case of the *Eudemus* the appropriate subject was the immortality of the soul as urged in Plato's *Phaedo*. Still other writings followed: *On the Poets*, *On Truth*, *On Wealth*, *On Nobility*, *On Justice*; perhaps, however, their content was less Platonic than might appear from their titles.

There is a tradition, probably apocryphal, but familiar to us from the Epicurean Philodemus, that Aristotle, who in this period taught rhetoric in the Academy, observed that it is shameful to be silent and let Isocrates speak. But whether the story is true or false, it should not lead us to suppose that Aristotle's attitude to Isocrates was purely critical and polemical. As we have seen, Aristotle developed a different attitude to literature from that of Plato, and this is already visible in his writing *On the Poets*, which, together with essays on *Political Matters* (perhaps also called *The Statesman*) and the early parts of the *Rhetoric* itself (1.5–15), was composed during the earlier parts of the 350s (135ff below). Plato, who wrote the *Sophist* about the year 359, still pursued his attacks on those charlatans who preyed on rich young men, deluding them by logical sleight-of-hand and seducing them with flattery. But for Aristotle a literary education, such as Isocrates offered, need not be worthless. Plato's strictures are valid, but an honest 'rhetoric' is possible; indeed Isocrates is right to think that such a rhetoric can be morally valuable.

Aristotle's *Rhetoric* itself reads at times like preliminary drafts of moral philosophy, and perhaps Aristotle already thought that poetry, though imitative, could purge the soul. If so, then literature and an 'ethical' rhetoric are part of the concern of the politician, and Aristotle's writings on all these subjects at this time are cast in an idealized or reformed Isocratean mould. However critical Aristotle may have been of the assumptions and behaviour of the rhetoricians in the *Gryllus*, rhetoric need not be sophistry in the bad sense, need not be merely profitable flattery. Presumably the rhetoric which Aristotle himself taught, and of which the early sections of *Rhetoric* I are a memorial, is to be seen as such a purified version (136–44 below). Plato too, we recall, was now thinking about similar questions. His *Sophist* (ca 359) was followed in about 353 – perhaps after Aristotle's 'Isocratean' efforts in ethics and politics – by the *Statesman*, with which Aristotle does not seem to have been familiar in his 'Isocratean' period. In that period, and notably in his analysis of political constitutions, Aristotle still looks back to the *Republic*.

But such debate about the practical side of the good life, spiced, as it was, by the view of Eudoxus that the pursuit and achievement of intellectual pleasure are the highest good, by no means comprised the sum of Aristotle's intellectual pursuits in the Academy. As we have seen, quite un-Isocratean concerns with making sense of complex problems of Platonic metaphysics, and sorting out their logical implications, were high on the Academic agenda. Aristotle is said to have taught logic in these years, and such teaching included, as a primary component, the detection of fallacies. But the chief material he put at the disposal of his hearers were *topoi* or common modes of argument: how in discussion we can use 'more and less', or 'contrariety', or forms of predication, or genus and species; and how such items can be used both constructively and destructively. The activity in which Aristotle says he is engaged when doing such work – the raw material of which is drawn not from truth but from current opinions – is later dignified with the name 'dialectic,' which Plato had reserved for metaphysics. What we have under the title of the *Topics* is a growing record of this part of Aristotle's life in the Academy, and the earliest sections (2–4, 7.1–2) date from the mid-350s. The process of compilation of 'our' *Topics* was long and can only be roughly charted. If Aristotle began collecting the material and using it in courses as early as, say, 353, he put the finishing touches to it as much as a dozen years later (ch. 4 below, 76–82).

Yet the existence of parts of the *Topics* in the 350s shows us something important about Aristotle's mentality. Unlike Plato's 'logical' writing, the *Topics* is rather formal. Aristotle is classifying methods of argument, and using common opinion as the raw material with which to work. The search for classification, as we have seen, had been a concern of the Academy for some years, but emphasis on the methodology, on the forms of thinking, is less well attested. Certainly Aristotle did not work in a vacuum. What he talked about, when he lectured on *topoi*, would have been known to his Academic colleagues, and discussed by them. His own writing provides evidence that he was perhaps talking especially to Xenocrates, his rather older contemporary from the north. Nevertheless, in his concern with method and with the forms of argument, we can detect something of Aristotle's own that is beginning to surface. Such special interests may explain why as far back as the *Parmenides* (ca 364), Plato had assigned Aristotle a role in a text which must be viewed in part at least as a training in mental gymnastics.

Concern with method and discussion of the modes of thinking are bound to involve the introduction of specialized terminology. One of Aristotle's major contributions to western thought has been the construction of a philosophical language which is largely still in circulation, and we can see this process beginning in the early parts of the *Topics*. 'Genus,' 'species', and 'accident' are terms in common use, but it would be mistaken to assume that Aristotle already deployed the whole range of technical vocabulary to be found in the *Metaphysics*, *Nicomachean Ethics*, or *De Anima*. Aristotle's technical terminology developed, and some of it may be due not to Aristotle himself but to his fellow Academics. Answers to such questions are unattainable, but that the terms grew, that they did not spring forth fully grown as from the head of Zeus, is clear in the case of one of the most famous: *energeia*, meaning 'actuality' in late Aristotelian writings, does not have this sense in earlier days. Originally its etymological connection with notions of action, of movement, is very apparent; it means 'activity' (ch. 6 below).

Aristotle's family background was 'Ionian,' and 'Ionian' in spirit are some of his early works. In pre-Socratic times we can isolate as separate questions: (1) What is there (in the world)? and (2) Why is there what there is? Clearly in a logical sense (1) is prior: if we do not know what there is, we can hardly explain its origins. Now one of the vicious features of the Sophistic movement, at least according to Plato, was that the Sophists took advantage of unclarified popular speech; and from logically unanalysed speech false distinctions could be read into the world. It might be supposed, for example, that human beings can be divided into Greeks and barbarians, but this is mistaken, for barbarians are merely non-Greeks. To say that A is a barbarian is to say nothing positive about him. Such problems arise for classifiers, and the Academy encouraged classifiers. It encouraged Aristotle to classify too, and we can see him classifying and organizing modes of argument in the early books of the *Topics*. But the primary subject of classification is the world itself; and the primary question is: 'What is really there?' Sharp distinctions between logic and metaphysics had not yet been drawn, perhaps deliberately so, in Platonic writings, even in a text like the *Sophist*. But there were already those in the Academy who were worrying about whether 'logical' distinctions might have metaphysical implications. If Goodness is a Form, a substance, what about Earth or Fire? Is Goodness the same kind of thing as Horse or Man? Or, putting the question somewhat differently, is 'X is a man' the same kind of proposition as 'X is good'? Or are we to say, as Aristotle says in the *Categories*, that a man (e.g., Socrates) is a substance while goodness is a quality? Declining an explicit rejection of Plato's metaphysics, but presenting a theory of the priority of individual substances which depends on an ontological devaluation of universals – since they indicate kinds, not particulars – Aristotle proceeds to compile lists of substances, lists of qualities, and lists of various other sorts of subjects too. In so doing, he is beginning to sort out the world and to arrange it, to some extent, in order of importance. Substances are more important than anything else, but qualities, quantities, and the rest are necessarily separate and distinct in kind: no quality can ever be a quantity. Thus we may say that in the *Categories* (2–9) Aristotle was trying to compile what may be identified as a kind of descriptive metaphysics, an intelligible, pre-scientific guide to the kinds of contents the universe possesses.

But it is a static account that Aristotle gives us in the *Categories*, and in non-polemical terms. Although his arguments that particulars are in fact primary substances imply criticism, indeed rejection, of the theory of Forms, there is no direct attack on Plato, Platonic Forms, or Platonism. Rather, substance-universals are still dignified as secondary *substances*. And what Aristotle offers in the *Categories* is in no sense a complete metaphysical statement. There is nothing about final or efficient causes, nothing about matter, nothing about potentiality and actuality, nothing explicit about accidents.

So while saying very unplatonic things about substance, the *Categories* neither indicates whether Aristotle had ever subscribed to a theory of Forms, nor explicitly urges its rejection. Aristotle's notion of secondary substance has Platonic overtones, but in his concern with words and their 'combinations' ('man,' 'runs,' 'man runs,' etc.) he reflects some of the more technical questions of Plato's *Sophist*, completed not long before, rather than those of the *Parmenides*: the 'Third Man' argument and the open warfare about transcendent realities. In fact there is nothing in the available evidence to suggest that Aristotle had ever accepted any kind of Platonic theory of Forms, only that he was concerned about the problems Plato had revealed about the proper status of 'secondary substances.'

It is entirely comprehensible that, even though by 353 Aristotle was convinced that the theory of Forms is defective, he would not yet say so directly. As the *Gryllus* indicated – and as his continuing presence in the Academy confirms – Aristotle was still deeply respectful of Plato, and, we may assume, an assiduous reader of his dialogues. As later texts, such as the *De Generatione et Corruptione*, make clear, the *Phaedo* and the views of 'Socrates in the *Phaedo*' particularly impressed him; and in 354, when he heard that his friend Eudemus of Cyprus had been killed fighting for justice at Syracuse, it was to the *Phaedo* that Aristotle turned for inspiration. A fair number of fragments of the *Eudemus* (ca 353) survive, and they show us an Aristotle who, though no advocate of the theory of Forms, is certainly a believer in the substantiality of the soul, in its pre-existence, and in its coming separation from the body. Platonic too is the inclusion of a myth, that of Midas and Silenus; and, like parts of the *Phaedo* itself, the *Eudemus* argued for personal survival, refuting in passing alternative theories of the nature of the soul, such as that which held it to be an attunement (or harmony) of bodily phenomena. Aristotle's objection to epiphenomenalist theories of the soul was to outlast his view of the soul as a separate substance, recurring even in the late *De Anima*; but it appears that, as we might expect from the author of the early parts of the *Topics* and of the *Categories*, his arguments in the *Eudemus* were already presented more systematically than Plato's.

But Aristotle's mind was soon recalled to an earlier battle. In the *Antidosis*, also published in about 353, Isocrates set out a further challenge to the Academy as an educational institution. Aristotle produced a reply that was Isocratean in form but Platonic in content. The *Protrepticus*, or *Exhortation to Philosophy*, a work of vast influence in its time and, especially via its use in Cicero's *Hortensius*, right down to late antiquity, is formally in the Isocratean or even Sophistic mode (48ff below). Addressed as an open letter to Themison, a mini-prince in Cyprus, it aimed to encourage those seeking understanding to do it the Academic way. Aristotle's personal love of truth, his excitement at contemplating the physical world and trying to understand it, appear strongly in the substantial fragments which have come down to us. There is little metaphysics in the *Protrepticus*; what is advocated is a loving inspection of the natural universe: Pythagoras and Anaxagoras are held up as models, as princes of human speculation. Yet in addition to its *lack* of metaphysics the work exhibits certain ultra-Platonic, even therefore unplatonic, characteristics. Like the *Eudemus* it presents a radical dualism of soul and body, and urges the cultivation of the soul (167–70 below). But that cultivation is by study, by 'settling down' in the study to think about the world, an activity which may seem uninviting to the layman but which those who have experienced it know to be the most pleasurable, the most satisfying, activity available to man. The spirit of Eudoxus's intellectual hedonism is unmistakable. Aristotle seems to be advising the Platonic philosopher not to go back into the Cave, or at least to realize that the pleaures of staying outside in the world of contemplation and science are unbeatable. It is a tone which Plato himself at times seems to wish to adopt, but eventually always refuses to adopt. Yet for Aristotle in the *Protrepticus* man is constructed by God to contemplate and understand nature. Philosophy, viewed as the contemplation of nature, is the highest life; it can be pursued regardless of one's place of residence. Metics, therefore, like Aristotle in Athens, can pursue it as well as citizens, and it is quite free of that sense of servile labour which deadens the soul. In pursuing such philosophy man seeks and best achieves the Platonic goal of attaining likeness to God.

The *Protrepticus* was always one of Aristotle's favourite works. It came back to his mind when he wrote an introduction to his *Metaphysics*, and when he offered a description of happiness at the end of the *Nicomachean Ethics*. But soon after its composition a bomb exploded before the young philosopher in the Academy, detonated by Plato himself: in about 352 Plato produced his *Timaeus*, a work which defied Eleatic strictures on general explanations of nature, which completed one part of the anti-Eleatic project Plato had been engaged on in the *Parmenides* and *Sophist*, and which was bound to strike Aristotle, the admirer of natural science, as of immense importance. Soon afterwards, in a further burst of energy, Plato tossed the *Philebus* into the renewed debate about the relation of pleasure, thought, and happiness which Eudoxus had stirred up; and at about the same time twelve books of *Laws* began to appear, representing a new and, as Aristotle recognized, significant development in Plato's ethical and political thinking. Some time during these years, perhaps in response to 'popular demand' among his colleagues in the Academy, Plato also delivered the famous lecture *On the Good*, which, like the *Timaeus* to which it is related, aroused immense interest. Some of its subject-matter also underlies the *Philebus*, and arguments about its worth, or even its intelligibility, persisted for decades. Almost the only point on which our sources agree about the lecture is that all the leading members of the Academy heard it.

Book 5 of the *Topics* marks the beginning of Aristotle's lifelong interest in the *Timaeus* (80f below). Already disputes were arising as to how Plato should be understood. Did he mean to be taken literally in speaking of the beginning of the world, as Aristotle himself believed, or was he speaking in metaphor, as was the view of his 'orthodox' or 'conservative' defender Xenocrates? What is the relation between a transcendent God (or Demiurge) and the Forms (above all the Form of the Good)? Does God think, and if so what about? What else could he do? In what sense does the *Timaeus* offer an adequate account of matter? Such questions, the roots of Aristotle's own theory of four 'causes' in nature, dominated the Academy in the last years of Plato's life. Those, like Speusippus, who rejected Plato's Forms, were drawn into the debate. Cosmology had become important; new theories of the origins of the universe, diverse but influenced by Plato's, began to grow. But amid the renewed intellectual excitement, the world of politics was becoming dangerous and peculiarly threatening to Aristotle himself.

Aristotle's devotion to study seems to have kept him clear of personal involvement in the affairs of Sicily with which Plato, and his nephew Speusippus, the most senior member of the school, were much concerned. Those affairs, from an Academic point of view, had gone badly. Plato's friend Dion, failing to be reconciled with his kinsman Dionysius II despite Plato's intervention, had resorted to force, and with the help of friends in the Academy had recruited mercenaries, set off for Sicily, and seized Syracuse. But his success did not last and he was eventually murdered, by Callippus, another member of the Academy. From Sicilian politics, though it doubtless provided much debate in the School, Aristotle could stand aloof, as he could from various other overtly political schemes pursued by his friends and associates; but the growing power and activity of the Macedonian king Philip was another question. Philip, we recall, was probably known to Aristotle since boyhood, as were many of his associates in the Macedonian ruling class. In the later 350s, after the decline of Thebes, relations between Athens and Macedon steadily worsened. The crisis came in 348, when Philip besieged Olynthus, chief city of the Chalcidian confederacy. In Athens Demosthenes urged, and eventually secured, the sending of troops, but they arrived too late. Olynthus fell, and most of the neighbouring towns submitted to Philip; Stagira, Aristotle's birthplace, had already resisted and been destroyed. At about this time, in the year 347 when hostility to friends or supposed friends of Macedon was strong in Athens, Plato died.

It is uncertain whether Aristotle left Athens before or after Plato's death. Ancient evidence is divided, and it cannot be denied that as a man known to have important connections with Macedon – though less notorious in this regard than he was to become later – Aristotle would have had little reason to risk staying in Athens once Plato himself was dead. It is possible that he left for political reasons before Plato died, but more likely that, with Plato gone, no claim of loyalty remained to keep him in Athens at considerable personal risk. Speusippus, son of Plato's sister Potone, succeeded to the leadership of the school. His kinship with Plato and, especially at this time, his Athenian citizenship – not to speak of his seniority in age to Aristotle, or even Xenocrates – made him the obvious choice. His philosophical differences with Aristotle were perhaps already substantial, but there is no reason to think that this had anything to do with Aristotle's departure.

Nor, of course, did Aristotle break off relations with the Academy. On the invitation of Hermeias of Atarneus, a 'prince' from the Troad and former visitor to the Academy, he moved to the town of Assos, in Hermeias's territory, in the company of his fellow northerner Xenocrates. It was an 'outpost' of the Academy to which they journeyed, for in Assos, under the patronage of Hermeias, a small philosophical circle had assembled around two local notables (and former members of the School in Athens), Erastus and Coriscus. Hermeias himself, a Greek from Bithynia, seems to have been a self-made man (enemies said that he was a castrated ex-slave) who rose to power under the banker Eubulus and succeeded him as 'tyrant' or 'boss' of Atarneus. His earlier days were probably marked by savagery and crime ('some by poison, others ...'), though also by a certain success, for though nominally subject to the king of Persia, Hermeias extended his territory in the Troad to include various of the neighbouring cities, including Assos and Scepsis. By the time of Aristotle's arrival he had probably become aware of the way the political wind was blowing, and was beginning to think of shifting his allegiance from Persia to Macedon, which he eventually did in the form of a military pact. At some stage he made a deal with Philip to allow the Macedonians to use his territory as a bridgehead for their assault on the Great King.

But Hermeias, as we have seen, had taken an interest in philosophy, and even hostile testimony allows that under the influence of Erastus and Coriscus he had modified many of the excesses of his former government and acquired popularity and further territory by so doing. In the circumstances it is not difficult to see why Aristotle and Xenocrates accepted his invitation to join the philosophers at Assos. It should not be deduced from this acceptance, of course, that members of the Academy were uniformly pro-Macedonian. Indeed one of them, a certain Cleon, defended Byzantium stubbornly against Philip in 340, and possibly such political rifts within the Academy provided additional incentive for Aristotle to leave when he did. At Assos he could settle down.

The years which Aristotle spent in Asia Minor and on the neighbouring island of Lesbos were of great importance in his intellectual development. New philosophical friendships were made which were to last a lifetime. Coriscus is frequently mentioned in Aristotle's writings and his son Neleus followed in his father's footsteps, eventually inheriting Aristotle's library. Doubtless at this time too Aristotle began his association with Theophrastus, from Eresos on Lesbos, who was to be his closest philosophical collaborator and eventual successor as head of the school in Athens. What is more,

Aristotle, who became an intimate friend of Hermeias, was later to marry Pythias, a relation of the 'tyrant' himself, probably his sister, though some sources suggest she was his niece (and adopted daughter). Aristotle spent about three years at Assos, and then crossed the narrow strip of water to Lesbos where he remained for something more than a further year.

As we have seen, Aristotle seems never to have accepted Plato's theory of transcendent Forms, and already in Athens he had published theories quite incompatible with it. His doubts about Plato's progress as a philosopher were strengthened by the appearance of the *Timaeus*, which, while retaining transcendent Forms, would add a transcendent God and a strange account of matter and the construction of the physical universe (191–207 below). Aristotle's own tendencies in physics were, as we have seen, in the opposite direction and, as he progressed in years, he naturally grew in confidence too. At some point near the time of Plato's death, now writing as his own philosophical master, he offered extended criticisms of Platonic 'transcendence,' as represented both by the theory of Forms and by the notion of a Demiurge. The works in which this criticism was expressed – and which mark Aristotle's full emergence as a philosopher in his own right – were two books *On Ideas*, a book *On the Good*, and three books *On Philosophy* (38–46 below). Whether they appeared before or after Aristotle left Athens we cannot tell, and it matters little, since even if they were published after Aristotle had left, the subject-matter would have been familiar to his philosophical colleagues. Certainly they were written for the Academy or for people associated with the Academy, but Aristotle was later to think of them as more popular compositions when compared with his technical lecture-notes. Unfortunately they survive only in fragments, but our knowledge of them, though incomplete, is fairly extensive. *On Ideas* and *On the Good* present what we may call specifically Aristotelian themes (such as the distinction already found in the *Categories*, between being a 'this' [i.e., a particular] and being a 'such' [i.e., a member of a kind]), and they probably enable us to locate Aristotle's original reason for proposing the primacy of concrete individuals in his understanding of the 'Third Man' argument against Platonic Forms. But the main *purpose* of these new treatises seems to be critical. Those criticized are Plato and Eudoxus; both the 'original' theory of Forms and Plato's later speculation about the derivation of beings from the One and the Dyad are considered. There is apparently little attention given to personal contributions by Speusippus or Xenocrates – which suggests at least that both works are to be dated around the last years of Plato's life, before Aristotle felt it particularly necessary to reject the views of Speusippus, and before his philosophical goal had shifted from conceptual criticism of Plato and the Academy to more independent development of new theories of his own, especially about the world of nature. Interestingly enough, many of the criticisms in *On Ideas*, on the participation of particulars in Forms, on the numbers of Forms, and on the reification of objects of thought, had already been considered by Plato himself in the *Parmenides*. Perhaps Plato's placing of Aristotle in that dialogue had been prophetic; he was to come back to some of the criticisms yet again in *Metaphysics* A, M, and N.

We cannot know for sure whether these texts were first made available to a wider audience at Athens or in Assos. Were Plato's Sixth Letter certainly genuine, it would suggest that Athens was the more likely. We may only conclude that, wherever the critical books first appeared, Aristotle and Xenocrates were now deeply engrossed in debate over some of the most basic structures of Platonic metaphysics, and deeply divided. Whether Aristotle had yet attacked Plato's theory of the soul as well as his theory of Forms is not certain, but it is unlikely.

On Philosophy is in many ways a more ambitious work than *On Ideas* or *On the Good*. It is much more than a critique of Plato; it is a statement of the present condition of philosophy, with some historical material dealing with both Greek and non-Greek thought, including that of Zoroaster. *On Philosophy* also contains a certain amount of physics: it discusses final and efficient causes, denies a transcendent God, and identifies the highest principle of the cosmos with an immanent World-Mind. The world and its immanent God are eternal, but the nature of the eternal God is to be a self-moving cause of the movement of the heavens, as Plato had taught in the *Laws*. Also following the *Laws*, Aristotle argues for star-souls which choose their own movements. What the *Protrepticus* has already foreshadowed, the treatise *On Philosophy* declares openly: nature (its mind and body) is the highest subject of human contemplation and study. The stage is set by *On Philosophy* for Aristotle's ambitious programme to map out and scrutinize the world around him. But while the *Protrepticus* and the *Eudemus* are still governed very largely by admiration for the other-worldly spirit of Plato's *Phaedo*, *On Philosophy* is inspired by detailed scrutiny of Plato's attempt to expound nature in the *Timaeus*. For the time being, at least, not only has 'metaphysics' been put aside, but the Platonic insistence on the priority of ethics over physics has receded too. Final causes, as in the *Phaedo*, are still important, but it is final causes *in nature* which are Aristotle's primary concern. In Plato's *Republic* men in the Cave fail to grasp the Form of the Good which lies outside the physical cosmos; in Aristotle's *On Philosophy* they are deluded into false beliefs about the nature of *this* world and its divine but immanent causes.

During his years at Assos Aristotle began two major projects. The first, which was probably in two parts called *On the First Principles of Nature* and *On All Natural Motions* (or *On Motion*), led eventually to the formation of books 2–7 of our *Physics* (though perhaps book 7 was written first). Aristotle's aim was to give an account of the general principles of nature, to expound the causes and to introduce notions of potentiality and actuality, as well as theories of time, space, void, infinity, and motion; and to refute, where necessary, alternative explanations. Simultaneously he began the collection of material for a study of the animal kingdom, in particular of the differences between different sorts of animals. This was a huge project which was soon to produce at least the largest sections of *Historia Animalium* 1–4, *De Respiratione, De Incessu Animalium,* and *Historia Animalium* 5–7 (212–18 below). Such undertakings will have taken years to complete, and the work on animals involved an enormous labour of collecting evidence, from books, from talk with country people, and from observation. A good deal of this was achieved in Assos, on Lesbos, and in Macedonia. The work was not completed until 339, and even then only approximately in the case of the *Historia Animalium*; zoological additions were apparently made to the 'file' – and not only by Aristotle – for many more years. It is important to emphasize that in addition to observing phenomena, and talking about them, Aristotle also read about them – Plato had apparently already nicknamed him 'the reader' – and, oddly as it seems to us, he seems to have made little distinction between phenomena he read of in books and phenomena he observed himself (or with the direct help of friends like Theophrastus). Hence in his biological writings we find a curious mixture of acute and detailed observation, together with errors of fact which we might suppose he could easily have checked and found inadequate.

All the work on animals, including the psychology, will from Aristotle's point of view have been regarded as work in 'physics,' for at this time he probably subscribed to the thesis, current in the Academy and attributed to Xenocrates, that all 'science' could be distinguished as physics, ethics, or logic. For many years after the anti-Platonic *On Ideas* Aristotle's entire concentration of effort was thus put into 'physics.' Not only did he work on what was to become *Physics* 2–7 and the *Historia Animalium*, but he soon set about two more specialized or 'applied' writings, the *De Caelo* and *De Generatione et Corruptione*. The theses of these books in their original form were less radical than they are in the form in which they have come down to us; as yet they taught no theory of a Prime Unmoved Mover of the universe, relying still on the self-moving immanent God of *On Philosophy*, which had been written not many years earlier. But *De Caelo* also offered an important new proposal, that of the *aether* or fifth element of the world above the level of the moon, distinct from the earth, water, air, and fire of our sublunary universe, with a natural circular movement, different from the upward and downward movements of the other four; and especially in the *De Generatione et Corruptione* Aristotle developed a new account of 'prime matter.' Thus he could both resolve the ambiguities and paradoxes of Plato's 'Receptacle' or quasi-material cause, and improve on the cosmology of Democritus who, he believed, had failed in his account of the separating and combining of atoms to give an adequate explanation of qualitative change and of the difference (if viewed in the terms of the *Categories*) between substance and accident. Doubtless Aristotle was working on the '*Physics*' and the *De Caelo* simultaneously, and doubtless his material was reworked many times throughout his career, so that sometimes passages of the *De Caelo* will appear ignorant of more sophisticated arguments in the *Physics* as we have it; but by and large it can be said that Aristotle planned to give an account of the general principles of nature, of the causes of motion and rest, in what was to be *Physics* 2–7, before he moved on to the more specific areas of the supralunary (*De Caelo*) and sublunary (*De Generatione et Corruptione*). At any rate it is sensible to suggest that the whole project was thus originally conceived. It was completed by 339, when a further stage (three books of *Meteorologica*) was added.

Throughout the whole of these physical writings we can see Aristotle striving for a unity in the cosmos, for general explanations of all 'phenomena,' and for basic physical substances which are to 'underlie' (as 'matter') or 'overlie' (as God – the final or efficient cause). A search has begun not only for a single concept of a 'divine' final cause, but for a single physical substance which shall help account for the phenomena of the physical universe, both – in our terminology – animate and inanimate. The identification of *aether* in the *De Caelo* is an important step in that process, and indications are beginning to appear that there may be something analogous in the sublunary world (127–34 below).

In 343 Aristotle moved again, with his works in physics still incomplete. Philip of Macedon, with whom he had been acquainted since boyhood, with whom Hermeias was now in negotiation for a military pact, invited him to return to Macedon to act as tutor to his son and heir Alexander. It was an obvious choice. Aristotle was a known sympathizer with the king, and his father had been the personal physician to Philip's father Amyntas. His fame among philosophers was growing; Plato had already recognized it, and doubtless Hermeias added an enthusiastic report. Aristotle, as a good member of the Academy, was interested in the education of rulers. He had already addressed his *Protrepticus* to a prince in Cyprus, and lived with and admired a prince in Asia Minor. Now he had a different task – to influence a prince still in his teens – and he seems to have taken up the offer with alacrity. He moved to Macedonia, probably with Theophrastus and other friends, and maintained a close association with Alexander for some three years, until 340, when Alexander was appointed regent during his father's campaign against Byzantium. After that, contact with the prince became less and less frequent as royal duties increased, and Alexander succeeded to the throne in 336 when his father was assassinated. Some time during these years Aristotle secured the restoration of his home city of Stagira.

Aristotle's position as tutor did not stop him from pursuing his researches. The physical treatises begun at Assos and continued in Lesbos reached completion; and soon after arriving in Macedon Aristotle began the second stage of what was increasingly to look like a project to write authoritatively on all the major areas of 'science'. Physics was well under way; logic came next, and Aristotle began to enlarge the *Topics*, adding an introductory book 1 (in what was to become a regular way of expanding on existing texts) and carrying the series of *Topics* through to 8.1, with a final book on the refutation of sophistries (*Sophistici Elenchi* 3–34). The new material is much more sophisticated than some of the earlier sections of the *Topics*, containing in book 1 an elaborate introduction to definitions, a thesis about predicables, further work on categories, as well as a discussion of different kinds of propositions, while in book 6 we find further development of the peculiarly Aristotelian concept of activity.

Aristotle, as he says himself at the end of the *Sophistici Elenchi* (= *Topics* 9), was very proud of his achievement. He was sure that it had not been done before. Still further material was to be added to the *Topics* a year or two later: a new section was inserted, namely our *Topics* 8.2–14 and *SE* 1–2. But the *Topics* themselves pale into insignificance beside the major 'logical' constructions of this period: the completion of two books of *Prior Analytics* and two of *Posterior Analytics* (82f below). They represent, without a doubt, the accumulation of many years of thought – sparked in part by reflections on a famous paradox in Plato's *Meno* about the possibility of knowledge – and they are not fully coherent internally. They are concerned with inductive and deductive reasoning and include for the first time an almost complete account of the three-term syllogism as normally taught in our logic textbooks. But Aristotle has not sorted out the relation of syllogistic reasoning to the broader area of deductive inference in general; hence the unevenness of parts of the *Analytics*. What he has done, however, in his discussions of understanding, definition, and demonstration in the *Posterior Analytics*, is to distinguish the modes of reasoning appropriate for discovering new facts (largely inductive) from those which are particularly valuable for giving an exposition of truths already available (largely deductive). What is more, the *Posterior Analytics* lays the foundations, though Aristotle does not yet complete the structure, for what was to become a new sort of metaphysics or theory of substance. Unlike the cautious Aristotle of the early sections of the *Categories*, the Aristotle of the *Analytics*, as we should expect from his work in the *Physics* and the *De Caelo*, is no longer merely concerned with identification of what there is in the world, but primarily with what can be determined from the furniture of the world about why there is what there is. Description in terms of genus and species and differentia may be existence-blind, for goat-stags may be a species for the logician. But goat-stags do not have a realized nature which can be understood in terms of the 'causes': material, formal, efficient, and above all final. But Aristotle is not prepared to talk about 'first philosophy' (metaphysics) in the *Analytics*. On the contrary he assumes that the only possible such 'philosophy' would have to deal in Platonic Forms or other such suprasensible realities proposed as prior to particulars by the Academy, and still stoutly defended there by Xenocrates. Since such 'beings' are fantasy, as the *Analytics* bluntly puts it, there would still seem to be no future, as Aristotle saw it, for metaphysical theories of substance.

Such reflections – perhaps unintelligible to the young Alexander – were interrupted, or shortly followed, by tragic news from Asia Minor. Hermeias, Aristotle's former patron whose sister he was soon to marry, was entrapped by Mentor, an officer in the employment of the Persian king, shipped off to Susa, tortured in the hope that he would reveal details of his negotiations with Philip, and eventually crucified. Aristotle was deeply affected by the fate of a man who had died saying, as the story ran, that they should tell his comrades and friends that he had done nothing weak or unworthy of philosophy. In Athens Demosthenes exhibited unconcealed delight at the fall of Hermeias, gloating over what he hoped to be a serious setback for the plans of Philip. Aristotle, however, went to great lengths to honour Hermeias's memory: he erected a memorial in his honour at Delphi, with an inscription denouncing the godless treachery of the Persian king, and wrote an ode, probably to be sung at a Delphic memorial service, in which Hermeias is glorified as a hero who has run the straight race of virtue like Achilles and Ajax: his memory will be immortalized by the Muses, who honour his enduring friendship and devotion to Zeus the Hospitable. It was not a poem to win friends among the Greek enemies of Macedon, and Aristotle's detractors kept it in mind for future use – along with the memorial service. Aristotle's nephew Callisthenes of Olynthus composed a second encomium.

At about this time (if not perhaps even earlier) Aristotle married Pythias, Hermeias's sister, and a daughter Pythias was born soon after; she was almost of marriageable age (as Aristotle would have understood that age) when he wrote his will. Some time later, perhaps after other unrecorded infants who did not survive, there was born a son Nicomachus (named for Aristotle's father) who was still a child at the time of Aristotle's death. Aristotle's wife, however, probably died in Athens after his return there in 334. She too was honoured, and again his enemies remembered it. He had sacrificed in her honour, it was said, as the Athenians do to Demeter.

After completing the *Analytics* and rewriting the *Topics*, and with the *Meteorologica* bringing to an end the series of writings about 'physics' which he had begun in Assos, Aristotle would without doubt have turned his mind to the third great area of 'science,' that of ethics. The death of Hermeias can only have encouraged such an interest, and Aristotle, who had hardly written on the matter since the days of the *Eudemus* and the early parts of the *Rhetoric* more than fifteen years before, embarked on a new project which was to produce, during his remaining years in Macedonia, eight books of *Eudemian Ethics* (perhaps in the intended order 1, 2, 3, 4, 7, 5, 6, 8 – where friendship is thus closely linked with justice) and four books of our *Politics* (2, 3, 7, 8) (146–9, 170–3 below). To this time too probably belongs the lost treatise *On Monarchy* addressed to the young Alexander, who was to become king in 336, more quickly than Aristotle would have expected.

In the year 339, Speusippus, successor to Plato as head of the Academy, had died in Athens. It was no moment for Aristotle to be elected successor even if he had so wished. With the offensive ode to Hermeias in circulation, and the nationalists of Demosthenes about to precipitate the disastrous war with Philip which led to the rout at Chaeroneia in 338, Aristotle would have been even less secure in Athens than he was in 348–7. Xenocrates, his former friend and colleague, was elected by the school; Aristotle could have been neither surprised nor disappointed. Though Xenocrates was not an Athenian, he was less obviously pro-Macedonian than Aristotle, though sympathetic enough to the Macedonians to be able to render considerable service to Athens later on, in 322, as member of an embassy from Athens to the regent Antipater.

So Aristotle stayed on in Macedonia, probably, as some sources suggest, well subsidized from the royal treasury and in close touch with the rich and powerful. Alexander would have had little time for philosophy now, but at least Aristotle's new directions in ethics and politics would have interested him, not least when he heard or read what we find in *Politics* 7, that Greece, if only she were united, could rule the world. And Greece *should* so rule, Aristotle might have added, with his view of the Persian monarchy confirmed by the killing of his friend Hermeias, and his opinion of despots in general summed up with the remark that it is a delusion to believe that being lord of land and sea will make a man happy.

The *Eudemian Ethics*, like the *Posterior Analytics*, is strongly anti-

Platonic in metaphysics: the Form of the Good is a fantasy, and in any case of no significance for ethics. But Plato was right in seeking for happiness for the individual, and for unity and harmony in the larger community in which the individual can develop. The *Eudemian Ethics* urges 'nobility' as the highest good for man, most productive of happiness as well as of pleasure; its most honourable component is the service and contemplation of God, the immanent mind of the universe. For the first time, in the *Eudemian Ethics*, Aristotle writes systematically about the good for man, the virtues (especially justice), the relation of pleasure to happiness, friendship, weakness of will, and happiness itself which is a human activity. In the course of his work he also takes further steps towards developing his overall conception of the 'sciences'. Just as the *Posterior Analytics* enables Aristotle to begin rebuilding a non-Platonic account of substance, the *Eudemian Ethics* begins to expand the non-Platonic concept of *energeia*; now, through developing the analysis of pleasure which he had touched on in the *Topics* (book 6), Aristotle is able to separate *energeia* from its roots in motion, to talk about activities of rest, or – and better translated – the actuality of rest. The new concept of actuality begins to move towards a meeting-point with the new concept of substance, just as potentiality had already, as far back as the '*Physics*' (book 2), been brought into immediate connection with the specifically Aristotelian concept of matter.

The first version of the *Politics* (2, 3, 7, 8) is not formally tied to the *Eudemian Ethics*, as its revised version is eventually to be tied to the late *Nicomachean Ethics* (book 10); but Aristotle, who had already written about statesmen himself and had soaked himself in Plato's *Republic*, *Statesman*, and *Laws*, could never have thought about ethics and politics in isolation. Now, especially, living in Macedonia and friend of the powerful, he could see the connection: how important it is, as *Politics* 7 says, that the good of the individual and the good of society shall be one, that claims of 'Realpolitik' or appeals to 'raison d'état' shall not override the claims of morality. But individualistic ethics, as Plato had seen, was of no avail either, and the Greek cities were destroying themselves in faction. If a unified society could be found, Greeks could rule the world – and the rule Aristotle had in mind was not merely political but cultural. So, in the first version of the *Politics*, Aristotle sets out, like Plato, to examine existing societies that may approximate more or less to the ideal, and the conscious attempts of Plato and others to construct Utopias. All are defective, he believes. Plato had diagnosed much of the illness of Greek society, but his prescriptions, such as communism of property for the Guardians and the destruction – in that class – of the traditional family, could only make matters worse. In general Aristotle believes that revolutionary changes are dangerous, that Mirabeau will always yield to Robespierre,

Kerensky to Lenin. The aim must be stability, the achievement and maintaining of an ideal society through slow and careful reform.

Aristotle is certain that whether or not the Macedonian kings succeed in acquiring a huge empire, human life can flourish best in city-states (presumably protected where necessary – against themselves and others – by benevolent suzerains who would allow a maximum of self-government). For it is his firm conviction that, if the state becomes too large, then the title of citizen is meaningless; within a large society no citizen can participate directly in the passing of laws and the administration of justice. So after outlining the theory of citizenship, and analysing the failures of others, Aristotle too sets about describing the ideal society. But the work breaks off, with little more than the (admittedly basic) regulations for marriage and part of the educational system described in detail. For in 334 Aristotle decided to return to Athens; book 8 of the *Politics* remained, and was to remain, incomplete.

Philip was murdered in 336. Alexander, succeeding him, quickly secured his power and put down revolts. Athens was lucky to escape the fate of Thebes, which Alexander razed to the ground, leaving only the house which had once belonged to the poet Pindar standing. But Aristotle, left in Macedonia while his former charge roamed the Greek world, may have felt like a stranded whale. Despite the presence of Theophrastus and other philosophical friends, not to speak of political and military associates old and new, he may have thought by 334 that there was no longer any particular reason to stay in Macedonia. Philosophic debate was still hottest in Athens, and it was now quite safe to return. Philo-Macedonianism, once a cause of unpopularity, would now be an advantage, as the sycophantic Athenians would be not unhappy to receive back a man who could stand them in good stead with the new and fearsome ruler of Macedon and master of the pan-Hellenic League of Corinth. As a learned man at court Aristotle could leave behind his nephew Callisthenes, who had collaborated with him some time after 340 in compiling, for the people of Delphi, a list of victors at the Pythian games, and had shared in an honour decreed by the Delphians for so doing. Callisthenes remained with Alexander, to immortalize him, he claimed, by writing the history of his campaigns in Asia, and to meet a mysterious and violent end.

Aristotle celebrated his return to the 'famous land of Cecrops' with an elegy in which he speaks of himself as having 'piously founded an altar of reverent Friendship' in honour of Plato, a man 'whom it is wrong for the base even to praise.' Friendship, as his writings (*EE* 7: *NE* 8–9) tell us, and as his relations with Hermeias, Theophrastus, Antipater, and Plato himself make clear, was of great importance for Aristotle. It makes life worth living; only the demands of truth override it. 'It goes against the grain,' he was later to write, 'to criticize the theory of Forms, for those who introduced the Forms were friends of mine. But truth must come first, especially for a philosopher.' Now, in 334, Aristotle was returning to Plato's city, where the Academy was in the hands of Xenocrates, his former travelling companion on the boat to Assos. Aristotle did not rejoin the School, presumably thinking that his own interests were too different from those still there, and perhaps not wishing to interfere in a society where he might appear to be trying to undermine Xenocrates' position. At any rate, he began to teach independently in the covered walk (*peripatos*) of a gymnasium called the Lyceum. As Diogenes Laertius put it, he discussed philosophy there with his pupils until it was time to be rubbed down with oil. Nearby must have been a house for books – Aristotle was notable for his collection – rooms for study (and dissection), and a dining-room where those engaged full-time in philosophy could meet. But the operation was small-scale, in no way comparable in size with the Academy, and was probably regarded by most Athenians as a somewhat 'heretical' offshoot from it. However, it would be wrong to think that Aristotle's arrival in Athens passed almost unnoticed. Though the number of his pupils and close associates may have been small, a much wider group of intellectuals – not to speak of politicians – will have been well aware of his presence.

Aristotle did not finish the *Politics* (book 8) when he first came to Athens; perhaps he already had in mind that new kinds of work based on further collections of data for political analysis were required. Instead he began a programme of enlarging and completing a number of his logical and physical writings in the light of new thinking and new teaching since they were originally composed. He assembled a compilation known as *Methodics*, concerned largely with the forms of reasoning, perhaps including within this general heading the contents of what we now call *De Interpretatione*, and an enlarged version of the *Categories*, including the so-called *Post-Praedicamenta*. Our *Categories*, including the *Post-Praedicamenta* and the vaguely related material in chapter 1, may have obtained its present form as the result of being thrown together and tagged (by someone or other) as a bit of the *Methodics*. All the material was assembled, as it were, within single covers, though later it circulated separately in segments which were not necessarily homogeneous. At about the same time appeared the *Poetics*, probably in two books, and a vastly enlarged *Rhetoric* in three, which, besides containing allusions to nearly contemporary events, shows a knowledge of the *Analytics*, of which the earlier parts of the *Rhetoric* are quite innocent. It should not be assumed, of course, that all the ideas in these revised versions were the product of Aristotle's last Athenian period, only that this was the time when the material we have under the titles *Poetics* and *Rhetoric* was finally compiled (144–6 below). In book 1 of the *Rhetoric* Aristotle attempts to fit rhetoric into the broader framework of scientific enquiry in which he now wishes to work.

After the 'logical' material came revision and expansion of the '*Physics*,' *De Caelo*, and *De Generatione et Corruptione*. What we call *Metaphysics* α was added as an introduction to various basic 'physical' writings, now perhaps first labelled *Physics*, and followed by *Physics* 1, with its special emphasis on 'privation' of form as a concept in physics which should not be overlooked, and its particular preoccupation (evident in some of the later logical material also) with problems posed by the Eleatics (230–1 below). Then came *Physics* 8, where for the first time Aristotle criticized and rejected his earlier theory of a self-moved mover as God (which he had taken over from Plato); he replaced it with an Unmoved Mover as the necessary first cause of motion. References to this Unmoved Mover were also added to earlier parts of the other physical treatises (thus producing our present sequence, *Physics* 1–8) and to the *De Caelo*, where they exist (notoriously) alongside the earlier theory of self-motion. In most of our *Physics* Aristotle maintains a consistent account of the origins of motion, though he apparently retained the earlier book 7 alongside our book 8 which largely replaces it. In the *De Caelo*, however, contradictions between the earlier and later accounts are more obvious within particular books themselves. Why Aristotle did not 'clean this up' is not clear; possibly, since he still used the material in lectures, he thought it worthwhile to retain the earlier view and explain as he went along why he had come later to advocate the newer theories. Thus the retention of material dealing with a self-moved mover would be by way of an *aide-mémoire*. In the case of the *Physics*, however, the whole of book 7 could serve that purpose.

The *De Generatione et Corruptione* was also revised. Here, as in the '*Physics*,' Aristotle employs the technique of adding material to the beginning or the end, in the case of the *De Generatione et Corruptione* at the end of book 2. The earlier text of the *De Generatione et Corruptione* ended rhetorically and appropriately with an attack on the views of 'Socrates in the *Phaedo*'; the newer chapters at the end, long recognized as looking a bit like an appendix, introduce the new theory of an Unmoved Mover of which the original *De Generatione et Corruptione* was innocent. A few such references and other additions were also inserted into earlier sections of the book.

But the introduction of the Unmoved Mover involved Aristotle in a good deal more than the composition of *Physics* 8 and the insertion of new material in other physical treatises already in circulation. It involved him in a re-examination of his whole framework for scientific work, in a reappraisal of the Academic or Xenocratean thesis of the division of the sciences into physics, ethics, and logic, as well as the accompanying rejection, in the *Posterior Analytics* and the *Eudemian Ethics*, of 'metaphysical' problems outside those areas as arising from conceptual confusions. Previously Aristotle had thought that 'metaphysics' is concerned with hypothetical, useless and muddled 'Platonic' beings; now his own theory of motion had led him to believe that there is indeed an unchanging immaterial substance. And with such substances, he had himself said, physics has no concern, for physics deals exclusively with the causes of motion and rest. Thus the existence of an Unmoved Mover may be a postulate of Aristotelian physics, but consideration of its nature, of its actuality, will be material for what he was to call 'first philosophy.' First philosophy is metaphysics, but metaphysics need no longer be Platonic.

At this time, therefore, Aristotle began to assemble 'metaphysical' material and perhaps first envisaged compiling a complete course, made up of a number of mini-courses, on 'first philosophy.' His first attempt, on what seems to be the most plausible explanation of the data, was broken off in mid-stream. It is represented in our *Metaphysics* by A.1–6 and 10 and K (231–3 below). The project was to be linked closely with the *Physics* and to be dominated by reflection on the four causes which had already proved their worth in physical analysis. It was to be systematically set out, and the first step (as in our *Metaphysics* A) was to be an historical examination of what earlier philosophers, down to and including Plato, had said about causation. But comparatively little emphasis was to be put on polemic against the contemporary or near-contemporary Academy, on the views, that is, of Speusippus and Xenocrates. Perhaps Aristotle, newly returned to Athens, preferred to minimize his disagreements with the Academy, leaving much of his critique not very different from what he had composed long ago in *On Ideas*. For whatever reason, however, he broke off the scheme, abandoning and later completely rewriting the metaphysical sections of K, and expanding A by the inclusion of further material from *On Ideas* as well as new sections designed in part to consider Academic theses of the post-Platonic period. But, as has often been noticed, Aristotle still speaks of himself as a member of the 'Academic' tradition, even when treating of notions which he had for years considered misguided.

At about this same time, that is, about 331, and for a number of succeeding years, Aristotle also turned his attention again to biology, which included psychology. As the unfinished state of the *De Generatione Animalium* indicates, the huge project was left incomplete at his death. It began with *De Partibus Animalium*, probably put together in the years 330 to 328. Like the *Metaphysics*, *De Partibus* is a rather formal composition with an elaborate introduction, in this case partly concerned with defining the 'dignity' and worth of the subject-matter. More important, in *De Partibus Animalium* 1 – note the parallel with *Physics* 8 – Aristotle comes to the conclusion that in the case of psychology too we are confronted with material which cannot be subsumed within the general framework of physics; for the study of psychology, as of theories of motion, brings us up against non-material substances. Thus substance in general will need examination, not merely those substances which involve the presence of form in matter. But *De Partibus Animalium* is not the place for work of that kind.

While the *De Partibus Animalium* was in course of composition, Aristotle began to assemble metaphysical material once more. Some of it, no doubt, had been in his mind for a time, but most for not too long, for only a few years earlier he had denied any point to such enquiries. The *Metaphysics* as we have it, in other words, is an accumulation of material of partially undatable origin; but not much of it – apart from the critiques dependent on *On Ideas* – can go back long before Aristotle's arrival in Athens for his second stay. In the *Eudemian Ethics* Aristotle had still, it appears, not emerged from his non-metaphysical frame of reference, even though, in that work, he makes use of what was to become one of his basic tools in metaphysics, the notion of 'focal meaning' – a notion in the first place about intelligibility – which he was to apply not to all concepts (not, for example, to concepts like man or green or double, which refer to the physical contents of the sensible world), but to concepts like being or good: these are neither dependent on Platonic Forms nor merely equivocal. Rather the definition of a star instance of being (say, God) could be included in the definition of other beings in so far as they are beings. God, that is to say, would fulfil the necessary conditions for being, and all else that is called being should be understood with reference to him. Similarly, to use an earlier Aristotelian example, the true nature of friendship can be found in a primary and perfect type.

The *Metaphysics* can be broken up into sections (such as M, N, which Aristotle called 'On Substance,' and Z, H), and the material in these sections may not have been in the order in which it now appears. But the sections can be shown to form a coherent sequence of metaphysical books, and they seem to have been composed by Aristotle when he had a general theory of a proper unfolding of metaphysical enquiry in his mind. So that whatever 'chapters' within these sections were written down first, given first as lectures, or circulated first as lecture-notes, Aristotle had the raw materials for an intelligible presentation of metaphysics as a whole available to him after about 330. At that time he began to present the material in a sequence which can be reconstructed on the basis of the texts we have. The order of books as they were assembled for our *Metaphysics* (omitting, as we have seen, α and K) can be established largely on the basis of 'non-philosophical' evidence, that is, on the basis of cross-references and of the development of purely biological theories to which Aristotle alludes from time to time in the course of the *Metaphysics*: theories about the role of male and female partners in the process of conception.

In the year 330 or thereabouts, we conclude, while proceeding with the four books of the *De Partibus Animalium*, Aristotle began the 'metaphysical' sequence again (225–41 below). By the year 328 he seems to have completed A, B, Γ, E.1, Δ.1–12, I, E.2–4, which should be arranged in that order. Obviously an exact time-scale cannot be specified, but he seems to have finished the next group of metaphysical treatises (M, N, Λ) soon after completing the last book of the *De Partibus Animalium*, and by this time to have returned also to the ethical and political concerns of his Macedonian period. Two projects in this area can be identified. First came a large collaborative scheme to collect information on scores of city constitutions of the Greek world and beyond, which were to provide raw material for comment on politics in the same way as the early *Historia Animalium* provides and organizes raw material for the study of zoology. We do not hear how many such constitutions were written; only one, the *Constitution of the Athenians*, plausibly revised by Aristotle himself in about 328, has come down to us – and that only by the discovery of a papyrus fragment in Egypt about a century ago.

At this time also, Aristotle began to rewrite his ethics, bringing out the new books 1, 8, 9, and 10 of the *Nicomachean Ethics* to replace parts of the earlier *Eudemian* version (182–6 below). These texts, still not reflecting the very latest phase of Aristotle's psychology, were 'built into' the *Eudemian Ethics* to make a version which would run as follows: *NE* 1, *EE* 2 (1220A to end), 3, 4, 5, 6; *NE* 8, 9, 10. The last book of the *Nicomachean Ethics* (10) refers to the collection of constitutions on which Aristotle had been engaged, and, unlike the original *Eudemian Ethics*, is designed to lead directly into the *Politics*. It is to these years too, therefore, that we should assign the second phase of the composition of our *Politics*, that is, the composition of what have been called the 'Machiavellian' books, namely books 4–6, which are concerned with value-free political analysis, with political science as it is sometimes now understood, rather than with the more value-laden political philosophy which Aristotle had treated earlier. *Politics* 4–6 is largely concerned with analysis not of how to make a constitution or society better, but of how a ruler or rulers (of whatever stripe) can maintain themselves in power. It is a discussion of what the Greeks called *aretē* (and Machiavelli *virtù*), not in its moral sense, but as designating the 'successful' achievements of politicians without reference to the moral quality of their behaviour: a study, that is, of Cesare Borgia, rather than of Socrates, once described by Plato as 'the only real politician among the Athenians.'

The appearance of these books of the *Politics* must have more or less coincided with the news from far away in Asia that Aristotle's outspoken nephew Callisthenes, the intended historian of Alexander's wars and immortalizer of Alexander himself as the new Achilles fighting the barbarians, had first declined to kowtow to the king by performing an act of prostration, and had then been eliminated by Achilles on an apparently trumped-up charge of conspiring against the king's life. We do not know – despite stories from antiquity – what Aristotle thought of his nephew's behaviour. We do know, as we shall see, what he thought of other aspects of the new policy Alexander was beginning to adopt towards the defeated Persians. But his view of the fate of Callisthenes can be surmised from the fact that at some later stage his associate Theophrastus published a work entitled *Callisthenes or On Grief*. Alexander can hardly have come out of this favourably – though we do not know when it was written – but whatever Aristotle thought about Callisthenes, there is no reason to assume that his opinion weakened his ties with other powerful Macedonians, such as Antipater. Indeed Antipater himself, by the end of the reign, was under suspicion from the increasingly paranoid and arbitrary ruler of the world. By the time of Alexander's death in 323, there must have been many senior Macedonians relieved that it was so.

Pythias, Aristotle's wife, was almost certainly dead, even assuming she was the mother of Nicomachus, before the execution of Callisthenes, and probably even before Aristotle had begun the *Metaphysics* in about 330. Aristotle did not remarry; his household in Athens was now supervised by a freedwoman Herpyllis, probably originally a maid of Pythias, possibly even a distant poor relation. Aristotle's recognition of her devotion is apparent in the dispositions of his will, but the external circumstances of his life, particularly after the death of Callisthenes, encouraged an increasing sense of loneliness of which we get occasional glimpses.

Meanwhile he continued with the *Metaphysics*. After the completion of E, he began the central sections on non-material substance (M, N, Λ) – which necessarily entailed a re-entry into the world of public disagreement. Xenocrates, his old comrade who now headed the Academy, was one of the targets, but Aristotle had come to have increasingly less respect for Xenocrates' philosophical competence; he was in general a conservative Platonist who tended, in Aristotle's view, often to compound Plato's errors without emphasizing his philosophical virtues. But since Xenocrates undoubtedly discussed non-sensible substances, the subject-matter of Aristotle's own *On Substance* (*Met.* M, N, Λ), he could not be neglected. The more serious opponent, however, was the now dead Speusippus. For Aristotle Speusippus represented a challenge in two important respects. First his theory of principles, in Aristotle's view, seriously compromised the unity of the cosmos: Speusippus was a fragmenter. Secondly, his account of the metaphysical origins of the world turned Aristotle's position on its head. Speusippus thought that the potential precedes the actual, the egg precedes the chicken, the One precedes the Good. But curiously enough Speusippus's views on conception and the origins of human life – in which he tended towards the atomists' theory that a newborn (like Speusippus's universe) is the product of the mingling of two diverse seeds, two potentialities – led Aristotle to the development of his own later theory of conception. And this theory, visible in an unambiguous form for the first time in *Metaphysics* Z, but of which *Metaphysics* N, Λ, and *De Partibus Animalium* 4 already provide foreshadowings, and which asserted that the male provides the human form, the female the matter formed only to the level of vegetable life, offers the most important tool for our study of the chronology of the *Metaphysics* itself.

Speusippus was no advocate of Platonic Forms, but a firm believer in non-sensible substance, which for him meant mathematical objects. Aristotle, who had long disapproved of his claims in ethics, especially his view that all pleasure is evil, had attacked such notions as far back as the *Eudemian Ethics* (book 6). But M and N of the *Metaphysics* are more fundamental in that they attack Speusippus's 'Platonism' in mathematics, thereby also providing Aristotle with a new opportunity further to develop his own view that mathematics describes the structural properties and relations of physical objects. Since Speusippus was for Aristotle the worst offender of those who turned philosophy itself into mathematics, to attack his theory of 'mathematicals' was to attack his 'first philosophy' as well. And now, with such (Platonist) accounts of non-sensible substance out of the way, Aristotle was finally free in *Metaphysics* Λ to do what *Physics* 8 and *De Partibus Animalium* 1 had predicted, that is, to give an account of the nature of an eternal, unchanging 'actual' Unmoved Mover (or God, for short). Such a being is substance par excellence and to be identified as a transcendent Mind, causing movement in virtue of his mere existence, as an object of desire for the soul of the first heaven. His nature is self-directed: he thinks of himself, since thinking is the nature of being and of life, as well as the 'source' of perfect pleasure and happiness. Aristotle does not pursue his Unmoved Mover as the source of existence, however, though his existence guarantees the possibility of the definition of other existents, and hence their suitability as the subjects of metaphysical enquiry of the sort they will receive in

Metaphysics Z. In Λ itself Aristotle's concern is with God as thinking, as the unifying factor in the cosmos (hence the rejection of Speusippean diversity and fragmentation), not as a being whose substance is identified with his realized nature.

After the completion of Λ, Aristotle continued with Θ, a book concerned with potentiality and actuality, with substances which are not purely actual, with natural objects which can be studied not merely as the subject-matter of physics, but as beings in so far as they are beings, that is, metaphysically, or in terms of 'first philosophy.' For although all particulars are a 'compound' of form and matter, or, more correctly, phenomena of informed matter or emmattered form, they are, in virtue of their matter, endowed with potentiality for change of some kind, and often, of course, for change of 'substance,' that is, for generation and destruction. In the course of his analysis of potentiality, Aristotle also finds it necessary to engage in further polemic with contemporaries, this time with Megarians – not necessarily a closely knit school, but perhaps the intellectual heirs of Euclides – who denied the reality of the potential, holding that all possible X's are actual X's. It may not be coincidence that one of Aristotle's earliest philosophical calumniators in antiquity was a 'Megarian': Eubulides, the inventor of various paradoxes and logical puzzles, including the Sorites, also impugned Aristotle's relationship with Hermeias, his marriage to Pythias, and his dealings with Plato.

By now (ca 327) the *De Partibus Animalium* was certainly complete, and Aristotle, while still continuing with the *Metaphysics* – Z, H, and Λ.8 come next (239–41 below) – began contemporaneously to work on the second stage of the new 'biological' scheme, namely the works of psychology, *De Anima* 1–3, followed by various studies we classify as the *Parva Naturalia*: *On Sense and Sensibles, On Memory and Recollection, On Sleep and Waking, On Dreams, On Divination in Sleep, On Length and Shortness of Life, On Youth and Old Age* (245 below). The *De Anima* is perhaps the most well worked of all his later writings, with a very elaborate book 1 which, like *Metaphysics* A, offers detailed analysis of theories current in the field, in this case theories about the nature of the soul and the mind.

As we have seen, these psychological works and the last books of the *Metaphysics* are roughly contemporary; and some of their most difficult theories are interrelated. Even linguistically there are interesting comparisons between, for example, *De Anima* 2 and *Metaphysics* Z. But the most striking feature of this stage of Aristotle's psychology is that *Metaphysics* Z and the *De Anima* offer similar definitions of the soul. In contrast to Aristotle's earlier view in the *Eudemus*, the soul is now the form of a living body. Thus not only is psychology brought within the scope of Aristotle's general theories in physics, it is also developed in an entirely unplatonic direction. There can now be no question of the soul's surviving the body. Yet Aristotle's anti-Platonism is not complete. The 'productive intellect' – that mind from outside, as he later names it in the *De Generatione Animalium* – which separates us from higher animals and enables us to think, is not itself part of the body-soul complex. Rather it is the Unmoved Mover itself, for the God whose mere existence is the cause of the movements of the first heaven, the sphere of the fixed stars, is also the cause of our own thinking. Naturally this productive intellect is immortal as well as immaterial; naturally 'we,' our body-soul complex, are not immortal (177–82 below). But *De Anima* 3.5, where the productive intellect is alone discussed by name and in relation to the processes of thinking, would be hardly intelligible without the light shed on it by the discussion of God in *Metaphysics* Λ (and the comments of Aristotle's associate Theophrastus). But if such an intellect is in us, but not of us, what is to become of the ethical implications drawn from an earlier psychology in *Nicomachean Ethics* 10, where Aristotle spoke of mind as primarily 'us'? Aristotle's further progress in psychology was to lead him to begin to redraft his *Ethics*, or parts of it, once again – if he can live to do it.

Long ago in Lesbos and in Macedonia, Aristotle had begun to think that just as there must be some kind of Mind to act as the first cause of the cosmos as a whole, so there must be some kind of material substance which is, somehow, common to the physical universe. He had begun the identification of that physical substance when, in the *De Caelo*, he had proposed, in addition to the four material elements, earth, water, air, and fire, a fifth element, *aether*, which was to embody the eternal, circular movements of the superlunary heavens. But below the moon something similar is required. That need is only spelled out in the *De Generatione Animalium*, and its problems still remained partially unsolved when Aristotle died. But in the *De Anima* and the consequent *Parva Naturalia* progress is being made in this area. Traces of it were to be found back in the *De Respiratione*, in Mytilene days, but substantial progress in the theory of what he came to call an analogue of *aether*, namely *pneuma*, is still only implicit in the *De Anima*.

The *De Anima* and the *Parva Naturalia* actually form a continuation of the Aristotelian parts of the *Historia Animalium*. In the entirely Aristotelian parts of that text (that is, books 1–7), there is no discussion of psychology, but the authors of 8–10 have 'obligingly' helped us out, though often with unaristotelian material. When we come to Aristotle's next biological work, however, the *De Motu Animalium*, we are dealing not with an addition to Aristotelian parts of the *Historia Animalium*, but with a replacement. *De Motu* is a replacement, or at least a radical restatement of *De Incessu*, which was itself, as we have seen (16 above), part of the original project of the *Historia Animalium*.

The *De Motu* is much more than a book on biology; it contains a fresh treatment of the theory of human action, which Aristotle had handled confusingly in *Eudemian Ethics* 6 – not to speak of material on motion in general, which is dependent on the Unmoved Mover of *Metaphysics* Λ. But before starting it, Aristotle had to complete the *Metaphysics* itself. The last two books, composed about 326, and dealing with substance as realized nature, are Z and H. Λ.8 is the last chapter of H and treats of the number of heavenly compounds of form and matter, the matter in them being *aether*. At the same time Aristotle produced further material which later editors, perhaps rightly, included with Δ; that is, Δ.13 to the end of the book. Thus by about the year 326, after some four years of labour, Aristotle had completed what we may call his final book of metaphysics. The complete sequence (excluding the earlier α and K, as well as the final late section of Δ) is A, B, Γ, and E.1, Δ.1–12, I and E.2–4, M, N, Λ, Θ, Z, and H + Λ.8. Λ.8 completes the task by picking up Aristotle's theme about wondering why the heavenly bodies are as they are from *Metaphysics* A. Now, he says, he has explained, at least approximately, why they are as they are, and others more technically competent than himself can finish the job. For Λ.8 is a product of Aristotle's dealings with professional astronomers, first his old master Eudoxus, then Callippus whom he met when he returned to Athens from Macedonia. Λ.8 attempts to assimilate the latest astronomical theories into Aristotle's physical universe and metaphysical structure. For it might seem, though to think so would be a mistake, that the plurality of movements of the heavenly bodies would compromise Aristotle's plan for a unified cosmos with a single final cause. Speusippean disintegration threatened the scientific universe once more, and Λ.8 is Aristotle's final attempt to impose, in the Homeric phrase, 'one lord' over the universe.

What remained for Aristotle to complete of his gigantic scientific and philosophical programme? By about 325 he still needed to finish the zoology (that is, to write the *De Motu* and *De Generatione Animalium*), to comment also on botanical matters (a book of this period *On Plants* is lost, though some knowledge of its content remains), and to rewrite parts of the *Ethics* in the light of the new psychology of the *De Anima* – not to speak of the *De Motu*'s treatment of human action (182–4 below). Finally there was a need to integrate the writings on politics, for Aristotle's growing awareness of the unity of the living cosmos was to have startling repercussions on his account of the relation of man to his society, and offered him, in an enlarged concept of nature, the opportunity to resolve a number of questions about human beings: what a slave is, what a woman is relative to a man (apart from her different role in reproduction). It is difficult to organize these late texts in sequence, for several of them were left unfinished: the *Politics*, the revised *Ethics*, the *De Generatione Animalium*. At least we know that the *De Motu* was finished (245–6 below). As we have seen, it contained not only zoology, but ethics and general use of metaphysical theories about the Unmoved Mover.

But the *De Motu* is important in another respect too. For here Aristotle makes use of his theory of *pneuma*, that highest of the material elements, as part of his explanation of human behaviour, as the physical means by which human and animal action – commanded by the soul – is effected. *Pneuma* is, in a way, the hormone-system of Aristotelian man. Aristotle does not help us much in understanding how it works – his scientific equipment is quite inadequate to provide such explanation – but he is certain that it works, and that it is needed to account for the phenomena of human and animal (and possibly even plant) behaviour.

In the incomplete *De Generatione Animalium* – the original intention was to include discussion of nutrition and growth as well as reproduction – Aristotle pursues *pneuma* further. Now it is used to explain the phenomena of reproduction and to give a 'biological' account of the difference between men and women, a question which preoccupied Aristotle greatly in his last years (246–9 below). Why should he think it important? To understand that we have to go back once more to Plato. In the *Republic* and elsewhere Plato had insisted that the physiological differences between men and women had minimal psychological counterparts, at least in an ideal society. Women could often do men's work (except in so far as it depended on physical strength) almost as well as men, and sometimes better, provided their reproductive urges were properly channelled off. The psychology of men and women need not be seriously affected by their differing roles in reproduction.

For Aristotle such claims were puzzling. They offended against his view of the interrelation of soul and body. Bodily differences would prima facie seem to affect the soul in more significant ways than Plato would allow. Why is it that women seem (in Aristotle's culture) to be less able to behave in a rational way? Is it because they are less intelligent? Is it even because they are a different species, as many Greeks seem to have half-believed? For Aristotle, in the *De Generatione Animalium*, the difference lies in the *pneuma*. Women are less able to produce this hormone-like substance in its most effective form. That is why they cannot produce 'pure' seed, only menstrual blood which cannot provide the human *form* of an embryo. Thus *pneuma* enables Aristotle to say that males and females are the same in species; but that Plato was wrong to suppose that physiological differences between men and women do not also indicate (or report) psychological differences. For in some sense women are not only different but also defective – and that too, *pace* Plato, must have social and political implications. If *pneuma*, the 'analogue' of *aether* in our sublunary world, is present, in some strength, throughout nature, the degree of its strength will be related to the height of its possessors on the scale of nature.

A curious coincidence, and for Aristotle a disturbing political fact, occurred in 324. Just when Aristotle was thinking again in *Politics* 1 about the relations of man and woman, Greek and barbarian, free and slave, Alexander, his former 'pupil,' was in Susa celebrating a new marriage, this time with the daughter of the Persian king Darius. Many of his generals (some doubtless known to Aristotle) and, so it is said, ten thousand Macedonian soldiers were similarly engaged, at a gigantic and well-staged ceremony, with Persian and other Oriental women. The whole affair was to symbolize the linking of Greece and the Orient under a single monarch and to celebrate Alexander's new 'racial' policy. Gone is the ideal of Alexander as the Achilles conquering a new Troy; growing is the figure of a new Hercules, son of Zeus, ruling the whole of human society, the universal benefactor, drawing his leading, but humble, servants from Greeks and 'barbarians' alike. From such similar treatment of Greeks and 'barbarians' Aristotle attempted at some stage to dissuade Alexander in a writing *On Colonies*. Perhaps it was composed in these years, for Aristotle would certainly not have read Alexander's behaviour at Susa as giving dignity to Persians, but rather as degrading the Greeks. For Aristotle in *On Colonies* the Greeks should be ruled by a leader, the 'barbarians' by a master. In *Politics* 1 Aristotle thinks of 'barbarians' as natural slaves. Susa would have looked to him like another instance of what had perhaps disturbed Callisthenes: equal slavery for all. Callisthenes had already paid the penalty for refusing the (largely but not entirely) oriental habit of prostration before the monarch, and perhaps for other 'wrong-doings.' He, and probably Aristotle, would have viewed the weddings in Susa as indicating the reduction of Greeks to 'barbarians' and the elevation of Alexander to a master of men not only 'naturally' but also 'unnaturally' enslaved.

Politics 1 is much more than an introduction to the two earlier sections of the *Politics* (2, 3, 7, 8, and 4–6) (146–64 below). It is also an attempt to put the growth of a society into the context of the growth of man. In contrast to sophists who think that cities are a device of the weak to gang up on the strong, or others like Thrasymachus in the *Republic* who consider them to be institutions designed by their rulers to secure their own rule, Aristotle argues that cities come into being as families and villages unite to protect themselves and to survive, but continue in existence, indeed find the raison d'être of their existence, in being the only means to human fulfilment. Hence, contrary perhaps to the ideas of Alexander, they must not grow too big. If they do, they cease to be cities and become mere agglomerations, probably of slaves or near-slaves. But *Politics* 1 not only describes the growth of the city-state; it deals with the relations between the several groups which compose it. Man is a social animal, though, unlike bees or ants, possessed of reason and speech which allow the possibility of morality. Men and women come together to form households; slaves help out where necessary with the manual labour. The family unit is a society in miniature where the man's relation to his wife is constitutional government, for as we have seen, though women are as capable of reasoning and deliberating as men – sharing equally in the enlightenment of the productive intellect – they are at the 'practical' level less satisfactory. Though they can deliberate equally well, they are less fitted to impose the results of their deliberation on their emotions – for the most part. Hence their 'virtue' will be different too. As for slaves, some are conventional, that is, acquired by force, others 'natural.' The natural slave is a man or woman who, for whatever reason, is not enlightened by the productive intellect (249–52 below). The light from outside, as it were, is blocked off and the natural slave thus needs a natural master. Nowadays we should call natural slaves, or some of them, mentally defective.

Politics 1 is a major and vastly influential treatise. Aristotle would probably have made further changes in the *Politics* (one or two additions are certainly visible), and he would certainly, if he had had time, have finished book 8 (163 below). But for a second time he did not manage to do so. A similar fate awaited what was perhaps his last new undertaking, the rewriting of the *Ethics*, to take account of recent work in psychology and the theory of action. Books 2 to 4 of the *Nicomachean Ethics* were now completed, with 2 containing new material about capabilities in man; and something was done to revise book 5, on justice. But this too was not completed and further studies of the intellectual virtues, of weakness of will in the light of the *De Motu*, and of happiness itself, were never even begun. Our *Nicomachean Ethics* 10, still deeply influenced by the early and now rather outdated psychology of the *Protrepticus*, was to be seen as his last word on the subject.

Whatever Aristotle may have thought of Alexander's doings in Asia, they at least provided him with leisure to talk with his close associates, to write endlessly, and to teach the general public later in the day. But in the summer of 323, contrary to all expectation, Alexander died. Here at least is part of the reason why Aristotle left three major works (*Ethics*, *Politics*, and *De Generatione Animalium*) unfinished. His last year was full of strains and anxieties. The news of Alexander's death was not believed at first, but by September eyewitnesses reached Athens and the political storm broke. Throughout Greece, not least in Athens itself, anti-Macedonian feeling swelled to the point of war. Friends of Macedon were in danger, and even the regent Antipater could do nothing immediate to help. A certain Eurymedon brought a charge of irreligion against Aristotle: his alleged impious ode to Hermeias and the honours paid to his wife Pythias provided the pretext. Aristotle, who, unlike Socrates, was no Athenian, had no legal ties to the city, and no reason for not seeking to save his own life. He retired to his mother's ancestral home at Chalcis in Euboea. Herpyllis, in charge of his household, and the rest of his family went with him. In the turmoil there must have been little time to work, and further irritations reached him from abroad. At Delphi they voted to deprive him and the dead Callisthenes of the honours voted them for organizing the list of victors at the Pythian Games. Amid these anxieties, after less than a year at Chalcis, Aristotle died. Theophrastus, who had remained in Athens and was thus already in effect running the Lyceum, continued to do so. One of his first tasks may have been attempting to bring some order into the disorderly sets of notes Aristotle left behind. Our text of the *Nicomachean Ethics*, together with its dedication to Aristotle's son Nicomachus, is probably among the results of this work.

Aristotle's will survives. It begins 'All will be well, but in case anything happens, Aristotle makes the following dispositions.' Antipater is appointed executor. Theophrastus, for the time being, is to look after Herpyllis, Aristotle's children, and the estate. Nicanor, son of Aristotle's sister Arimneste, at present absent – he returned to Greece and was in charge of Antipater's garrison at the Athenian port of Munychia in 321 – is to become the husband of daughter Pythias when she comes of age. And if anything 'befalls' him – it did: he was executed in 318 – she shall be married to Theophrastus, if he wishes, or, if not, arrangements are to be made in consultation with Antipater. Herpyllis is to be looked after financially, and if she wishes to marry, she is to be found a worthy husband. Various other dispositions are made about slaves, some of whom are to be freed; none is to be sold. Images are to be set up to Nicanor, to his guardian Proxenus, to Arimneste, Proxenus's wife and Aristotle's sister, and to his brother Arimnestus who had died without issue. A statue of his mother Phaestis is to be dedicated to Demeter at Nemea or some other suitable place. When Nicanor returns safely, life-size statues to Zeus and Athene the Saviours are to be erected at Stagira, in fulfilment of a vow Aristotle had made. He himself is to be buried where the executors see fit, and the bones of his wife Pythias, at her request, are to be moved and laid beside him. There is no mention of the disposition of his writings or of his library; they seem, in fact, to have passed – as was fitting – to Theophrastus.

2

Platonism without the Forms?

I The Problem of Aristotle's Attitude to Platonic Forms

Any discussion of Aristotle's philosophical development must begin by identifying his attitude to Plato during the years from 367 to 347. It needs above all to clarify his relationship to Platonic metaphysics, but questions of psychology, logic, and rhetoric are also important. Such clarification is the primary and overriding purpose of the next four chapters of this study.

When Plato developed a theory of Forms in the *Symposium*, *Phaedo*, and *Republic*, he intended to solve at least two important philosophical problems:[1] why are things as they are; what is the source of value. Both themes already occur in the *Phaedo*. We learn that it is 'by beauty' that beautiful things are beautiful (100D), and it is the failure of Anaxagoras's supposed attempt to show how mind orders all things *for the best* (98A) that is said to have impelled Socrates to seek refuge in the hypothesis that eternal and unchanging realities exist. A third, obviously not unrelated point is added in the *Republic* (6.508E): Forms, and above all the Form of the Good, not only account for the existence of things, but render them intelligible.

By the time Aristotle composed the *Posterior Analytics* and the *Eudemian Ethics* – an ethical work which alludes regularly to the *Posterior Analytics* – he sharply denied these claims.[2] In the *Posterior Analytics* the Forms are described as fantasy (1.83A33). Strictly speaking, Aristotle should perhaps have limited his dismissal to Forms falling outside his own category of substance; for such Forms 'which do not denote substance' cannot exist independently – and clearly without independent existence they cannot be causal. And even if they do exist, he adds, they are irrelevant, because demonstration, i.e. 'scientific' reasoning, is concerned with quite different sorts of predicates. So much for Plato's claim that the Forms somehow contribute intelligibility.

A similar charge of irrelevance is brought in the *Eudemian Ethics* against the Form of the Good, that Form which in the *Republic* is particularly identified as the source of value. To propose the existence of any Form, let alone the Form of the Good, is abstract nonsense (1.1217B22).[3] Even if the Forms and the Form of the Good exist, they are of no use for the good life or for behaviour. In the *Eudemian Ethics* Aristotle tells us he has dealt with such matters elsewhere, and we notice that in the course of explaining the inadequacy of the Good, he offers an analysis in terms of the categories: 'Good' has as many meanings as 'being.' Hence, like being, it cannot be the subject of a single science.

Such matters, says Aristotle (*EE* 1.1217B23–4), have been discussed both in writings for the general public[4] and in more technical philosophical texts. Which texts he has in mind must remain somewhat uncertain, but we know that in at least three major writings composed, let us suppose, about the time of Plato's death or even slightly before, the theory of Forms had come under attack: *On the Good*, *On Ideas*, and *On Philosophy*. We do not know the exact dates of these works; from the fragments which have survived we can only obtain a limited notion of their contents. But in discussions of Aristotle's 'break' with Platonism, which since Jaeger has been claimed as the main subject of *On Philosophy*, a significant fact seems to have been given insufficient attention: although in these writings Aristotle attacked the theory of Forms – both in the versions of Plato and in those of others in the Academy – and although he made a number of 'metaphysical' claims, these claims fall far short of a complete replacement of the whole range of Platonic metaphysics.

Jaeger's discussion is odd in that he makes only one passing reference to the work *On Ideas* (*Aristotle*, 172), says nothing about *On the Good*, misinterprets the *Eudemus* as preaching a theory of transcendent Forms, and insists that *On Philosophy* was certainly composed after Plato's death because 'for the sake of the Academy' Aristotle would have avoided as long as possible a public exhibition of the internal controversies of his school on logical and metaphysical questions. But even a limited examination of these works will yield conclusions different from those of Jaeger.

II Forms in 'On Ideas' and 'On the Good'

First let us consider *On Ideas*. Most of our evidence comes from Alexander of Aphrodisias, the Aristotelian commentator of the late second century A.D. *On Ideas* apparently consisted of two books,[5] which are sometimes carefully distinguished by the ancient commentators from books M and N of the *Metaphysics*. Our primary source is Alexander's commentary on *Meta-*

physics A, and the commentator remarks that a number of the objections to Plato's theory of Forms found in *Metaphysics* A appear in a lengthier version in *On Ideas*. Unless we have been misled by the unrepresentative nature of the passages quoted by Alexander, *On Ideas* was intended primarily as a critique,[6] and Aristotle's chief activity seems to be conceptual analysis. New claims about the status of universals and about predication can be discerned in the analysis, and Aristotle's discussion of relative terms is particularly damaging to at least one version of the theory of Forms – at least if too exuberantly or carelessly expressed. But although possible outlines of a new account of being are certainly visible, it is hard to obtain much information from *On Ideas* about Aristotle's own solutions to the problems about value or causation which the theory of Forms was originally supposed to solve. On being itself it is true that Aristotle utilizes a distinction between individuals and kinds – a distinction which, arising from the 'Third Man' argument against Platonic Forms, propelled him elsewhere towards his own explicit assertion of the priority of the concrete individual or primary substance; and he appears also to reject a crudely nominalist account of universals. But depending on which fragments we allow to come from *On Ideas*, we are on firmest metaphysical ground when showing Aristotle's dissent from (and arguments against) specific Platonic theses. On the more generous collection of fragments allowed by Ross,[7] for example, we can see that Aristotle does more than reject an inadequately expressed and apparently early version of the theory of Forms; he also claims that the theory is both inadequate in itself and in conflict with a theory of 'first principles' (the One and the Indefinite Dyad) on which the Forms themselves are supposed to depend, and which Plato worked out in the latter part of his life. The incompatibility of the two theories is also emphasized in the much later *Metaphysics*.

In the treatise *On the Good* we find little further evidence of the growth of Aristotle's own philosophical views. Again much is said about Plato's One and Indefinite Dyad, with some reference to the account of matter in the *Timaeus*, but there is comparatively little allusion to Aristotle's own position except the complaint that Plato's metaphysics neglected final and efficient causes (fr. 4 Ross). Perhaps a further text which may help (though it is very uncertain whether it does) is the notorious comment of Aristoxenus. He purports to be quoting Aristotle (perhaps indeed from the work *On the Good*) to the effect that according to Plato the Good is one.[8] If that is indeed the nature of Plato's claim (remarks in the *Metaphysics* also support it), the point of Aristoxenus's (or Aristotle's) objection may be that it is false to suppose that good is a univocal term. We shall see in our discussion of categories that Aristotle comes to that conclusion both in the *Posterior*

Analytics and in the *Eudemian Ethics*. Perhaps he had already reached it in the work *On the Good*; but in any case we can advance no farther.

III The Content of the Treatise 'On Philosophy'

Turning to *On Philosophy*, a work praised for its style by Cicero (fr. 20 Ross) – hence probably one of the more popular 'essays' referred to in the *Eudemian Ethics* (1.1217B23–4) – we find ourselves both on firmer ground and in more wide ranging controversy. There is little doubt that a good deal of new philosophical speculation was to be found in this essay, but scholars differ greatly as to what Aristotle had to say. Jaeger's reading is clear: *On Philosophy* was an anti-Platonic manifesto; but this suggestion depends on the view that Aristotle subscribed at an earlier stage to all the most important parts of Plato's philosophical programme. We may accept a minimal version of Jaeger's analysis: in *On Philosophy* Aristotle did more than *imply* theses of his own in the course of an onslaught on Platonic positions; he advanced his own specific claims directly. But what do the fragments tell us these claims were?

Certainly in *On Philosophy* Aristotle talked about the gods, and some thought that his account differed greatly from that of Plato;[9] and he certainly attacked as unintelligible both the notion that the first principles are the One and the Dyad, and the Platonic account of the relationship between 'form-numbers' and mathematical numbers.[10] It seems that *On Philosophy* contained no attack on the 'classical' theory of Forms, that of the *Phaedo* and the *Republic*. What it does seem to have included, however, was an account of the 'cosmic' situation of human beings: the theory of Forms is not mentioned, but human life seems to make good sense without them. And the literary form of this account was a rewriting of Plato's own myth of the Cave in the seventh book of the *Republic* (Cic. *ND* 2.37.95ff = fr. 13 Ross). The cave-dwellers are now depicted as surrounded by works of such magnificence as to induce them to believe in the existence of some sort of godly organizer. On reading this, we might suppose that Aristotle's view of the gods is very different from that of Plato in the *Timaeus*. If so, could the new theory also have been intended to displace the Forms from their causal role? A brief digression on what Plato says about gods and Forms, together with a look at Aristotle's own ideas about the nature of the gods, will shed light on this question.

Plato's thinking about the Forms, beginning with the *Symposium* and the *Phaedo* and culminating with the attempt to organize the Forms as products of the One and the Dyad, as described by Aristotle, developed *originally* in separation from his reflections about the gods. I shall assume – and argue in a later chapter – that Aristotle's evidence that Plato always somehow maintained a theory of Forms must be accepted, and that whatever alterations Plato may have made after the *Parmenides*, he at no time abandoned the belief that Forms are separate from particulars. I shall also assume, however, that the originally distinct contexts of Plato's theory of Forms on the one hand and of the gods on the other made it easy for Aristotle (in *On Philosophy*) to maintain certain parts of Plato's metaphysics, viz., a suitably adapted version of his account of God as Self-moved Mover, while consistently rejecting the notion of separate Forms.

Let us summarize Plato's later ideas about the gods, leaving aside, at this point, the problem of the relation between God and Form. Briefly, in late Platonic metaphysics, God is what Aristotle would call an efficient cause: he is the Craftsman of the *Timaeus* and the 'Cause of the Mixture' in the *Philebus*. He is some sort of Mind, who fulfils Plato's desire – expressed as far back as the *Phaedo* (98D) – for a being able to arrange things for the best. Thus in Aristotelian language he supplies the final cause, as well as the efficient cause, though Aristotle thinks that he 'supplies' neither satisfactorily. And his handiwork, the physical, living universe, formed, it seems, at the beginning of time,[11] may itself be called a visible god, with body, soul, and mind. Such visibility, in fact, transforms astronomy – an atheistic science in the hands of such men as Anaxagoras (*Laws* 12.967C) – into Platonic theology. The world itself, once formed, will continue in being as an eternal and – in the heavens – unchanging reality.

Let us highlight a few features of this scheme. First there is the mode of God's action. God is a planner, a craftsman, a begetter. In the *Timaeus* at least, he plans in accordance with a model. Now notice what may seem a striking omission: there is little comment in the *Timaeus* about the nature of God himself – except that we are told he is good; in particular, there is no attempt in the *Timaeus* to identify God as self-moving *soul*; rather God is mind.

In the *Laws* self-movement is discussed by Plato in the context of the soul's immortality and of why things are in motion rather than at rest. Plato identifies the 'movements' of the soul: thinking, planning, etc. There is a sense, of course, in which all this can be viewed as related to (or derived from) what he says in the *Timaeus*. Plato's Demiurge in the *Timaeus*, and his Cause of the Mixture in the *Philebus*, are not defined as self-movers, or indeed as souls at all, but the Demiurge in the *Timaeus* does arrange things because he is good and because he wants to. God as a self-moving efficient cause is what the *Phaedo* projects as desirable; this is not inconsistent with the God of the *Timaeus* and with the *Philebus*, and it is developed further in the *Laws*.

Let us now identify, so far as we can from our limited selection of fragments, what Aristotle is ready to offer the public in *On Philosophy*.[12] The discussion of theology was apparently to be found in book 3. There Aristotle discussed evidence, both popular and philosophical, for the existence of God. Simplicius records his argument that where there is a better, there is also a best,[13] and it is at least clear from a confused passage of Cicero that in book 3 of *On Philosophy* (among other theological claims) Aristotle identified God with mind.[14] This identification seems reasonable enough; similar ideas occur in the *Eudemian Ethics*, the *Nicomachean Ethics*, and the *Metaphysics*.[15] It is also Platonic enough, reminding us of the Demiurge of the *Timaeus* and of other Platonic figures. But inspection of the *activity* of the primary God-Mind reveals differences. For Aristotle already in *On Philosophy* the world is unambiguously eternal. Whatever Plato may have thought on this subject – I have indicated my own support for the view that the making of the world by the Demiurge is fact not myth (11 above) – Aristotle's position is certain. According to Cicero he differed markedly with Plato in *On Philosophy*, book 3; here is a likely point of contention. The world, he thought, had no beginning; the defence of the claim for the beginning of our world-order is impossible.[16] So Aristotle's God is neither creator nor organizer in the manner of Plato's Demiurge. To put the point in Aristotle's developed language (though such terminology does not occur in our fragments of *On Philosophy*), he is no external efficient cause. It would, of course, be anachronistic to attribute to Aristotle the Neoplatonic view that God is the 'ground' of being; hence we must assume that although the cave-dwellers think that the cosmos reveals signs of God's handiwork, they should not be misinterpreted. If the evidence points to an efficient cause at all, it is not to a *transcendent* efficient cause but to an immanent one; that is, a world-soul, or rather World-Mind.

We come then to the question of Mind's action. First, since there is no doubt that the star-gods of late Platonic theology occur in *On Philosophy*, what is Mind's relationship with them, if any? The star-gods are self-moved movers in some sense in Aristotle's later *De Caelo*. There is therefore no reason to think that self-movement has already been eliminated in *On Philosophy*. Yet in the *De Caelo* as we have it there is evidence both for some sort of self-movers and for a transcendent unmoved mover. Is such a possibility available for *On Philosophy*? Jaeger thought so, and others have followed him.[17] But although, as we have seen, there is evidence of God as Mind in *On Philosophy*, there is no evidence that he is *especially* concerned with the movement of the sphere of the fixed stars. That does not mean, however, that he has no kind of cosmological function at all.

An attempt has sometimes been made to find the theory that God is a transcendent mover of heavenly bodies (or star-souls) in the evidence from the *Physics* that in *On Philosophy* Aristotle discussed the nature of final causes (*telos, to hou heneka*).[18] But it has also been observed that this discussion is not linked in the fragments to the various theories of *motion*.[19] God, it has sometimes been suggested, may be some sort of object of aspiration (perhaps to men) in *On Philosophy*, as in the *Eudemian Ethics* (8.1249B9–19), but that is another question. We are on safe ground if we conclude – so far – that Aristotle's theology in *On Philosophy* is limited. There is a first or highest God; he is both Mind and World as a whole, that is, he is a World-Mind. There is no fifth element,[20] though in holding to a theory of star-gods Aristotle (like Plato) is open to such a development. What there is, according to Cicero's *De Natura Deorum* (2.16.44, fr. 21 Ross), is an analysis (partly inspired by related work in Plato's *Laws*) of different types of motion. Motion is of one of three kinds – natural, enforced, and voluntary – and the star-souls engage in voluntary motions; that is , they choose to move. Why do they so choose? Here perhaps, it has sometimes been suggested, is the place for God to be seen as a final cause only. For, as we have seen, final causes are discussed in *On Philosophy*.

If we knew that in *On Philosophy* God himself did not move, we should know that the supposed difficulties of a self-moving first cause had already been faced directly. But we do not know, and there is good reason to think they had not. At *De Caelo* 1.279AB Aristotle suggests that, according to *On Philosophy*, the highest divinity is unchanging, but in unceasing motion. Why, one might ask, should the God be in motion anyway? Answer: because Plato's star-gods were in motion. Soul *is* that which moves itself. It is highly likely that the God or Mind of *On Philosophy* was, in a rather Platonic mode, a self-moved being. But was he a Self-moved Mover of others and, if so, how?

The star-gods of *On Philosophy* are self-moved. They choose to move. The relevant question therefore is: Why do they choose? Why do they *want* to move? Only a Platonic answer will do – and an appeal to final cause. It is because it is *best* to do so. Were Plato to give this answer we should interpret the notion of best with reference to the Forms, and in particular to the Form of the Good. With Aristotle we cannot assume a reference to the Forms. Are we to assume, however, that the good which the self-moving star-gods choose is the nature of a *transcendent* God, which would thus, as Jaeger held, move as a final cause? There is no evidence for Jaeger's view either; it depends on the assumption that a final cause *implies* a transcendent God. Yet all our evidence thus far would point to an *immanent* God. Such a God could still be a final cause for the movements of the stars, and, as self-mover, both a final and an efficient cause for the rest of the universe. We conclude, therefore, that there is no transcendent God in *On Philosophy*, but rather an immanent Mind which functions as both final and efficient cause. There is no transcendence of any kind. 'Nature' is the highest reality; the *Protrepticus* took a similar line (B47–51). Self-movement (as immanent Mind) is the highest God.

Our discussion of *On Philosophy* has necessarily been based on the interpretation of disparate fragments; it would be strengthened if we could show that even in the original version of the later *De Caelo*, God is still a self-mover, still not yet either transcendent or unmoved. A digression to achieve this seems unavoidable. Generally speaking, scholars have realized that most sections of the *De Caelo* point to the absence of an Unmoved Mover, but that a few passages favour its presence. These are usually – and rightly – disposed of as interpolations into the original text of the treatise.[21]

In the *De Caelo* we find a new fifth element whose *natural* movement as a self-mover is circular. Without other changes from the theory of *On Philosophy*, a further transcendent mover would still be unnecessary. Nor does Aristotle develop an *analysis* of self-movement in the *De Caelo*; that has to wait until the last book of the *Physics* (see 74f below). The absence of analysis too should indicate that the demand for an *Unmoved* Mover in the original *De Caelo* is premature. What the original text of *De Caelo* contained, I believe, was a fifth element, intended to perform naturally the movements induced by the Self-moved Mover still advocated in *Physics* 7. Let us therefore look at those sections of the *De Caelo* which are said to contradict this since they presuppose the existence of an *unmoved* first principle which itself moves other bodies. There are only a very few such passages.

1 *De Caelo* 2.6. Here we have discussion of the motion of the 'outside' sphere of the heavens. A number of proofs are offered, designed to show that its movement must be constant. Two of these, the second and the fourth, depend on the existence of an Unmoved Mover. This is even said to be incorporeal (288B6). If these two arguments were removed from the text, they would not be missed. They certainly could be interpolated, as has often been recognized, and the second of them seems to imply (288A28) the analysis of self-motion to be found in book 8 of the *Physics*.
2 *De Caelo* 4.3. At 311A9ff there is a clear reference to the theory of the Unmoved Mover complete with a reference to 'our first writings' (*en tois prōtois logois*), by which Aristotle seems to mean *Physics* 8.[22] Again the sentence can be removed without danger to the argument, and indeed it looks like an 'updating' of the text.

Perhaps it might now be sufficient to observe that the *De Caelo* in its original form had no transcendent Unmoved Mover, and leave it at that. But there is a further complication. It is often thought that the *Physics* is largely earlier than the *De Caelo*.[23] There are several references to some form of our *Physics* in the *De Caelo*, but no such references to the *De Caelo* in the *Physics*. This latter could be coincidence, and all the references in the *De Caelo* could be later insertions into what is certainly an interpolated text. But the number of passages to be explained is considerable,[24] and we should not forget that our *Physics* was not composed as a single treatise, and that the original *De Caelo* does not refer to *Physics* 8, with its rejection of the Platonic doctrine of self-motion.

There are three passages which might seem to invalidate this last claim: one, a text we have already discussed, is a late addition to the *De Caelo* itself (4.311A11); the other two (1.273A17 said to refer to *Physics* 8.8, and 1.275B21 said to refer to *Physics* 8.10) are more controversial, but even if not later additions need not refer to *Physics* 8.

De Caelo 273A17, indeed, does not specifically refer to the *Physics* at all – the text merely remarks that 'it has been shown previously ...,' and the subject-matter under consideration appears in *Physics* 8. The form of the reference is such that even if it does refer to the *Physics*, it could certainly have been an addendum. In any case, the reference could be to *Physics* 7.242B19. As for *De Caelo* 275B21, which refers to Aristotle's book 'On Motion' (i.e., to what eventually became the later books of the *Physics*), we read that 'there is an argument in the writings "On Motion" suggesting that no finite body has infinite potentiality, and no infinite body finite potentiality.' This sentence is not only unnecessary to the argument; it does not flow smoothly from its predecessor. It appears to be an addition. We conclude that in the original *De Caelo* there are no references at least to book 8 of the *Physics*, that is to the analysis of the concept of self-motion.

There is a further problem. There *are* references in *De Caelo* to *Physics* 6, and *Physics* 6 is often said to have been written together with *Physics* 7 and 8, all comprising *On Motion*. Yet a close look at the evidence provides nothing to support such an interpretation. *Physics* 6 (called *On Motion* at *De Caelo* 3.299A10) begins with backward glances at earlier books of the *Physics* and its closing gives reason to suppose that further discussion of motion is to follow. But book 7 follows book 6, and similarly, at the very least, avoids rejecting the notion of a first Self-moved Mover. This book, in fact, was probably *replaced* by our present discussion of unmoved movers in book 8. At any rate books 6 and 7 may have been the original *On Motion*, to which 8 (possibly intended to replace 7) was later added. As for the opening of *Physics* 8 itself, it contains no backward-looking glances at book 6. We may notice, moreover, that at *Physics* 8.251A9, book 3 is referred to as 'in the *Physics*' – that is, book 8 is somehow not 'in the [original?] *Physics*.'

Let us sum up. If the sequence of texts on motion is (a) *Physics* 6–7, (b) *De Caelo*, (c) *Physics* 8 (often referred to in Aristotle himself as *On Motion*), then the difficulties about self-motion disappear. Most important, the analysis of self-motion in the last book of the *Physics* follows the original *De Caelo*; and evidence thus accumulates that the original text of the *De Caelo* (as well as the bulk of our present text) knows nothing of an *Unmoved* Mover. Returning then to the reason for the digression: if there was no Unmoved Mover in the first version of the *De Caelo*, or of the earlier books of the *Physics*, as Easterling has shown,[25] we have *further* strong reason to deny one in *On Philosophy*.

So far then, in a brief examination of *On Ideas*, *On the Good*, and *On Philosophy*, we have found the groundwork for a new theory of universals and of predication, criticism of the theory of Forms itself, and of the notion of the One and Dyad as principles, as well as a substantive modification of Plato's theory of a *transcendent* Mind – though as yet no attack on self-moved movers despite the discussion of final causes in *On Philosophy*. But this discussion, as far as the fragments allow us to see, is in no sense a full-scale analysis of causation.

IV The Content of the 'Eudemus'

Topics and *Categories* aside, there still remain substantial fragments of two works which have been thought of as important sources for positive metaphysics in the early period of Aristotle's career – earlier in fact than the works we have discussed so far in this chapter. The first of these, the dialogue *Eudemus*, was written to commemorate a friend of Aristotle's killed at Syracuse in 354: its subject is the immortality of the soul. Frequently since Jaeger the *Eudemus* has been combed for Platonic teaching. It is sometimes believed to have urged not only the immortality of the soul, but the theory of Forms and the doctrine of knowledge as recollection. According to Jaeger (*Aristotle*, 40), 'the Neoplatonists' used the *Eudemus* and the *Phaedo* as equally valuable sources for Plato's doctrine of immortality. But a glance at the evidence for this rather startling conclusion shows that it is unfounded.[26]

What, then, can we be sure of about the *Eudemus*? First, Aristotle attacked the notion that the soul is a 'harmony' (fr. 7 Ross), as Plato had done in the *Phaedo*, and as he himself was to do again in the *De Anima*. Secondly, Themistius says that Plato's arguments for the immortality of the soul (and those of Aristotle's *Eudemus*) really imply that the *mind* (*nous*) is immortal[27] – a position perhaps akin to that which Aristotle takes in the *De Anima* (not to speak of *On Philosophy*). Thirdly, however, Elias, in his commentary on *Categories*, says several times that Aristotle 'in his dialogues' proclaims the immortality of the soul.[28] Fourthly, Proclus, in his commentary on the *Republic*, speaks of the soul coming here 'from there' and forgetting the 'sights' (*theamatōn*) there. This idea he attributes to the 'inspired' Aristotle, though he says nothing specific about where in Aristotle's writings it is to be found.[29] (Proclus's lack of specificity, however, is partly remedied elsewhere, for he says that the descent of the soul into body and related matters are discussed 'in the dialogues'.)[30] Finally Philoponus, in his commentary on the *De Anima*, while discussing the *Eudemus's* rejection of the theory that the soul is a harmony, says that for Aristotle the soul is some kind of form (*eidos*),[31] a notion which Simplicius repeats.[32] What is to be made of all this? First, that not one text says that Aristotle accepted Platonic Forms. Nor do we read that the *Eudemus* was regularly used as a *substitute* for the *Phaedo* in discussions of immortality, though it was widely recognized that both the *Phaedo* and the *Eudemus* attacked the theory of the soul as harmony. Secondly, that Aristotle's talk of the soul as a form cannot *by itself* tell us that it is a Platonic *separate* form rather than a soul *for* a particular body as in the *De Anima*.

By far the most remarkable texts are those of Proclus which suggest that the doctrines of pre-existence and survival of the soul are to be found somewhere in Aristotle's dialogues. Furthermore, according to Proclus, the soul forgets the sights (*theamata*)[33] which it knew in an earlier existence. We may ask: what are these sights? There is no reason to assume that they are Forms; sights which are not Forms are visible before birth according to the *Meno* (81C1), a favourite dialogue of Aristotle's. Indeed the *Meno's* very *unclarity* about the nature of the 'sights' we see before birth would suit Aristotle's scepticism about Forms. Nothing that Proclus says suggests that Aristotle associated pre-existence with *recollection*, let alone with recollection of Forms. On the contrary, Aristotle is held to have explained *why* the soul *forgets* what it saw in earlier times and in some earlier existence 'there.' When it lived 'naturally' (the phrase is a foretaste of the language of the *Protrepticus*), it was healthy, and it knew its 'lessons' (*grammata*). When it became sick, and was born into the 'unnatural' life here, it forgot them. Hence in this life we have to learn all over again – presumably by induction and deduction.

In sum, then, the soul is immortal. (Themistius's reduction of this to an immortality of mind *might* be question-begging.) But there are no Forms as there are in the *Phaedo*, even though one of the arguments of the *Eudemus* (the attack on harmony) recalls that Platonic text, as indeed does the whole theme of Aristotle's work. But Aristotle's position is not unusual. After all, others (e.g., Pythagoras) held that the soul is immortal, and Socrates is depicted in the *Apology* (perhaps with historical accuracy) as regarding the survival of the soul as a possible outcome – but without benefit of a theory of Forms. So in the *Eudemus* Aristotle believed in the immortality of the soul (or if Themistius is right, of the mind) – though this solution cannot be deduced merely from the remarks of Simplicius and Philoponus that the soul is a separate substance. Now if in the *Eudemus* it were the mind which is immortal (or perhaps, as we shall see, ensouled mind), then we should have an interesting precursor of Aristotle's later thought – with which the *Protrepticus* will also provide many parallels. But if we accept this solution, then we must remember that in the *Eudemus* the mind is capable of remembering and forgetting, for, as Proclus says, it *remembers* after death its experiences in this life (fr. 5) – which makes it a creature very different from the impassive 'productive' intellect of *De Anima* 3.5. But even if it is the mind which is immortal in the *Eudemus*, its relationship to the body is different from that expounded by Aristotle in later days.

Perhaps the solution to the problem of the soul in the *Eudemus* is that Aristotle, following the *Phaedo*, did not distinguish clearly between soul and mind, but only urged that the soul (mind) did pre-exist the body. The ambiguity suggested by Themistius shows that Aristotle perhaps maintained the Platonic theory that *minds* exist in souls, and are therefore presumably affected by them. In any case, the *Eudemus* gives us no reason to revise our view of Aristotle's attitude to Platonic Forms. In 353 (or thereabouts) there is no evidence that he accepted them.

V The Content of the 'Protrepticus'

What about the *Protrepticus*?[34] That too was composed in about 353, more or less contemporaneously with the *Eudemus*, and was probably stimulated by Isocrates' remarks on philosophy in his *Antidosis*.[35] It was very well known in antiquity, both directly and as a major source of Cicero's *Hortensius*. Designed to promote philosophy among the unenlightened, it took the form of an address to a Cyprian princeling named Themison, whom we may suppose to have been a small-town 'tyrant.' It seems to have provoked a feeble reply from one of Isocrates' pupils.[36]

There is no mention of Platonic Forms in our extensive fragments of the *Protrepticus*, though the work is Platonic in some respects and gives a defence of what Aristotle seems to see as the Platonic spirit, the Platonic vision of philosophy. Aristotle's aim is to set down the nature of the best (and the second best) life, to praise the life of thought (*phronēsis*), and to argue that one ought to philosophize in the spirit not of Isocrates but of the Academy. Thinking and 'looking at' things (*theōria*) are the tasks of virtue and most worthy of human choice (B70 Düring). They are to be chosen for their own sake. Nature is the model and art imitates it (B13). Art is useful to complete nature: a theme to be expanded, along with much else, in the second book of the *Physics*. There is a purpose in nature, that is, a final cause, on which we should do well to reflect. Pythagoras was right to say that God 'constructed' man to contemplate and understand nature.

As Jaeger saw, there are Platonic themes in the *Protrepticus*, as there are in the *Eudemus*. But Jaeger often misses Platonic themes that are there and invents those that are not. He suggests, for example, that Aristotle already makes use of a 'Platonic' or 'Academic' division of the sciences into something like physics, logic, and dialectic.[37] This suggestion is quite misleading. Aristotle says that philosophy is concerned with: (1) things that are just and advantageous, and (2) the science of nature and the rest of truth. Aristotle continues by identifying the nature of the philosopher, the *phronimos*, as that of a man who can determine what the greatest goods are, probably by the application of his mind to nature: 'For what rule or more accurate limit of goods is there than that of the philosopher?' But Jaeger's attempt to make this 'limit' an absolute norm is misguided, based only on his assumption that in the *Protrepticus* Aristotle 'is still completely dominated by the conception of *phronēsis* in the old sense,' which '*must* [Jaeger's italics] have been based on Plato's ethical metaphysics, that is, on the unity of being and value.' Jaeger assumes that Aristotle's unity of being and value entails the Platonic Theory of Forms (*Aristotle*, 87), hence that Aristotle promoted ethics and politics as examples of 'exact science' – a view which Aristotle rejects in both versions of our *Ethics* and of which the *Protrepticus* itself gives no indication.

Jaeger's argument that in the *Ethics* Aristotle reverses himself about goodness is fantasy, but fantasy based on a truth, namely that Aristotle was impressed by the ideas found in Plato's *Philebus* – a work probably a little later than the *Protrepticus*.[38] But Jaeger misreads the *Philebus* too, as teaching that ethics is part of an 'exact and mathematical' science. Now of course Plato is interested in limit and measure in the *Philebus*; he thinks that to understand them is to approach the Good itself (65A). But this is not the same as making ethics an 'exact and mathematical' science. And when Aristotle remarks in the second book of his *Statesman* that 'the Good is the most exact measure of all things,'[39] he is probably foreshadowing Plato's remark in the *Laws* that 'God is the measure of all things' (*pace* Protagoras).[40] In the *Protrepticus* and *Statesman*, Aristotle presumably agreed with Plato that God is good (a view he held throughout his life), or even *the* Good; but he also probably thought that God is to be identified with Mind – and it is of God as Mind that Plato speaks in the *Laws*.

Jaeger's basic error, repeated again and again throughout his treatment of the *Protrepticus*, is to assume that wherever Aristotle speaks of 'nature' he refers to Platonic Forms, presumably because Plato does speak of Forms as what exist 'by nature' and in other such ways. Hence whenever Aristotle talks of theoretical wisdom (*theōrētikē phronēsis*) dealing with nature itself and with truth rather than imitations, or saying that the 'best law is that which is disposed most naturally' (B47 Düring), Jaeger assumes that the Forms are in question, that the philosopher looks not to imitations but to Platonic Forms. Aristotle himself speaks in a quite different way. He speaks, as we have seen, of Pythagoras's reply to the questions with which Aristotle himself is concerned till the end of his life: What is man for? What is his final cause? Why did nature and God beget us? (B18). Pythagoras's answer is: 'to contemplate the heavens' (*ouranos*). Man has come into this life to be a contemplator of nature. Aristotle then cites Anaxagoras for a similar reply. Man would choose to be born to watch the heaven and the stars and the sun and the moon. Man, says Aristotle in the same passage, is the most valuable of the animals here, so that it is clear that he has been born by nature and in accordance with nature. And again 'intelligence' (*phronēsis*) is for us the end by nature: *phronēsis* is the 'most final' of the parts of the soul, and 'thinking' is the best and the highest (*akrotaton*) of all things (B23–5). As to what we think about when we think best, 'whether the object of knowledge (*gnōston*) is the cosmos or some other nature, perhaps we must consider later'.

The last comment is particularly interesting. Aristotle throws open the possibility that there is something higher than the *cosmos*, but says nothing here of what it is. Just possibly it might be a Platonic Form, but in view of Aristotle's constant repetition of the notion that thinking itself is the highest natural end and the highest thing in nature, it is much more likely that he is thinking of some manifestation of Mind. 'Mind is our God,' he quotes (B110). The *problem* to which he alludes is whether that Mind is *in* the cosmos, as he tends to assume in much of his earlier work, or outside. It was to be a long time before he resolved the matter to his own satisfaction.

There is one Platonic strain in the *Protrepticus* which we cannot pass over. Interestingly it is exactly what we might expect given the contemporary *Eudemus*. Aristotle is greatly impressed by the moral asceticism of the Platonic Socrates. Just as the *Eudemus*, in its paean on immortality, its myth, and the universally recognized moral starkness of its 'other-worldly' ethics, recalls the *Phaedo*, so the apparent attack on the beauty of Alcibiades in the *Protrepticus* recalls the *Symposium*, but in an earnest and humourless way. Strength, size, and beauty are a laugh, worth nothing (fr. 10a). If we had the eyes of Lynceus, says Aristotle, we would see that Alcibiades' most beautiful body concealed the vileness 'in his guts' (*introspectis visceribus*).[41] The 'model' for Alcibiades is an obscenity produced by Etruscan pirates who bind together the living (mind) and the dead (the body). Perhaps one could go further. The *Phaedo* and the *Symposium* are more or less contemporary works of Plato's, designed to exhibit the two sides of the great philosopher, the Platonic 'lover' personified by Socrates. In the *Phaedo* he overcomes pain and death; in the *Symposium* he overcomes pleasure.[42] Pain and pleasure are the twin enemies of philosophy and the good life.

In Aristotle's *Eudemus* and *Protrepticus* we detect a similar, probably consciously similar, thesis. The *Protrepticus* challenges us to philosophy, and with its emphasis on the power and importance of the mind indicates that we have the divine energy required. By substituting the mind for Plato's *erōs*, however, Aristotle has made a fateful decision which will in the end affect his most basic notions of God and man. He argues endlessly in the *Protrepticus* that mind at its best is *not* productive of anything outside itself (B68–70 Düring). But the implications of that argument are to be discussed later (117, 160 below). For the present let us look at his own description of philosophy or contemplation: we go to Olympia for nothing more than to 'see' (and seeing is better than many possessions); we do not go to the Dionysia to get something from the actors – indeed they cost money – but to watch. Seeing must be valued higher than many seemingly useful things. We ought not to resort to men on the stage who 'imitate silly women and slaves, or people who fight and rush about.' There is no point in making great efforts to see play-actors and not the *nature* of things itself; and we must not think that there is no reward in watching the truth (B44). If we could be transported to the Isles of the Blest we would need nothing. We could simply think and watch (*dianoeisthai kai theōrein*). If we had such a choice and did not take it, that would be really shameful (B43). And even on the practical level the pursuit of philosophy is rewarding, for the philosopher looks at nature, not at stage-plays or similar things, but at the world. As law-giver he looks not at second-hand copies of constitutions such as we find in Sparta and Crete, but at nature itself which is divine (B49).

Philosophy is its own reward: it is easy and can be practised everywhere and without equipment. So speaks Aristotle the non-citizen resident in Athens. It is pleasurable and without any sense of servile labour (*ponos*) (B56, cf. B85, 87). All men seek – not the Forms – but to think and to know (B72, 73), says Aristotle in anticipation of the opening lines of the *Metaphysics*. If for a man to be is to live the life of the mind, then when a philosopher thinks, he *is*, is real, apparently in the strictest and most authoritative sense of the word. The pleasure of living comes from the use of the soul: thinking is 'really living.' Düring holds that the last words of the *Protrepticus* were the ones we quoted above:[43] 'Mind is our God …' and 'Mortal life (*aiōn*) has a portion of some god. Therefore we ought to pursue philosophy or say farewell to life and depart from here, since all else is a lot of rubbish and drivel.' In the *Eudemus* Aristotle had talked about whether being born is worthwhile. Now he affirms that it is, if we do the right thing – not of course if we engage in what Isocrates calls 'philosophy.' That is part of the drivel.

The philosopher is free, for he pursues thoughts for their own sake (B25 Düring). In doing so he is like God (B36). Aristotle leaves it open, in the manner of certain passages in the *Topics*, as to whether fire or air or number or other natures (perhaps Forms) are the causes and principles of things. In the *Protrepticus*, as in the *Eudemus*, we can see that Aristotle is a lover of wisdom; but we cannot see that he adopts Platonic Forms. The nearest he comes to adopting them is the present passage (B36), where Forms may be lumped in with other implausible candidates like air or fire as the possibly basic causes of the world.

When Aristotle came to the Academy in 367, the *Parmenides* had probably not yet been written, but it was soon to come, and there still seems no reason to deny that Aristotle himself is the young interlocutor of the second part. Indeed the lack of *specific* citation of the *Parmenides* by Aristotle may be connected with that fact. Be that as it may, we know that Aristotle arrived at the Academy when major debates about Forms among the leading members of the group seem to have prompted Plato into his baffling piece of self-examination. Eudoxus offered what appeared to Aristotle an impossible solution to problems of the participation of particulars in Forms. Aristotle probably alludes to it in the *Topics* (2.113A25ff), and Plato himself rejected the Eudoxan way out. With this sort of intellectual turmoil in the school it is highly unlikely that Aristotle would have been an instant convert to any version of the theory of Forms in 367. Our examination of the works written about 353, as well as those of the few years later, indicates that at no point did he put himself forward as an orthodox disciple of Plato in this regard. What really impressed him, as the *Protrepticus* shows with the utmost clarity, was Plato's idea – emphasized again in a section of the recent *Theaetetus* (176C) – that man should seek to attain likeness to God as far as possible. It was an idea which, in some form, Aristotle was to retain till the end of his life. We find it in sections of book 10 of the *Nicomachean Ethics*, much of which is an incompletely corrected version of the *Protrepticus*.

VI A Metaphysical Alternative to Forms: The First Steps
(*Posterior Analytics*, *Metaphysics* A, E)

About the time of Plato's death Aristotle moved from the studied refusal to speak of the theory of Forms, which is visible in the *Categories*, to open and forthright criticism. Our next concern is: When did he feel the need to develop a consciously metaphysical alternative more fully and more openly? When did he move from sketching rival accounts of universals and of predication (which he probably considered matters of conceptual analysis) to a new theory of cause, of being, and of intelligibility? Let us return to the passage of the *Posterior Analytics* with which we began (1.83A33) – the passage where Aristotle makes two comments, first that there are no Forms, and second that even if there are, they contribute nothing to knowledge: they are irrelevant. The second point had been discussed by Plato himself in the *Parmenides* (133Eff): Mastership may be related, says Parmenides, to slavery, but not to slaves. As we observed earlier, the most basic objection raised against Plato in the *Posterior Analytics* is that the Forms are not *causal*, and this brings us to the question of Aristotle's first formal *identification* of causation as deserving exact explanation. For, perhaps more than anything else, this identification eventually led Aristotle to develop further the alternative metaphysics of substance, of which the *Categories* is the first stage.

One of the examples which Aristotle uses in the *Posterior Analytics* is the proposition 'Man is white.' Aristotle cannot explain this by reference to Forms. The introduction of Forms does not help him understand why the man in question is white. In a Platonic world it *would* be helpful, for by whiteness things are white. Now that this explanation is rejected as inadequate, the causal question remains. In its most general formulation the problem is: why are things as they are? In one sense, this is a question of physics, and Aristotle develops his theories of causation in the early books of the *Physics*, the *De Caelo*, and the *De Generatione et Corruptione*. But it also has near-metaphysical implications, though at this stage Aristotle would have preferred to call such enquiries 'logical'.

Aristotle does *not* take up the question of cause in the *first* book of the *Posterior Analytics*, but in the second book it arises at once. In fact there are four questions (2.89B23ff), of the following types:

1 Is the sun eclipsed? (Aristotle calls this question of fact [Does X occur?] a *hoti* question.)
2 Why is the sun eclipsed? (Here is the causal question for which we were looking. Aristotle goes on to ask about the cause [*aition*] of the eclipse.)
3 Do centaurs or gods exist? (Aristotle calls this question about the existence of a subject a 'whether-it-exists' question.)[44]
4 When we know that X exists, we may ask questions like 'What is a god, what is a man?'

In the following discussion, as commentators have frequently observed, Aristotle tries to reduce his four questions to two: Does it exist? What is it? The reduction seems to suggest that both about events and about possible subjects we can ask either, does such and such exist/occur? or why does such and such exist/occur? We thus have a clear distinction between questions of fact and questions involving causes and explanations of fact. The formalization of this distinction marks both an advance on Aristotle's early 'metaphysics' in the *Categories* and a claim that problems of cause/explanation are not merely physical questions: they have necessary metaphysical implications. The 'metaphysics' of X, that is, involves knowing what there is and why there is what there is. As we shall see later, there is for the first time in our *Posterior Analytics* a great deal about what is often called 'essence' (*to ti ēn einai*); I shall prefer the translation 'realized nature.'

At the earlier stage of Aristotle's 'metaphysical' activity, which is represented by the *Categories,* direct discussion of causation is absent. In the *Categories* Aristotle is concerned with what kinds of things there are and how these things can be classified. As is generally recognized, such reflections continued the activity of the Academy and indeed are themselves part of that activity. There is no discussion of the processes of causation in the *Categories;* the question as to why things are as they are is not raised, even though it is noted that substances are receptive of contraries (4A11ff). Indeed, we may note that even in the list of subjects for discussion in *Metaphysics* B, although the words *aition/aitia* occur, the principal themes are formal and material causes and the nature (and principles) of non-sensible substance. There is no clear assertion of the importance of the '*four* causes' – which indicates that 'metaphysics' is still proposed as the study of the nature of possible non-sensible substances. But, as we shall see, appearances are also deceptive: although *metaphysics is to be dependent* on a theory of non-sensible substances, it is not limited to it. Neither the old 'classification' of the *Categories* nor the Academic version of non-sensible substance properly indicates the subject-matter of metaphysics.

The opening section of *Metaphysics* E sounds much more like the *Posterior Analytics* – not, however, the 'anti-Platonic' parts of that work, but the constructive schemata Aristotle has begun to build. In *Metaphysics* E we find that the same intellectual activity (metaphysics) is concerned with *what* a thing *is* and *whether* it is. And chapter 2 of the same book, opening with the famous account of different senses of the word 'being,' identifies two particular ways in which metaphysics can approach the question: either through the categories, as we might expect, or through potentiality and actuality. Both these will be considered in later chapters. For the time being let us return to the identification of a formal metaphysical analysis of causation.

We begin with *Metaphysics* A. Looking back once again to Plato, we may assume that one of his first worries about particulars was epistemological.

How can the ever-changing particular be the object of knowledge? The search for the abiding Form and the consequent interest in classification grew out of that concern. Through the Form, according to Plato, the particular can be known, and the search for classification brought enquiry to the stage of Aristotle's categories. What things are there? What things exist and what are their logical and metaphysical relationships with one another? But in *Metaphysics* A we find, almost from the outset, quite a different tack. Wisdom, we learn, is concerned with certain principles and causes (1.982A1), for those who are experienced but not wise know facts but not the reason why (981A28). So far, the approach of *Metaphysics* A could lead us to a merely Platonic and Academic concern with the Forms or the One. But Aristotle turns rapidly to the *origins* of philosophy. Philosophy, he tells us, begins with wonder (982B): We are first concerned with the more obvious perplexities, then we advance to consider the sun, moon, and stars and the origin of the cosmos (as did the philosophers in the *Protrepticus*). First we are puzzled and wonder why things are as they are, but if we ever reach our conclusions, we shall be perplexed and full of wonder if things are *not* as they are: the learned geometer would be annoyed 'if the diagonal were to be commensurable.' And since it is *explanations* that we seek, Aristotle holds that philosophical knowledge is concerned with the original 'causes' of things – of which he recognizes the four types he has already deployed in his 'physical' treatises.

But we face an obvious methodological difficulty. There is no immediate reason to *assume* that the entire *Metaphysics* was compiled in short order. It may be a gradual collection of lecture courses and notes. Its very title *Metaphysics* is not due to Aristotle himself. How then do we know that the material which appears as book A of the *Metaphysics* is really 'metaphysical' in our sense of the word? Is it not more likely that the study of the four causes is really a problem in *physics*, in the philosophy of nature? If so, then wonder at why things are as they are is not proposed by Aristotle as a *metaphysical* anxiety at all – except in so far as he tells us he wants to decide whether the four causes are in fact the only *causes* there are (983B6, cf. 993A12). Indeed, a remark in *Metaphysics* A itself (983B) might seem to confirm the suggestion that the study of causes is non-metaphysical: Aristotle tells us that the question of causes has already been well analysed in his writings about nature, that is, in the *Physics* (2.3; 2.7). But such a conclusion would be strange in the light shed by the remaining sections of *Metaphysics* A, for there Aristotle considers far more than causes and their role in the world of change. His investigations and criticisms range widely over such obviously metaphysical problems as the nature and mode of existence of the Platonic Forms. In fact, in the next few words, after Aristotle has referred to the *Physics*, he lets us know what he has in mind: we must consider, he says, what our predecessors have said about beings (*tōn ontōn*) and truth. The latter word, in such a text, should involve consideration of the possible nature of non-physical beings. Indeed it becomes clear from later parts of the *Metaphysics* that Aristotle thinks that the existence of at least one such suprasensible being is necessary if a complete causal account even of *physical* beings is to be produced.

How do the role and nature of causes in *Metaphysics* A relate to that central theme of the *Posterior Analytics*, namely the dismissal of Forms as irrelevant? It is clear that analysis of causes is meant to do all that the Forms did – and more – to provide explanation of particulars, indeed to *complete* that explanation. In the *Categories* Aristotle is interested in showing how what he calls primary substances are the essential part of the subject-matter of philosophy – and in identifying what *are* primary substances. Now he begins with these primary substances themselves, hoping to show not just what can be listed as a primary substance, but how the world of primary substance can be *explained* – without reference to Platonic Forms. In *Metaphysics* A itself there is no direct answer to the question of *what* a particular *is* – a question which will eventually lead to the identification of a substance and its 'realized nature.' We are still dealing with the preliminary stage of asking *why* the world of particulars is as it is. But Aristotle has advanced well beyond negative criticism of Plato and beyond rival accounts of universals and predication. He is ready to develop new metaphysical proposals about causation; the *Posterior Analytics*, as we shall see, has paved the way. Aristotle wants to consider the metaphysical implications of his own *Physics*.

Aristotle does not provide all the answers in *Metaphysics* A. He identifies the four 'causes' as the way to proceed, but advances by a method he was more and more to favour, that of critically assessing his predecessors: it is a method he uses magisterially in the *De Anima*. Nevertheless by the time of *Metaphysics* A (that is, as we shall see, in the last ten years of Aristotle's life) there is a new programme for what he will call 'first philosophy' to take the place of the Platonic programme. Much preliminary work has been done. Already in the *Topics* Platonic dialectic, the queen of the sciences, has been dethroned; dialectic is now a more humble occupation. But now Aristotle's early approach, that of the *Categories*, the identification of what there is, must also be superseded. For the primacy of substance (already clear in the *Categories*) and the identification of substances in a manner free of Platonic confusions have led Aristotle to ask *why* things are as they are. Plato had explained in the *Republic* that Forms account both for the existence and for the intelligibility of the world, and that the Good does the same for the Forms (6.508E). His later metaphysics developed those themes. Now in *Metaphysics* A Aristotle is ready to propose an alternative thesis, for the Forms account neither for our knowledge of other things – as the *Posterior Analytics* and *Eudemian Ethics* have already asserted – nor for their existence (*einai*, 991A13). They do not even subsist in the particulars – not that subsistence would be enough to explain why particulars are, and have become, what they are.

One reason for Aristotle's denying the causal role of the Forms was their transcendence over particulars. It was not a new difficulty. According to the earlier *On Ideas*, Eudoxus had already tried a clumsy immanentist remedy which still confused particulars with kinds.[45] But if we no longer know what forms (or Forms) are like, then the metaphysical problems which Plato had tried to solve remain unsettled. The study of causation, which might seem to be only a problem in physics, is a metaphysical problem after all. We need to know more than the mechanics of causation; that is, we need to know the relationship of the causes themselves. For we now have no complete answer to the problem of why things are as they are, or, as Aristotle more readily expresses it, to the problem of their 'realized nature.' In the *Physics* Aristotle had hardly touched on the question of the relationship between causes – and the little treatment he gives the question occurs mainly in the late book 8.

The metaphysical analysis of the *Categories* is quite incomplete, and the opening of *Metaphysics* E shows us something of how Aristotle eventually intended to proceed. If *Metaphysics* A suggests that Plato's (and others') failure to explain causation requires a re-examination of the whole subject, of such 'simple' questions as how A can become B, *Metaphysics* Γ and E point the way forward. The opening chapter of book E indicates a concern with the principles and causes of beings, and this is quickly followed by the repetition of some of the ideas of book Γ: we are to be concerned with being qua being and with a 'demonstration' of being. Such a demonstration would be unnecessary were the Forms still available as explanations, but in the next chapter we begin to see beyond them – and beyond the virtual denial of 'metaphysics' in the *Eudemian Ethics*: 'being' is not a universal term; it has many senses. Four senses are listed: being as accidental being; being as truth; being as defined by the categories; being conceived as potential and actual. As the discussion continues throughout *Metaphysics* E, we discover that there is no science of accidental being and that being as truth is not primary: it should be studied in connection with thought rather than with things; or, as we should say, it is for the logician rather than the metaphysician. That leaves us with being as defined by the categories, as we should expect, and above all with substance (in the question of what –

after all – a substance is); and being seen in terms of potentiality and actuality.

Substance, of course, was not a new topic, though Aristotle's theories in *Metaphysics* Z and H certainly are. But by the standards of the early Aristotle, the more interesting new development is the importance to be given to potentiality and actuality. These concepts are hardly mentioned in *Metaphysics* A, but their development is of the greatest importance from the time of their first significant use in the *Physics*. Substance, actuality, and God or Mind, these are to be the future of the new Aristotelian metaphysics. Their fuller development will be charted in subsequent chapters. There is little trace of substance and actuality (but a certain amount on God) in the 'anti-Platonic' early writings with which this chapter has been primarily concerned. But the demolition work of those writings provided a basis for Aristotle's advance from conceptual critic of Platonic Forms to 'Aristotelian' metaphysician.

3

Forms, Numbers, and Aristotelian Development

I 'On Ideas'

I have argued earlier that Aristotle's work *On Ideas* is to be dated to about the time of Plato's death (14–15 above). The Sixth Platonic Letter, though probably not genuine, seems to give some idea of the argument about Forms going on in Plato's old age. Plato is made to say that he still upholds the theory.[1] Of course, we know that the theory had been under attack in some quarters since the time of the *Parmenides,* that is for some twenty years, but the letter to Erastus and Coriscus, friends of Aristotle from Scepsis, and to the 'tyrant' Hermeias who was to be Aristotle's host is, if not genuine, at least *ben trovato.* At the time of Plato's death at least some members of the circle around Aristotle are among the most severe critics of the theory. That is not to say, however, that they were its only critics; the view that Speusippus had already *abandoned* it, often repeated, may be correct, but lacks evidence.[2] Indeed, we have no evidence that he ever held it at all. The testimony of Aristotle might suggest that he did not; unlike Eudoxus, Speusippus is never named as a 'corrector' of Plato's theory. Rather he is the proponent of a 'Platonic' theory of mathematical objects and of a theory about first principles of a Pythagoreanizing sort.

Whereas Xenocrates' identification of Forms and the objects of mathematics could be a conservative rendering of Platonic notions of number, based ultimately on a reading of the *Phaedo* and of the sixth book of the *Republic,* the 'mathematics' of Speusippus and his theory of principles need have little connection with the theory of Forms in Plato's dialogues. Rather than Plato having influenced Speusippus on these questions, the truth could even be the other way round. There is nothing in our texts which would preclude the possibility that Speusippus first suggested to Plato that the objects of mathematics cannot be Forms, and that in his own theory of principles he encouraged rather than followed the 'Pythagoreanizing' of Plato's later work. All that stands in the way of such an interpretation is the unfounded assumption that all ideas in the Academy were either generated by Plato himself or were produced by those wishing to escape the consequences of attacks on Plato's original proposals. This is particularly unlikely to be true in the case of Speusippus, a man who was already sixty years old at the time of Plato's death. Xenocrates then was forty-nine and Aristotle a mere thirty-seven. In the work *On Ideas* there is no attack on Speusippus by name or on any theory which looks to be unique to Speusippus himself. That would make a lot more sense if Speusippus never accepted the theory of Forms, or at least if he had given it up long, long ago. The latter of these two suggestions is less likely, for if Speusippus had abandoned the theory, he would probably have replaced it with something else, or modified it as Eudoxus (who *is* mentioned in *On Ideas*) or Xenocrates attempted to do. It is worthwhile bearing these points in mind while looking again at what Aristotle has to say about different versions of Platonism, first in those limited parts of *On Ideas* which have survived.

One point is clear at the outset: *On Ideas* is about Forms, as far as we can see, not about mathematicals. It cannot therefore be aimed at Speusippus. There is a short section dealing with the theory of first principles, the One and the Dyad, which might include Xenocrates as well as Plato, though there are no particularly Xenocratean features visible: no description of the One as the Monad, or as Mind, or talk of different species of the 'great and small,' as there are in the *Metaphysics*.[3] This absence, however, may not be significant; Xenocrates, as well as Plato, could be the target. But if so, he would be only an incidental target; there are only very limited portions of *On Ideas* which would seem to have any special reference to Xenocrates. The most interesting section, however, deals with the relation of Forms to Numbers (85.24ff, fr. 4 Ross). Aristotle is arguing that the Dyad cannot be a principle, because number is prior to it. It is predicated of it as a Form, he says. Thus the Dyad would be a number, i.e., Two (as in Twoness is 2). For, continues Aristotle, Forms are basically numbers (*keintai*) for them. Thus number would be prior, since it is a kind of Form. If we could determine the meaning of ths passage, we should be rid of long-standing puzzles about the relationship between Forms and Numbers.

The first thing to note about Aristotle's reasoning here is that he knows that one version of it would not be acceptable to Plato (cf. *NE* 1.1096A19–20), for he knows that those who first introduced the theory of Forms did not offer a Form of Number itself. This is probably signalled in the *On Ideas* passage when Aristotle says not that his opponents regard number as a Form *simpliciter* but that it is a 'sort' of Form. Thus Aristotle probably does not wish to conclude from the fact that Twoness is a number (and Threeness is a number) that since numbers have something in common, there *should* be a Form of Number. We shall consider how else he might reach that conclusion without violating what he says in the *Nicomachean Ethics*.

Why or in what sense can Aristotle say that the Forms are numbers? Various scholars have denied that Plato ever identified all Forms with numbers, and some have attempted to answer the further question of how Aristotle could say that he did.[4] On this question, we shall consider some misinterpretations of a section of Theophrastus a little later. For the time being let us be content with noting that in the *Philebus* Plato does in a sense identify the Forms as numbers. It is not simply a question, as Annas proposed, of seeing how many species there are in a genus, and of awarding number characteristics accordingly. Rather it is a case of noting that Plato speaks of the Forms as henads and monads (15AB), that is, as units.[5] In that sense each Form is a perfect unity; it is numerical in that it is a perfect unit. No particulars are numerical in this sense; they are not perfect units. To the objection that 'one' is not a number, but the source of number for the Greeks, the answer is, 'not always.' Thus Xenocrates called his first principle odd (*perittos*) (fr. 15 Heinze), and indeed it would be absurd to suppose that if a Greek were asked how many cows he could see, when he answered 'two,' he mentioned a number, but if he said 'one,' he mentioned something else. The solution to such dilemmas is presumably that when (Pythagoreanizing?) Greeks were discussing the 'origin' of numbers, they might speculate on whether 'one' is really a number, but when they were counting they treated it like all the rest. At *Theaetetus* 185CD Plato speaks of 'one and the rest of number.'[6] If that is so, then all Plato need have meant when he said that Forms are numbers is that they are units. His problems arise precisely because this seems to involve him in talking 'mathematically' about Forms. If Forms (as units) are derived from first principles, and if 'mathematicals' also so derive, then what is the relationship between the two? The temptation would be to identify Forms and mathematicals – which is what Xenocrates in fact did, but which Plato declined to do.

The problem is even more complicated in that *some* Forms *are* numbers in another sense. Thus although Threeness is three, no non-numerical Form is three. In brief all Forms are units, and some Forms (of numbers) are also numbers in this additional sense. With this clear we can see that Aristotle's argument in *On Ideas* does not involve attributing a Form of number to Plato in the sense denounced in the *Nicomachean Ethics* of a Form of 'prior and posterior' (2, 3, 4, etc.). It merely involves saying that twoness, threeness, etc. have something in common, that is, they are unities, therefore there is a sort of Form of number, which is unity, for all unities have something numerical in common. Let us assume, therefore, that the main, perhaps the only purpose of *On Ideas* as we know it is to attack the earlier and later views of Plato himself.[7] As we proceed to other texts we shall notice the appearance of other obvious targets, and this will have repercussions for the dating of sections of the *Metaphysics*.

II 'Metaphysics' A

Few would dispute that Aristotle's next major effort to criticize Forms and numbers is to be found in the first book of the *Metaphysics*. Further, as we shall argue, *Metaphysics* A is later than the *Physics*, as is indeed obvious from references in the text itself (e.g., 993A11). In proposing a new investigation of causes, Aristotle knows that there are difficulties involved (993A25ff). These, no doubt, are partly at least the difficulties of the *Analytics* (and the *Eudemian Ethics*), where the possibility of a science of metaphysics seems to have been ruled out. Aristotle alludes to this clear negative at 992B29: 'Some say that there is a science of all things.' He does not say that he himself had argued *against* a Platonic version of that science in the *Analytics*. He does, however, allude to induction in the immediately following section, and, as we shall see,[8] chapter 1 of *Metaphysics* A comes very close to the *Posterior Analytics* in its account of memory and experience. Those methodological questions, also found in book 5 of the *Eudemian Ethics*, are still in Aristotle's mind. Perhaps *Metaphysics* A (at least in its original version) is to be dated not too long after the *Posterior Analytics*.

A second text points in the same chronological direction: the high-point of Aristotle's polemic in chapter 9 (992A22–B1) is the attack on those contemporary thinkers who have turned philosophy into mathematics. These people, Aristotle says, claim to be following (Plato's) methodology in using mathematics as a prelude for philosophy, but really they are doing it for its own sake and have substituted it for philosophy itself. Above all, as has been commonly recognized, this critique is aimed at those around Speusippus, himself, we recall, now dead in 339. But it could also reach his successor Xenocrates, who, by identifying (perhaps all) Plato's Forms with the objects of mathematics, similarly invited philosophers to treat the principles of mathematics as identical with the principles of metaphysics.

It is well known that Jaeger thought that the passages in *Metaphysics* A in which Aristotle speaks in the first person plural are passages in which he still thinks of himself as an advocate (though a puzzled advocate) of the theory of Forms. They were replaced, according to Jaeger, by third person plurals ('They say') when Aristotle rewrote these sections of book A and used them again in books M (4–5) and N. But the appearance of 'we' passages in other sections of books M and N greatly weakens Jaeger's case, as Cherniss pointed out. Jaeger's reply would have to be that at these sections (M.1086B19, N.1091A32) Aristotle is committed to Platonic positions also – which is impossible if our interpretation of Aristotle's early attitude to Plato is correct.

In *Metaphysics* A Aristotle uses 'we' forms in close proximity both to theories he accepts and to those he rejects: '"We" have ignored the cause in visible things, and "we" speak vainly about this, for "participation", as was said before, explains nothing. On the other hand Forms have nothing to do with the cause which "we" [i.e., Aristotle himself] hold to be one of the principles' (A.992A26–32).[9] Nevertheless, Jaeger was right to draw our attention to the first person plurals. There is no doubt that Aristotle does at times use 'we' when, on my interpretation, he is speaking of theories held not by himself, but by others, by supporters, in fact, of the theory of Forms. This usage cannot simply be dismissed as an oddity; an explanation is called for.

There is at least one obvious approach. In 334, when Aristotle returned to Athens, he had been away from the Academy and its philosophers for twelve years; he had been in Macedonia since 343. There he had probably been separated even from many of his friends from his years in Asia Minor and Lesbos. He seems to have composed an elegy to mark his return to Athens and the happiness it brought him.[10] But, on returning to Athens, he found himself back in a new atmosphere. Speusippus, who represented more than anyone else the 'mathematicization' of philosophy – but also the old days of Plato's lifetime – was dead. So, presumably, was Eudoxus, but Callippus, a pupil of Eudoxus's friend Polemarchus,[11] was at work there, as we shall see. The senior figure in the Academy was Xenocrates, Aristotle's old friend, but a much more conservative thinker and, in Aristotle's view, much less able than Speusippus. In a sense, therefore, Aristotle was coming home, but the situation, academically as well as politically, was uncertain, and in that uncertainty what could have been more natural than that he should tread warily? Not for now the harsher dismissals of Forms (though they are still misguided and irrelevant, e.g., A.992A33) which characterize the *Posterior Analytics* and the *Eudemian Ethics*, products, let us say, of the Macedonian period. The scene in life, as in philosophy, has changed. Aristotle is back among the Platonists and has begun to come round in philosophy to the view that there may be some kind of 'first philosophy,' though not of the Platonic sort, after all. Let us see what he does in those sections of *Metaphysics* A (chapters 6 and 9) which deal with 'Platonic' problems. If our thesis is right, Aristotle in *Metaphysics* A is stating his position vis-à-vis Plato in the Athens after 334, just as he stated it in the Academy near the time of Plato's death.

We have already touched on Aristotle's attack on those who wished to mathematicize philosophy. Let us now identify those whom he does *not* attack, and how his attacks can be distinguished from one another. The first to survive untouched, in *Metaphysics* A as in *On Ideas*, was the astronomically minded Philip of Opus, perhaps because he was not in charge, perhaps because as a representative of the Eudoxan tradition of astronomy plus theories of high-grade pleasure – as well as being, according to tradition, some sort of literary executor of Plato's – he was more or less philosophically acceptable. Perhaps Philip had earlier been a pupil or associate of Eudoxus.[12] A more likely explanation is that Philip did not accept the theory of Forms in any version (and never had); hence he is irrelevant. Even Eudoxus himself, discussed as teaching a deviant version of the theory of Forms in *On Ideas*, is absent from *Metaphysics* A.6 and only gets a replay of the rejection found in *On Ideas* – in passing – in chapter 9.

Chapter 6 of *Metaphysics* A gives Aristotle's version of the origins and history of Plato's Forms. The main influences on Plato are said to have been Pythagoreans, the Heraclitean Cratylus and Socrates. Nothing is said of Eleatics; Forms were introduced because of problems arising in propositions (*en logois*), as the *Phaedo* had told us. Separate objects of mathematics are discussed (987B15–18), as are the principles of the Forms, the One and the 'great-and-small.' Plato is mentioned by name again in 988A8; no other Platonist is mentioned. The theory proposed is substantially similar to that demolished in *On Ideas*. The only important difference is that the *Metaphysics* mentions the objects of mathematics as part of a specifically Platonic theory. That we know to be true. Though they are not identified as such, they must be the objects of the philosophical arithmetic of the *Philebus* (56D).[13] They are probably mentioned in *Metaphysics* A (and not in *On Ideas*) because Speusippus and Xenocrates had, in Aristotle's view, so badly misused them – apart from the fact that *On Ideas* is about Forms alone. Perhaps it was what Aristotle judged to be the sheer bad mathematics of Xenocrates and Speusippus which led Aristotle to prefer to say nothing of them. At any rate, Speusippus (also Xenocrates) is not yet discussed; even when One and Being are mentioned as first causes, the reference is to the Eleatics (988B12). And in that part of chapter 7 where Plato's 'great-and-small' rates a mention (988A26), nothing is said about the alternative name

Speusippus gave Plato's term (i.e., 'plurality'). Interestingly enough, however, Aristotle goes out of his way to refer to the 'realized nature' (988A34) so prominent in the *Posterior Analytics*, and to bracket it with substance (*ousia*). The members of the Academy, in keeping perhaps with Aristotle's more eirenic mood in Athens, are treated leniently here; Forms are an *attempt* to identify the 'realized nature' of things.

In chapter 12 I shall argue that sections 7–9 are a slightly later addition to the original text of *Metaphysics* A; certainly section 9 is more complicated. Aristotle re-uses, in a very casual fashion, some of the specific arguments against Forms from *On Ideas*. 'We' expressions occur in this section, as we have noticed. But a new group of people (*tines*) is now introduced; this can scarcely refer to Plato. These people, by developing the (original) theory of Forms, have generated a number of (other?) serious objections to the original version.

We have a fairly limited knowledge of much of the content of *On Ideas*, so we cannot tell whether, when Aristotle proceeds in the *Metaphysics* (990B23) to query Forms outside the category of substance, he is raising new objections. At any rate he continues with a series of arguments, down to 991B, which *could* apply only to the Platonic version of the theory of Forms, in the condition it had reached by the time of Plato's death. Homonyms ('category-material') recur (991A6–8), and Eudoxus's doctored version of the Forms, now compared with the theory of Anaxagoras, again reminds us of *On Ideas* itself. More interestingly Aristotle mentions odd Forms, such as 'house' and 'ring,' of which 'we' say there are no Forms. Aristotle does *not* say that Plato himself denied such Forms, either here or in *On Ideas* – in fact the argument is continued quite differently in *On Ideas*, where 'house' is given no prominence and 'ring' is not mentioned at all.[14]

At 991B9 a completely new point appears, which we found briefly discussed in *On Ideas*, but which demanded explanation. Furthermore, says Aristotle, 'if the Forms are numbers how will they be causes?' The context of this in *On Ideas*, we recall, was whether Two or Number is prior. As we indicated before, such passages are frequently taken to show that all Platonic Forms are Numbers. But not only was Cherniss right in denying that Plato ever held such a view – a view with such unpalatable philosophical consequences that it should not be forced on him unless the evidence *demands* it; there is also no evidence in Aristotle which compels us to assume that Forms (except Forms of numbers, e.g., the Form of two) are numbers in any other sense than that they are perfect units, henads and monads. Aristotle never attributes anything else to Plato himself in the *Metaphysics*.[15] This is indeed what we might expect. In *On Ideas* Plato is made to identify Forms with numbers somehow, but the manner in which he did it has always been a mere invention of Pythagorean scholars, ancient and modern. Up to this point in *Metaphysics* A, the only substantive addition to the theory of Forms outlined in *On Ideas* is the view that mathematicals are separate from both Forms and particulars. Since, as we have seen, *On Ideas* is almost entirely about Plato's theory of Forms, there is no reason why his theory of mathematical objects should have been introduced.

But now, at *Metaphysics* A.991B9, Aristotle has gone through the arguments against the original theory of Forms and alluded to the problems the Dyad caused for Plato (discussed already in chapter 6), as well as to mathematicals (991A5); he has concluded discussion of the theory which in chapter 6 he has attributed to Plato. He now moves on to new ground (991B9), to the theory of those (mentioned, we recall, in chapter 6) who identify the Forms with numbers. He does not say here, or anywhere else in *Metaphysics* A, that this is Plato's theory. In fact the identification of Forms and numbers was the work of Plato only in the special sense we have outlined; but there was also a stronger theory of Xenocrates that at least some Forms are also the objects of mathematics.[16] At 991B9, therefore, Aristotle is probably going beyond what he did in *On Ideas* and certainly beyond what he has said in chapter 6. He is now discussing the post-Platonic position in the Academy. No names are named, but it would be appropriate if the first views to be considered were those of its current leader, Xenocrates.

III Modern Fictions about Forms and Numbers

Let us briefly return to the question of why Plato himself was ever held to support the view attributed to him (by some commentators) that all Forms are numbers – and not merely as units. A number of further points should be made. First, Plato undoubtedly did propose Forms of Numbers, e.g., the Form of 2, which in the *Phaedo* is still confused with mathematical twos, but which, after the recognition of separate mathematicals, must be kept distinct. So there are *some* Forms *of* Numbers in Plato. Xenocrates, probably worried by how both ordinary Forms and Form-Numbers (which have quasi-mathematical features) could be derived from a common *One* as first principle, identified *all* Forms with numbers, not simply as unities, but with mathematical numbers.[17] There is no reason why Plato should be supposed to have taken this step, and Aristotle does not say in *Metaphysics* A that he took it.

The second source of confusion on this matter is a passage from Theophrastus's *Metaphysics* – which also enables us to see something of the dilemma which Xenocrates tried to resolve so drastically. At *Metaphysics*

6B11ff Plato is said by Theophrastus to 'refer' (*anagein*) things to the first principles (viz. to the One and the Dyad). In doing so, says Theophrastus, he *seems* to treat of everything when he links (*anaptein*) particulars with Forms, and Forms with numbers. Notice that Theophrastus does *not* say that Plato 'reduces' Forms to numbers, only that he links them. He continues by saying that 'from there' (presumably from the numbers) he proceeds to the first principles. In this scrupulous account both the *problems* left by Plato *and* Plato's own position are clear. Numbers and Forms are linked, and numbers derive from the One and the Dyad. It is easy to see how Xenocrates could assume similar statements to mean that any numbers may be identified with Forms, that Forms are numbers *more Pythagorico*: easy, but probably a false solution by Xenocrates of the Platonic dilemma. Plato certainly derived Forms from the One and the Dyad (though it is 'limit' and the 'unlimited' with which he operates in the *Philebus*, using 'more-and-less' as an equivalent for 'unlimited'). We shall return to this later; it will shed further light on the problem of Form-Numbers. For the moment let us note that Plato certainly derived numbers from the One and the Dyad, but that there is no evidence in Theophrastus that he succumbed to the 'simple' solution of Xenocrates and identified Forms themselves with different numbers. In fact in Plato's lecture on the Good, it was notorious that he only talked about 'mathematical' topics, including doubtless the derivation of the Forms of numbers; that might suggest that he said little about the derivation of other Forms, let alone about other 'good things.'[18] But such an interpretation involves trusting the liar Aristoxenus, and although liars do not always lie, their testimony is not secure.

Part at least of our trouble with the passage from Theophrastus is caused by the fact that Ross and Fobes translated *anagein* as 'reduce,' a term which suggests ontological reduction. This translation is followed by Annas, though she admits that she does not understand what the term means.[19] 'Refer' would be a better translation. Plato is speaking of explaining the Forms, not of accounting for their existence. Interestingly enough, just before alluding to Plato and his *seeming* to link everything together, but perhaps not *really* doing so, Theophrastus has mentioned Xenocrates (6B7): Xenocrates is the only philosopher who actually maps out the metaphysical universe *in toto*. What could be clearer evidence that Plato resisted the temptation to do so, despite the problems with which he was faced by not doing so?

Annas believes she has found in the *Philebus* (which is certainly the place to look) further evidence for attributing Form-Numbers to Plato, or at least for supposing that such an attribution – as a *reductio ad absurdum* of Platonic theories – might seem not unreasonable.[20] Plato has, as we have seen, already identified Forms as unities (16Dff). Now he wants to identify how many species each genus contains. It is no good saying that pleasure is a plurality; we need to know how many kinds of pleasure there are. Thus, presumably, if there are seven types of pleasure, pleasure is a unity and a seven – and the whole analysis of pleasure can be understood in terms of Plato's concern with classification. A superficial difficulty with this interpretation is that whereas some genera would be huge numbers – how many kinds of plants are there? – very many (all the *infimae species*) would presumably be identical as ones. So the numbering of Forms would be of little use. We might add that there is no evidence that other numerical identifications – made presumably by Pythagoreans – followed this route. Marriage, for instance, is regularly numbered as five, that is, the combination of the first odd and the first even number in one method of identifying odd and even (i.e., two plus three).[21] Admittedly this sort of identification is Pythagorean or Neopythagorean. Yet there is no evidence in or about Plato for any of the more scientific procedures Annas would need.

If more is to be squeezed out of the *Philebus* than I have already suggested, it seems that a passage of the *Metaphysics* itself (M.1085A7ff) may provide a key. Some people, says Aristotle (who is probably referring to Xenocrates), try to subdivide the 'great' and 'small' themselves as though they were genera. If the reference is to Xenocrates, and if he is understood correctly, he is interested in finding other species of the 'great' and of the 'small' than those which generate numbers; thus he can generate geometrical objects, from, say, the 'broad' and the 'narrow.' This extraordinary proposal is made odder still by the fact that its author seems to accord a priority of the 'great-and-small' to the 'broad-and-narrow.' For this priority would seem unnecessary if we take the 'great-and-small' to represent the 'more-and-less' of the *Philebus*, and this itself to be merely another way of referring to the 'unlimited.' Now if we turn to the Pythagorean column of opposites, we notice that 'limit' and 'unlimited' are at the top. The 'great-and-small,' on a 'Xenocratean' interpretation, could be viewed even in the *Philebus* as a *mode* of the 'unlimited,' suitable for generating numbers alone, not suitable for generating geometricals – and *a fortiori* not suitable for generating Forms which are not Forms of mathematical entities. Thus the passage in *Metaphysics* M may tell us that Xenocrates *was* being Platonic in generating everything from some species of the 'unlimited,' but was non-Platonic in assimilating the Forms of non-mathematicals to the Forms of mathematicals – if that is what he did. For we must also add that the obsession with the derivation of mathematical objects, whether the Form two or the mathematical two, could easily have led philosophers into speaking of Forms *as* numbers when they were only referring to the Forms *of* numbers.

There is a passage in the *Eudemian Ethics* which may shed further light on our text of Theophrastus. Aristotle says (1.1218A17ff) that the supporters of the Form of the Good (who perhaps include Plato, though he is not named) argue more or less as follows:

1 The One itself is the Good.
2 Therefore the Good exists in numbers and units.
3 Justice and health are arrangements and numbers.
4 Therefore justice and health are good.

Note first that justice and health are not identified as particular numbers, though Aristotle knew that *Pythagoreans* like Eurytus (N.1092B10) made such identifications. The theory against which he is arguing is probably that Forms are of single character (*monoeidēs*), as in the *Phaedo*, and therefore perfect unities. So 2–4 above should be interpreted as follows:

2a The good exists in numbers, that is, in units.
3a Justice and health are arrangements (of the elements or parts of the state or the soul) and units.
4a Therefore justice and health, being units, are good.

The conclusion would be that Forms are numbers as units, as the text of Theophrastus, when read carefully, also suggests.

IV 'Metaphysics' A Again

Returning at last to Metaphysics A, we can now bring our remarks on this section to a close. After 991B Plato is not mentioned again, except at 992A21 where it is said that he kept opposing the real existence of points; they are a 'teaching device' (*dogma*) of geometers. Plato is thus only introduced with reference to a specific problem in the philosophy of mathematics. Though some of the general observations about Forms (992A25ff) would apply to him, they equally or better apply to the Academy of 333, and that is why they are introduced. General criticism of the theory of Forms (apart from numbers) seems only offered at this point so that Aristotle can work up to an attack on the 'mathematicians.'

Aristotle proceeds via references to the failure of Forms to provide final causes (992A30) 'through which all Mind and the whole of nature work.' Perhaps Mind is mentioned rather than God so that the special final causality of the Prime Mover can now be signalled; this text may be the first Aristotelian reference to Mind as unambiguously only a final cause. As we shall see later (75, 172–3 below), in the *Eudemian Ethics* its causation is still 'efficient'; and something of that attitude still persists even in *Physics* 8. But it is final causes with which Aristotle is concerned in *Metaphysics* A.992A32. His phrase 'on account of which cause' could be ambiguous, but

Aristotle makes clear that he is thinking of final causes by his immediate reference to Forms. Platonic Forms, in Aristotle's opinion, cannot provide the final cause; and in any case, for 'present day thinkers' they are confused with the objects of mathematics.

In a passage of the *Eudemian Ethics* to which we referred earlier (1.1218A25ff), Aristotle argues that it is fallacious to claim without qualification that numbers aim at unity and that therefore unity is good. If it were, of course, it would be a final cause in mathematics, and hence for those who identified the objects of mathematics with Forms, for philosophy too. But it is not, and the 'turning of philosophy into mathematics' is then worse than useless if we as philosophers hope to identify Forms as the final cause. As the *Posterior Analytics* puts it (1.75B18), it is not the business of a geometer to identify the most beautiful kind of line. With this final broadside against mathematicizing philosophy (992B1ff) Speusippus as well as Xenocrates is damned. The remaining lines of chapter 9 on the 'great-and small' are probably aimed chiefly at Xenocrates also – Speusippus used a different term. Plato himself might also fall under the attack, but the rest of this section tells us nothing more specific about Aristotle's view of Plato's *published* philosophy.

V **'Metaphysics'** M, N, Λ

Having clarified Aristotle's attitude to the number-theory of Plato and others in the Academy in *Metaphysics* A, chapters 6 and 9, let us now turn to books M and N. I shall not attempt to break this material up, as Jaeger and others have done, for they have largely based themselves on mistaken interpretations of passages in the text in which Aristotle speaks of what 'we' or 'they' say or believe. On the contrary I shall accept Annas's overall account of these books,[22] that they comprise a loosely knit whole dealing successively with three topics: 1, the objects of mathematics; 2, Forms (M.4–5, largely based on A.6 and 9); and 3, (with digressions) the claim that numbers and/or Forms are the principles of things.

In the whole of books M and N Plato, as we should expect, is in the background. The views considered are primarily those of Speusippus and Xenocrates, though the targets are not named. We can assume that the date is later than that of book A. Only at one place is the theory that Forms are numbers ascribed to Plato, and we shall touch on this subject again. Aristotle's primary aim, as Annas sees, is to criticize Academic mathematics, and he treats of Forms only in so far as they become mixed up with mathematical principles. Books M and N are a continuation of the discussion begun with the Academy in the later sections of A.9. Let us consider a few significant texts.

1 The conclusion of M.2 is that if 'mathematicals' exist, it is in some special way, for 'being' is equivocal. They are not prior in existence to sensibles and have less claim to be called substances.

2 Goodness is distinct from beauty. Goodness is only in action (*praxis*). Beauty exists in 'unmoved' things. Mathematicians point to the beauty of symmetry and arrangement (M.1078A31–1078B6). Further discussion of this is suggested, but is apparently not forthcoming in the *Metaphysics*.[23]

3 In chapter 4 Aristotle explains that Academic mathematics has historically been connected with the theory of Forms. Hence he gives an account of the growth of the theory, based on book A, chapters 6 and 9, but with significant differences:

(a) Plato is not mentioned at all.

(b) Dialectic is referred to both in M.4 (1078B25ff) and A.6 (987B32–3). Clearly in book M it is given an *Aristotelian* gloss; it concerns inspecting contraries apart from substance.

(c) Socrates' role in the history of philosophy is related (1078B30) to the starting-point of understanding (as worked out in the *Posterior Analytics*).

(d) 'They,' in M, deny Forms of house and ring.

Regarding Plato, the only conclusion we can draw from this account is that Aristotle has nothing new to say about him; Platonic material is only introduced when it is needed as a background for more contemporary debate. This suggests that a certain period may have elapsed since book A. Interestingly enough Aristotle does introduce a new (unnamed) actor in the drama: a very old-style Platonist indeed who believes in Form-Numbers, but not in mathematicals. There is no need to follow Jaeger in excising this section of the text; a similar theory can be found by implication at least in the early Plato of the *Phaedo* and the sixth book of the *Republic*.

The material on the 'non-addibility' of the Forms of Numbers (M.1081Aff) is probably aimed, among others, at Plato himself, but problems which would arise if (all) Forms are in fact non-mathematical Numbers are kept separate (M.1083A18). Whether or not Aristotle thought that Plato *ought* to have held this view, and in a more damaging form than the one we have attributed to him, he at no point attributes it to him individually. In fact the question is introduced rather casually: Aristotle has nothing specific to say about what relation numbers and Forms might (even theoretically) have. The argument at M.1084A12, that if there are, say, ten Form-Numbers, that is not enough for all the Forms, is of the same almost frivolous sort. It is unclear who, if anyone, held such a position.

The correct view of the situation among the Platonists can be retrieved from M.1086A. Aristotle here identifies three groups: those (presumably like Speusippus) who denied Form-Numbers, that is, even such items as the

Form of Two. They had in fact given up (if indeed they ever supported) all Forms – perhaps because they could not account for the 'numerical' ones.[24] The second group (the followers of Xenocrates) wished to make Forms numbers and to identify Form-Numbers with mathematicals. The last person in the section is Plato himself. He was the first to propose that there are Forms, that both Forms and mathematicals are numbers, and that Forms and mathematicals are distinct. This is the only passage in books M and N where Aristotle makes Plato specifically identify Forms and (some) numbers.

But the context seems to provide the explanation of this identification. Aristotle is discussing the Forms of numbers and their relationship with mathematicals. It is in this case that Plato posited both kinds: there is a Platonic Form of Two and there are mathematical twos. There is no need to read the text as suggesting that *all* Forms are numbers (though of course as units they are); here it is the Forms of numbers which are themselves numbers. Twoness is two, Plato means; not 'Elephantness' is seven. We can see the same point in a passage of book N (1090A16ff). Plato is not mentioned in this passage, while there are allusions to various people who say both that there are Forms and that they are numbers. From what follows it is clear that Aristotle is interested in the consequences of this claim in mathematics. It is the Forms of numbers which cannot be treated mathematically and cannot be used for demonstrating the existence of particular numbers. Aristotle has nothing to say about whether such Forms can generate sensibles; what he wants to show is that they cannot generate numbers. It is probably right, therefore, to take Aristotle to be asking, 'If there are Forms which are of numbers, how can numbers be generated from them?' A similar (mathematical) problem is posed for Plato at N.1090B33ff. In the case of those who propose both a number which is Form and a number which is mathematical, how does the mathematical derive from the other? This is a new problem for Plato himself, which could have been offered in book A, but which adds nothing further to our knowledge of Aristotle's understanding of Plato's theory of numbers and Forms.

So far we have failed to find metaphysical attacks on *Plato's* theory in books M and N which are not also available in book A. Books M and N, as they set out to be, are a treatise about the use and misuse of mathematical ideas and their identification as substance. But we have noticed a brief digression (M.1078A31–B7) about the possible goodness and beauty to be found in mathematics. Naturally Plato would have found them there, since in some sense he identified goodness, beauty, and the One itself. And in N.4 Aristotle returns to a related topic, a topic discussed neither in the *Eudemian Ethics* (where we might have expected it) nor presumably in *On the Good.*[25]

Speusippus had denied that the Good is a first principle, and this leads him to a problem and indeed, in Aristotle's rather strong phrase, to discredit inasmuch as he failed to take the difficulty seriously (N.1091A30ff). His view, says Aristotle, is like that of the old mythologists (*theologōn*); they do not allow us to speak of the first principle as the Good itself and the Best (as Aristotle would speak of the Prime Mover). Notice that Aristotle uses the 'we' form here. 'We speak of the Good and the Best.' That does not identify Aristotle as a Platonist. He is speaking in his own name. His own Good and Best (in Λ) will be seen to be quite different from that of the Platonists.

Speusippus's grotesque notion, it seems, has arisen from his attempt to avoid a difficulty for those who speak of the One as a first principle. Such people, of course, would include Plato himself. The difficulty arises not because such people treat goodness (*to eu*) as an attribute (*hyparchon*), but again because of their attempted derivation of number. It would make far more sense, says Aristotle, to make goodness prior to unity as a first principle than the other way round. In fact, of those who postulate 'unmoving realities' (this surely includes Plato himself), some say that the One and the Good itself are the same, but give priority to the One as primarily the substance. From this follow all kinds of absurdities both in number-theory and in the theory of Forms itself. It is interesting to see how at this presumably late stage in his life Aristotle has reverted to an attack on the perversion of the original theory of Forms as it had been developed in Plato's later life. Plato went off the rails, in fact, by subordinating goodness to unity; the *Eudemian Ethics* had already emphasized this point (1.1218A24–32). That being so, we may conclude with some more general remarks about the ramifications of Aristotle's developing reactions both to Plato's treatment of unity and to later developments in the Academy.

In the light of Metaphysics Λ Aristotle's attempt in book N to salvage goodness as a primary metaphysical notion is important. At *Metaphysics* Λ.1075A11ff, after describing the Prime Mover, Aristotle turns back to goodness in a quite unexpected fashion. Where do the good and the best reside in an army: in its order (its mathematical arrangement, to use a Platonic phrase) or in its commander? In both, replies Aristotle, but primarily in the commander on whom the order ultimately depends. This is (metaphorically) Aristotle's last word on the good in metaphysics – a topic he had discussed with his friends for most of his life. The end of book Λ is written to explain that the good is prior in the universe, and that this is to be found primarily in the source of order, namely Mind. Aristotle's own Mind goes back, among others, to Anaxagoras, as had Plato's as early as the *Phaedo*. And as book Λ rambles to its close, Aristotle devotes the last section to attacking once more that 'Platonist' who had 'given up on' goodness, as he had also rejected the primacy of Mind, namely Speusippus. Speusippus's world, based on the primacy of mathematical reality, is ill-governed. Quoting Homer, Aristotle condemns Plato's successor: 'Many rulers are not good, let there be one ruler.'

The analysis of such questions of goodness and unity provides good evidence for the close connection of books Λ and N of the *Metaphysics*. They mark the last stage of Aristotle's thought on the interrelations between unity and the good, both present outside the categories, but, alas, not both predicable of all that is. In *Nicomachean Ethics* 1.6 too Aristotle repeats one of his old examples from the *Eudemian Ethics*: in the category of substance, good can be predicated of mind and of God. Books M, N, and Λ of the *Metaphysics* (apart from Λ.8) were probably completed before Aristotle's later concern that a possible plurality of unmoved movers might seem to threaten ochlocracy once more.[26]

Let us close therefore with Aristotle's emotional words about Plato in the sixth chapter of the first book of the *Nicomachean Ethics*. There is nothing like it in the earlier *Eudemian* version, while the *Nicomachean Ethics* also contains a striking tribute to the dead astronomer Eudoxus (10.1172B15–18). Aristotle has now, as we have argued, reasserted the notion of goodness, but in a new de-mathematicized form. Parodying the last book of the *Republic* he says that is difficult for him to enquire into the notion of a *universal* good, because those who introduced the Forms were his friends. But perhaps it would be better, especially for philosophers, to sacrifice even personal ties for the preservation of the truth. Both Plato and the rest are dear to him, but it is his duty to prefer the truth. The sense of urgency which created the spirit of the Academy is still alive in this tribute, just as in the words attributed many years before to Hermeias, facing crucifixion: 'Tell my friends and companions that I have done nothing weak or unworthy of philosophy.' The subject of the urgency is the relation between goodness and truth.

APPENDIX
ARISTOTLE'S PHILOSOPHICAL WORK IN ATHENS 334 BC

In this chapter I have suggested that Aristotle began work on the first book of the *Metaphysics* when he returned to Athens in 334; but this may not have been his first and most pressing task at that time, for the account of motion in the *Physics* needed to be rewritten, and *Physics* 8 is that rewriting. In this book, self-motion is analysed with far greater precision, and it is argued unequivocably that the first mover must be unmoved. There is nothing in *Physics* 8 about the *nature* of that mover, since such an enquiry would be first philosophy, not physics, and that is to be discussed later. But a few pointers to what is to come in *Metaphysics* Λ can be detected even in the earlier *Eudemian Ethics*, two books of which (6 and 8) end with discussions of God's nature. In book 6 God is identified as activity (1154B25ff), and he is said to enjoy a single and simple pleasure of immobility – the mover of *Physics* 8 is also immobile – while in *Eudemian Ethics* book 8 he is identified as a 'mover of the universe' (1248A26ff), a mover as efficient cause (172–3 below, and for further activities after 334 BC, 163 below). In one sense, however, he is also unambiguously a final cause, for he is the object of our contemplation (1249B14–15). As Mind, he is our good; for his sake wisdom (*phronēsis*) gives commands.

These remarks about God harmonize with the material from *Physics* 8, where the Prime Mover, not in fact actually called God, is still envisaged as moving the world, somehow, from the edge of the universe (267B9), though he is non-material (267B19). But no mention is made of any other than the efficient causation of pushing and pulling. Aristotle certainly leaves bafflingly loose ends to be cleared up; and, as we have seen, God is to be identified wholly as final cause, without fuller explanation, in *Metaphysics* Λ.

Why then do we wish to locate this last book of the *Physics* in Athens? Could it not have been composed in Macedonia, along with the *Analytics* and the *Eudemian Ethics*? That is, admittedly, possible, but one piece of evidence makes composition in Athens more likely. It was a feature of *Physics* 8 already emphasized by Jaeger (Aristotle, 358–9). At 258B11 Aristotle raises the possibility that there is more than one unmoved mover, and at 259A11ff he concludes the discussion by arguing that it is better to assume as few causes as possible, and that one Unmoved Mover is enough in this case. The point about this problem, which Aristotle was later (in *Metaphysics* Λ) to take more seriously (1071B22 and chapter 8), is that speculation about a possible plurality of unmoved movers (and a single Prime Mover) was intensified by the astronomical speculations of Callippus – which Aristotle himself later developed. Callippus, whose new Attic calendar came into force in Athens in 330/329, seems to have been personally acquainted with Aristotle,[27] but the two probably did not meet until Aristotle returned to Athens in 334. Hence it is likely that Aristotle's concerns about a plurality of movers developed at this time rather than in Macedonia.

4

The Chronology of Aristotle's Logical and Rhetorical Works

I Introduction to Cross-References

It is an ungrounded hypothesis to suppose that all cross-references in Aristotle were added by later editors. They may be useful for purposes of dating and should be rejected only when there is good reason.[1] In fact they enable us to construct an unexpectedly intelligible sequence for the texts of the logical and rhetorical works, a sequence both intelligible in itself and easily accommodated to the chronology of other Aristotelian writings such as the *Eudemian Ethics* and the *Poetics* which can be established independently of cross-references.

II The Core 'Topics'

Topics 2–4 is the earliest phase of our *Topics*. There are no cross-references or allusions in these books of the *Topics* to other writings of Aristotle. For the time being I shall leave book 5 aside. Unlike *Topics* 6, books 2–4 contain no references or allusions to Plato's *Timaeus*, nor do they provide material to be used *against* those who favour Plato's Forms. Like the *Eudemus* and the *Protrepticus* they are silent on this matter (46–50 above). They allude to notions to be found in the *Phaedrus*: on envy (2.109B36),[2] and on the soul as self-mover (4.120B22, and cf. 2.111B5ff); and in the *Meno* (2.111B28ff): on recollection (i.e., on how we cannot recollect the future). They perhaps allude to the *Parmenides* at 2.113A25ff, or more precisely to the attempt of Eudoxus to salvage the Forms (But if Forms exist 'in us', then they are in movement).[3] There may be allusions to the *Sophist* on non-being (4.121A22) and just possibly on acting and being acted upon (4.120B27). We hear of the view of the *Theaetetus* that knowledge is perception (4.125A28) and of its tagging of spatial movement as *phora* – in a section (4.122B27) where Plato is mentioned by name (cf. *Tht.* 181D5); we hear also of the tripartite soul (2.113B1ff, 4.126A8–9, cf. 5.128B38ff) and of the belief (denied in *Eudemian Ethics* 1) that everything aims at the good (3.116A20). There are references too to the views of Xenocrates on the soul as a *daimōn* (2.112A37), probably to the soul as a number (3.120B3–4, 4.123A13ff), and to Xenocrates' defence of Plato's indivisible lines (4.121B20).[4] Finally we may note a reference to pleasure being placed in the genus of motion (4.121A31), as in the *Republic*.[5] If, as I believe, the *Timaeus* must be dated no later than about 352 – and in the *Topics* there may be new evidence to place it after the *Theaetetus* and *Sophist* – then *Topics* 2–4 could well be earlier than that. This is an argument *ex silentio*, but it is a fact that whereas book 6 indisputably refers to the *Timaeus*, books 2–4 do not. There is certainly nothing to prevent the whole of this set of *topoi* from being earlier than 352.

But some parts of the *Rhetoric* seem to be earlier still. Whereas in *Topics* 4.121A31 Aristotle seems prepared to deny the validity of the claim that motion is the genus of pleasure, he accepts it (at least as plausible) in *Rhetoric* 1 (1369B33ff). There are at least some indications too that at least parts of the *Categories* are earlier than *Topics* 2–4. In *Topics* 4, in particular, Aristotle uses the concept of accident, of which (oddly) the *Categories* makes no explicit mention; and the notion of transcendentals is at least foreshadowed in the same book of the *Topics* (4.121A18, cf. 4.127A33): 'Being and one are predicated of all that exists and good and evil are not in genera but are themselves genera' (4.123B12–13). For what it is worth, *Topics* 4 also contains some of the earliest discussion of the notions of *energeia*, *dunamis*, and *hexis* (4.124A32–4, 125B15–27), while the *Categories* has nothing about *energeia*. Certain passages of *Topics* 2–4, however, are *similar* to material in the *Categories*: 2.109B5ff on paronymous terms – though 'accident' occurs here too; 2.115B8, where the use of *legomena* for 'words' sounds like *Categories* 1A16. In a similar vein *Topics* 4.121A38 uses the phrase 'particular man' (*ho tis anthrōpos*, cf. *Cat.* 1A22, 2A16, etc.), but adds the alternative formulation (not in the *Categories*) 'individuals' (*atoma*), which 'partake' of genus and species. 'Partaking' too is not used in this way in the *Categories*; we shall consider this term later (82 below). Secondary substances (and 'secondaries' in other categories, especially quality) seem to be implied at *Topics* 4.120B36ff, as in the *Categories*, but we shall notice later that whereas in the *Categories* the first category is only called substance (*ousia*), in *Topics* 4 we find both *ousia* and *ti esti* (*what* it is, 4.120B21, 120B38).

All in all one could agree that *Topics* 2–4 (presumably in that order) are later than the *Categories* (though not necessarily than the *Post-Praedica-*

menta), but not by much. Some of this early material *may* refer to Plato's *Sophist*, as we have seen, and may have been complete by about 353. Of course it may not *refer* to the *Sophist*; it may merely *reflect* similar ideas: then it could be earlier still. But it is worth noting that Aristotle refers to the *definition* of a sophist at 4.126A3ff (and, interestingly, to the definition of a secret thief in the same breath). It is hard to date the *Sophist*, but it is difficult to put it much after 355 – and that is very probably too late. Be that as it may, it seems reasonable to suppose that *Topics* 2–4 are earlier than the *Eudemus* and the *Protrepticus*, the latter of which perhaps marks a fresh Aristotelian start. The opening of *Topics* 2 ('Some problems are universal, others particular') could easily be the beginning of a lecture course. Both books 1 and 6 of the *Topics*, as we shall see, involve elaborate discussion of theories of deduction and induction. For many reasons they must be dated much later – closer in time to our *Analytics*. By contrast, *Topics* 7.1–2 has no such material, and Maier, who links *Topics* 7.1–2 with book 4, is probably right.[6] But book 6 is an intruder, and we shall return to book 5 shortly.

III The Growth of the 'Topics'

It can be shown by cross-references (assuming that these are not mere misleading interpolations by person or persons unknown) that during Aristotle's Macedonian period he composed (or reorganized) logical works in the following order: *Topics* 1–6, 7, 8.1, *Sophistici Elenchi* (= *Topics* 9) 3–34, *Prior Analytics*, *Posterior Analytics*, *Topics* 8.2–14, and *Sophistici Elenchi* 1–2. The evidence is as follows: *Prior Analytics* refers to *Posterior Analytics* many times (1.24B13, 25B28, etc.). No reference suggests that our version of the *Posterior Analytics* was written first. *Prior Analytics* 1 refers to *Topics* 1 at 24B12 and to *Topics* 8.1 at 47A21. *Prior Analytics* 2 refers to *Topics* 8.1 at 64A37 and to *Sophistici Elenchi* (as *Topics*) at 65B16.

Topics 8.11.162A11 refers to *Prior Analytics* 2.53B26ff, and 8.12.162B31ff refers to *Prior Analytics* 2.64B28ff.[7] It is therefore necessary to split *Topics* 8; the break is easiest made after chapter one, where there is a sharp change of subject. My thesis, therefore, is that 8.2–14 was inserted into a complete text of the *Topics* (including most of the *Sophistici Elenchi*) after Aristotle had finished the *Analytics*. At this time he also added the first two chapters of the *Sophistici Elenchi*: *SE* 2.165B9–10 refers to the *Analytics* and to the *Topics*.[8] Thus it would appear that some time before working on the *Analytics* Aristotle added book 1 to his original *Topics*, as well as book 6, the rest of 7, 8.1, and *SE* 3–34. In fact *Topics* 8.1 is probably the misplaced beginning of the *Sophistici Elenchi*.[9] Thus the state of the *Topics* immediately before the *Analytics* would be books 1–7, 8.1, and *SE* 3–34; I refer to these as *Topics*² to distinguish them from the original or core *Topics*, that is *Topics* 2–4, 7.1–2. It is also part of my thesis, however, that we now have not only some sort of sequence of texts, but that *Topics*² and our *Analytics* were composed within a fairly short period while Aristotle was in Macedonia. This claim does not mean, of course, that some unascertainable amount of the material in the *Analytics* is not older, perhaps in some cases considerably older. It does mean that in our postulated version of *Topics*² and the *Analytics*, with some significant exceptions, we should expect to find something of a philosophical unity.

Let us now consider what Aristotle has added to his core *Topics*; that is, what do we find new and interesting in books 1, 6, 7, 8.1, and *SE* 3–34? Again I shall leave book 5 for the time being. The chief characteristic of the new material is reference (absent in the core *Topics*) to a system of deductive reasoning (*sullogismos*) and induction. I shall argue that although there is no reference to what is now called 'syllogistic' (or 'the syllogism') – such as is found in the *Analytics* – yet that absence only gives worry if we *mistranslate* Aristotle's claim in the *Posterior Analytics* about the relationship between 'syllogistic' and deductive reasoning in general (82–3 below).

Before glancing quickly at some of the material from *Topics*², however, let us merely observe that there is no reason why *Topics* 8.1 should not be followed immediately by *SE* 3–34. *Topics* 8.1 *completes* the treatment of 'order' (*taxis*), and has no necessary connection with what follows in the rest of *Topics* 8. Similarly, of course, there is no *necessary* connection between the early *Topics* 7.1–2 and 7.3–5. 7.3 reverts to the questions of book 6 (to which it seems like an addendum), dealing with how to *establish* a definition. As for *SE* 3ff, this indeed can be seen as rounding off the destructive and constructive uses of *topoi* which 8.1 (with its discussion of arrangement) has not yet completed. Aristotle's references to the *Sophistici Elenchi* as part of the *Topics* show that he had no particular concern to write a special treatise on the refutation of sophistries. Nevertheless, such material is certainly appropriate for inclusion in a general account of 'dialectic,' and when he has finished it, Aristotle summarizes his writing on dialectic in general (183A37). It is an achievement, he thinks, without precedents, and he is proud of being the first to complete such a programme (184B). Rhetoric has been handled by others; dialectic has not. The reader should be grateful for what he has got.

*Topics*² then represents our complete nine books without the block 8.2–14 and *SE* 1–2. Let us note what, besides talk of deduction and induction, has been added. The following are the more important points (I am still leaving book 5 aside).[10]

1 The term 'dialectic' is used regularly in an unplatonic sense, referring to

inference from 'generally agreed' premisses.[11] This is especially true of books 1 and 8.

2 There is frequent reference to demonstration (*apodeixis*) (1.100A27, 1.105A8, 1.108B19, 6.141A30) as well as to deduction (1.100A25, 103B7, 105A18, 108B8, 7.3.153A15, 154A29 [cf. 154B34], etc.) and to *to ti ēn einai*, which, respecting the *einai*, I have said I shall generally (but not in the *Topics*) translate as 'realized nature', for the form is the realization of the matter (1.101B38, 102A18, 103B10, 6.139A33, 6.143A18, 7.153A15). (I shall defend this translation in a later chapter [265–6 and note 25 below].) There is also reference to premisses (*protaseis*, 1.101B16, 104A3, 104B18).

3 There is a threefold division of premisses into logical, physical, and ethical.[12]

4 *Energeia* is identified as the use rather than the mere possession of a faculty (e.g., of sight at 1.106B16ff).

5 'Good' is said to be simply equivocal (1.107A5ff); it is predicated in all the categories (cf. 6.144A14–19). The same is the case with 'being,' 'one,' 'same' at *SE* 169A24. The discussion of the differentiae of colours at 1.107B29 perhaps depends on *Timaeus* 67DE, but it is more probably based on a 'school' definition.[13]

6 Allusions to the content of the *Timaeus*, perhaps beginning in book 5, continue in book 6 (see 6.139B33 on the 'nurse' of becoming and 6.143B31 on the 'ideal living creature').

7 Material for use *against* those who advocate Platonic Forms is now offered regularly (6.143B24–32; 6.147A5–11 [a passage which does *not* predate the *Sophist*];[14] 148A20ff; 7.154A19ff).

8 Knowledge is said to be (perhaps) an 'incontrovertible notion' (6.146B2, cf. *APo*.1.72B3–4).

9 There are attacks on 'auto-' phrases, that is, on the *language* of the ideal theory (6.143B31, 148A17). This is continued (and generalized) at 8.162A7ff.

10 There is marked interest in Zeno (and Parmenides), especially in the *Sophistici Elenchi* (172A9, 179B20, 182B26), in Melissus (*SE* 181A27ff), and in Parmenidean ambiguities on 'being X' versus 'being *simpliciter*.'

11 The 'Third Man' argument is invoked at *SE* 178B36, echoing *On Ideas*,[15] and confirming nos. 7 and 9 above that Aristotle has now passed from implicit to explicit opposition to the theory of Forms (52–3 above).

Our conclusion is that *Topics*² is substantially different from the original core *Topics*. It is later than the *Timaeus*, and is approaching the logic of 'realized nature' which Aristotle developed in the *Posterior Analytics* – though, as we shall see, *Topics*² is cruder. In general, however, it employs much of the language of the *Analytics*. Its division of science into logic, physics, and ethics, and its rejection of Forms, also remind us of the *Analytics* – not to speak of the slightly later *Eudemian Ethics* (for the chronology, see 170–1 and 262 below). It is not, of course, certain that the whole expansion of the *Topics* was pushed through in the late 340s. Aristotle himself says at the end of the *Sophistici Elenchi* that it has taken him a long time (184B2). Perhaps a little more light can be shed on the growth of the *Topics* by returning to book 5, which we have so far left on one side.

Book 5 seems to begin in the manner of the core *Topics*, but new material is soon introduced:

1 There is *doubt* about the tripartition of the soul (133A32).
2 The phrase *to ti ēn einai* occurs three times in 133A.
3 The description of knowledge as an 'incontrovertible notion' occurs at 133B30 and 134A35.
4 There is an apparent allusion to the *Timaeus* at 137B12, and probably to the *Sophist* at 139A6.

We can conclude from this new material that at some time after the *Timaeus* (to which, as we have seen [80 above], passages of book 6 also allude), Aristotle resumed work on the *Topics*; he probably continued it intermittently right up to the end of *Topics*², finishing the new material by about 343 and incorporating the early section of book 7 as he went along. It is possible that, as we shall see happened later on with the *Physics* and the *Politics* (148f, 231 below), book 1 was written last (or at the same time as the *Sophistici Elenchi*). But this time Aristotle had not quite finished. He still had *Topics* 8.2–5 and *SE* 1–2 to add, as the cross-references indicate, after the completion of the *Analytics*.

Before we turn to the *Analytics* themselves, one rather extraordinary feature of the *Topics* remains unconsidered. I shall argue later that *to ti ēn einai* should generally in Aristotle be translated as 'realized nature,' because it refers to the actual *existence* of particulars, and I shall defend that translation for the *Analytics* and for all the later works including the *Metaphysics* (82, 265–6 below). But the translation does not work for the *Topics*. Here, as we shall see, the traditional translation 'essence' seems right, where it is wrong for the *Analytics*. Barnes has observed that at *Topics* 7.153A12 Aristotle offers to deduce definitions[16] – which in the *Posterior Analytics* he denies can be done directly (2.3–8). But the difference between the *Topics* and the *Posterior Analytics* runs considerably deeper. The phrase *to ti ēn einai* occurs in books 1, 5, 6, and 7 of the *Topics*, and from the relevant passages a theory alien to the *Analytics* can be perceived. Of course there are similarities too. Definitions show (*dēloun*, 7.155A22–3) or tag (*sēmainein*, 1.101B20, 101B37) the 'essence,' but 'essence' in the *Topics* is almost verbal, certainly a phenomenon of logic (or dialectic) rather than of physics. Things available 'by participation' (*kata methexin*, 5.133A1–2, 5–10) 'contribute' to the 'essence' – a notion quite alien to the *Analytics*, and perhaps indebted to Eudoxus's attempts to save the idea of participation in Platonic Forms. No attention is paid here to the question of whether entities exist or not, as it is in the *Posterior Analytics*, where clear distinctions between the *ti esti* (roughly the kind) of a thing and its realization (*to ti ēn einai*) are drawn. In the *Topics* it is assumed that things exist, for they show their own existence (*einai* 5.135A11). Certainly one 'states' (*eirētai*) the essence in the *Topics* (e.g., 6.141A25, 143A17–19), but if the *genus* is omitted, one does *not state the essence* (6.143A17–19). Definitions in fact tag the essence, and can be used instead of a *name* (1.101B37). Thus a name tags the essence, and Aristotle is simply not concerned with whether *naming* something (or listing it in a category) may or may not be useful in determining whether it actually exists.

Aristotle could not have exhibited such unconcern after the opening chapter of *Posterior Analytics* 2. In the *Topics*, he has introduced the term *to ti ēn einai*, but he uses it without distinguishing it from *ti esti*, or perhaps originally intending it to replace *ti esti*, for *ti esti* also has to serve in various places (1.102A32, 103B27, etc.) for the name of the first category; that is, of the category which, in the *Categories* itself (and sometimes in the *Topics*), Aristotle calls the category of substance (*ousia*). Be that as it may, the fact that in the *Topics to ti ēn einai* does seem to mean something like 'essence,' i.e., that in virtue of which an individual 'partakes' in its species and genus, may have something to do with the common habit of scholars of translating it this way in the *Analytics* (or the *Metaphysics*), where such a translation, as we shall see later, is at best neglectful of distinctions Aristotle is careful to make, and at worst wildly erroneous: in these later texts, as I have observed, 'realized nature' is satisfactory as a translation, while something like 'kind' and 'substance' (like *ousia*) will do for the broad and narrow senses of *ti esti*.

IV Dating the 'Analytics'

At *Rhetoric* 1.1355A35 we are told that the theory of understanding (*epistēmē*) is developed for teaching.[17] Although this may be slightly overstated if it is correct that some of Aristotle's definitions are not analytic (but necessary *de re*),[18] it is largely true that demonstration (*apodeixis* is not as wide a term as 'proof') rather than induction is what Aristotle believes to be required to make us *understand* what we have learned or what we know; for it 'demonstrates' or 'lays out' the causes of things.

Internal evidence suggests that our text of the *Prior* and *Posterior*

Analytics was composed at a particular period in Aristotle's life. That does not mean that none of the ideas is earlier. Certainly Aristotle had been interested in induction and deduction for many years, but distinct chronological layers within the *Analytics* cannot be discovered. The recent attempt by Barnes, following Solmsen, to separate out 'apodeictic' from 'syllogistic',[19] that is, to argue that an overestimated theory of 'syllogistic' is imposed on an *earlier* 'apodeictic,' or general programme of deductive reasoning, depends in part on assumptions about Aristotle's view of the relationship between such 'syllogistic' and deductive reasoning in general. But if there is no necessary tension *in Aristotle's mind* between the two in our *Analytics*, it is hard to see why the 'apodeictic' should be earlier, except perhaps on more general considerations such as the absence of 'syllogistic' in non-Aristotelian (i.e. Platonic) logical writings and the fact that whatever one's *theory* of *apodeixis*, it is impossible not to talk about *apodeixis*. However, there is no particular reason to reject an alternative view to that of Barnes – which equally accounts for the present state of the text of the *Analytics* – namely that before our text was compiled, there was a period in which Aristotle was developing theses about 'syllogistic' and about 'apodeictic' reasoning in a wider sense simultaneously, but that as far as we can see from our *Analytics*, he never achieved an overarching theory.[20] If so, however, then the discovery of chronological layers within our *Analytics* becomes impossible.

We have already argued that our *Analytics* presupposes most of the *Topics* and the so-called *Sophistici Elenchi*. But without reference to the *Analytics* themselves, it is hard to be very precise about what that implies. The interest in the Eleatics, and in particular in Zeno's arguments about motion, which is shown in the *Topics* and the *Sophistici Elenchi*, suggests a date somewhere in the region of that of the *Physics* or later, and there is good reason to suppose that the *Physics* was begun in Mytilene and continued in Macedon. We have argued that *Topics*[2] should be dated provisionally to about 343. The *Analytics* – despite the problem about the sense of *to ti ēn einai* (essence or realized nature) – should be dated fairly shortly thereafter.

Barnes has pointed out that a passage in *Prior Analytics* 2 (68B41–69A11) refers to the relations between Athens and Thebes:[21] should Athens make war on Thebes? For Aristotle such a discussion would be absurd (except as the topic for merely trivial debates) after the alliance between Athens and Thebes which led to the battle of Chaeroneia in 338; still more so – and in poor taste – after the destruction of Thebes by Alexander in 335. It seems in fact to refer to debate *before* the alliance of Athens and Thebes (yet to post-date 346, for the same passage also includes a reference to an attack by Thebes on Phocis in that year). The most plausible date, therefore, for *Prior Analytics* 2 is about 341/0, which is just about the date we should expect from its relationship to the *Topics*.

V The 'Methodics' and the 'De Interpretatione'

Probably some time after the *Analytics*, but before the final version of the *Rhetoric*, Aristotle seems to have composed a work called *Methodics*.[22] I have suggested that it was concerned with the form (rather than with the *topoi* or content) of such activities as dialectic, rhetoric, and demonstration. A passage of the *Rhetoric* also suggests that Aristotle stated there that rhetoric uses both syllogisms and inductions, and/or their analogues enthymeme and example. One might speculate that our *De Interpretatione* was part of the *Methodics*. And if so, we have a date for it – depending on the date of the *Rhetoric* which we shall discuss below – just after Aristotle returned to Athens in 334/3. Certainly the *De Interpretatione* refers back to the *Topics*, apparently to 8.7 (at 20B26), that is, to a section which we have suggested was the very last Aristotle added; not *Topics*², but the final *Topics* with the added material 8.2–14 and *SE* 1–2 which was included after the completion of the *Analytics*.

There are a few other pieces of evidence which connect *De Interpretatione* with the period immediately preceding the *Rhetoric*, or, if it does not belong to the *Methodics*, to about the same time:

1 16A3–5. Words are not merely 'symbols' (as in *SE* 165A8), but symbols in the soul and a kind of sign. The reference to residence in the soul cannot be to the *De Anima*, but must point back to the *Eudemus* (or *On the Soul*). The passage offers a description of a name as a sound which signifies; the matter is treated very similarly in the *Poetics* (1457A10ff).[23] The remarks in the *De Interpretatione* look rather more developed than those in the *Sophistici Elenchi*, but this could lack significance. But signs have been discussed at length in the *Prior Analytics* (2.27), and that discussion itself is quoted in the same chapter of the *Rhetoric* (1.2). Goat-stags also crop up in the *De Interpretatione* (271–2 below).

2 The famous sea-battle of chapter 9, indicating that the future is contingent, can be seen as improving the 'Perhaps cultured Miccalus may perish tomorrow' section of the *Prior Analytics*. Certainly it is clearer. And Aristotle's purpose will be to develop a theme of the *Posterior Analytics*, that proper understanding, though possible of the present and past (18A35ff) – because there truths are necessary – is not possible (even presumably with foreknowledge) of future singulars. If future events are necessary, there would be no chance (18B9).

3 23A33ff seems to allude to the metaphysical situation of Aristotle in the last Athenian period: there are actualities without potentiality (like the 'primary substance'). That is not, of course, the first substance of the categories, but (e.g.) the Prime Mover of the *Metaphysics*.

There seems, then, to be a reasonable case for including *De Interpretatione* with the *Methodics* and for dating the work shortly before our *Rhetoric* in Aristotle's latest period. The *Methodics* probably also provides an explanation for our 'floating' book *Categories*; in compiling it, Aristotle collected and reproduced an early set of material on predicate-lists and their 'metaphysics' (our *Categories* 2–9), squeezing it between discussion of synonymy, paronymy, etc. (our *Cat* 1, with general but rather unspecific connection to the lists of predicates) and the so-called *Post Praedicamenta* (*Cat* 10–15), which again are only loosely connected to the *Categories* itself. If all these (followed by *De Interpretatione*) were sections of the *Methodics*, the form in which they have come down to us is made more intelligible. The material on the categories themselves, however, is certainly a version of earlier data, probably going back to before the earliest core of the *Topics*. If that is so, then the discussion of categories in the *Categories* is the earliest treatment of the matter in the Aristotelian writings.[24]

VI The Original 'Rhetoric' and Some Final Observations

I shall discuss the *Rhetoric* at some length later in this book (136–44 below), but a few words now will help to set the chronological stage. Like the *Topics*, the *Rhetoric* has an early core. The problem is how much of a core, and the safest answer is chapters 5 to 15 of book 1 (86, 136–41 below). That the work was completed in Athens in about 334 will be argued later. That it contains material apparently earlier even than *Topics* 4, such as the unexamined remark that pleasure is a movement (1.11.1369B33), seems to indicate that it was one of Aristotle's earliest efforts. Much of the *Rhetoric* reads like an early draft of an *ethical* treatise; an ethics, that is, in the Isocratean mode.[25] This is what we might expect from Aristotle's early interest in rhetoric and the prominence of Isocrates in the field (as noticed even by Plato in the *Phaedrus*). For Isocrates the teaching of rhetoric included a teaching of ethical and political wisdom.

It would therefore not be inappropriate to find other 'ethical' writings coming from Aristotle's hand at this early time. And indeed we do. *Rhetoric* 1.8 contains a list of constitutions which, I shall show later, seems to pre-date Plato's *Statesman* (138f below); and in a discussion of expediency in the same chapter we find reference to the 'Political Writings' (1.1366A26ff). Since this cannot be our *Politics* – any of it – it must refer to a work on politics to which *Politics* 7 itself also refers (160 below), and which we know, from other sources, that Aristotle wrote. Indeed we have fragments of the so-called *Statesman*. Whether that was the actual title is unclear. More probably 'Political Writings' was the title, as *Rhetoric* 1 suggests, and, as the fragments may indicate, the subject of the nature of a true statesman occupied a fair amount of the work.

Very probably Aristotle's early work *On the Poets* (*Rh.* 1.11), containing a discussion of comedy, appeared at about the same time. Poetry was ever a matter for political reflection. If the early core of the *Rhetoric*, the early *Politica*, and *On the Poets* are more or less contemporaneous, they probably appeared before the core of the *Topics*, and not too long after the *Gryllus*, known to have been Aristotle's first work – and concerned with rhetoric. The core of our *Rhetoric*, at least in part, is from after 366, for events of that year (concerning Callistratus and the town of Oropus) are mentioned in *Rhetoric* 1.7 (1364A19). This is fair enough; the *Gryllus* had not yet been written.

Why cannot parts of *Rhetoric* 2 be as early as this? Perhaps some of it is, but if Aristotle followed a common habit when revising of adding in not lines but chunks of text – a habit which I shall mention again (161, 206 below) in chapters 8 and 10 – it is impossible to sort the material out. Certainly 2.3 (1380B8ff) seems to refer to the events surrounding the 'Peace of Philocrates' (346 BC). If so, that is part of a revised *Rhetoric*, completed in about 332. *Rhetoric* 2.8 refers to the death of Diopeithes in 340, and the same chapter, with its detailed treatment of pity and terror, looks like the *Poetics*. Material in the later chapters of book 2 is later still: 2.23 refers to the treaty of Corinth of 336. It is safe to conclude that only the later chapters (5–15) of the first book of the *Rhetoric* are early, in the form that we have them.

We can now compile, however, a provisional schedule for a number of Aristotle's rhetorical, poetical, and logical writings:

Gryllus (ca 361)
Politica, On Poets, Rhetoric 1.5–15 (ca 358–4)
Categories 2–9, *Topics* 2–4, 7.1–2 (ca 353)
Topics 5 (ca 349)
Topics 1–8.1 completed, *SE* 2–34 (ca 343)
Prior and *Posterior Analytics* (ca 341/0)
Topics 8.2–14, *SE* 1–2 (ca 340)
Methodics (including *Categories* and *De Interpretatione*) (ca 334)
Poetics (ca 333)
Revised *Rhetoric* (ca 332)

One might consider the gap before *Methodics*. It will appear that at this stage Aristotle's attention turned to ethics and politics. The death of his father-in-law Hermeias at the hands of the Persians may have been in part the catalyst: Aristotle wrote an ode in his honour.[26]

APPENDIX

'DEMONSTRATION IN THE STRICT SENSE'

It will be helpful for our later enquiries into the specifically Aristotelian concept of metaphysics to comment briefly on the relationship in the *Analytics* between deductive reasoning in general and 'syllogistic' in particular, and on the phrase 'demonstration in the strict sense' (*haplōs*). Aristotle's general drift is rather unclear. *Prior Analytics* 1 begins (24A10) by telling us that it is his intention to discuss demonstration (*apodeixis*) and the understanding (*epistēmē*) that results from it: 'We will begin by defining the terms premiss, definition, and deductive reasoning (*sullogismos*). We shall identify "perfect" and "imperfect" forms of such reasoning.' He then proceeds to a definition of deduction (*sullogismos*): it is a structure in which given certain assumptions a conclusion necessarily follows; it is perfect if it is self-contained. Aristotle seems to assume, but need not assume, that such structures will be three-term deductions. The necessity of the conclusion in such cases flows from the premisses themselves and does not require the interposing of other propositions which themselves derive necessarily from the premisses (24B). Chapter 2 proposes to deal with three sorts of premisses: when an attribute 'applies' (*huparchein*), 'applies necessarily' (*ex anagkēs*), or 'may apply.' Clearly Aristotle envisages forms of deductive reasoning with premisses of all three types. Within the types, furthermore, some premisses are universal (positive or negative), some particular, some indefinite.

Chapter 4 begins the task in earnest; the rest of the *Prior Analytics* is concerned with deduction. Demonstration (*apodeixis*) will follow later (in the *Posterior Analytics*), for every demonstration is a sort of deduction, but not every deduction is a demonstration. So there are different kinds of deduction, and different kinds of demonstration. *Prior Analytics* 1 then proceeds to discuss what is now called 'syllogistic', with very little further comment on whether the premisses are true or are necessarily true. That distinction is not employed in the *Topics* either (book 1 only referring to true – without comment on the possibility of necessarily true – premisses, 100B1), and it is unnecessary for the general account of deductive reasoning in the *Prior Analytics*. As we shall see, however, it *is* necessary, and *apparent*, in the *Posterior Analytics*; for there we need to know the *use* of different sorts of demonstration and their application; that is, which would be useful in physics, ethics, mathematics, or even (though not yet) metaphysics.

Nevertheless, Aristotle gives us pointers in the *Prior Analytics* as to where he is going. Only deductions in the first 'syllogistic' figure are perfect, though others are valid (26B28ff, 27A1–2, 28A16, 29A30). But in chapters 4 to 7 he has nothing to say about whether the premisses themselves are true or necessarily true. There is no attempt to integrate that distinction with the subordination of later 'syllogistic' figures to the first. Chapters 4 to 7, in fact, apply to all deductions, not merely to those with necessary premisses.

In 1.8 Aristotle returns to the difference in premiss: the true and the necessarily true. The deduction, he says, is different if the premisses differ:

some deductions are from necessary premisses, some from true premisses, others from possible premisses. He still does not relate the different kinds of 'syllogism', let alone of deductive reasoning in general, as thus differentiated. But the conclusions will be different: while all will be valid, some will be true, others necessarily true (1.30A1–4). In the next few chapters he goes through the different figures of deduction, to indicate the effect on the conclusion of whether the premisses are necessary or not (1.9–12). At the end of chapter 12 he concludes that as regards necessary deductions with necessarily true premisses, he has said enough.

It would be false to call Aristotelian *sullogismoi*, without comment, 'syllogisms', where 'syllogism' means a deductive scheme with necessary premisses. And it is commentators (such as, recently, Barnes), not Aristotle, who say that 'in a *demonstration* [my italics] all the propositions are necessary.'[27] What Aristotle says is that with regard to demonstration 'strictly speaking' or 'in the proper sense' (*haplōs*) all the propositions are necessary – but that is in the *Posterior Analytics* (1.73A24). In the *Prior Analytics* (e.g., 1.31B14ff) he rather speaks of the 'necessary deductive schemata' (or 'necessary syllogism', if you will). Or again, at 1.36B20ff, in the midst of discussion of deductive schemata with 'problematic' premisses, Aristotle points out that similar arrangements of the terms will produce a valid deduction, both when the premisses are true and when they are necessary (cf. 39A1).

Aristotle in the *Analytics* discusses various forms of deduction, of which 'syllogisms with necessary premisses' are one variety, albeit in some perhaps *metalogical* sense the most important variety. But to follow from premisses necessarily is not the same as to follow necessarily from necessary premisses.[28] In fact, in a passage with undoubted connections with the sea-battle of *De Interpretatione* 9, Aristotle begs to suggest (1.33.47B30ff) that 'Cultured Miccalus [an odd, perhaps Macedonian, name] may die tomorrow' is not universally true, that is, not necessarily true. For, as Aristotle says, there is a difference between saying 'X is true of Y' and 'X is true of all Y.' Statements about future possibilities are not in the latter class.

Much of the rest of *Prior Analytics* 1 is concerned with proofs of deductions beyond the first syllogistic figure – and with the selection of premisses – and is not our immediate concern. We may note, however, that in 1.31 Platonic divisions are called 'weak deductions' (cf. 87 above). Divisions do not allow us to demonstrate 'about substance' and 'what it is.' (That means that classification in the Platonic sense has nothing to *say* about *why* things are as they are.)

I shall spend little time on book 2 – much of which is concerned with formal proofs and with what is deducible from false or partially false premisses – except to repeat, as is necessary, that the book is concerned with deduction in general, not specifically with deductions with necessary premisses. Again, as in book 1, the relation between such deduction and other deductions is left aside. We may now repeat that this is also the position in the *Topics*. Even in the *Topics* our problem is not whether Aristotle is innocent of the 'syllogism' – which we do not know – but it resides in the fact that (as in most of the *Prior Analytics*) he refers to deduction in general, not to deductions with certain kinds of premiss. Of course, the 'dialectical' deductions of the *Topics* will *not* have necessary premisses, though the premisses may (or may not) be true.

Prior Analytics 2.23 sums up the whole discussion of deduction, before moving to induction. The figures which Aristotle has described, he says, are significant for all kinds of deduction, whether they are dialectical, or demonstrative, not to speak of rhetoric and any other form (*methodos*) of reasoning (68B12) which may produce conviction.[29] Note how induction is called 'inductive "syllogism"'; the broad sense of *sullogismos* supports my interpretation of the term. But inductions have no middle term. Induction, therefore, is not an instrument for 'demonstration' but for learning, for getting to know. The same idea is visible in chapter 27, in the discussion of signs: signs, says Aristotle, are demonstrative premisses *either necessary* or generally accepted (*endoxa*). Thus again non-necessary premisses are going to be acceptable as premisses for (some sorts of) demonstrations. And further evidence follows. Deductions (like signs which are deductions with only one premiss, 70A24ff) cannot be refuted in *the first figure* if it is true, since it is *universal*, but deductions in other figures, even where the conclusion is true, can be refuted. The point seems to be that there is an important *difference* between first-figure deductions which are 'universal' (that is, necessary) and other first-figure deductions. For the former are irrefutable. But Aristotle does not *spell out* the formal relationship between the refutable and the irrefutable deduction.

What in fact is the connection (for Aristotle) between 'syllogisms' in the first figure which are true and 'universal' (that is, with premisses which are both true and necessary) and other 'deductions' (even) in the first figure? The answer is not given in the *Prior Analytics*, but perhaps it can be discerned. Could it be that deductions with premisses both true and necessary are somehow the point of reference for other deductions? The 'intelligibility' of other deductions is preserved by reference to the logic of deductions from necessarily true premisses. That we shall find indicated much more clearly in the *Posterior Analytics*. Irrefutable 'syllogisms' in fact turn out to be deductions which are universally true (as in mathematics),[30] or 'necessarily true' in that they deal with the present or past, or with reference to the future viewed *as if* it were the present or past, that is, in such propositions as '*All* eclipses are (theoretically) predictable.' The *De Interpretatione*, echoing the *Prior Analytics*, as I have suggested, will show that in this sense 'This sea battle will happen tomorrow' can never be a premiss in the 'strictest' 'syllogism' (or deduction). The *Posterior Analytics* will enable us to identify different kinds of deduction and different kinds of 'demonstration.' Some demonstrations will be 'necessary' in the strongest sense; those whose premisses are not necessary will (at best) merely be true.

Like the *Prior Analytics*, the *Posterior Analytics* is much concerned with paradox: such as that of the *Meno*, that one cannot learn anything because we either know it already or because we would not realize it when we had 'learned' it.[31] Both deductive and inductive arguments, says Aristotle, produce instruction through the use of pre-existent 'knowledge' of some kind. Deduction here, as in the *Prior Analytics*, is not limited to 'syllogistic'; it works from assumptions while induction displays the universal because of the self-evident character of the particular. Both deduction[32] and induction are considered in the *Posterior Analytics*, though induction only appears at the end (2.19). Clearly Aristotle is telling us that the nature and value of deduction depend on the reliability of the premisses on which it is based. We know that if there are merely 'agreed' premisses, we shall have a piece of 'dialectical' reasoning, whereas if they are true (or probably true), we shall have understanding of what is before us (provided, or course, that we accept probability as probability).

What we should expect to find, therefore, are different sorts of understanding, different sorts of 'demonstration', and therefore of course different sorts of deductive reasoning. It would be typically Aristotelian if we found that one of these types was regarded as superior to the others and in some sense normative – unless there are no common types of reasoning underlying the different sorts of 'understanding'. And we do indeed find such notions of normativity already in chapter 2 of *Posterior Analytics* 1, where Aristotle immediately introduces the notion (not used in the *Prior Analytics*) of understanding in some 'strict' sense (*haplōs*),[33] which is more 'authoritative' (1.86A23). Such understanding comes *inter alia* from an understanding of the cause, and a realization that the fact 'cannot be otherwise,' that is, that it is a necessary truth. We conclude that 'complete understanding' will ensue only from demonstrations with necessary premisses, as we have already suspected.

But Aristotle does not immediately pursue that line. After noting that there may be 'other modes' of understanding (71B16), he proceeds to a general account of *all* deductive reasoning and 'demonstrative understanding'. It deals with premisses which are true, primary, immediate, more familiar, prior, and causative of the conclusion. They are *not* said here to be necessary (though they will be, as we have seen, if 'complete understanding' is to be obtained). Not all understanding is *demonstration*, of course – such as that of immediate premisses (72B20).

We have already found 'proper [or strict] understanding'. We quickly meet its associate at 72B25: 'proper demonstration' (for *apodeixis*, see also 75B23, 76A14; and cf. *Met.* Δ.1015B8); there is also another kind of demonstration, which is not 'proper' (72B31). So we now have proper understanding generated by proper demonstration. The phrase 'proper deduction' ('syllogism') does not occur, but we quickly hear again of the necessarily true premisses of such 'syllogisms' (73A24–5). Such 'syllogisms' can even deal with individuals and events, provided that such things are treated universally (73B) as explicable by necessary truths. They are then 'properly understandable' (73B16ff). Mathematics is certainly an important (but not unique) model for Aristotle in his treatment of 'proper' (or strict) understanding in these sections, and we soon find him asking 'When do we know properly?' (74A33).

It is sections like the beginning of 1.6 which have confused the commentators. Here Aristotle uses the phrase 'demonstrative understanding' and says that it derives from 'necessary first principles'. But we know by now that he means that 'proper' demonstration and understanding – that is, that form of understanding to which other forms refer *because* it is *proper* (*haplōs*) – derive from 'necessary first principles'. The prior nature of this strict form, and its limited application to necessary (though probably not merely analytic) truths, seem to be a claim in metalogic as well as in logic. And its application to the future is to be maintained only in so far as the future can be *assumed* to be necessarily like the past. Such assumptions explain how Aristotle could use proper demonstrations to found understanding not of the eclipse qua particular (for which special knowledge would be required) but of eclipses qua eclipses (75B34), that is, through 'tracking down what the thing is' by an exposition of its causes (79A25). If there were 'metaphysics' in the *Posterior Analytics*, 'proper demonstration' would be needed for that too; but there is not. Each science has its own first principles, related only analogously (1.76A39).[34]

There is no need to pursue the matter further through the *Analytics*. We can now see why the *Prior Analytics* (not to speak of the *Topics*) has little to say about the subordination or reduction of deductive argument in general to 'syllogistic'. So-called 'syllogistic' is merely the form of deductive reasoning (*sullogismos*) necessary for certain specified tasks, and to which, since the premisses are necessary, other deductive reasoning is referred 'metalogically'. It cannot do the job of other types of deduction, which have their own spheres. Generally, remarks about deductive reasoning have nothing to imply about the role of complete demonstrations within the whole class of demonstrations. Such questions, I suppose, are strictly matters of the philosophy of logic, and their undeveloped state in the *Topics* and *Analytics* reflects Aristotle's (persistent) lack of concern with such a study. Indeed an investigation of it might have involved him in a 'metaphysical' discussion of the whole theory of 'focal meaning' – which he would not (and could not) have undertaken until he had developed ideas to be found in certain books of the *Metaphysics* (especially Λ). Meanwhile in the *Analytics* Aristotle uses rather than defends an application of such metalogical thinking in relating the various forms of deductive reasoning and demonstration. For such application helps us grasp the *limits* of our understanding of particular phenomena in the past, the present, and the future, and of mathematics on the one hand or physics on the other.

It seems thus to be misleading to talk about an attempt by Aristotle to reduce deductive reasoning to 'syllogistic'. *Sullogismos* in Aristotle should normally be translated as 'deductive reasoning'. The importance of three-term syllogisms with necessary premisses is that they are said to be (or are assumed to be) productive of complete understanding. They are not privileged instruments of discovery. The fact that *epistēmē* means 'understanding' does not, of course, suggest that Aristotle denies *knowledge* of particulars. Collectors of sense-data *know* the fact, Aristotle tells us, but (among others) mathematicians know the explanation (1.79A1–2). And people who study the universal may *not know* the particular well enough (79A6); they may not investigate carefully enough.[35] Knowledge thus comes through the senses, but understanding requires more (1.87B28ff).

5

Categories

I The 'Categories'

We may now begin to apply some of the results of our study of the chronology of Aristotle's logical and rhetorical writings. It seems, first of all, that *Topics* 1 is not among the earliest sections of the *Topics*. Yet *Topics* 1.9 contains a list of 'kinds of predication'[1] which supply material for sentences indicating definitions, properties, genera, and accidents. Such kinds of predication were certainly listed by Aristotle (and perhaps by others in the Academy), and the number of such kinds, in the *Topics*, is ten. Only in one other work, named the *Categories* in the tradition, though probably not so named by Aristotle,[2] is a set of ten kinds to be found, and there is little doubt that parts at least of the *Categories* are much earlier than *Topics* 1. But earlier sections of the *Topics* also refer to similar subject-matter: we read of substance (*ousia*), quality, and relation in *Topics* 4 (120B36ff). But *Topics* 4 also uses an apparently later phrase for the first kind: at 122A32ff (and at 127B28ff) we find the phrase *ti esti* (what it is). In the *Categories* itself, however, *ousia* is the only term used in this connection – which probably indicates that this was the earliest term for 'kind' number one (substances); and that originally the 'kinds' were not of predications but of 'things' and of the words which somehow name 'things.'

Let us therefore open our discussion with the *Categories* itself, on the assumption that it is a genuine work of Aristotle's[3] and that there is a *prima facie* reason to begin with this text rather than with *Topics* 1.9, the only other place where a list of ten 'categories' is provided and in some degree explained. Since we have argued that *Topics* 1.9 in its present form was composed about 343, the alternative would be to admit that we have no account of Aristotle's theory of 'categories' (whatever they are) before 343 –

which in view of the use of 'category-material' in earlier parts of the *Topics* is a solution only to be embraced as a last resort. Indeed we shall find a number of features in the text of the *Categories* which seem to link it with Plato's *Sophist*, a work which can most plausibly be dated after Plato's final return from Sicily; that is, to about 359. The exact date of the *Sophist* is unimportant for our considerations; the approximate date is certain.

Chapter 1 of the *Categories* is only rather loosely connected with the theory of the central chapters of the book. A treatment of homonyms and synonyms is relevant to the discussion of terms and the objects which they name, but can be left aside in our present discussion. I have suggested above that this material (along with the so-called *Post Praedicamenta*) may have later been packaged with the original *Categories* by Aristotle when he compiled the *Methodics*. Be that as it may, chapter 2 introduces us to 'things said' (*legomena*) either in combination (i.e., 'man runs,' 'man conquers'), or uncombined ('man,' 'ox,' 'runs,' 'conquers'). Commentators have regularly and rightly associated the discussion of the combination of terms with the *Sophist* of Plato, where in sections dealing with such 'combinations of kinds' we read of 'Theaetetus sits,' 'Theaetetus flies'; while 'Theaetetus,' 'sits,' and 'flies' are uncombined. In what follows Aristotle includes phrases like 'in the Lyceum' as uncombined utterances. As in the *Sophist*, however, 'runs' and 'conquers' are taken as without combination, like 'flies' and 'sits' – that is, they are considered somehow grammatically rather than semantically. For Aristotle would apparently approve the translation of *trechei* as 'runs,' rather than as 'he runs,' presumably because by itself *trechei* gives us no information as to who (he, she, or it) is doing the running.

What does *ta legomena* mean? Normally 'what is said' (i.e., words, phrases, sentences, etc.) or 'what is referred to'; these are quite possible meanings of the word *lego*. But the latter meaning is impossible, for then *ta legomena* would be identical in meaning with *ta onta* (the items or events listed or named) – and there would be no point in Aristotle's distinction. The *legomena* must therefore be words, names, phrases, or sentences uttered. But they are not *merely* linguistic items; they must refer to existing items in the world, and the structure of the words or sentences must reflect or indicate (or purport to reflect or indicate) the objects in the world or their structures in relation to one another. Thus it is mistaken to assume that the *Categories* is simply about words, or even simply about logic;[4] it is also concerned with the identification of the contents of the universe as being of different sorts. The *Categories* is a sort of inventory of items of phenomena which can be named; thus it is both logical (in that it distinguishes different ways in which predicates can be said of a subject), and metaphysical in a weak or descriptive sense in that it tells us what is important and what is subordinate in the world itself.

The title of our book, viz. *Categories*, has no claim to Aristotelian origin, and the word *katēgoria* occurs rarely in the text itself – and nowhere in the key chapters 2 and 4 about uncombined terms.[5] We hear of words being 'predicated', of course. Nor does the notion of 'kinds' have much claim to be regarded as a title for the text, despite references to the *Categories* as a book about '*ten kinds*' in writers like Porphyry or Simplicius. Doubtless *one* of the topics of the book is what Aristotle later called 'kinds of predicates,' but the original Aristotelian description of his subject-matter – if it ever existed – is lost. What the book comprises is an analysis of words and their objects listed under certain heads; it seems to deal with the modes of naming (*schēma prosēgorias*, 3B14) rather than of predicating (*katēgorias*). And its purpose seems to be to identify the kinds of true and false statements which can be made by linking words in the different lists (or by confusing them, 2A6ff). Leaving aside, therefore, the question of the title, we will do well to consider what is actually listed in the *Categories*, and see what purpose the lists might serve. The table of items is as follows, and it is repeated with only trivial differences in *Topics* 1.9 For the time being I shall leave aside the first kind, which in the *Categories* is called substance (*ousia*) and in the *Topics* either substance or 'what it is.' Apart from substances, then, uncombined terms indicate (*sēmainei*) phenomena under one of the following heads:

Categories	*Topics* 1.9
Quantity (2 cubits, 3 cubits)	Quality (white)
Quality (white, grammatical)	Quantity (a cubit long)
Relation (double, half, greater)	Relation
Place (in the Lyceum, in the market)	Place
Time (yesterday, last year)	Time
Position (is lying, is sitting)	Position
State (is shod, is armed)	State
Activity (burns, cuts)	Activity
Passivity (is burned, is cut)	Passivity

According to the *Topics* the number ten comprises the total number of kinds.[6] If this is so, the next question is why there are ten, and how Aristotle arrived at such a figure. In answering this we cannot hope for certainty, but an inspection of the examples Aristotle gives and of the uses he makes of the lists may help us make limited progress. It is clear that the primary substance of the *Categories* is not a predicate; indeed such substance is not 'said of any subject nor is it in any subject.' So the lists, as *originally* conceived, cannot be lists of predicates, but lists of naming words of various types which may be used for various purposes, including, in many cases, predication. When we realize this, progress on the nature of the kinds is easier. Two of them, 'substance' and 'relation', date back to basic logical concerns of the Academy. Certainly Aristotle's use of these terms is idiosyncratic, but he himself makes use of the old Academic dichotomy even in his latest works. Thus there is a contrast between things 'in themselves' (*kath' hauto*) and 'relations' made at *Metaphysics* A.990B16–17, precisely in the context of the 'more exact' arguments offered for the existence of Forms.[7] *Nicomachean Ethics* 1.6 (1096A20–2) is even more explicit; here substance is identified as 'the in itself' (*to kath' hauto*) and contrasted with 'relation', which latter more or less stands for all the other categories as offshoots of substance. The old Academic distinction between 'in itself' and 'relation' was maintained by Xenocrates (fr. 15 Heinze), and seems not only to lie behind two of Aristotle's own categories, but also to help us understand why substance and relation could both be listed as kinds despite their different ontological status. Aristotle is merely following Academic practice in *distinguishing* what cannot *exist* apart (*chōris*, 1A25). Where he comes to diverge from the Academy, however, is that he *lists* a category of relation and distinguishes eight other sorts of non-substance items which would originally have simply been classed as relatives in some (imprecise) way.[8]

We can proceed to the identification of three further kinds by their uses, especially in the physical treatises. Quality, quantity, and place are regularly employed by Aristotle to identify different kinds of *movements* (growth, alteration, locomotion). Perhaps the earliest such passage in the physical treatises (*Phys.* 3.201A9), however, introduces a problem which appears neither in the *Categories* nor in the *Topics*. Aristotle says that there are as many kinds of motion and change as there are of being (*tou ontos*); and this immediately follows an identification of motion in respect of quality, quantity, and place. Now Aristotle does not normally consider other kinds of movement in terms of categories. Nevertheless his point here seems to be that substances can change (hence there can be so many senses or uses of 'is') in a definable number of ways; however many such ways there are, so many will be the 'categories'. The lists of items other than substances will thus in effect be lists of the modes of alteration or of 'movement' of substances. But if Aristotle suggests that the non-substance categories are modes of change in *Physics* 3, he must be assumed by *Physics* 5 (225B5ff) either to wish to retract this, or to indicate that the changes of *Physics* 3 are to be understood in a very broad sense, for in *Physics* 5, again after discussing movements, he lists *eight* categories (position and state being dropped), and observes that only three of them (quality, quantity, and place) refer to modes of movement.

At least we can reasonably conclude that Aristotle started with two

Academic categories and added three more to account for movement understood in fairly obvious senses. We may recall that it was a concern of Plato at the end of his life to identify different kinds of movements: ten are recognized in book 10 of the *Laws* (893B–895A). Aristotle's 'categorizing' does not seem entirely out of place. At any rate we may not unreasonably add a further kind (that of time) to those categories generated by the search for classification of modes of movement. For time, *Metaphysics* Λ.1071B9–11 tells us, is either identical with motion or an affection (*pathos*) of motion, and both these suggestions are far from alien to the treatment of motion in Plato's *Timaeus* (which we need not assume to be a totally original treatment). So perhaps we can see from this passage of the *Metaphysics* why time has come to be among Aristotle's kinds – and *Timaeus* and motion apart, there is yet another Academic phenomenon which must be related to it. Plato had long since been thinking of a contrast between 'being' and 'time': the philosopher-king of the *Republic* is an observer of both (6.486A). Indeed the Academic contrast between substance and relation could be viewed as another (more general) formulation of the *Republic*'s distinction between being and time.

Substance, quantity, quality, relation, place, time: there remain four more kinds unaccounted for in the version of 'categories' urged in the *Categories* and *Topics*. We must discuss activity and passivity as well as position and state. The first pair, however, are also of Platonic origin. In the *Sophist* (248C), to which we have already claimed that the *Categories* is connected, being is said either to act or to be acted upon. Position and state, however, are not to be identified so easily in non-Aristotelian sources, and have always proved difficult to account for. In the last century Trendelenburg attempted to argue that the categories as a whole derive from a grammatical analysis,[9] but there is no evidence for this in the earliest texts dealing with the subject, that is, in the *Categories* and the *Topics*. (The general references in the *Physics* and *De Generatione et Corruptione* are quite inadequate for Trendelenburg's purposes.) The claim must remain, therefore, an interesting but unsubstantiated guess.

Some similar suggestions offered by Benveniste as part of an interpretation of the categories as a whole may take us a little further.[10] According to Benveniste too all the categories are of grammatical origin. The first six are 'nominal', having to do with what Greek would call *onomata* (nouns, adjectives, or adverbs used adjectivally – as in 'the men of the present day' [*hoi nūn*]); the last four are verbal (connected with *rhēmata*). That the distinction between an *onoma* and a *rhēma* may be invoked is entirely plausible; Aristotle uses it in the *Categories* itself, and speaks of locutions combining *onomata* and *rhēmata* as 'said in combination.' Furthermore, I have observed that in the *Posterior Analytics* Aristotle considers that the two sets of phenomena deserving explanation are objects and events (54 above). Be that as it may, however, one should also notice that if all the non-substance kinds are modes of what other members of the Academy would have preferred to call 'relations', then the distinction between the 'nominal' and the 'verbal' relations might have appeared less striking than it does to us: the nominal categories deal with a substance's circumstances, the verbal with its acts. Both concern what is perhaps non-intrinsic.

It is certainly in favour of Benveniste's view (or of one something like it) that the examples given by Aristotle himself for the last four of his kinds are all verbal in form. Now the Greek verb is not only active and passive; it is also middle. Perhaps position and state are meant to represent the middle force of such 'doings'. The examples given can all be construed as perfect middles. Now perfect middles are also grammatically aspectual; the form of the verb is perfective, representing an enduring state resulting from prior action or experiencing. Thus *anakeitai* means 'is lying as a result of having lain'; *kathētai* means 'is sitting as a result of having sat'; *hupodedetai* means 'is shod as a result of having been shod'; *hōplistai* means 'is armed as a result of having armed oneself.' Such verbs may be described as half verbal and half adjectival-descriptive. If this analysis is on the right lines, then perhaps Aristotle is *expanding* on Plato's description of being as that which is capable of acting or being acted upon, in line with a grammatical feature of the Greek language. But if that is the case, why did he abandon the experiment? The answer is probably because position and state can easily be seen simply as qualities or relations. In a dubiously genuine section of the *Categories* (11B11–12), position is already identified as a kind of relation,[11] and in the *Post Praedicamenta* (ch. 15), we note the disappearance of state (*echein*); state has many modes, says Aristotle, and the first mode he selects is 'disposition and condition and some other *quality*.'

What we have in the *Categories* then are sets of items in the world and in speech which can be related to concerns in the Academy. The interests of the Academy were metaphysical, so we should expect the *Categories* to have metaphysical implications, and indeed it does in its account of the priority of primary substances, i.e., of individual concrete particulars, to species and genera. We shall discuss this metaphysical question in a later chapter. For the moment we shall content ourselves with the following observations:

1 The assertion of the priority of the concrete particular is anti-Platonic in the sense that it denies the priority of the Form.
2 The existence of items called secondary substances – which may have some connection with 'Platonism' if only by virtue of the name 'substance' – indicates that Aristotle is not yet prepared to adopt the position on

universals – especially on substance–universals – which he adopts, for example, in the *Posterior Analytics*.

3 There is no discussion of 'realized nature' (*to ti ēn einai*) in the *Categories*, and the account of primary substance would most naturally be taken to imply that Aristotle had not yet developed that notion. In this respect the *Categories* resembles the earliest parts of the *Topics* (books 2–4).

4 There is no deployment of form and matter, or explicitly even of accidental being, in the *Categories*. Again this situation is compatible with Platonic (or Academic) investigation of classes. The specifically Aristotelian account of what it is to be a substance, with its concomitant theory of causation, is missing.

5 In brief the *Categories* is a rather Platonic exercise in descriptive metaphysics. Its lists of kinds of things suggest nothing of the first philosophy of the *Metaphysics* or even of the *Posterior Analytics*. There is no reason to claim that the identification of the concrete individual with its 'realized nature' is implied in the *Categories*.[12] On the contrary the *only* metaphysical points Aristotle seems concerned to make are that it is important to separate substances from (e.g.) qualities ('man' from 'just'), as Plato had failed to do; and to emphasize against Plato that the concrete individual is not less but more real than the kind (the secondary substance) to which it belongs. For the secondary substance only identifies the *kind* of thing on the list (3B15–16), not what it is in the strictest sense. To designate X as a primary substance is to tag it as a real being, a part of the furniture of the universe, a *kath' hauto* in the old Academic classification. Thus a simple listing of the contents of the world becomes what we have called a descriptive metaphysics. Substances are the most important things and the other kinds indicate ways of dependence on substance; of substances themselves some are primary, others (the species and genera) are not second but secondary.[13] It is a bold claim for the young philosopher in the Academy, but a limited one. For even the theory of 'categories' itself is far from complete in the *Categories*.

But as he developed his theory of 'kinds', Aristotle moved away from some of the metaphysical implications of this original programme. For he eventually came to believe that demonstration, not Platonic-Academic classification, is the technique which, grounded on induction, is necessary for expounding first philosophy or metaphysics. As for the *Categories*, Aristotle wishes only, but firmly, to insist that what is not itself a substance (that is, a concrete individual) is either the species or genus to which such a substance belongs (the status of these is rather uncertain) or something merely present 'in' the substance itself.

II From the 'Categories' to 'Topics' 1.9

Between the *Categories* and *Topics* 1.9 we find an important development. We meet, for the first time, the notion that some items cannot be put on the lists because they apply to items in all of them. These free-range entities are of great metaphysical importance, though in the early parts of the *Topics*, where the matter is first raised, such implications are not stressed. The items involved are 'being' and 'one' (*Topics* 4.121B4–8, 127A26–34, 5.130B17); they are said to be unlistable and ambiguous. Later on Aristotle comes to think that this ambiguity has been traded on by metaphysicians, especially by Eleatics (*Phys.* 1.185A21, 185B31, 186A24). For the time being we may merely observe an extension of the uses to which the lists are put in the *Categories*, and an indication of what is to come in *Topics* 1.9, namely their application to increasingly logical rather than metaphysical purposes.

Although almost certainly later than *Physics* 5 (where at 225B5–16 only eight kinds are to be found, of which substance – *ousia* – is the first), *Topics* 1.9 gives us the complete set of ten as found in the *Categories*. The discrepancy need not disturb us: *Physics* 5 does not claim to be complete; *Topics* 1.9 does. But *Topics* 1.9 is no mere repetition of the *Categories*. First of all the kinds are now introduced as 'kinds of predication,' among which definitions, *propria*, genera, and accidentals can be found. Among these kinds of predication further novelties may be itemized:

1 There is no discussion of primary substances (i.e., subjects) in *Topics* 1.9, though their existence is assumed in what is discussed.[14]
2 'What it is' is a name of the first kind, indicating what in the *Categories* was called a secondary substance. The latter term has disappeared. The first kind still indicates or tags the substance.
3 The kinds as a whole give answers to questions that ask 'What is it?'
4 'What it is' is thus ambiguous: it is the question being asked every time we try to identify something, and it is also the name of the first kind.
5 The kinds indicate what is predicated of something 'set before us' (*ekkeimenon*, not *hupokeimenon* as in the *Categories*).

In sum we have now a theory of predication. The lists tell us the different ways in which predication of concrete individuals is possible; it identifies their qualities, etc. The categories (as the earlier material on 'one' and 'being' foreshadowed) have become a tool for the logician and have largely lost their metaphysical importance. There is no hint of an interest in the older metaphysics of primary and secondary substances. Classification in category-lists is now inadequate for metaphysical purposes; as we observed in the previous chapter (81 above), Aristotle is now also using the notion of *to ti ēn einai*. This is quite beyond the world of arguments in the old Platonic context, for although Aristotle's account of primary substance in the *Categories* is unplatonic, the framework of the discussion derives from Platonic divisions, Platonic classification. With the loss of interest in primary substances as subject-matter for anti-Platonic metaphysical claims, Aristotle is preparing the ground for a quite different account of what a substance is; his discussion in the *Metaphysics* will eventually bring this work to fruition. From now on Aristotle's *logical* interest in categories will only be in the relationship of the 'later' categories to the category of substance; this will eventually establish that the *metaphysics* of substance will also be relevant to all the other lists. It will be for metaphysics itself to deal with the nature of that relevance.

We should notice that although *Topics* 1.9 indicates that the categories provide sets of answers to questions that ask 'What is it?' (What is this? It is a substance, a quality, etc.), it was not by the random posing of this question that the category-lists were originally compiled. For that compilation we have offered quite another explanation. It is only in the *Topics*, that is, after the lists have been compiled, that the 'What is it?' question is brought to the forefront. This observation does something at least to help Aristotle face the charge that the *number* of categories (produced, it is sometimes claimed, by asking 'What is it?' questions of differing phenomena) is arbitrary or random. But the lists were not established by asking 'What is it?' questions; rather, their existence enabled such questions to be answered. By the answers each list acquired more and more members.

III The Verb 'to be'

The evidence of *Physics* 3.201A9 indicates that Aristotle had begun to connect his category-lists with different senses of the verb 'to be,' or different uses of the verb 'to be,' even before *Topics* 1.9. *Physics* 5 (227B4) is perhaps the first indication of a feature of Aristotle's category-theory which came to be connected with these ideas: the notion of forms (*schēmata*) of predication (*katēgorias*), not, as we observed in the *Categories*, of naming (*prosēgorias*, 3B14). In this text, however, Aristotle is only concerned to identify the ambiguity of the phrase 'one movement.' 'One', as the early parts of the *Topics* had shown, has many senses, and a movement is 'one in genus' when it belongs to a particular mode of predication. So the formalization of the 'category-system' seems to spring from Aristotle's concern in the first instance with kinds of movement. Yet this passage also indicates that a formal structure of predication is available, and it would seem at least to clear the ground for the application of that structure to propositions other than those concerning movements.

This, in fact, seems to be the position of Aristotle in the *Prior Analytics*, when in 1.37 we find the general, formalized notion that we can say 'X is Y' and 'it is true that X is Y' in as many ways as 'predicates' can be distinguished. But even here we have neither the formal phrase 'forms of predication' nor the *direct* reference to the different uses of the verb 'to be.' Nor is this spelled out even in the *Posterior Analytics* (1.83A)[15] where there is discussion of the distinction between those predicates which indicate a class (e.g., 'A man is an animal') and those which indicate accidents (e.g., 'A man is white'). The passage reminds us of the *Categories*, though the term 'accident', absent before, now appears, and the phrases 'said of a subject' referring to class-membership in *Cat.* 1A20ff and 'present in a subject' (referring to predication) are missing. It is perhaps also the earliest text where the number of categories is reduced to eight. We have already indicated, however, that this reduction has no great significance for understanding the nature or the purpose of the categories themselves.

Thus in the period between the earlier books of the *Physics* and the *Metaphysics* we can form little notion of the uses to which Aristotle is going to put the categories in the *Metaphysics* itself, where they occur repeatedly. Indeed, as we shall see, there is in this period a decidedly anti-metaphysical purpose to which they are sometimes directed. The overall situation, however, is roughly as follows:

1 Aristotle uses the phrase 'modes of predication'.
2 He begins to connect the 'categories' with senses or uses of the verb 'to be,' perhaps first through reflection on the different ways in which we can say 'This *is* changing.'
3 The *Prior Analytics* seems to indicate an attempt to use the categories to promote something of a formal theory of all modes of intelligible discourse based on subject-predicate logic.
4 The *Posterior Analytics* seems to suggest that the theory of predication so produced removes the conceptual unclarities which have generated Platonic Forms. Meaningful propositions which can be used in demonstrations are constructed and understood by anyone who can handle the categories properly. Platonic Forms do not fit into any of the categories and can therefore serve no role in demonstrations (1.83A24–35).
5 Eight categories are listed, and that is the complete set (*APo.* 1.83B15–17).
6 Last but by no means least: with Platonic Forms gone we should not be surprised to find in the *Eudemian Ethics* (1.1217B27) that the 'extra-categorial' identification of 'being' is extended to 'good'. As is typical of the *Eudemian Ethics*, there is no attempt to dissolve the claim that 'being' and 'good' are thus simply ambiguous.[16] The conclusion is that no Platonic variety of ethics is possible. Since the *Eudemian Ethics* agrees with the

Posterior Analytics that no metaphysics is possible if no Platonic metaphysics is possible, it follows that no relationship between ethics and metaphysics is possible. The categories are used here to assert that the ethical 'good' cannot be identified with any metaphysical goodness. No primary sense of goodness is available, any more than any primary sense of being.

IV The Last Stage of the Theory

The *Metaphysics* repeatedly identifies the modes of predication and the corresponding use of predicates as indicating different modes of being, as do other late Aristotelian texts.[17] Assembling all these texts – with the exception of the latest sections of book Δ[18] – we find that Aristotle still maintains the eight categories as listed in the *Analytics*. Now it is easy to see how the first six categories, taken as answers to 'What is it?' questions, can be viewed in this way. What is it? It is a man, an animal. What is it in size? Big. What is its location? In the Lyceum. But, we ask, what about 'activity' and 'passivity'? In an important passage of Δ.7.1017A23–30) the answer is given. There are just as many uses of the verb 'to be' as there are forms of predication. Then follow the eight forms; and activity and passivity are explained. To say 'a man recovers' (*hugiainei*) and 'a man is recovering' (*hugiainōn esti*) is to say the same thing. Similarly with '*is* walking,' or '*is* cutting.' And with the categories of position and state already eliminated, all the kinds now correspond with uses of the verb 'to be.' Furthermore, in the *Metaphysics* there is, of course, a primary sense of being: this is the category of substance (Γ.1003A33–B6 – where other categories are affections of substance – and Z.1028A14ff). This thesis is repeated in the *Nicomachean Ethics* (1.1096A22ff), as we have seen: the 'in itself' and substance are prior by nature to relation. Relations, and the others, are like offshoots of substance. So that now, contrary to the situation which obtained in the *Eudemian Ethics*, 'being' and 'good' are no longer merely ambivalent. There is a primary sense. Hence study of the being and goodness of substance will help us to understand other kinds of being and goodness. The categories, the modes of predication, have taken a renewed lease on metaphysical life. As in the *Categories*, but unlike what is in the *Posterior Analytics* and the *Eudemian Ethics*, they have a clear and *positive* metaphysical role. At least they can forward one of the original metaphysical purposes of the *Categories*. There, a doctrine of primary and secondary substance is discussed; now, it is only the metaphysics of primary substances (understood, however, as individuals and their 'realized natures') which is important. The function of the categories is to show that other features of the world, and predicates of sentences, must be related to the primary substances and can be so logically related. But if logically related, then they are metaphysically related.

I argue in chapter 12 that Δ.13–30 is much later than the rest of Δ (235 below). This reading may (but need not) be supported by a final development of category-theory.[19] Δ.13 deals with quantity; Δ.14 deals with quality; Δ.15 deals with relations – but here *poiētika* and *pathētika* are treated as varieties of *relation*. They are so called because they have an active and passive capability and corresponding activity. This would seem to eliminate the separate *categories* of activity and passivity altogether – as a final development of their resolution in Δ.7 into modes of the verb 'to be.' For if 'to walk' is 'to be walking' and 'to cut' is 'to be cutting,' then one is dealing with the capacity and activity of walking and cutting. Δ.15.1021A15ff deals with heating and cutting viewed as the ability to heat and be heated, to cut and be cut: hence as relatives. Time and place are not discussed in this section of Δ, but there is no reason to think that they too have been dropped. The number of categories seems now to be six.

And there, with the implicating of some of the categories with potentiality and actuality (*energeia*),[20] this chapter on the development of Aristotle's category-theory comes to an end. It is interesting to notice that of the four senses of substance which Aristotle is prepared to identify in the *Metaphysics* (Δ.7, E.2), the two that matter for metaphysics itself are being as distinguished in accordance with the forms of predication and being as potential and actual. In fact the primary instances of each kind coincide. The primary and authoritative example of a substance turns our to be the Prime Mover (understood as Mind) – which is also the only being entirely in act without potentiality. An important theme from the *Categories* thus asserts itself again in the *Metaphysics*, though in a new, even transcendent, guise. There is indeed a being which is 'said most authoritatively, primarily, and especially' (*Cat.* 2A11), though it can no longer be a particular *composite* individual.

6

The Development of *Energeia*: Activity and Actuality

Throughout this chapter I shall refer to *energeia* by its Greek name, though arguing that in Aristotle's *developed* theory 'actuality' seems to be the best available rendering in English.[1] My main aim is to shed light on the origins and growth of the concept of *energeia*, a subject which has received surprisingly little attention in view of the intense interest at some periods of the twentieth century in Aristotle's philosophical development.

Aristotle has two separate words for actuality/activity, *energeia* and *entelecheia*, though the former is by far the more frequently used. Only in the *De Generatione et Corruptione* is *entelecheia* the more usual (eighteen instances to four according to Blair).[2] There is often assumed to be no basic difference in the meaning of the words, but this is not entirely true. *Energeia* seems to be the earlier of the two, for *entelecheia* occurs neither in the fragments of the dialogues nor in the *Organon*, apparently appearing first in the *Physics* (fifteen times in book 3). A search for the origin of the concepts involved can be concentrated first, and primarily therefore, on *energeia*. I shall return to the meaning of the words later.

Energeia does not occur in Plato, or indeed in any other Greek text before Aristotle, though Aristotle himself says that other thinkers used the word, claiming that an *energeia* is a process (*EE* 6.1153A16). The *Protrepticus* (frs. B79, 87, 91 Düring) provides some of the first Aristotelian examples, all of which are translatable as 'activity', as are those from the early books of the *Topics* (4.124A32–4, 125B15–19). Neither do we find *entelecheia* before Aristotle, though *endelecheia* is older, and there have been suggestions that this was the form Aristotle originally used. Nothing commits us to accepting this, however, and I shall leave it aside. *Endelecheia* does not contain the significant root *telos* (goal) which is essential to the special Aristotelian sense of *entelecheia*.

De Strycker has argued that the Aristotelian distinction between *energeia* and *dunamis* (in the sense of 'capacity') derives from a distinction made by Plato in the *Euthydemus* – and used by Aristotle in the early *Rhetoric* 1.1361A23 – between possessing and using some external good.[3] This may be correct, but a more probable Platonic source can be found in the *Theaetetus* (197B). Here Plato makes a distinction between possessing knowledge and having it available (i.e., using it). It is, says Plato, similar to the distinction between possessing a coat and wearing it, or possessing birds in an aviary but not having them in the hand. This is a better Platonic exemplar, because some of the earliest instances of *energeiai* are concerned with the question of knowledge (or of sensation). In the *Topics*, as De Strycker rightly observes, Aristotle distinguishes between having and using knowledge (*epistēmē*, 5.130A21) and between having and using sensation (5.129B33ff). It is true that the word *energeia* does not occur in this passage, but that De Strycker is right to think of these texts as important for the development of the concept is borne out by a section of the *Protrepticus* (fr.B79 Düring), which De Strycker does not notice, where both *energeia* and *dunamis* occur in just the sense required. 'We say,' says Aristotle, '... that living has a sense *kata dunamin* and a sense *kat' energeian*.' Similarly with knowing how and knowing that (*epistasthai, gignōskein*); we speak of *using* knowledge (i.e., thinking) and 'having knowledge,' i.e., possessing the capacity, etc. Thus in the *Protrepticus* the distinction made in the *Topics* is given the technical terminology. (A similar point is made in the later *De Anima* [2.417B8–9].) But, as Ackrill has pointed out,[4] passages dealing with the *expression* of an acquired capacity do not provide the *normal* philosophical sense to be attached to the notion of *energeia*.

To advance further we must turn to what the word *energeia* means elsewhere. In an early part of the *Topics* (4.125B15ff) movement is an *energeia*. Even in the comparatively late *Rhetoric* 3.1412A10, we read that an *energeia* is a movement. That this is what a Greek speaker might expect is borne out by a paragraph of the *Metaphysics* (Θ.1047A30ff): 'The term *energeia* ... has come from motions, where it most properly belongs, to other things as well; for *energeia* seems to be primarily motion.' In other words an *energeia*, as one might expect, is an action, a movement, and this is the original and quite natural Aristotelian sense of the word. A further passage of the *Topics* emphasizes the point (4.124A31ff), bringing us back to the ideas of possession and use that we have already noted, and this time employing the word *dunamis* (capacity) as well: 'Similarly with capacities and uses. For if a capacity is a disposition, then to be capable is to be disposed [to something]. And if the use of anything is an activity (*energeia*), then to use is to be active (*energein*) and to have used is to have been active.' There is no doubt that 'activity', not 'actuality', is the correct translation here. Some scholars, like Owens, seem to want to translate *energeia* by 'actuality' in all instances. Owens argues thus: 'The word [for *energeia*] has to be applicable to separate substances and to forms that are not in motion. Also for this reason 'activity' does not seem to be correct. 'Activity' expresses clearly enough the original notion of work in contrast to idleness. But can it really be suited to what is immobile? May one say that an Aristotelian separate substance is an "activity"?'[5]. But this approach begs the question of the growth of the concept of *energeia* assuming, as it does, that the complete doctrine of the *Metaphysics* can be found in the *Topics* or the *Rhetoric*, where there is no evidence for it. As we shall see, the *Topics* indicates that the meaning of *energeia* develops from 'activity' to the wider 'actuality' approved by Owens.

Consider the following text from the *Metaphysics* (Θ.1050A22): 'The term activity is used in relation to action [*ergon*].' In the *De Anima* we are told that when a carpenter works, he changes from inactivity to *energeia* (2.416B2–3). We conclude that when Aristotle began to talk about activities (quite understandably) all activities are movements and all movements are activities, and that he was prepared to maintain this language throughout his career.

Aristotle never wavered in his belief that all motions are *energeiai*, though he also came to think that there are *energeiai* which are not motions. Such views are clearest in the *Metaphysics* and in *Eudemian Ethics* 6. We shall come back to their significance later. First let us try to identify what made Aristotle alter his original and 'ordinary language' view of the nature of an *energeia* – and if possible to discover *when* he made the change. The *Topics* provides the best evidence. In an early passage we have just considered, Aristotle introduces what was to become a significant distinction of tenses: he talks about acting, and having acted, using and having used (4.124A31ff). But when we come to a later section of the *Topics* (6.146B13ff), composed about 343, this distinction is given a new and important twist. Indeed *Topics* 6.146B13–19 is so important for the development and history of the notion of *energeia* that it must be subjected to detailed analysis. By the time *energeia* is discussed in *Topics* 6, we may assume that movement has already received detailed treatment in the early books of the *Physics*.

The context of the passage is a discussion of the definition of relative terms; in this context we must consider both 'coming-to-be' (*genesis*) and *energeia*. Here, as might be expected from the fact that *energeia* is connected with *ergon*, with doing things, the translation again appears to be 'activity'. In the important sentences which follow we hear nothing further of 'coming-to-be', though it may turn out that thinking about 'coming-to-be' directed Aristotle's attention to a particular example, or alleged example, of 'coming-to-be', namely pleasure. Before reaching this, however, Aristotle introduces the notion of an end or goal. 'Coming-to-be' and 'activity', he says, point to a goal; they are not themselves goals. First, notice how even at this early stage Aristotle emphasizes goals; secondly, and perhaps more relevantly, notice how he immediately moves to correct himself, for he then wishes to check whether it is in fact true that all activities are directed to goals *outside* themselves. Perhaps some activities involve their own goal in their very performance. For, he continues, most people prefer to be pleased rather than to have finished (i.e., achieved) being pleased.

Interestingly enough, although Aristotle has introduced the concept of an end into the discussion of activities, that is, although he views activities as purposive, when he comes to notice that there are certain activities whose nature itself embraces the accomplishment of that end, he does not introduce the word *entelecheia*; he stays with *energeia*. (Indeed, as we have seen, the word *entelecheia* does not occur at all in the *Topics*.) Nevertheless its relevance to change is obvious enough, if changes are goal-directed, and we may recall that in the *De Generatione et Corruptione*, in a work dedicated to the nature of 'coming-to-be', we find instances of *entelecheia* uniquely outnumbering those of *energeia* – by the striking margin of eighteen to four.

Leaving *entelecheia* aside, however, we return to the *Topics*. Two points should be made at once. First, Aristotle's concern with activity and *genesis* has drawn his attention to goals, to ends. Secondly, the example that makes him think twice about asserting or assuming that all activities are directed to ends beyond themselves is that of pleasure, a subject much discussed shortly before *Topics* 6 was composed, that is, in the last years of Plato's life. Aristotle's account here suggests that pleasure is viewed by some, and presumably himself, as an activity; but activities themselves are not clearly distinguished from instances of 'coming-to-be' or at least, if they are to be thought of as different, the difference is not spelled out and seems unconnected with the problems of ends or goals. What Aristotle seems to mean is that instances of 'coming-to-be' and activities are normally directed to external goals (so that they are similar in that respect), but that apparently pleasure is a special case. The logic of this is that, though pleasure is an activity, it is not a 'coming-to-be', for it is hard to see how instances of 'coming-to-be' could *not* be directed to goals outside themselves.

We know that sometime in the late 350s, according to Plato's *Philebus*, 'clever' people said that pleasure is a 'coming-to-be' (53c4–7); and in the same dialogue it is suggested that this 'coming-to-be' is the restoration (*katastasis*) of an organ to its natural condition (*eis tēn hautōn phusin*). This suggests again that pleasure is at least related to goal-directed activity, as

Topics 6 agrees; and a similar idea can be found (though it is not certain whether Aristotle would have owned it himself) in an early section of book 1 of the *Rhetoric*.[6]

Whatever Aristotle thought in the *Rhetoric*, our passage of the *Topics* seems to show that he had come to think that the 'clever' people (even if they included Plato) who identified pleasure as a 'coming-to-be' are mistaken. And if pleasure is an *activity*, it is an activity of a special kind, unlike, say, building a house; for the goal of a house-builder is to have completed his house, the goal of a pleasure-enjoyer is to carry on enjoying his pleasure. Pleasure then is not only not a 'coming-to-be', it is an activity of an unusual kind. And in terms of the linguistic facts of tense, to which Aristotle refers again in the *Topics* (6.146B) in the case of pleasure, to feel pleasure is not necessarily the same experience as to have felt pleasure. (For I can say I have felt pleasure when I feel pleasure, but to say that I have felt pleasure does not entail that I am still feeling it.)

But there is still something odd about the analysis. Although Aristotle has realized that (for example) the goal of a pleasure-enjoyer is of a different order from that of a house-builder, he might still be thought to speak as though pleasurable activities can be described in the same way as physical activities such as house-building or running. But pleasure is, as it were, parasitic on other (often physical) activities. We get pleasure from running, satisfaction from having built a house; we say we do things for pleasure, or get pleasure from doing things. We do not say that we do pleasure. Yet Aristotle seems to speak in this passage of the *Topics* as though that is what we do. He speaks of feeling pleasure as 'acting' (*energein*) in some way, apparently as he might speak of running or house-building as acting.

Yet since this *is* what he does, he would apparently be ready to speak of pleasure as activity (which is, of course, what he does openly in the rather later *Eudemian Ethics* 6).[7] For Aristotle's position in *Topics* 6 appears to be that feeling pleasure is something we do, something we engage in, and the engagement itself is the pleasure. The fact that the *goal* is achieved in the activity itself awaits exploitation in later texts. The chief point of this text, however, seems to be that pleasure is an activity, but *not* a 'coming-to-be' or process of change, because its goal is achieved during the time we feel it, not after. Hence we shall not be surprised to find that from now on Aristotle has no truck with descriptions of pleasure as a process (*genesis*). Even though a movement (*kinēsis*) may still be recognized as an activity, a process is a special kind of movement which is not an activity. Thus since processes are movements, it follows that the terms 'movement' and 'activity' are not necessarily unambiguous and synonymous – which accords with what we find at the end of *Eudemian Ethics* 6 (1154B25ff).

Aristotle seems to assert that pleasure is not a *process* of change in the *Topics*; he does not suggest that it is not a movement of *any* kind. This may be more important than it seems not only for clarification of Aristotle's notion of *energeia*, but for a more general understanding of the fourth-century debates about pleasure. The view that pleasure is a process (and therefore, according to the doctrine of the *Topics*, not an *energeia*) appears in Plato's *Philebus*; it is repeated by implication in the *Topics* and is explicitly mentioned in *Eudemian Ethics* 6. The view that pleasure is a *movement* (*kinēsis*), which in Aristotelian terms might also allow it to be an *energeia*, appears in Plato's *Republic*, and in *Rhetoric* 1 (1369B33), and it is only refuted in *Nicomachean Ethics* 10 (1173Bff). *Nicomachean Ethics* 10 in fact takes us a stage beyond the account of *energeia* we have observed so far. Here Aristotle refutes both the view that pleasure is a movement *and* that it is a process. Against the notion that it is a process (already rejected in the *Eudemian Ethics*) new arguments are adduced. Those who hold such a view, he says, derive it from imagining that all pleasures are comparable to the pleasure of eating, which depends on the preceding state of emptiness. But some pleasures are not replenishments and are not preceded by pain, e.g., the pleasures of knowledge. Therefore pleasure is not to be identified as a process of generation from a preceding (painful) state of deficiency. The *Eudemian Ethics* has already shown us that pleasure (though still possibly a movement) is not a process of change; *Nicomachean Ethics* 10 goes further. Pleasure is not a movement in any sense. For, says Aristotle, movement is quick or slow, and although it is possible to change into a pleasurable state quickly or slowly, it is not possible to *energein* in a pleasurable state quickly. The Greek is odd here and Aristotle seems to gloss his own words. It is not possible to function [*energein*] with pleasure quickly, he says, and then adds, 'I mean, "to be pleased".' Thus *energein kath' hēdonēn* would seem to be equivalent to *hēdesthai*; and in view of the contrast with *metaballein eis tēn hēdonēn* ('to change into a pleasurable state'), with its associations of 'becoming', of 'process', *energein* seems to mean 'to be in a certain condition,' viz. a pleasurable one.

At first the passage looks like our text of the *Topics* (6.146B) again. There too 'to feel pleasure' is to *energein* in a certain way. But while in the *Topics* there is no reason to translate *energein* as other than to *act*, to *function*, in the *Nicomachean Ethics* the sense is developed so that *energein* almost means simply 'to be.' I would propose that this is because in the *Topics* all activities are still movements, whereas in *Nicomachean Ethics* 10 Aristotle argues that since all movements involve 'quickly' or 'slowly,' there are some activities which are not movements; rather, if my argument is right, they are non-variable states of being. This view, it should be added, does not entail that Aristotle would deny that every movement (unless viewed merely as a process) is an *energeia*; what it does is to show that if an *energeia* cannot be said to occur 'quickly' or 'slowly,' it cannot be a movement.

I do not propose to continue the investigation of the nature of pleasure in the light of the developing sense of *energeia*. What I shall do is show how the new *meaning* of the word *energeia* (i.e., non-variable state of being) visible in *Nicomachean Ethics* 10 is to be associated with the distinction made by Aristotle of different types of *energeiai*, and with his recognition that there are certain states of being which have no intrinsic connection with motion at all. This means, of course, that we must comment briefly on the Unmoved Mover and on pure form in general, but before that let us return to the *Organon* to see how Aristotle further developed his analysis of *activities* in terms of the distinction between present and perfect tenses. For this is at least one of the roads he followed as he began extending his concept of *energeia*.

We have already noticed how, in *Topics* 6, Aristotle's attention is drawn to the fact that being pleased is unlike house-building in that a man's goal is to *be* pleased in the one case and to *have* completed the house in the other. Aristotle's reflections on the relationship between the present and perfect tenses of verbs were developed elsewhere in the *Organon* – in a passage certainly related to the problem of *energeia*, but not directly associated with it by Aristotle himself. In the *Sophistici Elenchi*, most of which, as we have seen, is later than most of the *Topics*, we find the following (22.178A9ff): 'Is it possible to be doing and to have done the same thing at the same time? No. But surely it is possible to see and to have seen the same thing at the same time and in the same conditions.' A similar point is made in the *De Sensu* (446B2ff), which I take to be a much later composition.[8] Here Aristotle remarks that everybody at the same time hears and has heard, and in general perceives and has perceived, and there is no 'coming-to-be' of them, but they *are* without 'coming-to-be.'

This latter passage is especially interesting because although it seems very close to the nearly contemporary *Metaphysics* Θ.6 – the long discussion of the relevance of the present and past tenses of verbs to questions of *energeia* – there is no specific mention of *energeia* in the text of the *De Sensu*. What there is, however, is an implicit contrast between what is (without 'coming-to-be') and what is as a result of 'coming-to-be.' Readers of Plato's *Philebus* will immediately recognize the theme: Plato makes a significant distinction there between *ousia* and *gegenēmenē ousia* (27B) and *gegenēmenē ousia* is clearly the product of the *genesis eis ousian* of 26D. I suspect that Aristotle makes use of this Platonic distinction in the *De Sensu*, but even if he does not follow Plato directly, his thought moves on similar lines. Thus hearing, and in general perceiving, are modes of being and activity without *genesis*, while other activities are beings with *genesis*. This in turn looks like what we found in *Nicomachean Ethics* 10, where Aristotle seemed to be thinking of some sorts of *energeia* as modes of being, as distinct from the activities of a movement or 'coming-to-be'.

Although the *De Sensu* does not specifically mention *energeia,* or call hearing and perceiving activities, I take it that the analysis of present and perfect tenses of such verbs as 'to hear' in that treatise may be assumed to refer to the *energeiai* of *Metaphysics* Θ and of *Nicomachean Ethics* 10. But when Aristotle deals with such questions in the earlier *Sophistici Elenchi,* his position is less clear. At this stage of his career, we do not know whether he already wanted to call seeing an activity – though he probably did – or, what is more important, whether he already recognized that seeing is in some sense an activity which is *not* a 'coming-to-be'. What is clear is that activities which are not in instances of 'coming-to-be' are recognizable in *Metaphysics* Θ and in *Nicomachean Ethics* 10, and discernible through the *beings* which have no becoming of the *De Sensu.* In texts of this sort, then, the word 'activity', so easy a translation of *energeia* in *Topics* 6, for example, is misleading – for indeed by now Aristotle has recognized not only activities which are not instances of 'coming-to-be', but activities which are not movements at all. *Eudemian Ethics* 6 seems to present the first clear acknowledgment of this recognition.

The importance of *Eudemian Ethics* 6 as a turning-point in Aristotle's thought about *energeia* cannot be overestimated. The context once again, as in *Topics* 6, is pleasure – which cannot but help confirm the suspicion that it was thinking about pleasure which impelled Aristotle to develop his notion of *energeia.* Our nature, says Aristotle, is not simple (6.1154B21ff), for if men had a simple nature, then a simple action (*praxis*) would be most pleasing. God, however, does enjoy a single simple pleasure, because he has a single, simple nature. We might expect that Aristotle would say that a single *action* (*praxis*) is in accordance with God's nature but, in fact, he avoids attributing action to God. Rather he says that 'there is not only an *energeia* of movement, but also of rest ...' Change is sweet for us only because we are corrupt in some way. What we draw from this passage is that there is no *praxis* for God, but an activity without movement or change of any kind. Since God's nature is unchanging, his activity (which is not a *praxis*) is also unchanging. It is an activity which does not involve motion at all.

If we assemble all the information thus far obtained about the notion of *energeia,* we have the following picture. *Energeia* originally meant activity. Hence all *energeiai* were movements and all movements *energeiai.* Gradually Aristotle reached the position that all movements (unless viewed merely qua processes) are *energeiai* but not all *energeiai* are movements. On the contrary some *energeiai* are totally dissociated from movement and change. By the time we reach *Eudemian Ethics* 6 Aristotle has identified at least three different kinds of activity:

1 The activity of change. This is the sort of activity which is formally defined in the *Physics* (and *Metaphysics*) as 'imperfect activity' or 'activity of the imperfect.' Its end is outside itself.

2 Certain physical activities such as that of the ears when they hear, the eyes when they see. Seeing does have a beginning and end, but, in Aristotle's language, 'seeing' is compatible with 'having seen,' and such activities (or should we already say states of being in these cases?) are not directed to a goal beyond themselves. Theoretically (and indeed in fact in Aristotle's physics) such activities can be of eternal duration, without beginning or end; and since at an early stage of his career Aristotle accepted the Platonic theory of a Self-Moved Mover (necessarily spatially located), the movement of such a mover would be of this sort.

3 The activity, or better actuality (state of being), of whatever is eternal and cannot change *because immaterial and non-physical*: God, the Prime Mover, etc.

It is easy to understand why with classes like these Aristotle can sometimes speak as though the 'activities' of class 2 or 3 can be *contrasted* with class 1 movements (e.g., at *Met.* Θ.1048B34ff), even though both actualities and movements are *energeiai* (cf. *De Anima* 3.431A6ff). Aristotle puts the matter slightly differently at *De Interpretatione* 23A23: there are 'activities' without capability, like the primary (i.e., unchanging and eternal) substances; and there are activities with capabilities (for example, things that grow). In these cases the capability precedes the activity in terms of time, but the activity is 'prior by nature.'

The central reference of the word *energeia*, therefore, in Aristotle's mature thought comes to be that of the nature of an eternal, immaterial, hence unchanging being. Since the word 'activity' is an appropriate translation for Aristotle's original understanding of the word *energeia*, for it is indubitably tied up with the notion of movement (whether changing or unchanging in its nature), we suggest that it is inappropriate as a translation of *energeia* in Aristotle's later work, when Aristotle wants to identify *energeia* as the nature of beings which do not perform *activities* as 'activity' is normally understood.

The special Aristotelian concept of *energeia* develops from ideas about movement; in its later stage the 'focal meaning' of *energeia* indicates the nature of non-moving things.[9] Since Aristotle eventually comes to recognize activities with potentiality as intelligible in terms of actuality without potentiality, it is easy to see why he was unimpressed by the 'Megarian' notion that 'capability' makes no sense (*Met.* Θ.1046B29ff), for capability is a form of potentiality (The same word is used in Greek for both terms): if a man is capable of building a house, he is potentially a house-builder. The Megarian view seems to have depended, as did Megarian doctrine in general, on the Eleatic denial of becoming: either one builds, in which case one is a builder, or one does not build, in which case one is not a builder. The consequences of this, as Aristotle points out, seem absurd: if I stop building, I cease to be a builder. If in five minutes time I start again, I have in the meantime acquired the art. How did I manage that? The man who shuts his eyes will be blind – until he opens them again! Those who talk in this way, in fact, have forgotten the distinction between having something and using it, which, as we pointed out, is one of the blocks from which Aristotle's own doctrine of an *energeia* is built up – though Aristotle does not point this out in his rebuttal of the Megarians in the *Metaphysics*. Rather he concentrates on the anti-Eleatic side of his case: they destroy motion and generation, for they in fact identify potentiality with actuality. Thus Aristotle's position helps eliminate such Eleatic paradoxes, though our discussion of the growth of his thinking suggests that he did not *develop* his account of *energeia* as a specifically anti-Eleatic position. Rather, in the *Metaphysics*, he finds himself obliged to defend it against attacks by Neo-Eleatics.

Before closing this discussion, we should consider how Aristotle's development of *energeia* from motion significantly affected his more general metaphysical doctrines: for it helps explain why Aristotle never came to grips with the metaphysics of existence as such. As we have shown in our discussion of categories, at an early stage in his career Aristotle was led, perhaps through the influence of Plato's theories of classification, into attempts to determine what there is in the universe, and to organize the contents of the universe into classes. At a later stage, it seems, he began to raise questions not only about what there is, but why there is what there is, and he attempted to answer these questions in terms of an analysis of 'causes'. In particular Aristotle inherited from Plato the question of why there is movement, and his first researches on this, following those of Plato, led him eventually to his theories of the First Unmoved Mover and its nature. The Platonic belief (shared and adopted by Aristotle) that movement – especially in the heavens – *needed* explanation helps us understand why Aristotle thought that the most immediate physical/metaphysical question is not 'Why are there things?' but 'Why are things as they are?'; not 'What is it to exist?' but rather, as in *Metaphysics* A, 'What is movement?' or 'Why do things (especially heavenly bodies) move?' These are also the questions of *Metaphysics* Λ.

It is true that Plato's pre-Socratic past inclined philosophers to find motion peculiarly puzzling: the Heraclitean Cratylus thought that all is in motion;

Eleatics thought that all that is 'real' is at rest. The argument between Heracliteans and Eleatics might seem at bottom to turn on whether the concept 'motion' is intelligible. The questions 'What is motion?' and 'How are motions caused?' were urgent in the context of fourth-century philosophy. In book B of the *Metaphysics*, where Aristotle reviews the state of metaphysical enquiry, primarily in the Academy, his questions and perplexities constantly revolve around the theme of whether there are (or are not) eternal *unchanging* substances; and the question of the existence or non-existence of such substances is closely tied to deciding whether proposing such substances in any way helps solve problems about generation and corruption (that is, about change) in the physical world. For Plato movement without an unchanging cause is unintelligible.

But it was from the movement, not from the existence of particulars, that Aristotle was led towards his doctrine of actuality.[10] We have seen how pleasure, defined as movement or 'coming-to-be' in Academic circles, is connected with the development of *energeia* in crucial passages of both the *Topics* and the *Eudemian Ethics*. We must now consider the most basic discussions of movement found in Aristotle (in the *Physics, De Generatione et Corruptione*, and *Metaphysics*), in the hope of getting further clarification. For despite Aristotle's defence of potentiality against Megarian logicians in *Metaphysics* Θ, the almost total absence of detailed discussion of activity/actuality in the *Organon* suggests very strongly what Aristotle himself observes, that the motivation for the development of the concept of *energeia* came not from logic but from thinking about movements or, in the case of pleasure, alleged movements.

In fact few texts from 'physical' treatises are very helpful in pursuing *energeia* further. An important passage from the *De Caelo* (2.286A9) associates the *energeia* of God with immortality, eternal life, and eternal movement. The highest reality, which is the highest life, is unchanging eternal motion. But the *Physics* and the *De Caelo* give us little inkling of the coming change in the nature of the activity of God. Clearly if he is unmoved, he must have a special kind of activity, but the implications of this are not considered in the *Physics*. The activity of immobility – advocated in *Eudemian Ethics* 6 – is not yet on the horizon of physics. It is only in *Metaphysics* Λ that we can see what Aristotle has tried to do, and it seems that, for all the exegesis the revelant sections (1071B2–1072B30) have received, enormous difficulties remain. Aristotle's arguments, let alone his presuppositions, are still apparently unclear at best and muddled at worst. By attempting to clarify parts of the passage, we shall, I believe, be able to shed further light on the development of the doctrine of *energeia*.

Chapter 6 of *Metaphysics* Λ begins by recalling that there are three types of substance, and draws our attention particularly to the type which is immovable and unchangeable. Arguing from the premiss that motion and time are eternal, Aristotle deduces that there must also exist substances in eternal circular motion. Since such motion demands an eternal cause, there must be an eternal causing principle which must *act* (*energēsei*), must indeed *function* and not simply have the capacity or potentiality of functioning. Indeed for Aristotle, since it functions *always*, it must function *necessarily* (cf. *De Caelo* 1.281A29ff). Its essence, therefore, must be *energeia* – so that it seems that for this principle to be is to do.

The reader of *Metaphysics* Λ up to this point might find little to surprise him about *energeia*. Aristotle rules out Platonic Forms; they are incapable of filling the requirements for a first principle (1071B15) since they cannot initiate change; they cannot provide efficient causation. We therefore expect that his own new principle will be more effective; indeed that its function will include the production of movement. And since Aristotle has also told us that his principle is immaterial, we expect him to confront the problem of how an immaterial could *act*, could *function* as an efficient cause. The solution which commentators usually attribute to Aristotle is that the Prime Mover is an efficient cause only in the odd sense of being a final cause, that is, indirectly.[11] The peculiarity which this solution generates in its turn is what it implies about the special sort of *energeia* which is God.

According to Aristotle (1072A5), Anaxagoras, who postulated Mind as a first efficient cause, was on the right lines, for 'mind is *energeia*'; as were, in their different ways, Empedocles and Leucippus. But it is not clear that any of these thinkers had a notion of immaterial substance, so the kind of problems Aristotle has with his first principle are less acute for them. Aristotle, therefore, attempts a quite different solution, though his passing remark that Anaxagoras's cosmic Mind is *energeia* is not to be forgotten. The first principle, he says, being immovable, may be viewed as an object of desire, in fact as *to kalon* and that which is choiceworthy in itself (*to di' hauto haireton*, 1072A35). (Note that in *Metaphysics* B.996A22ff Aristotle denies that the principle of motion and the nature of the Good can be in immovable things [though *praxis*, nor *energeia*, is used in this passage]). But in *Metaphysics* Λ questions seem to be begged, for the explanation Aristotle provides as to how the Prime Mover can be viewed as 'choiceworthy' is that it is the object of desire of the first heaven; it moves as an object of desire (*kinei hōs erōmenon*, 1072B3), and since the first heaven is rational, its object of desire must be 'the real good' (*to on kalon*).

It is hard to avoid getting the impression that the oddity of this explanation arises at least in part from the fact that, since Aristotle has determined that the first cause is immaterial, and that it must cause movement, he must insist that the first heaven is rational merely in order to treat the 'first cause' as an object of desire. In other words a mechanistic explanation is ruled out because a necessarily immaterial first cause cannot be an efficient cause in the ordinary sense. And Aristotle offers a teleological account of the origin of movement despite the fact that the immaterial first cause must be an *activity* of some sort: that it must *do* something, not merely *be* something.

Now if it does something and is the first good, presumably its action must be the best kind of action and not a *praxis* (though this word does not occur in Λ); and this action, as Anaxagoras hinted, must be thinking (1072B). Now thinking is an activity which we humans can engage in at times; and it brings pleasure. Hence Aristotle can say that the 'way of life' (*diagōgē*, 1072B14) of the first principle is available to us for short periods of time, and that the activity which it is is pleasure (*hēdonē*). I take it that this means that thinking brings pleasure.

The first principle is now designated as God (1072B29–31); that is, it is an eternal unchanging being enjoying an eternally unchanging pleasant life of thought. For, says Aristotle, the activity of mind is life. Clearly, of course, since for Aristotle not all living beings think, he means that, if 'God' thinks, he has life – and he is indeed thinking both because there is nothing else he can do (and he must do something) and because he must do the best thing, which is in turn the object of desire of the first heaven.

What Aristotle says can be put in another way: the activity of God's thinking is such as to induce the best embodied soul to cause movement. Put like that it seems odd. The Aristotelian God provokes movement not because he is there, but because he is there thinking. To see the activity of God in this way is the direct result of approaching the question via the problem of movement. The Aristotelian notion of *energeia*, even in its highest form, never leaves this basis. So perhaps, after all, it is never right simply to translate *energeia* as actuality. It always implies realized activity of some sort. Thus when Aristotle says that an adult is a man ('in *energeia*'), it means that he can do certain kinds of things which the boy in time will develop the capacity to do. What about the statue, however, for Aristotle also says that the statue is 'in *energeia*' what the block of marble is potentially? Are we to say that the statue too *does* things?.

It is clearly examples of this sort which lead scholars to translate *energeia* as 'actuality' or 'realized perfection'. But it is hard to see how such inanimate 'actualities' are on all fours with living 'activities', of which the Prime Mover is the star instance. But Aristotle does treat them as on all fours, at least in his mature works. What then is the assumption he makes to reach this conclusion? If thinking is the star instance of an 'activity', what can we infer?

First, of course, that not all activities are movements. It is possible to *function* without involvement in movement, even unchanging movement. Aristotle, as we saw, began by identifying all activities as movements, and he is even prepared in places (as in *Metaphysics* Θ) to *contrast* activities with movements, though this might be misconstrued. The correct position is that although all movements in the full sense are activities, Aristotle now thinks that some activities are not movements.

But this still fails to meet the main philosophical point about the 'activity' of a non-living item like a statue. The only assumption available to Aristotle, therefore – an assumption he must have made – is that to be complete is itself an activity, for activities need not act (even though the word is *energeia*), rather they must *be*. God, of course, is complete in a special sense, for in his case there is not only no development of perfection, there is no possibility of change at all. We have in God an example of perfect 'activity' which *can* never be otherwise. At this point one can see that the translation 'actuality' is justified after all, though Aristotle never spells out the justification. And the actuality is in fact God's act of being a certain kind of existent (namely a thinker), though Aristotle does not put it in those terms, and we may ask ourselves again whether the mode of existence, namely self-thinking, is not artificially imposed on God's nature by the development of the concept of *energeia* itself and its roots in the early Aristotelian belief that all activities are movements.

Not all 'actualities' think: statues do not think. But statues are *realized* (in the sense of 'derived') actualities. But pure actuality thinks and so the focal meaning of 'actuality' involves thinking. The oddity of this claim, of course, is that the non-thinking actualities may seem so different as not to be actualities at all. Thus we highlight the fact that Aristotle insists on pure actuality being not just an act of existing but also a mode of existing, an existing in a certain way, namely as thought. But the theory would be more coherent, the notion of actuality and the very translation 'actuality' more intelligible, if Aristotle had been able to concentrate on the act of existing itself, rather than on the act of thinking that exists. For statues exist (contingently, we might add) and do not think, while God both exists and thinks, and men exist (again contingently) and think inadequately and incompletely.

What I have argued is that the notion of *energeia* in Aristotle has a history, and that its history is a development in a certain direction. But even by the time of *Metaphysics* Λ (and indeed of other later Aristotelian texts) the *potential* development is not complete. Aristotle has not purified the notion of *energeia* so as to make its focal meaning unambiguous and coherent, though he has moved towards such purification and coherence. Of course, had *energeia* been intended only as a general word for 'activity', it would hardly have needed such purification. But Aristotle has attempted to use it in much more daring philosophical constructions. His failure to develop it fully may be seen as due in no small measure to his not grasping firmly that the concept of *energeia* could be used not merely to answer the questions 'Why is there movement?' and 'Why do things move?' It could be used – and he almost unwittingly began to use it – to answer the questions 'Why are there beings? and 'Why do things exist?' or even 'Why are there beings rather than just concepts?'[12] Aristotle's unclarity about the relationship between 'Why do things move?' and 'Why do things exist?' is brought out in a striking passage of the *Metaphysics*. Substances, he says, are first among existing things. If they are all perishable, everything is perishable. But motion is imperishable, etc. By motion, here, Aristotle must mean the motion of existent beings (*Met.* Λ.1071B5ff). But the discussion which follows is concerned with the origin of motion, not the origin of being.[13]

Let us finally return to humbler matters – the alternative word *entelecheia*. There are passages in Aristotle – of which *Met.* K.1065B15 is perhaps the most striking – where it would seem that Aristotle is grooming this word to mean 'actuality' (or perhaps 'realized potentiality'),[14] leaving for *energeia* its original sense of 'activity' (or perhaps 'process of actualization'). 'Since in every kind there is the potential and the realized potentiality, I call the actualization [*energeia*] of the potential as such movement.' But for some reason, despite the frequency of *entelecheia* in *Metaphysics* K and *De Anima* 2 – assuming Aristotle is the author of K – he did not persist in this apparently useful distinction which would have left *energeia* nearer its original and natural meaning. On the contrary his latest writings seem to insist that *entelecheia* return to the comparative obscurity from which it emerged. Although it occurs, according to Blair, twenty-two times in book 2 of the *De Anima* (as against twenty-seven for *energeia*), it can muster a mere six in *Metaphysics* Θ – which is concerned with actuality and potentiality – as against sixty for *energeia*. In the *Nicomachean Ethics energeia* scores 113 times to nil for its rival.

7

Teleology: From World-Mind towards *Aether* and *Pneuma*

Aristotle claims in *Metaphysics* A (988A) that Plato in effect only employs two of the four 'causes': he omits the efficient cause and the final cause. This comment has always puzzled his readers because they think that efficient causes appear, as desiderata or in reality, in a number of dialogues (e.g., *Phaedo, Philebus, Sophist, Timaeus*). Explanations of Aristotle's attitude will be offered later (193, 196 below); for the time being let us say that Aristotle must have concluded that Plato's apparent efficient or final causes are not really what they seem to be or 'claim' to be, or that they are the wrong sort of final and efficient causes. If Aristotle did reach such a conclusion, we might find vestiges of Plato's way of handling causation in Aristotle's earlier writings or, if not vestiges, some justification for the adoption of alternative positions. In fact, as we shall see, even when Aristotle had completed his development of the theory of final and efficient causes in nature, he continued to make statements suggestive of an earlier and more Platonic way of thinking.

In the *Phaedo* (98B) Plato comments adversely on what he took to be an attempt by Anaxagoras to explain how Mind ordered everything in the universe for the best. Aristotle interprets Anaxagoras, rightly or wrongly, in a similar way (*Met.* A.984B18). Anaxagoras is supposed to have marked a return to sobriety in that he postulated that just as in living beings, so in nature as a whole, there is a mind which is the cause of order and orderly arrangement. Plato makes a further, though also interestingly divergent, reference to this reading of Anaxagoras near the end of his latest writing, book 12 of the *Laws* (967B). Here we read that in the past there were people (sc. Anaxagoras) who said that Mind arranged everything *in the heavens*. Note that Anaxagoras is not credited here with arguing that everything in the whole universe was so arranged. Presumably Plato is alluding to what he now believed, namely that whereas in the heavens the construction of Mind can be seen in a comparatively unimpeded form, this is not so here on earth. Here, as the *Timaeus* regularly has it, the works of mind are more impeded by the brute fact of the 'material' or 'necessity' with which it is obliged to work. Nevertheless we can assert without hesitation that up to the end of his life Plato commended Anaxagoras for wishing to show that the world, or at least certain parts of it, is divinely ordered. As the *Timaeus* describes it at length, the crafting mind of God designs the world to exhibit 'goodness'. He is good and he wished the world to be as like himself as possible (*Ti.* 29E). Aristotle took this account of the Craftsman literally, and was, I think, right to do so.[1]

We may be certain, therefore, that from Aristotle's earliest days in the Academy it would be believed (at least by some) that Plato sought, and thought he had found, evidence that our universe is designed by God at a particular moment which marks the beginning of history, and that God is thus the maker (the efficient cause) of both the cosmos as a whole and (even if indirectly) also of its individual parts. Furthermore, God had designed the universe to be of a certain kind; and his design can be labelled providential. Above all human beings are designed to live in a certain way, that is, morally, and God is concerned to see that they do so. To deny this latter claim is impious (*Laws* 10.888C). To subscribe to such beliefs, in antiquity, was to be a believer in Providence (*Pronoia*). Significantly, we may note, Aristotle was widely held *not* to be a believer in Providence, that is, to deny the direct concern of God with nature.

Yet Aristotle was a believer in the importance of both final and efficient causes. Let us consider the development of his ideas in relation to those of Plato. In an earlier chapter we noticed that already in the dialogue *On Philosophy* both final and efficient causes are discussed (42–3 above). In *On Philosophy*, however, God is not a transcendent cause of the universe, neither final nor efficient. The universe, unlike Plato's, is eternal, and again, unlike Plato's, it depends on no model (such as the world of Forms) outside itself. Thus if there is design in the universe, this design is 'immanent'. Nature's patterns must be law-like rather than laws, if laws are made by an external law-giver. That, we found, is how we must construe a famous section of Cicero's *De Natura Deorum* (2.95; fr. 13 Ross), which is dependent on *On Philosophy*. In book 1 of *De Natura Deorum* (1.33) Cicero tells us that Aristotle (in *On Philosophy*) disagrees with his master Plato and offers a confused account of the nature of the world. In our present passage we are asked to imagine the inhabitants of a cave below the earth suddenly emerging and seeing the wonders of the heavens. Such a sight would surely, suggests Aristotle, induce them to think that gods exist and that this is their handiwork. But there is no evidence that Aristotle, in *On Philosophy* or elsewhere, argued that their explanation of the marvels they have seen is correct. For if the universe is already eternal in *On Philosophy*, it could only be made by the gods if Aristotle taught some sort of 'neo-Platonic' rendering of the *Timaeus* by which God is the eternal ground of existence; and there is no reason to believe he taught any such thing. Rather the cave-dwellers see design, and offer a mistakenly Platonic explanation of it. Aristotle did indeed disagree with his master in *On Philosophy*.

But although Aristotle rejected a Platonic transcendent craftsman in *On Philosophy*, he did discuss final causes, which is clear from the *Physics* (2.194A36; fr. 28 Ross). And it is probable that his discussion involved at least the following points, the first of which is certain, as the *Physics* tells us: 'A is done for the sake of B' can mean either that it is done for the advantage of B where B is the person advantaged, or A is done 'to secure B.' Thus a doctor both acts to the advantage of his patient and to secure health. Thus *On Philosophy* probably argued, as in the *Physics*, that in some sense final causes secure the best for the individual. In the *Physics* Aristotle says that the statement 'he has reached the goal for which he was born' does not mean simply that he has reached a final point (i.e., perhaps his death!), but that he has fulfilled himself. If final causes, as we argued earlier, are *immanent* in *On Philosophy*, Aristotle must already have thought that the development of living beings can be understood in terms of a thrust to develop whatever specific potentialities each individual has. Aristotle will say that it is *best* for an acorn to become an oak tree, a child to become a man.

As we have seen, it is in the *Physics* that we find specific reference to this notion that the final cause is concerned with what is best for the individual – and we have suggested that the distinction between the two senses of 'final' already exists in *On Philosophy*. Unfortunately we cannot expand on the matter much from demonstrably early Aristotelian works. We are obliged to do so not merely with the help of a work rather later than most of the *Physics*, namely the *De Generatione et Corruptione*, but even with one of the very latest of Aristotle's writings, the *De Generatione Animalium*. However, there is no evidence to suggest that once Aristotle had begun to talk of 'better' in the context of final causation, the general nature of his views came to change. Certainly unanalysed ideas about what is better or more valuable are widely scattered throughout the whole body of Aristotle's writings.

Nature always strives for the better, we read in *De Generatione et Corruptione* (2.336B27ff), and Aristotle goes on to tell us what this means: being is better than non-being. Similar ideas occur in the *De Caelo* (2.292A22ff); and at the beginning of book 2 of *De Generatione Animalium*, we hear that soul is better than body (731B24ff); being is better than non-being; that which has a soul (animals and plants) is better than that which has none; the male is better (i.e., more complete) than the female (732A), since the male is the principle of nature while the female produces the 'matter' for generated things. Thus we can see that the universe is graded: that which is 'best' is at the top; hence the principle of final causation comes 'from the top,' that is, by the time of the *De Generatione Animalium*, from the Unmoved Mover. Thus we can view the whole of nature as 'motivated' by a series of final causes. In so far as each item in motion can 'desire,' it will desire to be better, that is, it will desire being rather than non-being, life rather than non-life, etc. It might be supposed that Aristotle is envisaging that the whole of the cosmos is permeated by some kind of upward desire and aspiration, and in a sense this is true,[2] but the matter of cosmic desire is more complicated and a final resolution of the problem must await a later chapter. But a beginning is possible here. What, we must ask, does Aristotle mean by nature when he says that 'nature always strives for the good' (*Phys.* 1.192A16ff) and that 'We say that in everything nature always strives for the better' (*De Generatione et Corruptione* 2.336B28)?

The Greek word *phusis*, which we translate as 'nature', is connected etymologically with the notion of growth. So we might expect that the study of nature would have to do with the study of what is alive, and thus only embrace the whole of nature in our sense of the word *if* the whole world was supposed to be alive. Such may well have been the view of many of the earliest students of nature (*phusikoi*), the Presocratics. Aristotle's own view in book 2 of the *Physics* is related, but rather different. Developing ideas from the *Protrepticus*, he distinguishes the products of nature from those of art, and speaks of 'natural' objects as those which have the principle and cause of motion and rest within themselves primarily, not just accidentally. In other words, it might seem that nature is the realm of self-movers: animals, men. But Aristotle does not limit himself in this section of the *Physics* to animals and men; he also finds room for plants and the four basic sublunary substances (earth, water, air, and fire). These, however, are only examples (*hoion*, 192B10); the fifth element could also be included. All these, he says, have the principle of motion and rest within themselves. At a later stage (*Phys.* 8.255A5ff), of course, the elements are distinguished. Though 'natural' they are not *self-movers*, because they have no soul – and for other reasons too.[3]

But in *Physics* 2 the elements are included with living things without comment, as containing the principle of motion within themselves and intrinsically. And we should notice in this regard that plants are not distinguished from animals either. It seems that in their case too Aristotle clarified his views in the later *Physics* 8. Although he continued to believe that plants have souls, that is 'nutritive' souls, they cannot be self-movers as self-movers are defined in *Physics* 8 (where, as we have seen, the elements are also excluded), because although they grow, they cannot stop themselves from growing. For in *Physics* 8.255A5 the capacity to stop moving is required of whatever is to be a self-mover.

The fact is that although in *Physics* 2 the study of nature deals with those subjects which contain the principle of motion and rest within themselves intrinsically, Aristotle does not identify a class of self-movers (animals, men) within 'nature' and treat them separately from plants and the four elements. Yet according to *Physics* 8, these last groups, though natural and containing the principle of motion and rest within themselves, are not self-movers. Once Aristotle has made this distinction, of course, he should tell us in what other sense plants and elements 'contain the principle of motion and rest within themselves intrinsically'. (*Physics* 2.192B21ff). We shall return to this question later.

Before proceeding further, however, we should explain why it is that plants, though possessing souls, do not, as *Physics* 8 says, have the power to start and stop growing. It is because they have no sensation, and if no sensation, no possibility of desire. That plants have no sensation is emphasized by Aristotle, especially in *De Anima*, against many early thinkers.[4] But if plants (and *a fortiori* the elements) have no desire (and obviously no power of deliberation), how can they be said, as in *Physics* 2, to contain the principle of motion and rest within themselves? Has Aristotle changed his mind about the nature of plants and elements between *Physics* 2 and *Physics* 8? Or rather, has his thought developed between *Physics* 2 and *Physics* 8? The problem is presented in its sharpest form by a sentence not of *Physics* 8, however, but of *Physics* 1 (192A17ff), to which I have previously drawn attention: matter, says Aristotle, has a nature of such a kind as to desire (*ephiesthai*) and yearn for (*oregesthai*) the good. This passage, which contains what Ross called 'a bold metaphor,'[5] can easily be dismissed as isolated, or as Aristotle's echoing of a phrase of one of his predecessors, to which he would give no weight.[6] I do not think, however, that this is the correct approach, though my previous attempt to explain this sentence in *Physics* 1 must be modified.[7] It is not, as I previously suggested, *necessarily* supported by the opening of *Physics* 8 where we find the following series of questions: Did motion ever come into existence when it did not exist before? Will it pass away again so that nothing is moved? Or did it neither come to be nor will it ever cease to be, so that it has always existed and always will exist as a deathless and unfailing quality of things, like some sort of life belonging to everything constituted by nature?

Of this passage it might be said that Aristotle is merely appealing to the fact that if, as is the case, motion is from eternity and everlasting, it may *look* as though everything is alive – because movement is a feature of living things. But, of course, objects in motion need not have any intrinsic principle of motion and rest – let alone 'desire' – within themselves. For the time being, therefore, let us leave this passage of *Physics* 8 aside.

We are left with the 'bold metaphor' of desire in *Physics* 1. I explained the 'metaphor' previously by proposing unconscious desires; it has been objected that unconscious desires are unintelligible in beings without conscious desires.[8] Perhaps so in Freudian terms, but what would Aristotle, who, unlike Freud, always took the notion of a world-soul seriously, have thought? The general problem of a possible 'vitalism' in *Physics* 1, however, must be deferred, in part, until a later chapter. At the moment, before returning to a sketch of Aristotle's eventual answer to the question of the movement of plants and elements, and their intelligibility and relevance to his notion of final cause, we should recapitulate. Already in *On Philosophy* Aristotle had rejected the Platonic notion that a Demiurge has planned the nature and workings of the universe. That is not the way in which 'final causes' are to be understood. Now, in the account of 'nature' in *Physics* 2, the distinction between non-self-movers (plants, elements) and self-movers (animals, men) has not yet been emphasized, if indeed it has even been drawn – though it was later to be drawn in *Physics* 8; while in *Physics* 1 – which I have already suggested was the latest book of the *Physics* to be composed – we find the bold metaphor of matter striving for form.

Throughout Aristotle's writings, and with particular frequency in the biological works, we find the rule that 'Nature does nothing in vain, or to no purpose.' In a well-known passage of the *De Caelo* (echoing *Protrepticus*, B18, cf. B50 Düring), there is a variation on this: *God* and nature, Aristotle tells us, do nothing in vain (*De Caelo* 1.271A33). Obviously all such passages, including the unusual one from the *De Caelo*, refer to final causes. All the rest can, with difficulty, perhaps be explained away, as Sorabji would wish: 'Occasionally Aristotle personifies nature and talks of it as doing this or that. But this talk of nature can always be understood in terms of the natures of things.'[9] But thus to equate the final cause in nature solely with the final cause in the particular in question seems impossible in the *De Caelo* passage (or in the *Protrepticus*). If we rule out – as we have seen we must – the view that Aristotle is here thinking of a *transcendent* God as the designer of the universe and of its parts, this sentence must be construed as 'God, i.e., nature, does nothing in vain,' the *kai* being the *kai* of added explanation. That is, Nature, not only the natures of individual things but an immanent God (not dissimilar to that of *On Philosophy*), must work in a law-like fashion. There is more to final causes than individual substances seeking their own perfection (as the acorn developing into the oak). There is an object of reference, not merely a personification, in the word Nature. If that is so, we can attach more sense to our baffling sections of the *Physics* and especially to the 'bold metaphor' of *Physics* 1 where we found a comparable desire or striving for form inherent in matter as such. We may wonder whether that striving is a kind of ghost of the original immanent mind of the world. There are a few (but only a few) other passages which offer further help; but there are also objections:

1 We know that Aristotle evaluated and rejected the Platonic notion of a world-soul. Is not the present proposal, that of Nature as an immanent God, merely the Platonic idea in a new guise?
2 In the comparatively early *Eudemian Ethics* (1.1218A30ff) Aristotle observes that 'the statement that all existing things desire some one good is not true, for each thing desires its particular good, the eyes seek sight, the body health, and so on.'

The second objection is easily disposed of. Plato *was* wrong in supposing a single object of desire in the form of a transcendent Good. But that does not imply that it is false to suppose that there is aspiration immanent in all things. This aspiration is to fulfil oneself, to achieve one's own form and purpose. Plato would be condemned in the *Eudemian Ethics* for his usual mistake of *separating* the Form (of Good) from that of which it is the form.

The first objection is more serious, but what seems to be the solution has been generally overlooked. It is certainly true that Aristotle rejected the *Platonic* world-soul, conceived in the *Timaeus* as dependent on an external Mind or God. It is far from clear that he always rejected the related, but different idea of a World-Mind; in fact, I have already argued that he did not. For it exists not only in *On Philosophy*; its continuing existence in Aristotle's later thought affords the only mode of explaining, as distinct from explaining away, the passage of *De Caelo* (God, i.e., Nature, does nothing in vain), and indeed one or two other passages as well. I am not claiming that Aristotle held this view unchanged until the end of his life, only that he held it for some time after *On Philosophy*. There is little evidence for Aristotle specifically and with line-by-line reference correcting or modifying his earlier work in later texts. That does not mean that he did not do so. Indeed, he did so in the case of the nature of the human soul and mind.[10] In the case of the World-Mind we discover a similar progression.

There is specific evidence, as we have seen, that Aristotle accepted a World-Mind in *On Philosophy*; it is preserved in the well-known passage of the *De Natura Deorum* (1.33, fr.26 Ross) where Cicero is puzzled that in *On Philosophy* Aristotle seems to postulate both God as mind and God as 'the world itself.'[11] Cicero's reference fits exactly with the freakish text of the *De*

Caelo, which may be a survivor from this earlier way of thinking which Aristotle (in this one instance) has failed to exclude from the later text of the *De Caelo* itself. We also noted that within the *De Natura Deorum* Cicero appears to move from *On Philosophy* to *De Caelo*.

Let us assume a World-Mind in *On Philosophy*. That helps us to explain our text of *De Caelo* (1.271A33). It also helps with the origins of the much later *Physics* 1 (192A13–25), where we find the 'bold metaphor' of matter desiring form. As we have said, this could simply be written off as loose talk, dependent on Platonic echoes. But if Aristotle had once postulated a World-Mind (presumably considered Platonically as ensouled), then the relation of the matter of the world to its form would be that of potentiality to actuality; and matter, even in *Physics* 1, might be said to desire and yearn for form – and not just bits of matter, but matter as a whole. We shall recall again that at the beginning of the second book of the *Physics* Aristotle believes that there is somehow an intrinsic cause of motion and rest not only in man, animals, and plants, but even in the four terrestrial elements – and this belief is not out of keeping with the notion of the world as a whole being in some sense alive. And if the world is in some sense alive, then it may have some sort of overall 'purpose' as such: a purpose distinct from, though instantiated in, the purposes of its individual (living) entities. If there were a single basic and common 'element' within the four elements themselves, such a view would appear more plausible.

Further evidence for overall 'purpose' in Aristotle is available in a well-known passage of the *De Generatione et Corruptione*. The passage is interesting not only because there seems good reason to think that the *De Generatione et Corruptione* is largely later than *Physics* 2–7, but especially because it is one of those texts where Aristotle uses a principle of fittingness or nobility or the phrase 'what is better' to explain phenomena in the physical and biological worlds.[12] For in such passages, where the good aimed at in nature is not the survival or flourishing of a particular living creature, we must recognize, as Cooper saw, that for Aristotle nature tends to organize itself on pre-scientific (or non-scientific?) principles.

De Generatione et Corruptione 2.336B27ff reads as follows: 'Since we say that in all things nature always strives for [*oregesthai*] the better, and being is better than non-being ... but it is impossible that "being" be present in all things because they are too far away from the "principle". God ... completed the whole by making coming-to-be perpetual.' Here we have a number of themes: the superiority of being to becoming, so far as it can be achieved, the eternity of the changing world, and the role of God. Again two devices can be found for neglecting the last theme: it can be popular talk (though this is difficult to maintain for a technical work of this kind) or, if a transcendent

God is being referred to, it can be an echo of, say, Plato. But there is no *reason* for choosing only from *these* alternatives. And if there is other evidence, and we have seen there is, that Aristotle did at some stage think of God as immanent in the universe, that explanation would do here as well. As Aristotle knew well enough, it is interesting to note, the *locus classicus* for discussions of an immanent God in the world was Plato's *Timaeus*, a work which is frequently criticized in the *De Generatione et Corruptione*. But the world-soul itself is not criticized. Aristotle's general approach to the *Timaeus* can be well observed in 1.315A29ff, a passage where he complains that of his predecessors only Democritus has investigated coming-to-be and passing-away in other than a superficial way. Plato (in the *Timaeus*), for example, did not tell us how alteration or growth is present in things. Plato's attitude was too restricted; he made no comments on coming-to-be in general. In all this there is no complaint about Plato's remarks on *why* things happen; the emphasis is on his inadequate or mistaken views on *how* they happen.

A further passage which should be cited in favour of an overall (immanent) teleology at a rather unexpected stage of Aristotle's thought is from the *Politics* (indeed from the late book 1). At 1256B15ff we read that 'plants exist for the sake of animals, and other animals for the good of men (*tōn anthrōpōn charin*) … in order that (not simply with the result that) from them may come clothing and tools, since nature makes nothing imperfect or in vain …'[13] Clearly the 'nature' to which Aristotle refers in this passage as doing nothing in vain is not the nature of the individual animal; it is not the nature of the horse qua horse to become a beast of burden or a hide. The 'cause' must be outside the horse, and if not a transcendent God, then an immanent God or something in Nature somehow producing the same teleological effects which we have attempted to identify in the *De Caelo*.[14] Again regarding this passage we find attempts to explain it away: Aristotle 'is not writing biology' in the *Politics*, says Ross, though even he himself cites what may be a parallel in one of the biological works.[15] But the fact that *Politics* 1 is not a specifically biological text seems inadequate to explain why Aristotle should appear to present a principle (i.e., that there is a certain overall purpose in nature) which he supposedly rejected in work after work. It is simpler to conclude that this passage bears witness that even very late in his philosophical career (but nearly contemporaneously with *De Generatione Animalium* 2.731B25ff, in which we find related material), Aristotle wants to maintain at least some of the claims involved in his earlier theory of World-Mind as planner and some at least of the overall teleology which he held in his earlier life. The theory found in *Politics* 1 is a development in a late text (ca 324 BC), as we argue later (146, 161 below); yet a tantalizingly brief comment in the last book of the *Eudemian Ethics* (8.1248A25–6) suggests that a World-Mind was still surviving in more or less its original version at that stage of Aristotle's career (ca 338): *As in the universe* (*en tōi holōi*), Aristotle says,[16] so (in the soul) God moves everything. The context shows that an efficient, not merely a final cause is in question at this point.

I think it can be shown why Aristotle abandoned his original account of a World-Mind; that in *Physics* 8 he has already begun to do so; and that we can see what form the new theory eventually took in *De Generatione Animalium* and *Politics* 1. But it would be unwise to insist that Aristotle would have thought all problems about overall teleology could be made to disappear, as Sorabji suggests,[17] by assuming that 'talk of nature (personified) can always be understood in terms of the natures of things.' We have already argued that such talk cannot always be understood in this way. Two arguments, I believe, caused Aristotle to rethink and replace the 'immanent god' theory. First, while at the end of book 7 of the *Physics* (cf. 243A3ff) Aristotle is still arguing for a First Mover which is also moved, i.e., moves itself, in book 8 he has rejected that Platonic thesis in favour of an Unmoved Mover. Self-movers, as we have seen, Aristotle came to think must be (potential) self-stoppers. An Unmoved Mover would be free from such potentiality, thus free from the possibility of change, let alone of destruction. The Unmoved Mover for Aristotle in *Physics* 8 (276B9) must be located at the edge of the cosmos and must make its immediate effects felt there alone. In this respect, therefore, it will be different from the earlier World-Mind which would be present in some sense directly throughout the universe – and thus account for the 'overall' universal 'desire' in things. Perhaps Aristotle originally envisioned his Unmoved Mover 'semi-materially', something like a non-moving version of the fifth element in the *De Caelo*.

But a further difficulty remains. *De Generatione et Corruptione* is often thought to be later than *Physics* 8; it refers to *Physics* 8 at 1.318A3ff and possibly, though not certainly, at 2.336A16. If in *Physics* 8 the notion of an 'immanent god' has gone, why is it not removed from *De Generatione*? The answer is twofold: the Unmoved Mover is an addition to, not a substitute for, the 'immanent God' ('part' of which was associated with *aether*); and in any case *Physics* 8 is *later* than the original version of *De Generatione* – *De Generatione* 1.318A1–13 is out of place and is a later addition. Not only is the inappropriate reference to an Unmoved Mover almost unique in the original *De Generatione*, the reference to a (metaphysical) discussion of its nature by some 'prior philosophy' implies a distinction between physics and metaphysics quite alien to works long prior to the *Metaphysics* itself. The chronological order of the relevant physical works of Aristotle, in their original versions, is *De Caelo*, *De Generatione*, and *Physics* 1 and 8, 8 being the latest version of 'On Motion.'[18]

We noted the possibility that the Unmoved Mover may have been originally 'semi-material,' almost a non-moving version of the fifth element of the *De Caelo*. The nature of the Unmoved Mover remained somewhat uncertain until Aristotle attempted to clarify the relationship between *aether* and soul (the body and soul of the stars) on the one hand, and Mind itself on the other – which alone is what in the cosmos the Unmoved Mover was to *become*. The *separation* of Mind from all else has to await Aristotle's last Athenian period, and post-dates even *Physics* 8.

Aristotle's second reason for recasting his 'immanent god' was his conclusion of *Physics* 8 – the implications of which are not discussed – that whether or not plants and the four elements contain 'the principle of motion and rest' within themselves, they are *not* self-movers in the old sense – they are thus distinct from animals and men which are. Leaving plants aside for the moment – for though living (i.e., possessed of soul), they have no desire and *hence* cannot be self-movers – in *Physics* 8 we have a rough distinction between 'animate' and 'inanimate' substances. From now on when talking about teleology, Aristotle will frequently concentrate on the striving of *animate* beings to complete their 'form'.

Yet Aristotle thinks that even for 'inanimate' substances, such as the four elements, let alone for plants whose 'desire' to grow still needs to be explained, problems about natural movement remain. The re-examination of self-motion has not settled very much. For it still looks as though the whole of the cosmos is alive, as *Physics* 8 declares in that series of questions (250B11ff): 'Did motion ever come into existence when it did not exist before? Will it pass away again so that nothing is moved? Or did it not come to be and will it never cease to be, so that it has always existed, and will exist as a deathless and unfailing quality of things, like *some sort of life* belonging to everything constituted by nature?'

At first sight, as we said, the passage is easy to understand: 'It moves, so it looks alive.' But Aristotle does think that the elements have a tendency (a *dunamis*) to natural movement, air and fire upwards, earth and water downwards. This tendency is perhaps not now purposive, but necessary. It is certainly not purposive in the sense that there is purpose in 'the soul'; elements cannot stop themselves moving in the direction in which they move. They would only stop 'trying' to, presumably, when they had recovered their 'natural' places. This explanation becomes a little more difficult, however, when the 'first' element, the *aether* of *De Caelo*, is added. The appropriate movement of *aether* is circular, and it can never cease moving, for there is nowhere to which it is going. Here the movement which also looks like a sign of life is in fact identified by Aristotle as a sign of life, for the *aether*, like the later *pneuma* which it foreshadows, is the bearer of soul as form: but the stars, unlike the sublunary universe, are unambiguously alive. Where there is *aether*, there is life.

One of Aristotle's very latest works, the *De Generatione Animalium*, sheds light at least on the final stages of Aristotle's development of such ideas:[19] 'Animals and plants are found in the earth and in that which is wet because water is present in earth and *pneuma* is present in water, and in all *pneuma* there is present soul-heat, so that in a way *all* things are full of soul' (3.762A18–22). To say, as Skemp did, that this passage 'is closely related to the biological priority of *to thermon* and the doctrine of *sumphuton pneuma*' is of course true; but that is not to suggest, as Skemp holds, that it does not support 'the case for a kind of teleological "hylozoism".' Look precisely at what Aristotle says: '*In a way all* things are full of soul.' The phrase 'in a way' is necessary because *pneuma* itself is not soul, let alone Mind, like the earlier immanent God. It is only a 'bearer' of soul. 'In a way' though, *pneuma* is a partial substitute for the discarded 'immanent God' or Nature as Mind of Aristotle's earlier physics. What *pneuma* is is spelled out in another section of the *De Generatione Animalium*: *pneuma* is a substance analogous to that which composes the stars (2.736B37),[20] and, as I have suggested earlier, that substance, introduced in the *De Caelo*, may originally be a more limited version of the Self-moved Mover of *Physics* 7. Later, in *Physics* 8, when Aristotle thought it necessary, after analysing the concept of motion, to propose an *Unmoved* Mover, the 'fifth' element was still needed, and presumably remained as the element of the stars at the edge of the cosmos, the place the fifth element already occupies in the *De Caelo* itself. And if the fifth element embodies something of the purposiveness of the now discarded 'immanent God' in the 'heavens,' something else is needed to do the same on earth, and exhibit natural 'soul-like' behaviour. That something, I would suggest, is *pneuma*, which is thus 'in a way' the 'nature' of *Politics* 1.

Pneuma eventually exists in different 'strengths'; it is stronger, for example, in males than in females, though it exists in females. In Aristotle's latest view menstrual blood in women is the 'analogue' of 'pure' seed in men. But it lacks what he calls the 'principle' of soul (2.737A8) – which turns out, it seems, to mean the principle of sensible soul. For females do contain in their semi-pneumatized blood the principle of 'nutritive' soul (3.757B16ff). What this adds up to is that male animals can produce 'the principle' of sensitive soul, females and plants the principle of nutritive soul; and that there is a further weaker degree of soul-heat even in the elements, certainly in 'watery' earth and water and presumably in air and fire, since they are 'hotter' than the others. And of course there is something *pneuma*-like in the celestial element.[21]

From Aristotle's latest account of generation, where he requires the action of male on female, and (in the case of spontaneous generation) the activity of the sun on the earth (which contains *pneuma* indirectly in its water), we can derive further information on why he says that 'in a way' all things are full of soul. It is not reasoning soul, sensitive soul, or even nutritive soul that the elements contain, but it is something of a kind so special that when acted upon it ceases to be merely inert. Thus it is somewhat misleading to assert that at this stage of Aristotle's development there is no 'teleological hylozoism';[22] the four elements are not simply matter in some vaguely modern sense. Though they have no sensation, hence no desire, and hence can hardly be called self-movers, they have within themselves something of the raw materials of desire. Here we have another reason for Aristotle's refusal to draw sharp lines between different groups of phenomena in nature. As the compiler of *Historia Animalium* 8 explains it on Aristotle's behalf (588B4–6): 'Nature proceeds little by little from things lifeless to animal life in such a way that it is impossible to determine the exact line of demarcation, nor on which side of that line an intermediate form should lie.'[23] We shall return to the nature of the four elements in chapter 10.

One point should be clarified: there seems to be no reason to hold that what I have called the 'raw materials of desire,' the physiological basis of desire present in the elements, is merely a *picturesque* way of referring to the tendency of the elements to revert to their native places in the universe. For, as we have seen, if the four earthly elements could reach their place, they would no longer 'strive' to reach it, yet their nature would not change. Their *pneuma* would still retain its general 'desirousness' qua *pneuma*, so that there would be, in all things, a general and overriding teleological impulse 'for the best,' over and above the specific desire of individual matter for individual form.

Why then does Aristotle need the theory of *pneuma* at all? What exactly is its teleological role? Before trying to answer that question, let us summarize Aristotle's progression before the final stage of his thought is reached. Aristotle started from a view related to that found in Plato's *Timaeus*. Although he never subscribed to a demiurgic creator or orderer external to the universe, a planner or designer of the world and of man, he came to view the immanent power of nature itself as a variety of World-Mind. This view also he came to restate, and with its restatement comes the claim that none of his predecessors, including Plato (despite the *Timaeus*), gives an adequate account of final causes. For perhaps the final cause could be identified not as Nature itself but merely as the nature or form of the individual, or of some individuals. Rain, for example, does not fall so that crops can grow; rather crops grow if it rains (*Phys.* 2.198B18ff). With such remarks Aristotle might have rested content with a non-vitalist *scala naturae*, with a programme of listing the contents of the universe in descending order: man, animals, plants, elements. But since he wished, with one exception, to build up the faculties of the higher group from the lower, he looked for a common thread throughout the whole of nature. (The exception, of course, is Mind itself, which in *De Generatione Animalium* explicitly (2.736B28) and by implication in *De Anima* 3.5, comes 'from outside'; but Mind is not our concern here.) Hence we reach Aristotle's attempt to extend the activity of a physical substance akin to that which bears life in animals and men (the self-movers) to beings below that level. In the case of plants, perhaps, we can see something of Aristotle's intent: plants grow, or as Aristotle might put it, they strive for the perfection of their form even though they have no 'desiring faculty'. They do not want to grow; they tend to grow, we might say. So they must contain something which will account for this tendency, and in Aristotle's view this 'nutritive soul' is similar to the 'origin' of the nutritive soul possessed by female animals. This 'origin' can, in fact, be nothing more than *pneuma*, that common *pneuma* which somehow exists even among the four elements. Hence they too 'tend' or 'strive' both individually and 'communally'; for all things 'in a way' are full of soul; not of soul itself, of course, but of 'soul-heat', which is *pneuma*.

Pneuma, which will be discussed in more detail in chapter 11, and which is, of course, not a planner, has been introduced by Aristotle (after the discarding of the World-Mind) as a kind of 'mechanism' for teleology, as the bearer of desire in a new cosmological framework. Why does Aristotle need this 'mechanism' of desire? The only answer in the texts themselves is to be found in those passages in which we observed him speaking of 'being' as higher than 'non-being' and where Nature seems permeated with a desire for 'fittingness' and 'appropriateness'. Living things through their *pneuma* 'strive' for the perfection of their kind; to be rather than to become or not to be. Each thing strives for its own good – the eye sight; the body health, etc. (*EE* 1.1218A31ff). The *pneuma*, which is present as a *material* component of living things, is at least partially the origin of that striving. It is the 'mechanism' by which all things in some natural way desire the good as a final cause. Its role is again analogous to that of the *aether*. The desire of, or under the form of, the *aether* moves the first heaven; the desire of or under the form of, the *pneuma* unconsciously moves the sublunary world. Such striving for the final cause should, some might suppose, have been the subject of the last (unwritten) book of Aristotle's *Metaphysics*. Others might reply that Aristotle has made his intentions clear enough in *Metaphysics* Λ. In our sublunary world the striving which becomes explicit as growth in plants and as desire in animals exists everywhere, or at least wherever *pneuma* is to be found among the elements. Without it Aristotle would have felt forced to propose an unacceptable barrier between the animate and the inanimate;[24] his world, like that of Speusippus, would have fallen apart. *Pneuma* is a linking factor in the late Aristotelian cosmos. In living things it becomes the material mode in which the working of final causes is expressed. In the cosmos itself it is that which signals the ultimate unity, and hence, perhaps, the intelligibility of things.

We have come a long way from Plato's 'theodicy,' and Aristotle was rightly (in antiquity) taken in many quarters to be an 'atheist,' a man who rejected the providential ordering of the world. In a way his conception is the reverse of 'providential'. His notion that all living beings 'strive for' their completion and their form requires *pneuma* as a 'bearer of soul.' But Aristotle did not take the further step, which the Stoics took, of identifying the soul itself as *pneuma*, let alone thinking of Mind as *pneuma*. Had he done so, he would have become a 'providentialist'.

8

Rhetoric and Politics: Form and Content

I Early Political Writings

During most of this study of the development in Aristotle's thought, I have concentrated on those works of Aristotle which survive, rather than on those which are lost. Nowhere is this a more desirable procedure than in treating of his political writings. But in this area too we shall be unable entirely to separate philological questions about the order of Aristotle's texts from basic philosophical questions about the development of his thought. Consideration of philological and philosophical questions will have to progress *pari passu*. As Aristotle's early writings are identified, the nature of his early thought will become clearer.

Aristotle wrote two books labelled by doxographers or librarians as *The Statesman*, sometimes said, probably wrongly, to be modelled on Plato's dialogue of the same name – it was more likely dependent on Plato's *Republic*[1] – and four books of considerable size titled, according to Cicero, *On Justice*.[2] Philosophers of antiquity, like Plato, were liable to say more about justice than the other virtues. *Eudemian Ethics* 4 deals entirely with that subject, a fuller treatment than is granted to any other virtue anywhere else by Aristotle. Later, just possibly at Alexander's accession (ca 336), but probably considerably later, Aristotle sent him an address: *Alexander or on Colonies*. These books are largely lost; their fragments are valuable, but limited. Very different, however, was the fate of other texts related to political science. We have three books on rhetoric and one (of two) on poetics. I take it that these are both works related to the task of the statesman; for *rhetoric* this relation is affirmed by Aristotle himself (*Rh.* 1.1356A27). Poetry, as Greeks knew and Aristophanes said (*Frogs* 1009–10), is to make men better in the cities. The developing course of

Aristotle's mind on these issues is the subject of this chapter. Formally, I shall begin with chronological matters, but important questions of substance lie only just beyond the horizon; such as developing notions of happiness and the nature and proper form of slavery.

Aristotle's so-called *Statesman* is to be dated to the mid-350s; it is therefore slightly earlier than the *Protrepticus,* as its possibly Platonic-sounding title might indicate. It might be argued that after Aristotle's own exhortation to philosophy, he avoided using Platonic titles. Anger seems to have been one of the themes of the *Statesman* (fr. 3 Ross), but our only surviving *verbatim* fragment (fr. 2), from the second book, says that the good (which is unspecified) is the most precise measure of all things[3] – an idea also proposed in Plato's *Statesman* itself (cf. 293D), but which need not imply a theory of Forms in Aristotle, or even dependence on Plato's book. Similar notions occur in the *Protrepticus* (fr. B10 Düring), where Aristotle follows the distinction made in Plato's *Statesman* (as against the *Republic*) between the philosopher and the statesman himself. Thus the theoretical thought of the philosopher (*theōrētikē phronēsis*) is useful in politics, for the philosopher alone looks not merely to those conditions which exist in the world he inhabits (such as those of Sparta or Crete), but beyond them, as Plato was doing in the *Laws,* to what is not a copy but an original (fr. 13). Only the laws and actions prescribed by the philosopher are right and good. He alone looks to *nature* and the divine and lives accordingly. His knowledge is 'theoretical' but action in accordance with it is possible.

This is a striking passage, and helps us to understand why some in antiquity thought Aristotle believed in Platonic Forms. But for Aristotle the original the philosopher sees is nature, that is, reality: its quality is unspecified. All that Aristotle is committed to is that it is objective. In fact Aristotle's view is quite different from Plato's in the *Republic.* There to see the Good is to be able to act; but for Aristotle to have the theoretical understanding is to know the ground-rules for political action, not oneself to be able to carry them out. Such was the thesis Aristotle also advocated in his work *On Monarchy;* it is not necessary, indeed it is undesirable, for a philosopher to be king. But a good king will heed philosophers (fr. 2 Ross). *On Monarchy,* though arguably directed to Alexander, need not have been written, as Jaeger assumed (*Aristotle* 259), on his accession. More likely it appeared somewhat earlier, though certainly in Macedonia; Aristotle's own relationship with Hermeias coloured its contents.

II Ethics and Politics in Early Parts of the 'Rhetoric'

There can be little doubt that from his early days in the Academy Aristotle took an interest in rhetoric. That is not surprising. Plato's *Phaedrus* had been written not too long before his arrival, and the arrival itself followed fairly closely upon the 'digression' on life in the law courts of the *Theaetetus*. Plato's attitude to rhetoric was generally hostile. It is bitterly denounced in the *Gorgias* as an art of tarting up the goods, and mocked in the *Phaedrus* – not without polemic against Isocrates,[4] its most distinguished contemporary representative. Aristotle's *Gryllus*, now lost, certainly contained much of the same sort; it too is said to have been at least partially aimed at Isocrates. But it is possible that even at the time of writing the *Gryllus* Aristotle had begun to think more positively of the art of rhetoric. Certainly this is the case in his own *Rhetoric*; but in its present form the *Rhetoric* is a much later document, compiled after the *Topics*, *Sophistici Elenchi*, and *Analytics*, to all of which it refers or alludes.

Some of the material in the *Rhetoric* is much earlier, though how early we cannot be certain. I have argued that at least *Rhetoric* 1.5–end was composed before about 353, and tradition has it that Aristotle taught rhetoric in his first Athenian period. In order to show something of his attitude at that time, I will consider a few passages which almost certainly first appeared long before Aristotle's final years in Athens, when 'our' version of *Rhetoric* 1–3 was completed.

1. At 1360B14ff of book I in its final version, Aristotle has just explained that all men aim at 'happiness and its parts.' He proceeds to give some indication of current discussions of happiness, and it is often observed that it is hard, as here, to isolate Aristotle's own view in the *Rhetoric* from views which are popular and acceptable (*endoxa*, 1.1355A21; *koina*, 1.1355A27). Nevertheless the first account of happiness which he offers, that it is well-being (or well-doing) with virtue, is not dissimilar to the definition of happiness in *Politics* 7 (1325A33, 1325B15) as an activity (*praxis*) and a doing-well (*eupragia*). Note that in neither place is the happiness identified as an *energeia*. But here we meet the problem of the development of the word *energeia* itself (see chapter 6 above). The definition of *energeia* in *Politics* 7 *does* resemble that of the *Eudemian Ethics*, as we shall see; but it is more distinct from that of the *Nicomachean Ethics*. So the most that can be inferred from this passage chronologically is that it is not a very late composition of Aristotle's.

2. At 1361A24 we do meet the word *energeia* a little later in the same chapter. Here Aristotle is discussing being wealthy: it is to be understood rather in terms of using one's wealth than of possessing it. For wealth is the employment (*energeia*) and use (*chrēsis*) of possessions. We have already noticed the importance of this passage (106 above). It reflects an early stage of the history of the word, earlier than *Topics* 6, earlier than the critical

Eudemian Ethics 6. And we shall argue that the *Eudemian Ethics* is earlier than the *Politics*, which is itself (in part) earlier than our version of the *Rhetoric*. The present passage is thus a survival from an earlier period.

3. At 1362B6 pleasure is said to be a good because all animals naturally desire it. This argument occurs again in *Eudemian Ethics* 6 (1153B26ff), but with an interesting variation. The context now is the (Eudoxan) thesis that pleasure (or some pleasure) is the highest good, not merely a good, but *the* good. There is no mention of this context in our text of *Rhetoric* 1. If we accept the argument from silence, it suggests that 1362B6 represents a pre-Eudoxan stage of debate. The Eudoxan problem (represented also by Plato's *Philebus*) has not yet come up. Hence we have to push the early part of the *Rhetoric* back well into the 350s.

4. At 1365B27ff, we find the best evidence of all for an early date for parts of the *Rhetoric*. Aristotle identifies five types of constitution: democracy, oligarchy, aristocracy, monarchy, tyranny. Although a few lines later (1366A21), at the end of the section, he claims that such matters have been demonstrated in the 'Politics,' this is not our *Politics* – unless the reference is a later (and hasty) addition. For the list of constitutions in *Politics* 3.7 (monarchy, aristocracy, republicanism, democracy, oligarchy, and tyranny) is quite different from what we have in the *Rhetoric*. The list of constitutions in the 'Politics' (to which the *Rhetoric* refers) is unlike that available in other Aristotelian texts; nor is it even like that of Plato in the *Statesman*, which looks like an ancestor of the mature Aristotelian view. If anything, the list resembles that of Plato's *Republic*, but it is not identical with it. Plato's five are the ideal, timocracy (where the standard is honour), oligarchy, democracy, tyranny. Though Aristotle's list in the 'Politics' is not the same as Plato's it is much nearer to the *Republic* than to Plato's *Statesman* or to any of his later treatises. The solution is that when *Rhetoric* 1 refers to 'The Politics,' it refers not to Plato but to Aristotle's so-called 'Statesman,' that is, to his own early political writings.

5. At the end of 1366A we have yet another account of virtue and its parts. The parts are what we might expect: justice, courage, self-control. Virtue itself, however, is neither an action nor an activity; it is a capacity (*dunamis*) for providing and producing what is good. This is a possible definition of virtue for Aristotle, to be sure, but is innocent of his usual ideas on the subject and it exploits a quite unexpected sense of *dunamis*.

6. At 1367A33ff, we find a section with a quite different sort of interest. Here is a standard rhetorical theme: how to claim that a vice is a virtue; how to call the arrogant man magnificent, or the extravagant liberal.[5] Such misdescriptions of vice were by now an established fact of the Greek scene, both in politics and in rhetorical theory. Thucydides and Plato had

complained of them. But such material was to prove of exceptional use to Aristotle in his translation of what was presumably a medical theory of blending in the right proportions into an ethical doctrine of the mean in both the *Eudemian* and the *Nicomachean Ethics*. Some of the examples of virtue and vice from our text of the *Rhetoric* recur in the ethical works, and we may thus get some help from the *Rhetoric* in understanding how the complex theory of the mean should be interpreted. The vices of excess and defect are the realities which are often misdescribed as virtues. There are two ways of misdescribing (*EE* 2.1221B18ff): in one type of case, for example, an excess of boldness can be described as the mean, that is as courage; in the other type the matter is a little more complicated. An adulterer is not merely an *excessive* copulator but an excessive copulator with married women, and *any* such copulation may be held to be vicious. The adulterer has to claim that he did not know the woman was married (or that his action was against his will!), since 'adulterous' cannot be reduced to 'sexually active' in the way 'rash' can be reduced to 'brave'.[6]

Both the *Eudemian* and the *Nicomachean Ethics* (as well as the *Rhetoric* itself [2.1378A19]) tell us that Aristotle appealed to lists of virtues and vices (*EE* 2.1220B38; *NE* 2.1107A33). It is often said that the content of these lists is connected with long established rhetorical *topoi*, with the art of making evil behaviour seem better (and good behaviour, if necessary, worse). If that is so, then the material in *Rhetoric* 1 (1367A33ff) probably pre-dates that in the ethical treatises; indeed much of *Rhetoric* 1 almost reads like an (Isocratean?) ethical treatise. An incidental advantage of this interpretation, as I have suggested, is that it sheds a certain new light on the doctrine of the ethical mean itself. The three columns may at times represent the ways people *spoke* about virtues and their corresponding vices; precision in the original construction of the lists need not therefore always be expected; and problems as to whether Aristotle forced his virtues into a strait-jacket might thus be relieved. Aristotle may sometimes assemble 'rhetorical' rather than 'dialectical' versions of the mean. The man of practical judgment, of course, would deal with misdescriptions when he finds them and be able to identify both virtues and vices for what they are.

7. At 1369B33 a stipulative definition of pleasure is proposed, but one which even in *Topics* 4.121A31ff is refuted: pleasure is a movement of the soul and its conscious restoration to its natural state.[7] Such pleasures are mentioned in the *Eudemian Ethics*, and in Plato's *Philebus*, but it is significant that here in *Rhetoric* 1 the identification of pleasure, presumably of all pleasure, as some kind of movement is not denied, nor is any alternative offered. Certainly the passage can be explained away: these are popular views, not Aristotle's own. But that sounds like special pleading. Why should

Aristotle only attend to a view which he had just come to recognize as significantly false? The obvious answer is that the passage from *Rhetoric* 1 pre-dates, perhaps considerably, the discussion of pleasure in *Eudemian Ethics* 6, and even that in *Topics* 4.

8. At 1373B18ff Aristotle alludes to a famous speech of Alcidamas on behalf of the Messenians, former serfs of the Spartans: God has left all men free; nature has made no-one a slave. These, according to a scholiast,[8] were Alcidamas's actual words, and Aristotle alludes to the matter as part of an argument that there are unwritten natural laws, natural ideas of what is just and unjust. He cites Antigone, in Sophocles' play, as appealing to such unwritten laws. His allusion to Alcidamas might suggest that he accepted Alcidamas's view that there are no natural slaves – or it might not, for Aristotle remarks that there is no agreement about the content of such laws. Yet it is at the least surprising that if he rejected Alcidamas's view as whole-heartedly as he did in *Politics* 1, he gives no indication of that rejection here.[9]

9. An interesting and significant distinction between errors (*hamartēmata*), mere misfortunes (*atuchēmata*), and crimes (*adikēmata*) is drawn at 1374B4ff. Errors and misfortunes differ in that, while neither depends on viciousness (*ponēria*), the latter are unexpected, the former not (*paraloga*). In *Rhetoric* 1 the distinction looks crude: no 'errors' will be culpable. They are distinguished from crimes, which alone arise from viciousness. A seemingly similar passage occurs in the *Eudemian Ethics*, where again there is a distinction between misfortunes and errors (4.1135B12ff),[10] but here *some* errors *are* culpable. Now the matter occurs again in a famous and disputed section of the *Poetics*, where Aristotle says that in the ideal tragedy the hero falls into ill fortune not because of vice and wickedness, but through some sort of error (1453A8ff). It does not follow from this statement that the hero is never culpable, however, for 'vice' and 'wickedness' are overall characteristics, and as the passage in the *Eudemian Ethics* says, some '*crimes*' can be committed not through vice, but through anger and other necessary and natural emotions. A man who is neither vicious nor wicked *could* thus achieve by 'error' a culpable, but not strictly vicious act,[11] be it 'error' or 'crime'. This possibility is not left open, however, in *Rhetoric* 1, for there it seems that all crimes (*adikēmata*) do spring from vice, while errors are non-culpable. It is difficult to know what to conclude. Were the *Poetics* to be read, as some wish, as saying that all 'errors' are non-culpable, then it is identical with the *Rhetoric*, but if that is not what it says, then the themes of the two works are diverse. But if so, then we could conclude that this section of *Rhetoric* 1 probably derives from a different, and earlier, period of Aristotle's life than the *Poetics* – which is itself later than the *Eudemian Ethics*.[12]

Scholars have often discussed different 'layers' in our text of the *Rhetoric*.

Many of the details in these discussions often seem to be the product of subjective interpretations.[13] I do not think it possible to pin down Aristotle's *original* course on rhetoric. All I have attempted here is to show that there is material (often of an ethical sort) in *Rhetoric* 1 which is older, probably in some cases considerably older, than the *Eudemian Ethics*, which I have dated after 338, and that some of this goes back not only to the period of the *Philebus*, but earlier still, to a time soon after the so-called *Statesman* (to which *Rhetoric* 1 refers at 1366A21) – which would bring us back to the mid 350s. If this dating is right, then Aristotle's rhetorical interests, represented by his attempt to improve on Isocrates in the *Gryllus*, were an important part of his earliest philosophical world. That world would be built on Plato's *Phaedrus*, *Gorgias*, and *Theaetetus*, and on the claims of Isocrates to make rhetoric an education for ethics and politics. The earliest material in Aristotle's *Rhetoric* 1 is almost an Isocratean 'ethics', and such interests, as we know, soon also produced overtly political writing – probably the result of Aristotle's 'Isocratean' reflections on Plato's *Republic*.

Seeing then that the cumulative weight of the evidence assembled here – and much more could have been provided[14] – suggests that parts of the *Rhetoric* are to be dated well back into the 350s, is there any reason why the whole work should not belong to that period? Two sorts of data point decisively away from such a solution: the cross-references in Aristotle's texts, and the material available in other sections of the *Rhetoric*. Once again I shall produce only a sample of the available evidence.

There are a number of references in the *Rhetoric* as we have it not only to the *Topics* (1355A28, 1356B13, 1396B4, 1398A28, 1399A7, 1402A35, 1403A31) and the *Sophistici Elenchi* (called *Topics* at 1358A29), but also to both sets of *Analytics* (1356B10, 1357A29, 1403A5, 1403A12) and to their developed accounts of induction and deduction. At 1357A17 Aristotle refers to the 'first (presumably "basic") syllogism', and Aristotle's theory of enthymeme in the *Rhetoric* as we have it depends on that theory as a whole.[15] At 1357B15ff, in a sophisticated account of signs, Aristotle uses two examples that occur in the *Prior Analytics*: 'If she has milk, she has given birth; if he has a temperature, he is ill.'[16] The former appears in the *Prior Analytics* (2.70A13ff). The *Analytics*, as we have argued in chapter 4, must have been composed in their present form in Macedonia, probably before 340.

Our *Rhetoric* begins by coupling rhetoric and dialectic, and dialectic is clearly to be understood as the sort of logical procedures we find in the *Analytics* (1.1355A11ff). Like dialectic, rhetoric has no particular class of subject (1.1355B8ff); that is why, like dialectic, it could not appear in the table of 'sciences' later identified in *Metaphysics* E. Like dialectic too rhetoric has good and bad practitioners. In dialectic the bad are sophists:

sophists' arguments depend on the competence of the sophist and have nothing to do with his moral 'purpose' or 'intent' – an odd use of *prohairesis* (common in the *Rhetoric*) which reminds us more of the practice of Epictetus than of later ethical texts of Aristotle. Formally at 1.1356A30 in fact, rhetoric might be called an offshoot of dialectic (as the other categories are offshoots of substance in the *Nicomachean Ethics*, 1.1096A22) and of the science of ethics – so that we include rhetoric, like ethics, in the wider science of politics (cf. 1.1359B11). As we shall note later, however, such specific subordination of ethics to politics is not a marked feature of the *Eudemian Ethics*.

It can certainly be argued that *Rhetoric* 1.1–4 consists entirely of much later material, and that it is a new introduction to the earlier text of the *Rhetoric* which we have just been considering. All I need here, however, is to insist that these chapters, with their frequent references not only to developed syllogistic theory but to the *Analytics* themselves, are later than our *Analytics*, whose date is about 341. Evidence can also be found, however, – and it is generally accepted – that at least some parts of *Rhetoric* 2 are later still, that they were composed after Aristotle's return to Athens in 334.

The final sections of *Rhetoric* 2 are our best evidence. It has long been recognized that chapters 22 and following can only have been written by someone resident in Athens, and that they therefore date from Aristotle's latest period.[17] At 1399B12 we find a reference to the 'common peace' imposed by Alexander in 336, the latest datable reference in the *Rhetoric*. But these chapters abound with examples and themes from Athenian history and rhetoric and they contain numerous references to the works of Aristotle's friend, the rhetorician Theodectes, who had probably recently died.[18] We conclude, therefore, that these chapters, plus our version of the opening sections of book 1 and the majority of book 3 'on style and arrangement,' can only be parts of the revised version of the *Rhetoric* published soon after Aristotle's return to Athens. This version is later than our text of the *Poetics*, to which it refers on three occasions (1.1371B3ff, 3.1419B3ff, 3.1405A6).[19]

If my general thesis about the *Rhetoric* is correct (or indeed if any thesis of the development of the *Rhetoric* is correct), it would follow that, although our text was arranged soon after Aristotle's final return to Athens, when certain new material was added, and perhaps some of what was already written was altered and modified, yet some of the revising was left incomplete. Such additions to the 'finished' text of an Aristotelian work are not limited to the *Rhetoric*; the *De Caelo* shows in its strikingly different theories of motion that there too the process of assimilating material is left incomplete – perhaps even deliberately so for some pedagogical purpose if Aristotle wished to leave notes (to be expanded verbally?) on his philosophical past.

Two 'primitive' sections of our *Rhetoric* provide particularly striking examples of this phenomenon. Both are passages which have marked similarities (or dissimilarities) to sections of *EE* 6 – and both involve problems with the developing notion of *energeia*. The first is *Rhetoric* 1.1371A21ff, a section dealing with friendship. Aristotle starts by saying that it is pleasant to love (for you are not a wine-lover unless you enjoy wine), and that being loved is also pleasant. He then continues a little later by quoting a line from Euripides' *Orestes*, 'Change in all things is sweet,' which he also employs in the important discussion of *energeia* at *Eudemian Ethics* 6.1154B27ff. But the remarks on being loved in the *Eudemian Ethics* are very different. Not only do they make use of the notion of *energeia*, but the introduction of that idea produces a philosophically less intelligible position than is to be found in the *Rhetoric*. As in the *Rhetoric*, the *Eudemian Ethics* (7.1237A39) says that inanimate things (wine is not mentioned here)[20] are loved, but Aristotle does not say that 'being loved' is 'rejoicing' (*chairein*). This is because rejoicing is a display (*energeia*), a showing-forth of something; that is, it is an action, while being loved is not in this sense an action. Aristotle specifically says that the function (*ergon*) of a thing is its *energeia*. And since being loved is not such an 'activity', it is not rejoicing.

And therefore, one might suppose, being loved is not pleasant. But that supposition may be wrong, for in the previous book of the *Eudemian Ethics*, in the section whence comes the quotation from Euripides' *Orestes*, it is argued that not all *energeiai* are 'movements' – and that they are not, therefore, all 'actions' in the ordinary sense of the word. As we shall see, this doctrine is repeated in *Politics* 7 (159 below). Thus by the account of the *Eudemian Ethics*, even though 'being loved,' qua non-action, cannot be a rejoicing – and hence, it might seem, cannot be 'pleasant,' it *could* be a different sort of *energeia*, not of action but of immobility, and hence pleasant by another route. I do not know whether Aristotle would wish to extricate himself by taking this route. I would only say that the account in the *Rhetoric* avoids the tangles of the *Eudemian Ethics* precisely because the novel view of *energeia* in *Eudemian Ethics* 6 is not introduced.

In fact *energeia* is a rare word in the *Rhetoric*. We have already discussed one of the very few passages (1.1361A24) (106 above), where it occurs and noticed that this text offers a sense of *energeia* which seems old-fashioned even by the time of *Topics* 6; it refers to the employment of possessions. A similar use appears at 2.1378B11, where slighting a man is described as the employment, almost the acting out, of a certain kind of belief about him. But the most interesting section of all is in the third book (1411B25ff). Here we have a fascinating discussion of metaphor, in which a 'primitive' sense of *energeia* is still embedded: if we say a good man is 'four-square' (as Simonides did in a famous poem), we are using a metaphor, but the metaphor does not indicate *energeia*. *Energeia* is expressed, however, if we speak of a man having his prime of life 'in bloom' (as Isocrates had done in chapter 10 of his *Philip*). Metaphors which express the *energeia* indicate life and being animate. For Homer in a description of the sea gives it movement and makes it seem living, as he does when he speaks of a 'lusting spear' or a 'shameless stone.' For *energeia* is movement. Thus for a metaphor to express the *energeia* is for it to appear to express the vitality of a living substance.

This passage in *Rhetoric* 3 is both like and unlike the famous passage at the end of book 6 of the *Eudemian Ethics* about *energeia* and pleasure. It is easy to see in the light of *Rhetoric* 3 why Aristotle could come to say in the *Eudemian Ethics* that pleasure is an *energeia* of our natural state (6.1153A14ff), for the *Rhetoric* shows us how speaking of a man's 'blooming' is to speak of his vitality. Hence pleasure in the *Eudemian Ethics* could be identified as the appearance of such vitality – and if so interpreted the doctrine of the *Eudemian Ethics* is not very different in form, though different in terminology and in the sense of *energeia*, from that of *Nicomachean Ethics* 10. But in another respect the *Eudemian Ethics* neglects the language of *Rhetoric* 3.1411B27ff altogether. In the *Eudemian Ethics* pleasure is not a process of change (or a movement, presumably); but it *is* an *energeia*. For as book 6 goes on to explain, not all *energeiai* are movements – an outright denial of the meaning given in *Rhetoric* 3.

Hence, if our *Rhetoric* post-dates the *Eudemian Ethics*, as I believe it does, it has been augmented from its original form, but very primitive elements remain. *Rhetoric* 3.1411B27ff perhaps comes from Aristotle's early work on poetry. If so, the passage is a standing warning for us not to assume that Aristotle always uses his technical terms, in this case *energeia*, in a strictly technical sense.

III The 'Poetics'

There is no need to say much about the date of the *Poetics*. Cross-references enable us to pin it down to the last Athenian period. It is earlier than the final version of the *Rhetoric*, as we have seen, but later than parts of the *Politics*, for an unusual (even possibly interpolated) forward reference in *Politics* 8 (1341B37) tells us that Aristotle will have more to say in the *Poetics* about *catharsis*, about the purgation of the emotions of pity and terror. In our day, of course, it has been the *Politics* which has been used to illuminate the *Poetics*, but that is an accident of the history of scholarship. More modern critics have been interested in explaining Aristotle's account of tragedy in the *Poetics* than have troubled themselves about the *Politics*; and the *Politics* does indeed help explain Aristotle's account of tragedy. We learn in *Politics* 8 of the *catharsis* of pity and terror which can be generated by orgiastic music, and this helps to confirm the medical nature of the purgation of which Aristotle speaks in the *Poetics*. Pity and terror are not to be removed, but reduced to manageable proportions; physiologically they are an *excess* of black bile.[21] The topic of *catharsis* may pre-date the *Poetics*, perhaps appearing in Aristotle's lost work *On the Poets*. Certainly pity and terror are considered in not unrelated ways in the (later) *Rhetoric* 2 (1385B13ff). But there is nothing about purgation in this passage, or in 2.5. Aristotle tells us what is fearful and what is pitiable – and that we pity the undeserved troubles of others when we fear that we may suffer similarly ourselves. Yet it is not clear whether Aristotle thinks that such pity and fear are good for us, or merely that the arousal of such emotions is useful to the orator. An argument from silence would suggest that this undeveloped treatment of *catharsis* is another indication of early material in the *Rhetoric*; but there is no weight to such a claim. Aristotle's interest in the poets, in the lost book *On the Poets*,[22] may indicate that his positive evaluation of their work pre-dates the *Poetics*.

But there is both chronological and philosophical interest in the mere fact that *Politics* 8 seems to refer *forward* to the *Poetics*. For like rhetoric, poetry is not unconnected with the statesman's art, at least in a society which permits political life. Appropriately again, therefore, it is virtually certain that the *Poetics* (in our version at least) was composed soon after *Politics* 8, and during Aristotle's last Athenian period. Again, like the *Rhetoric*, the *Poetics* contains references to the work of Aristotle's Athenian friend and perhaps recently deceased contemporary Theodectes (1452A27, 1455B29), but the most interesting evidence on chronology is a comment about the history of comedy: both the Megarians 'here' (that is, on the Greek mainland) and those in Sicily claim to be the originators of the genre (1448A31). The sentence certainly suggests that Aristotle is writing in Athens (next to Megara), as most of the commentators have seen. The date, confirmed as we have seen by cross-reference, can only be soon after Aristotle's return in 334.

Aristotle, who shared Plato's view that drama was imitative, had long disagreed with him about its effect. The effect is purgation, which is good for the soul, and as a political philosopher Aristotle reckons to take cognizance of poetry in a more positive sense than Plato would allow. Aristotle had already made the point in his early work *On the Poets*,[23] where he first talked of the purgative effects of both tragedy and comedy. By watching other people's emotions, we purge our own and make them more moderate (*metriōtera*). In view of his rejection of Plato's approach on the effect of drama, however, it is interesting to note that Aristotle is nearer to Plato's *late* view of what constitutes the essence of a good tragic or comic plot. In the *Poetics* tragedy, as we have seen (140 above), is best represented by the possibility of the error, not necessarily culpable, of a man larger than life – though not beyond our reach. Comedy too thrives on errors. The laughable is some error or ugliness which does not, however, bring pain or death. Both 'errors' remind us of Plato's *Philebus* (50AB), where both tragedy and comedy are represented as depending on a man's lack of self-knowledge – doubtless leading to mistakes which are not necessarily culpable. And behind *Philebus* 50AB lies the closing section of the *Symposium* where Plato has Socrates argue that the same man ought to be able to write both tragedy and comedy. The *Philebus*, a work whose metaphysics and ethics had great influence on Aristotle, reminds us of the *Poetics* in another way too. Tragedy and comedy are providers both of pleasure and of pain – whether on the stage or in life. And Aristotle too thinks of the pleasure of tragedy; it has a peculiar pleasure all its own, and, we must assume, is by implication good for us (1453A36, 1453B11, 1459A21, 1462A16, 1462B13).

IV The Structure and Content of the 'Politics'

Our next step must be to consider the structure of the work called the *Politics*, which was known in Alexandria as a treatise in eight books and has come down to us in this format. Much ingenuity has been expended in identifying the various stages of its construction, but in this area much of Jaeger's original edifice remains more or less intact. Jaeger believed that our *Politics* is the conflation of two earlier books, a study of constitutions designed to lead up to an ideal state (reported by our books 2, 3, 7, and 8), and a treatise on political science, more or less value-free ('empirical' is Jaeger's term), which is our books 4, 5, and 6. This treatise betrays scant interest in the ideal state; it is an analysis of the workings of various sorts of political societies, and contains recommendations as to how they can be preserved. From these two treatises, according to Jaeger, our *Politics* was composed by a not entirely successful process of amalgamation. A new introduction was written; this is our present book 1. Jaeger is particularly impressed by the fact that the 'value-free' books 4 to 6 refer to the *Politics* as a whole, and that the 'utopian' set (2, 3, 7, 8) refer only to themselves (*Aristotle*, 267, 274); and this fact does seem to suggest that books 4 to 6 were originally composed separately, though it tells us nothing of Aristotle's intentions when (or if) he produced our current eight-book text.

Jaeger's thesis is incomplete (though it can perhaps be completed) in several respects:

1 His account of the relationship of book 1 to the rest is ill argued, and he gives us little reason to believe that this book was composed later than books 2, 3, 7, and 8 – though in fact it was!
2 It has been observed that the complete *Politics*, though apparently falling

into the two sections identified by Jaeger, does nevertheless fulfil the prerequisites for a book on politics such as Plato, for example, might have laid down.[24] For it could be argued that the political theorist must deal with two distinct, though related, fundamental questions: the description of an ideal state and of approximations to it; and a discussion of the root-problem of Greek politics, the *stability* of existing city constitutions. If, therefore, some thirty or forty years after Plato's *Republic*, Aristotle had concluded (as perhaps had Plato) that utopia is still far away, while the chronic problem of stability still remains, then it is understandable that he might wish to speak more realistically about how any constitution might reasonably be preserved – especially as his recommendations in value-free or empirical terms tend to make the existing constitutions 'better,' that is, more concerned to render all the citizens patient if not happy.

3 As Jaeger observed, it looks as though the *Politics*, in the form we have it, is designed to follow book 10 of the *Nicomachean Ethics*, though the programme of politics suggested by the last few lines of the *Nicomachean Ethics* does little justice at least to *Politics* 1. This objection, however, is not very serious. More important is that if Kenny is right – as I have assumed him to be, and as various further material in this book confirms – that the so-called books 5 to 7 of the *Nicomachean Ethics* belong to the *Eudemian* version, then the *Nicomachean Ethics* is an incomplete revision. It is certain that somewhere in the design of the *Nicomachean Ethics* there must be discussions at least of justice and of the intellectual virtues. In our truncated version of the *Nicomachean Ethics* these sections are missing. A possible solution to this problem is to say that Aristotle simply intended to plonk *Eudemian Ethics* 4–6 into the incomplete *Nicomachean* version just as we find occurs in the surviving manuscripts of the *Nicomachean Ethics*. But that is most unlikely to have been Aristotle's intention, for surely *some* changes in these books would have been necessary. Moreover, all the remaining sections of the *Nicomachean Ethics* are *revised* versions of the *Eudemian Ethics*, not mere copies. We have to assume that the *Nicomachean Ethics* was left incomplete by Aristotle and that the introduction to the *Politics* was left tacked on to the end of a still unfinished *Ethics*. This will look even more surprising if, as we shall argue, parts of the *Politics* were written as some sort of sequel not to the *Nicomachean Ethics*, but to the earlier *Eudemian* version. So that, as we shall see, our thesis will need a little modification, but we shall still be left with the fact that both the original and the revised version of the *Politics*, like the revised version of *Eudemian Ethics* 4–6, were never completed by Aristotle: he died too soon.

Nor, of course, would the situation be made easier were we to accept – as in fact we do not – the view of Kenny that the *Nicomachean Ethics* is an earlier version of the *Eudemian*, for then, of course, the earlier version was never completed and the *Politics*, apparently, was tacked on to a wildly incomplete *Ethics* by Aristotle himself well within his own lifetime, not merely near the end of his life or through the hand of a posthumous compiler.

These diverse questions about the unity and present state of the *Politics* are all in fact interrelated, and can be resolved if we determine first of all the relationship between the *Politics* (and especially *Politics* 1) and not the *Nicomachean*, but the *Eudemian*, version of the *Ethics*. First of all, as we have seen, Jaeger's reasons for detaching book 1 from books 2, 3, 7, and 8 are weak. They boil down to his interpretation of a single passage of book 1 (1260B8–13): 'As for man and wife and children and father, and the virtue of each of them, and of the right and wrong way they may have of dealing with one another, and how we pursue the right way and avoid the wrong, it is necessary to follow all this up *en tois peri tas politeias*' – which I take to mean in the sections dealing with the various constitutions. According to Jaeger, this passage 'at first sight looks like an incomprehensible failure in consistency and lucidity' (*Aristotle*, 272), for although the first book has raised three basic preliminary questions, dealing with the position in society of slaves, women, and children, only slavery is discussed in detail in book 1. This claim is not entirely true, in fact; there are substantial and important comments about women and children even in book 1. But leaving that aside, the attitude which Jaeger attributes to Aristotle is still unsatisfactory. Aristotle should have said much more about women and children in book 1, he thinks, but did not do so because he had already dealt with such matters in his account of the 'community of women and children' advocated by Plato, which he had already completed in book 2 – part of the original *Politics* and thus earlier than book 1.

Aristotle's remarks about dealing with women and children in the sections about constitutions can hardly refer only to the critique of Plato's *Republic*, as Jaeger wishes. They are probably to be understood more generally in the light of Aristotle's frequent claim that each sort of constitution will have an educational system appropriate to its needs, none of these of course being morally identical with the others. Hence we should expect what Jaeger calls the 'poor consolation' of finding a discussion of women and children in the section of book 8 dealing with the ideal constitution. In point of fact, of course, that section, and with it the *Politics* as a whole, is incomplete, and the problem of what has happened to the more detailed discussions of the proper role of women and children becomes part of the greater problem of the unfinished state of the *Politics* as a whole. We have to insist, therefore, that so far we are not justified in concluding that *Politics* 1 is a later addition, a new introduction to earlier treatises (2, 3, 7, 8, and 4–6) taken as a whole.

There are, however, further reasons which can be advanced in favour of Jaeger's thesis about *Politics* 1. It is possible to show that although the *Politics* as a whole is closer to the *Eudemian Ethics* than to the *Nicomachean Ethics, Politics* 1 enjoys a very particular and distinct relationship to the earlier ethical text: it tends to *replace* it. Kenny has drawn proper conclusions from a fact not unknown to earlier scholars, namely that the references in the *Politics* to the *Ethics* are almost certainly to the *Eudemian*, not to the *Nicomachean*, version;[25] and this point is strengthened if we believe that *Nicomachean Ethics* 5–7 were originally *Eudemian Ethics* 4–6. There are six such references altogether (*Pol.* 2.1261A30ff, 3.1280A16ff, 3.1282B18ff, 4.1295A35ff, 7.1332A7ff, 7.1332A21ff), and none of them is from book 1. Five out of the six are from Jaeger's 'earlier version' of the *Politics*, and only one (4.1295A35ff) comes from one of the 'empirical' books. For what it is worth, this might suggest that book 1 had not yet been composed.

At this point we should consider some parallels in thought between book 1 and the *Eudemian Ethics*, and between Jaeger's 'early books' of the *Politics* (2, 3, 7, 8) and the *Eudemian Ethics*.

1 *Pol.* 1.1257A9ff; *EE* 3.1232A1ff

Both passages deal with the use of shoes; they can be either worn (an intrinsic [*kath' hauto*] use according to the *Ethics*) or they can be sold or hired out for wearing – which is an 'accidental' use. The *Politics* offers a more sophisticated treatment. Now both the above cases are 'intrinsic' uses, but the sold shoe is used intrinsically in a different sense, and its use is thus no longer 'proper.' Whatever we think of the distinction in the *Politics*, it is a developed version of the distinction in the *Eudemian Ethics*; the matter does not arise in our texts of the *Nicomachean Ethics*. The same topic, however, also occurs in *Eudemian Ethics* 4.1133A20ff, where it leads on, as it does in *Politics* 1, to a discussion of the role of money in society. This part of the *Eudemian Ethics* has nothing to say about the 'proper' or other use of shoes, and its account of money differs also from that of the *Politics*. In *Eudemian Ethics* 4 money is thought of solely as a medium of exchange, and there is nothing about its 'natural' or 'unnatural' use – nothing, that is, about the topic of usury which is prominent in *Politics* 1. Again the *Politics* passage looks like a more developed version of what we find in the *Eudemian Ethics*. In the passages of the *Eudemian* version there is nothing said of acquisition for acquisition's sake, whether of goods or of money. I shall suggest that the *Politics* account depends on a more elaborate use of the concept of nature and natural behaviour, a concept which is more or less absent in the *Eudemian Ethics* (153–4 and ch. 9 below). At the beginning of *Politics* 1.9 Aristotle has already observed that acquisition is not always by nature; it may be the result of some 'art' developed by experience.

2 *Pol.* 8.1342A24ff; *EE* 7.1238B21ff, 1241B1ff

In these sections of the *Eudemian Ethics* Aristotle begins by distinguishing different kinds of friendship and explains them in terms of different sorts of justice. He claims that these forms of just relationship are visible in a family. For, he explains (1242A23ff), man is not only a city-living (*politikon*) animal, he is also a householding animal, not solitary but gregarious, and in these partnerships, even below the level of the city, some justice can be seen. For in a household we see the different kinds of 'partnerships' whereas the relation of master and slave is that of craft and tools (and soul and body). Relations between master and slave are not relations of justice or of friendship, but they are 'analogues' or 'counterparts' of them (1242A30–1).[26] But the relation of man and wife *is* a partnership – a sort of friendship of the lowest kind, based on utility – while that of father and son (like that of God and man!) is between benefactor and beneficiary or natural ruler and natural subject. The relation of brothers is based on equality. So that in the household we find the roots of friendship, political structure, and justice.

The earlier section of the same book of the *Eudemian Ethics* carries us a bit further. Again the relation between father and son is compared to that of benefactor and beneficiary (7.1238B24ff). That between husband and wife is similar in some respects to that of father and son (that is, they are both relationships between ruler and ruled) but distinct in other ways; for the wife's relationship to the husband is not only that of beneficiary; the wife, we are told later, needs the husband but is also needed by him – and the relation between master and slave is similar in this respect (7.1239B25ff).

Aristotle has more to say about the relation between masters and slaves later in the *Eudemian Ethics*. At 7.1241B18ff he repeats his view that the relation of master and slave is similar to that between soul and body, and between craftsman and tool. The body is an 'innate' tool of the soul, so the slave is a kind of part or separate tool of the master's, and an ordinary tool is a kind of lifeless slave. Aristotle then adds a new point: the household contains not only correct forms of constitution, but also the deviations. Now the father's authority is royal, that of husband and wife is an aristocratic relationship, while that of brothers is republican (*politeia hē tōn adelphōn*). Perverse versions of each of these are also available, and hellenically enough Aristotle makes a comparison at this stage between perverse constitutions and perverse musical modes. A similar but not identical comparison occurs in *Politics* 8, but here the perverse musical modes are said to be suitable for the perverse tastes of the perverse souls of workers and hired labourers (8.1342B20ff). It is interesting that this passage, though comparable with that of *Eudemian Ethics* 7, can in no sense be construed as a revised version.

Let us now turn to *Politics* 1, to look particularly at Aristotle's remarks about various household relationships, especially those between master and slave and husband and wife. The first and most obvious point is that the treatment in *Politics* 1 is more systematic, and that it is set in a biological context. Aristotle's project in *Politics* 1 is to show that the state is a natural growth, not only 'natural' in the sense that it regularly occurs, but that it is conducive to the survival of the human species in a way analogous to copulation. The point had already been made in the *Eudemian Ethics*, but more casually. Now Aristotle claims that the desire to reproduce brings together man and woman (1.1252A27ff) and the desire to survive leads to the foundation of cities. Since both the family and the city are in this sense natural growths, it will follow that the best sorts of relationships or partnerships within both families and cities will be those most conducive to the survival of the human species – with the additional point that in the case of the city, not merely survival, but well-being, is the final cause of the institution (1252B30). Let us consider the relationship of husband and wife first, then proceed to master and slave.

Males and females come to live together because they are unable to reproduce separately (1252A26ff). Such coupling, as with other animals, is instinctive, not (originally) intentional. Obviously Aristotle knows that marriages in his day were generally contracted to produce offspring. What he means here is that individual desire for intercourse is not necessarily desire for offspring, but offspring are the result of an instinct which has that effect. Thus the 'natural' purpose of male/female partnerships is the production of children. Such partnerships are different from master/slave partnerships because their *purpose* is different. 'Barbarians' wrongly regard the state of women and slaves as identical. (One of the disadvantages of being poor, Aristotle observes, is that one is obliged to treat one's wife and children as servants, proper slaves being lacking [6.1323A5–6].) Primitive societies reduce all relationships (at best) to monarchy: the Cyclops thus gives laws in a monarchical way to his wives and children (1.1252B23), and outside 'cities', says Aristotle, some such societies still survive.

The city is the form of organization in which men flourish best, and the city requires some form of justice. Man alone is capable of justice, and in this respect he is superior to other gregarious animals, whether cattle or insects like bees. In book 1 of the *Historia Animalium* Aristotle had already compared man with such creatures (487B33ff). But now he goes further. Man is differentiated from other gregarious animals by the possession of reason and its associate speech. Animals cannot speak; they can merely make sounds indicative of pleasure and pain. Further, man's reason helps him to identify (and indicate) what is to his advantage and disadvantage, hence what is just and unjust, good and bad. It is in virtue of this power of reason (and its concomitant speech) that men form households (*oikia*) and cities (1.1253A18). We should expect therefore that justice would be visible in the family relationships as well as in those of the city. Since the 'final cause' of the family and hence of the city is the survival and flourishing of the human species, we can see why Aristotle can now say that the city is 'prior by nature' to the household and the individual. It is prior in the sense that since a man (or woman) cannot reproduce alone, and since a household cannot survive alone, the goods of reproduction and survival will be achieved in cities whereas they will not be achieved in families and households. The priority of the city has nothing to do with claims that types of behaviour unacceptable in private life are acceptable for reasons of state – claims which in fact Aristotle denies.

In 1253B Aristotle returns to the basic household: man, wife, and slave. He observes that Greek has no word for the relationship between husband and wife, which he then calls the 'marital' relationship. By this he seems to mean that there is no word which describes the 'governmental' relationship in the way that 'masterful' describes the relationship between man and slave. The relationship between father and son similarly lacks description. Aristotle at this point deals with slavery (and other matters); we shall return to this. Discussion of the relationship between husband and wife is not taken further until chapter 12, where, in a fresh beginning, Aristotle identifies three kinds of governance, the 'despotic' (i.e., 'masterful,' not 'tyrannical') rule of master over slave, the royal rule of father over children, and the marital rule of husband over wife. This latter is similar to that of father over children in that both wife and children are free,[27] but its style is different. The relation is a 'political' one. Normally, continues Aristotle, the male is more fitted to rule than the female – unless something contrary to nature occurs, when presumably the female is fitter. Such 'normal' male rule, though 'political,' is not, however, patterned on the usual arrangements in 'political' constitutions, where ruler alternates with ruled. In this odd sort of political situation the males always rule.

What then is the virtue or goodness of the wife (1259B29ff)? Is she too capable of moderation, courage, and justice? The answer to this (as in the case of the slave) is put in 'biological' terms. The deliberative faculty of women is ineffective (*akuron*, 1260A13), while that of the slave is nonexistent and that of the child immature. This means not that women are less intelligent than men, but primarily that they are less able to impose their judgments on their emotions. It is not that they do not value self-control as men do, but that they have less capacity to exercise it effectively. Hence the best male will possess moral virtue completely (1260A17–18), and the best woman will be temperate, brave, and just in a different way – and in a lesser way. Socrates was simply mistaken on this point (in the *Meno*); Sophocles rather was right (1260A29ff) in distinguishing silence as an adornment for women, but not for men.[28]

Let us compare the accounts of husband and wife in *Politics* 1 with what can be gleaned from the *Eudemian Ethics*. In the *Politics* the relationship is spelled out both differently and more precisely. In the *Eudemian Ethics* it is aristocratic; in *Politics* 1 it is 'political', though political of a very special sort, for apart from freak cases the husband always rules. Nevertheless he presumably also rules in the aristocracy, because he is better. In *Politics* 1, in fact, by insisting that there is no proper name for the nature of the marital authority of the husband, Aristotle is trying, for whatever reason, to be precise. But the principal difference between the two accounts is that in *Politics* 1 the inferiority of women is identified as a recognizable inadequacy in their effectiveness, whereas in the *Eudemian Ethics* no explanation is proposed.

There is, admittedly, something relevant to the question in the *Eudemian Ethics* (6.1150B1ff), exactly where we might expect to find it, that is, in the discussion of restraint and unrestraint (*akrasia*). We do not really expect a man to give way to normal amounts of pleasure and pain unless he is ill or has some hereditary disability – but females will give way more than males. The impressionistic nature of the comment and the lack of explanation here is transparent; and the context is that of blameworthy failures rather than psychological incapacity. In *Politics* 1, however, Aristotle seems to allude to what he did not possess before, a *theory* of 'nature' to account for what he claims to observe, namely female inadequacy to attain the virtues of a ruler – and his remarks are presented in the course of a quasi-biological account of the development of human communities. In a later chapter we shall consider more precisely what his theory is (246–8 below). For the time being let us content ourselves with concluding that this rather lengthy discussion of Aristotelian husbands and wives supports my view that *Politics* 1 deals with some of the same topics as the *Eudemian Ethics*, but develops them in rather unexpected ways, whereas other early books of the *Politics* lack such surprising developments. This contrastive pattern tells in *favour* of Jaeger's view that, if the original *Politics* is designed in any sense as a follow-up to the *Eudemian Ethics*, book 1 was not part of the original project.

We have seen certain developments in Aristotle's treatment of husband and wife in *Politics* 1; let us now consider the master/slave relationship and see whether that too is distinct in *Politics* 1. In fact we have already observed that in this case too Aristotle introduces a psychological explanation. Slaves are totally defective in deliberative power. What more can be said? First that Aristotle believes slaves to be necessary for human flourishing, that is, for the flourishing of those of us who are not natural slaves (1253B33ff). Note, however, that slaves are 'originally' not for production but for assisting in action.[29] Furthermore, since we are 'intended' by nature to flourish, there must be natural slaves to allow for the possibility. That is not expressed, but it seems to be a vital hidden premise.

It is not only the master who benefits from his slave; the slave benefits from his master in that the two have a common interest (1252A34, 1254B22, 1255B6–7). The slave toils with his body (and in a sense is an extension of his master's body, 1255B11), the master foresees with his mind (1252A32–3).[30] Though the slave is compared to the master's body, however, Aristotle insists that friendship between master and natural slave is possible (1255B13–14).

Again this last point is somewhat different from, and more precise than, the version in the *Eudemian Ethics*. Friendship between natural slave and master is now possible; previously only an 'analogue' of friendship was allowed. In other significant respects, however, there is little difference from the *Eudemian Ethics*, except, of course, in the crucial matter of the psychological explanation of what a natural slave is, an explanation which in fact also allows for the different treatment of friendship. In other words the account of the natural slave's incapacity that we find in *Politics* 1 enables Aristotle to abandon his 'analogy' of friendship and replace it with a real friendship. This apparent replacement again would suggest that *Politics* 1 is a revised version, with additions, of matter in the *Eudemian Ethics* – and is thus substantially later. This suggestion looks all the more plausible because in the case of slavery there appear in book 7 (part of Jaeger's early version of the *Politics*) ideas about slavery which *Politics* 1 supersedes.

Before proceeding further, however, let us pause to consider whether what Aristotle says on slavery for the first time in *Politics* 1 is a coherent and complete account – something which looks to be the result of sustained intellectual effort over time. If it is, it will look like the work of an older and more mature thinker. Such sophistication, of course, is frequently denied of Aristotle's account of slavery, and a major source of error is identified thus: according to Aristotle, the relationship of master to slave is despotism, modelled on that of soul to body, but since the slave can be instructed by his master's reason, the real relationship is that between the rational and emotional parts of the soul. But if that is the relationship Aristotle has in mind, he is confused, for the rational soul rules the emotional part not as master, but as a monarch.[31]

According to W.W. Fortenbaugh, however, Aristotle denies slaves the logical or reasoning half of the soul but not the alogical or emotional half.[32] This means that the slaves can make the judgments involved in emotional responses and therefore have at least a minimal share in the cognitive capacity peculiar to man in relation to other animals. Fortenbaugh's interpretation, of course, is a version of the idea that the master/slave relationship is similar to that between reason and emotion – and leaves Aristotle open to the charge outlined above, that he in fact regularly compares master and slave to soul and body. But both Fortenbaugh and his critics have failed to analyse Aristotle's notion of 'being without the power to deliberate.' Let us therefore consider what it implies. Deliberation is necessary for making choices, and choice is a necessary component of *moral* virtue, the virtue of habit, in both the *Eudemian* and the *Nicomachean Ethics*. Hence the natural slave is not only incapable of the judgments made by the man of practical wisdom (the *phronimos*); he is incapable of the moral virtues as well. Moral virtue, in the *Eudemian Ethics*, is eventually defined in part as 'a disposition involving choosing' (2.1227B9ff) – and slaves cannot choose – 'for we deliberate about everything we choose.' Fortenbaugh therefore is precisely *wrong* in saying that the slave can make the *judgments* involved in emotional responses. If he could, then the master's rule could be regal, but Aristotle's point is that *of himself* the slave cannot make *any* judgments. To make them he receives reason from his master (1254B20ff, 1260B5–7). In his natural state he lives at the level of sensation alone, for (as *Politics* 3.1277A7 has it) the human soul is not reason plus emotion, but reason plus desire (*orexis*); that is why the natural slave *needs* a master. Without a master he is an animal; hence Aristotle can talk of 'slaves and animals,' and think of the master/slave relation as despotism (1254B16–19). With a master the slave can do some of the things men alone can do. Animals *only* obey their instincts (1254B23–4); slaves can obey *external* reason. When Aristotle says that the master/slave relation is to be understood as like that of the soul and the body, he is to be understood as dividing the soul into its 'animal' part (sensation and desire) and its human part (reason). The soul/body comparison is better than the reason/emotion one because only a proper and reasonable 'emotion' is specifically human.[33] Thus the soul/body distinction picks out those specifically human parts of soul, as against those parts which are present in an animal body. For, we remember, no animal body is without some sort of soul.

Thus the soul/body relationship, though not exactly what Aristotle wants, supplies a better model than that between reason and emotion, and we can thus see why Aristotle uses it. In biological terms slaves are 'dualizers'; the scale of nature is gradual, not in steep steps. Slaves are biologically men in the sense that they are generated by human beings, but definitely not men, and indeed definitely animals,[34] in that they do not possess *at all* that capability which enables men to achieve either the moral or the intellectual virtues. In this respect they are quite unlike women, who are capable to a degree of both intellectual and moral virtue, and children who will become so capable. Hence their ambiguous status. They are either men impaired beyond recognition,[35] or a special sort of animal. The former is a better description in so far as it does justice to the physiological evidence. A slave, or 'manimal', is a human so incomplete that left on his own he is an animal. We might expect to find in *Politics* 1 a biological explanation of the details of this psychological defectiveness, but it is not spelled out, just as the *Politics* itself contains no biological details about the ineffectiveness of women, only a quasi-biological context and comment on the psychological (rather than moral) results of a presumably biological situation. We shall consider the biology more closely in a later chapter, and the answer to biological questions about women and natural slaves to some extent supplied in other Aristotelian texts.

It is clear that Aristotle's discussion of slaves, as of women, in *Politics* 1 is *more* developed than what we find in the *Eudemian Ethics*. Let us look at one change in particular. In the *Eudemian Ethics*, as we saw, friendship between master and slave is not possible, but only something analogous to it; in *Politics* 1 this friendship is possible qua man, not qua slave. Aristotle's distinction has been widely ridiculed, but it is worth trying to see what he is getting at. If the slave were simply an animal – and that is how he functions qua slave – then obviously no friendship is possible. But Aristotle's whole problem with natural slaves is that they are not *simply* animals. When reason dominates them, they can act like human beings. It is clearly at this stage that friendship would seem a possibility. In other words when the natural slave is raised, by slavery to the right master, to capabilities of which he is incapable 'in the wild,' then he is capable of friendship. Thus when Aristotle says he is capable of friendship qua man, he means when he is exalted by his master to be more man-like than beast-like, capable of tolerating life in a *polis*. To say, however, that at any time the relation between master and slave is a relation of friendship would, in the account of *Eudemian Ethics* 7 (1242A30–1), suggest that there is some kind of justice in the relationship, that is, that the master has some obligation to the slave. I should presume that it is in virtue of this obligation that the Aristotelian natural master (who, it must be repeated, is not tyrannical, but will certainly consult his own advantage, not that of his slave) will not be and should not be what we would call an evil master. If he were, he would disadvantage both himself and his slave (1255B9). The 'good' master recognizes the fact that the natural slave is useful if ruled properly, and therefore deserves reasonable treatment. In this sense to maltreat a slave would be unjust because it would then be to deny him his desert.

Interestingly enough, there are several passages of book 7 which conflict with the theory of slavery advocated in book 1. Perhaps the most remarkable is at 1330A32–3, where it is suggested that the possibility of freedom should be available to all slaves as a reward for good service. If this refers to natural slaves, it is extraordinary, for according to book 1 it is not in the interest of the natural slave to be emancipated. (Nevertheless, although the possibility of emancipation might be available to all, the 'good' master might decline to award it to all, on 'good' grounds.) Interesting too is the attitude to 'barbarians.' According to book 1, they are all natural slaves (1252B9),[36] while according to book 7 (1327B27–9), there is a more traditional argument to the effect that they lack 'vigour' (*thumos*). The latter passage is particularly interesting, and it may afford a clue to the date of *Politics* 7. The Asiatics, says Aristotle, are intelligent and competent people (which surely means they can deliberate), but they lack vigour. That is why they are always slaves. The Greeks, in contrast, are spirited and clever. That is why they are free and politically developed and capable of ruling everyone – if they get a political unity. The reference here may be, *inter alia,* to Philip's League of Corinth of 338, but the implications are that the Greeks, though suited to universal rule, have not yet achieved it. It is a plausible assumption in these passages that Aristotle did not yet regard the Asiatics as natural slaves, and possible that, when he talks of manumission, his notion of a natural slave is not yet fully developed.[37] If this assumption is true, then we have further arguments for the later date of *Politics* 1 and its psychological theory of the relative inferiority of women and the gross inferiority of 'manimals'. It would not be at all unreasonable to suggest that, as often in Aristotle, development in ethics is related to development in biology. We have already observed that *Politics* 1 is given a marked biological framework though few biological details are given. Could it be that the development of the biology of female inferiority, which can be found in the *De Generatione Animalium*, is related to the psychology of female (and slave) inferiority in *Politics* 1, but not to that of *Politics* 7?

Without entering upon a general discussion of Aristotle's biology at this point, the thesis about the relation between ethical and biological claims can be pursued in two ways: first by looking at another class of subhumans, that is 'beasts' or 'savages'; secondly by seeing what the *Eudemian Ethics* has to say on these subjects. The opening of *Eudemian Ethics* 6 contains the longest discussion of 'beasts'. Beast are rare, says Aristotle, among men (1145A30) and are more frequent among barbarians than among Greeks – though they do occur. There are three types. Some are born as beasts, others become beasts by sickness, and others through some sort of maiming or evil habits. Bestiality is the opposite of godlike virtue, beneath our normal level. Beasts by nature, or what Aristotle calls an 'evil nature' (6.1148B18ff), are liable to perform horrendous and brutal acts (such as cannibalism, 1148B21ff). But bestiality is shown not only in cruelty; there are naturally bestial states corresponding to other virtues which may also be natural, that is, inborn. A man terrified of the sound of a mouse could be naturally bestial (1149A8ff). Here then we have another sort of subhuman condition, different from that of the slave, for there is no suggestion that the beast is devoid of the capacity for deliberation, but similar in that, being 'beyond vice,' he would appear quite unfitted for city-life. Aristotle does not, however, tell us what if anything is biologically *wrong* with natural beasts.

Beasts occur again in *Politics* 1, and they get treatment rather similar to what they receive in the *Eudemian Ethics*. The man who is unable to share, or needs nothing because he is entirely self-sufficient, is no part of a city; so he is either a beast or a god (1253A29). And again the man who is without a city by nature (which would include the slave) and not merely by chance is either a miserable specimen or he is higher than a man (1253A2ff). A beast, continues Aristotle, lusts for war; he is like a Homeric Cyclops. But that is all. Beasts are an accepted part of the human landscape, but they have no further part to play in the *Politics*. They do not occur in the *Nicomachean Ethics*.

The *Nicomachean Ethics*, however, provides evidence on slaves and women. Is it possible to fit this material into our proposed structure which would link the *Eudemian Ethics* rather loosely with *Politics* 2, 3, 7, and 8, but make *Politics* 1 later, perhaps contemporary with parts of the *Nicomachean Ethics* or even later still?

Some of the few remarks on slaves and women in the *Nicomachean Ethics* occur in a section about constitutional changes. At 8.1160B17ff Aristotle refers to the republican form of government as 'timocracy,'[38] a term not so used in the *Eudemian Ethics* or *Politics*. The discussion of government involved is similar, but by calling the state timocratic in the *Nicomachean Ethics*, Aristotle emphasizes that this limited democracy is distinguished by property qualification. This emphasis affects what he says about the relation between husband and wife, however, for that relationship in a 'proper' family has no connection with property but with 'worth' (*axia*, 8.1160B33). The family relationship thus resembles the 'aristocracy' of the *Eudemian Ethics*, in which there are separate spheres of worth for men and women, in a rather traditionally Greek fashion.[39] If the husband controls everything, then aristocracy collapses into oligarchy, for now the man acts contrary to worth. Of course if the wife is an heiress, she sometimes rules, again in an oligarchic manner.

Friendship between man and wife is called aristocracy in accordance with justice and virtue (1161A22ff). But in its handling of friendship between masters and slaves, it is noticeable that the *Nicomachean Ethics* goes with *Politics* 1 rather than with its *Eudemian* predecessor. Friendship is not merely by analogy; it is possible with the slave qua man.

In so far as this investigation gives evidence for a relative chronology, it supports the view that *Politics* 1 is later than the *Eudemian Ethics*. *Nicomachean Ethics* 8 agrees with *Politics* 1 on the substantive issue of friendship with slaves. It differs, however, on the relationship between husband and wife, reverting to the description of it in the *Eudemian* version as aristocratic, doubtless because the renaming of republicanism as timocracy (with its emphasis on the feature of property qualification) made republicanism seem a less suitable model for the marital relationship. In any case, as we have seen, even in the *Eudemian Ethics*, this relationship was a funny kind of republic, since the 'better' rules all the time.

V 'Politics' 7

There is another sort of material in *Politics* 7 which seems connected with what we find in the *Eudemian Ethics*: the remarks about divine and human nature. At first sight this may appear surprising evidence to cite, because in *Politics* 7 there is only a limited identification of happiness with *energeia* (1328A38), though this is an important theme in the *Eudemian Ethics*. *Politics* 7. 3 attempts to determine whether the life of politics or the life of the free (presumably independent) man is to be preferred. According to Aristotle, both views have something to be said for them, though supporters of the second group would be wrong to praise inactivity. For happiness is action (*praxis*, 1325A32) – at this time, we note, Aristotle does not employ the term *energeia* of the *Eudemian Ethics*.[40] Yet we should not jump to conclusions too quickly. Although static excellence is not enough, and the power to act is required (1325B11ff) for happiness, yet the well-doing (*eupragia*) which is happiness is not simply to be identified with outward acts, as some people think. The thoughts which lead to outward acts are themselves acts. Activity does not require relations with others. Internal life is itself an act. Contemplation (*theōria*) is a kind of act. So we see from Aristotle's argument that although the word *energeia* is absent from the description of happiness, the notion of an activity which has no necessary outside effects is present – an idea not too different from the activity of immobility which we have noted in a crucial passage of *Eudemian Ethics* 6 (112–13 above). In fact the argument in favour of a similar date for this part of *Politics* 7 and *Eudemian Ethics* 6 is strengthened if *Politics* 7 reflects

Eudemian Ethics 6 and if *Eudemian Ethics* 6 introduces a new and exciting notion of *energeia*, or at least a radically fresh development in its history, as we have argued earlier.

Nor does the similarity between *Politics* 7 and the *Eudemian Ethics* stop there. I have argued earlier that traces of the idea of the World-Mind are still visible in the *Eudemian Ethics*. What else can be intended in this same chapter of *Politics* 7 when, turning to the 'activity' of God, Aristotle remarks that, if his account of happiness and action is wrong, there would similarly be something wrong with God and the whole cosmos, who have no externally directed activities as distinct from their own internal (*oikeias*) ones (1325B28–30)? Not only do these remarks look something like the end of *Eudemian Ethics* 6; they also look very like a remarkable section of *Eudemian Ethics* 7 (1245B16–19) where, perhaps claiming for the first time that God thinks himself, Aristotle says that whereas our well-being depends on another, God is his own well-being. Action, of course, is not mentioned here directly, but thinking is mentioned, and it is thinking which in *Politics* 7.3 Aristotle identifies as one of the special and most important variants of 'action'.[41] *Politics* 7.1 has already made a similar point (1323B23ff). God is happy and blessed not because of external goods but because of himself and of the kind of thing he is of his own nature. That is, God is happy because he is what he is, not because of what happens to him, accrues to him, or even is done by him *externally*.

It might be argued that *Politics* 7.3 contains at least one text (1325A28–31) which tells against my general thesis of the relation of *Politics* 1 to *Politics* 7, for when speaking of the different kinds of authority Aristotle remarks that rule over free men is as different from rule over slaves as natural freedom (*to phusei eleutheron*) is different from natural slavery. But despite available mistranslations of this phrase, the irritating thing is that Aristotle here does not speak of natural *slaves*, only of a naturally slavish condition.[42] So that in fact the passage does *not* tell against the thesis that the theory of the natural slave is still in the future when Aristotle wrote book 7. The following section (which states, 'But we have discussed these matters adequately in the first treatises ...') makes matters clear. For in book 3 (1279A31) Aristotle alludes to a discussion of forms of authority which he has already issued 'in the published works.' Thus the 'first treatises' of *Politics* 7 refer not to *Politics* 1 but to some earlier work. Slaves are referred to strikingly in the *Protrepticus*, but this seems unlikely to be the origin of a detailed account of authority. The *Statesman*, originally in two books but now fragmentary, is probably the common source.

VI Our 'Politics'

Our examination, cursory as it has been, of parts of books 1, 2, 3, 7, and 8 of the *Politics* is obviously incomplete, even from the point of view of the development of Aristotle's thought. Nevertheless, as a result of a fairly detailed inspection of the new material in *Politics* 1, a certain amount of support for Jaeger's hypothesis about that book being a later addition has been assembled. These books as a whole, including book 1, seem reasonably well connected with the *Eudemian* version of the *Ethics*, but a series of indicators of varying strengths also suggests that 2, 3, 7, and 8 go together, while book 1 represents a later, more developed 'biological' phase of Aristotle's thought, a phase which would allow more specific explanations of the nature of true slavery and of the relationship of husband to wife in an ideal household. Jaeger's thesis about the late date of book 1 thus looks stronger than he himself made it appear. We may therefore now turn to the question of the relation of book 1 to books 4–6, the books which Jaeger calls 'empirical'; that is, those books in which the ideal or utopian constitution has receded.

Jaeger himself draws attention to an extraordinary 'biological' passage in the middle of book 4 (1290B25ff),[43] which begins 'If we were going to speak of the kinds of animal ...' Aristotle then draws parallels between the composition of animals and the composition of states. If we want to sort animals out, we first need to identify the essential parts (mouth, stomach, etc.) – mostly those parts required for movement. We will then realize that different combinations of the various different organs will present different sorts of animals. Such a presentation might be achieved on the basis of what Aristotle himself had undertaken in his *De Partibus Animalium*. The section of *Politics* 4 which this passage introduces appears to be an insertion into the original text. As Barker noted,[44] the sentence beginning at 1290B21 is repeated at 1291B14, and the whole passage, largely devoted to further criticism of Plato's *Republic*, could be removed from the body of *Politics* 4 without anyone realizing that there was a gap.[45]

If we suggest that this biological section of book 4 was added at the time of the original composition of book 1, where does that leave the order of the *Politics* as a whole? Jaeger is right to observe the importance of the fact that books 2, 3, 7, and 8 lack references to 4–6, though the contrary is not the case. It follows that we should present a modified version of Jaeger's theory. The original *Politics* comprised books 2, 3, 7, and 8. Books 4–6 are an independent composition which was included in the original version, and the whole was then given a new introduction (book 1) and probably various minor changes. The biological section of book 4 was one of these changes. But Jaeger overstated the degree of confusion the new work would produce. Rowe points out, as we have seen, that the two topics of the *Politics* are the ideal constitution and how to secure stability in earthly states. Roughly speaking, the latter is the subject of books 4–6. But these two topics had already been connected by political theorists. Both are very much in Plato's mind when he wrote the *Republic*. So that although Aristotle's final text of the *Politics* has rough edges, there is no need to suppose that he is trying to amalgamate two projects different by nature, or likely to be regarded by him as such. Granted that the original version of 4–6 was composed separately, the notion of combining it with the original version of 2, 3, 7, and 8 would not have seemed problematic. On the contrary it would conform with a tradition.

What then is the timetable of the *Politics*? If books 2, 3, 7, and 8 reflect some of the ideas of the *Eudemian Ethics*, though without being formally tied to it, they were probably begun in Macedonia (and perhaps temporarily abandoned when Aristotle returned to Athens in 334). The original version of books 4–6 (also apparently unfinished) was probably later, dependent as it seems to be on the collection of constitutions inaugurated by Aristotle after 334. We do not know the dates of these works (or even how many were written), but the *Constitution of the Athenians*, the only one which survives, was probably composed in the late 330s and revised in the first half of the 320s.[46] Further evidence about the composition of the *Politics* is provided by its latest historical reference, the one to the murder of Philip in 336 BC. This is mentioned without any suggestion that it was a very recent event (*Pol.* 5.1311B2).

What, finally, of the text of the *Politics* as we have it and book 1? It is clear from the end of book 10 of the *Nicomachean Ethics* that Aristotle intended the revised *Politics* to form a sequel to the *Nicomachean Ethics*, but that he himself never completed his project. Theophrastus may have published the *Politics* after Aristotle's death.[47] Some of the intended sections of the *Nicomachean Ethics* itself are missing, and parts of the *Eudemian Ethics* have been confusingly introduced to do duty on their behalf. In other words, although Aristotle wrote the end of the *Nicomachean Ethics* (book 10), he had not finished the work; he did not start at the beginning and write to the end. That need cause no surprise; many books receive their early drafts in this way. Yet what Aristotle says about the forthcoming *Politics* in *Nicomachean Ethics* 10 is remarkable in one particular respect: he presents a more or less satisfactory outline of much of our *Politics* (10.1181B16ff): the contributions of earlier critics (2); the analysis of existing constitutions and societies (4–6) – on the basis of his collected constitutions; the ideal state (7–8). Book 3, which certainly belongs with 7 and 8, could be more or less explained under the rubric for 4–6. But book 1 seems not to be accounted for at all. The only conclusion to be drawn from this is that as late as the composition of *Nicomachean Ethics* 10, Aristotle did not envisage the genetic account of the state in *Politics* 1 (and in the biological section of 4). We cannot yet be certain when *Nicomachean Ethics* 10 was written, though it must be in the early twenties of the fourth century, and I shall argue that it probably slightly pre-dates the *De Anima*. It seems plausible to suppose therefore that the present text of our *Politics*, including the 'biological' book 1, is one of the latest products of Aristotle's life, more or less contemporary with the *De Generatione Animalium*. If Aristotle revised the *Constitution of the Athenians* in 328 and completed *Nicomachean Ethics* 10 soon after, he must then have continued, as he says, with *Politics* 4–6. Eventually, after completing the later biological works (including *De Anima*), he came back to complete the joint project of ethics and politics in his last days. Both parts were left unfinished. *Nicomachean Ethics* 10, as we have it, has not been revised even to take account of the newly written introduction to the *Politics*; other parts of the *Nicomachean Ethics* remained in his mind alone.

There is a final extraordinary feature of the *Politics* – given our explanation of its chronology – to which we must refer. It is not surprising that book 8 is unfinished if we think that the ethical-political project as a whole was left unfinished at Aristotle's death. But *Politics* 8 is part of the original version of the *Politics*, and it was, on our (and Jaeger's) chronology, left unfinished then too. The only answer – and it is obviously speculative – which I can propose is that *Politics* 8 was unfinished when Aristotle left Macedonia for Athens in 334. He tells us in *Politics* 8, as we have seen, that he will discuss *catharsis* in the *Poetics* – which he does when he gets to Athens. But, for whatever reason, he did not, at this stage, go back to *Politics* 8 itself. Although he wrote the *Poetics*, and tidied up the *Rhetoric*, his attentions, once he was back in Athens, soon turned elsewhere – to finishing the *Physics* and working on the *Metaphysics*. Perhaps, in the realm of politics, his project to collect and analyse the constitutions of Greek states took precedence over earlier programmes. Only when he had established this project and almost completed the associated books 4–6 did he turn back to the remaining parts of the original *Politics*. At the end of his life he began to construct the *Politics* as we have it, but although he then composed some new material and made a number of alterations, he did not live to finish the work, thus leaving the end of the *Politics* (and even the end of book 6) still incomplete.

There is a final fascinating piece of evidence in a passage of book 7 which may serve to strengthen the date we suggest for the 'original' *Politics*. When we noticed Aristotle comparing the political with the apolitical life (51 above), we might have observed his curious remark that the apolitical life is that of a stranger, a foreigner in the city. Could this passage tell us of Aristotle's own thoughts when considering whether to return, as an apolitical stranger, to Athens, a less than friendly city, yet still the city for philosophy (7.1324A16)?

VII The Development of Aristotle's Political Thought

What can we say in conclusion of the development of Aristotle's political thought? Aristotle began with a Platonic view of politics as the art of constructing Utopia – a view accompanied by a certain Platonic suspicion of rhetoric as political sophistry. His view of rhetoric seems to have matured before his view of politics, and perhaps contributed substantially to a widening of his political concerns to include issues of survival in imperfect societies as well as an interest in the mechanics of those societies themselves. For to Aristotle, when used by decent men, the skills of the rhetorician are not politically useless; though they cannot legislate the ideal, they can improve the defective if the orator will follow the good as he sees it and as it is pointed out to him by the serious political observer.

Thus, practical ethics and practical politics come together. Aristotle's original *Politics*, though doubtless written soon after the *Eudemian Ethics*, is not formally a continuation of that work. Nor is the *Eudemian Ethics* described as a political text or as part of the art of politics. The good man is only discussed in the *Eudemian Ethics* as an individual, and book 8 culminates in the right attitude to God. Admittedly these features are part of all-round virtue (which would involve political life), but in the *Eudemian Ethics* there is little sense of ethics as a discipline being subordinate to politics – despite one remark about the chief good being the subject of the most authoritative practical science (viz. that which is political, 'economic,' and involving practical judgement [EE 1.1218B13ff]). Furthermore, details about happiness and the virtues are still described in *Politics* 7 (1323B39) as belonging to another science, viz. ethics.

But by the time of *Politics* 1 and the *Nicomachean Ethics*, above all of *Nicomachean Ethics* 1, all this had changed. *Nicomachean Ethics* 1.2–4 presents ethics as part of politics (1095A3, A16), just as the end of book 10 looks forward to the *Politics* itself. The science of politics is now the master science (1094A27ff) to which strategy, domestic economy, and rhetoric are subordinate. The good for (most) men is in the end the political act (1094B7). The true politician has studied goodness and happiness; they are part of his 'art' (1102A8–13). The culmination of this trend is the late *Politics* 1, where the relation between ethics and politics is ultimately spelled out as a 'genetic' one. Many, many problems are to be solved by the 'biological' or 'genetic' model, not least those of the relation of ethics to politics. For if we understand the latest model, we shall not only understand the relation of ethics to politics, but also such mysteries as the relation of men and women, and free and slave (in the 'natural' sense of that word); and perhaps even trade and usury will become clearer.

9

Soul and *Nous* in Psychology and Ethics

I The 'Eudemus' and the 'Protrepticus'

In considering Aristotle's various attempts to unravel the secrets of the final cause, the purpose of things, or their function, we have paid little attention to perhaps the most interesting area in which such theories are supposed to operate. For by saying in the *De Anima* that in some sense the soul is the form of a body equipped with organs (2.412B5–6) and having the potentiality of life, Aristotle is saying in passing that the soul is the final cause of the body and as final cause that it is inseparable from that body itself. But he did not always hold such a view, nor is it the whole story even in the *De Anima* that the soul is the form of body. Aristotle's various attempts to solve the problem of the relationship between the soul, the body, and the human being, that is, his developing theory of human nature, can also be shown to have repercussions in the field of ethics. These repercussions are not at all surprising, since there is no doubt that throughout his life Aristotle, like Plato, believed that moral laws are identifiable (in so far as they are rational ideals and not merely arbitrary commands) through an evaluation of the physiological and psychological nature of human beings. Normative ethics, therefore, is a flexible discipline (unlike mathematics and 'first philosophy') because the findings of physiology and psychology are subject to development. Not that this means, of course, that Plato and Aristotle are not objectivists in ethics; they certainly are. Rather it means that our knowledge of the objective truths of morality is dependent on advances in these special human sciences.

Much has been written about the development of Aristotle's psychology since the fundamental study of Nuyens.[1] Now that the dust has settled, and Nuyens's thesis can be modified in the light of the criticisms expressed in particular by Block,[2] Hardie,[3] and Lefèvre,[4] we can see what seems to have been accepted and what rejected. Briefly Nuyens proposed that there are three stages in the development of Aristotle's psychology: a 'Platonic' phase in which Aristotle held a view similar to that offered in Plato's *Phaedo*, that the soul is a separate substance; this was followed by an 'instrumentalist' period, in which the soul, located in the heart, used the body as its instrument; finally, we have the third stage, the fully hylomorphic theory of the *De Anima*. As a result of the work of Block and Lefèvre we have now learned to dispense with the separate instrumentalist phase; instrumentalist language can be found together with hylomorphic language, does not contradict it, and, at least in Aristotle's opinion, is a necessary part of the same theory. So on current orthodoxy we are left with two phases, the near-Platonic and the mature Aristotelian. The only difficulty that is not largely resolved by this hypothesis, even in Lefèvre's heroic attempt, is the problem of *nous*. And this problem has considerable ramifications.

But let us first go back to the beginning. The *Eudemus* and the *Protrepticus* are products of the 350s. As far as we can tell, they represent a similar stage in Aristotle's thinking about ethics and psychology. Briefly, in the *Eudemus* Aristotle holds that the soul is a separate substance (fr. 8 Ross),[5] a form in its own right, not merely the form of a particular body. It is not a harmony or attunement of any sort (fr. 7). It existed before coming into the body and will presumably continue to exist after its separation from the body (fr. 5). It had knowledge in its previous existence, which it has forgotten (fr. 5), but when leaving this life it will remember its earthly experience. Thus the soul is not only a separate substance; it has, at least until its reincarnation into another body, some measure of personal identity after death. This claim cannot be dismissed because it appears in mere 'consolation literature'; there is no reason why Aristotle should not have developed his view of the soul in a 'consolation' for his friend Eudemus, killed at Syracuse in 354. Consolation literature, if not philosophically serious, would hardly contain attacks on the *logic* of the theory of the soul as some kind of harmony. Nor need we worry much about the date: Eudemus, unlike Socrates, was not a man whose death could reasonably be commemorated years after it occurred. Later Aristotelians, like Themistius (*Eud.*, fr. 2), found the theory of the *Eudemus* puzzling. Used to Aristotle's later view (in the *De Anima*) that only mind is immortal, they tried to explain away the evidence of the *Eudemus*. What Aristotle, and even what Plato, says about soul should really, in their opinion, be said of mind. No better evidence could be found for the fact that in the *Eudemus* Aristotle talked not only of the immortality of the mind, but of the whole substantial soul. Nor do we even know whether he took any account, in the *Eudemus*, of Plato's development from the simple substance theory of the *Phaedo* to the tripartite soul of the *Republic*. But no matter: the soul in the *Eudemus* is basically simple (whatever it may be when in the body) and to a degree achieves personal immortality. As Plato puts it in the *Phaedo*: therefore our souls exist in Hades (71E2). So Aristotle, according to Elias, proclaims the immortality of the soul particularly in his dialogues (fr. 3). When the soul of Eudemus leaves his body, it returns to its true home (fr. 1).

Coupled with the soul-body dualism of the *Eudemus*, naturally, goes an ascetic variety of ethics. In the myth of Midas and Silenus we read that not to enter the world of becoming, of change, would have been the best lot for men and women (fr. 6), but if we are born into this wretched world of change, it would be best to die as soon as possible. Even the reference to men *and women* (*pasi kai pasais*) is Platonic; presumably a Platonic female guardian is good enough for escape from the cycle of births and deaths to be a genuine option. At least she can be a man next time. This is hardly in line with Aristotle's own 'mature' analysis of the view of women as defective males.

The *Protrepticus* is similar in many ways, but fills in important gaps in our knowledge which the fragments of the *Eudemus* leave unclear. In the repulsive story of the Etruscan pirates (B107 Düring), who chain their living captives face to face with corpses, we find Aristotle's disgust with a crudely hedonistic view of earthly life taking the strongest recorded form. The unwholesome torture of the binding of the living to the dead is an apt description, he suggests, of the relation of the human soul and its body. No wonder Iamblichus reported the story. Perhaps it seems too appropriate to the early centuries AD to be appropriate to the fourth century BC; but such suspicions are mere prejudice. The story itself, though admittedly without reference to Aristotle by name, certainly pre-dates Iamblichus: Clement of Alexandria is familiar with it a hundred years earlier, and Augustine, whose source is almost certainly *not* Iamblichus, connects the story with Aristotle by name, deriving his version, it seems, from Cicero's *Hortensius*. Cicero, we can be sure, had read the *Protrepticus*, on which his own *Hortensius* was explicitly based.

A dualism of soul and body is obvious in the *Protrepticus*; and from it is drawn the inevitable deduction of the superiority of the life of the soul to the life of the body – the theory of the *Eudemus*, it seems, in a more colourful form, though the *Eudemus* itself is colourful enough at times. But the *Protrepticus* apparently made a fateful change.[6] Plato had already tended to suggest the immortality of mind rather than of soul, and he was to do so again in the *Timaeus*. Apparently the same problem, whether it is mind or soul which is immortal, loomed for the author of the *Protrepticus*. Augustine tells us that at the end of the *Hortensius*, itself based on the

Protrepticus (C110: 1 Düring), Cicero praised *sapientia contemplativa*, in Greek presumably *theōria*; and certainly he spoke of our *aeternos animos ac divinos*. What is the *animus*? Mind or soul? There is prima facie reason from elsewhere in the *Protrepticus* to suggest that it is *mind*. For Iamblichus's text says that there is nothing divine and blessed in men except this alone, whatever we have within us of mind (*nous*) and intelligence (*phronēsis*). But this does not mean that mind has replaced soul as our immortal part in the *Protrepticus*; that is most unlikely, since Aristotle still holds at this time that, though mind is the most important part of man, indeed, as the *Nicomachean Ethics* will *also* put it, though we are *either* entirely *or* mostly that part (B62 Düring), yet mind is still 'immanent' in soul (B85). What Aristotle emphasizes rather in the *Protrepticus* is that the *pleasures* of the mind are superior to the pleasures of the body, and presumably also to all other pleasures of the soul (which are more 'bodily').

Mind is beginning to have a life of its own, and, as we shall see, the *Protrepticus* was re-used by Aristotle in discussing the pleasures of mind in *Nicomachean Ethics* 10. For in the *Protrepticus*, as Düring shows,[7] Aristotle is greatly influenced by Eudoxus's 'intellectual hedonism.' He does not think the good is pleasure; he does say at length that the pleasures of the intellect are immensely satisfying. 'Perfect and unimpeded activity has delight in it.' The activity of contemplating is the most pleasant of all (B87). When a man drinks, he both enjoys a pleasure and drinks with enjoyment: 'What are you doing'? 'Enjoying myself.' 'What you doing?' 'Drinking joyfully.' In fact we can see here in the same passage (B88) the origin of both the theory that pleasure is an activity of *Eudemian Ethics* 6 and the theory that pleasure accompanies activity of *Nicomachean Ethics* 10. For all movement (here equalling activity) can be pleasurable or painful. And there is a pleasure from life itself, if a man is wide awake and thinking (B90). For the pleasure of life is the pleasure of exercising the soul; that is real living.

There are several uses of the soul, but the most important is that of thinking as much as possible. It is a real incitement to philosophy that it is pleasurable (B92). Hence 'happiness' is either wisdom or some kind of wisdom *or* moral virtue, *or* the real pleasure, *or* all of them together. Here in fact we are very near the position of the *Eudemian Ethics* on pleasure. And whatever happiness is, whether one of these or all together, philosophers will have it. Philosophy is itself either the perfectly good life or primarily the cause of it for souls (B96). Philosophy is the good life rather than merely life, and we should make every effort to attain it. Most men are satisfied merely to live, but one should not go on living whatever the circumstances (B103). If a man's mind were destroyed, it would not be worth living (B99). Without reason man is a brute (B28).

It is clear that this view represents a Eudoxan 'asceticism': bodily pleasures are contemptible. Thinking is an activity: the proper and therefore most pleasurable use of the soul. The parallels with *Eudemian Ethics* 6, as well as with *Nicomachean Ethics* 10, are strong, though the concept of activity is little used (but note B87 where Aristotle speaks of perfect and unimpeded activity having pleasure in itself); rather he speaks of the use of the soul, for mind is still in the soul. Ultimately therefore the mind cannot have goods *separate* from goods of the soul.

Although Aristotle is tempted to sacrifice all for contemplation of the universe, his ideal in the *Protrepticus* is an 'inclusive' end, with philosophy being the most important element in the good life for those who can get it. However, the word *kalokagathia* (nobility), which describes this inclusive end in the *Eudemian Ethics*, is not found in our fragments of the *Protrepticus*, and we should also observe that the word 'blessed', which Aristotle particularly favours as descriptive of godlike happiness in the *Nicomachean Ethics*, is found in the early *Protrepticus* (B106, 108). Nevertheless, so long as mind is in soul, the only basic and unresolvable conflict can be between the life of the soul and that of the body – and that conflict, as we have seen, is as fierce in the *Protrepticus* as it is in the *Eudemus*. There is no separate mind in the *Protrepticus*; hence the conflict can be viewed as being not within the soul, but in the more primitive manner of Plato's *Phaedo*. It is important to realize that Aristotle's moral psychology at this time depends basically on the earlier Plato, and that, like Aristotelian physical thinking, it is untouched by the more sophisticated interrelations of soul and body that can be found in the *Timaeus*. For the *Timaeus* had not yet been written.

Nuyens thought that he could reinforce his account of the soul in the *Eudemus* and *Protrepticus* – which is largely endorsed here – by finding similar doctrines in other fairly early works of Aristotle, such as the *Topics* and the *Categories*; but these attempts are of little or no value. Even in the sixth book of the *Topics* (6.151B2) Aristotle speaks of the soul as a substance (*ousia*) receptive of knowledge;[8] but there is nothing in the passage to suggest that this is Aristotle's own view, rather than a view common at the time of the composition of the *Topics*. That it was a view held by some is beyond doubt; whether it was held by Aristotle himself is precisely what we want to know – and this sort of passage does not tell us. Use of evidence from the very early *Categories* is of slightly more help, but not much.[9] Aristotle speaks of sickness and health as existing in the body of a living being, whiteness and blackness in the body *simpliciter*, justice and injustice in a man's soul. And he seems to reject this way of speaking in the *De Anima* (1.408B11–15). But such material cannot tell us whether already in the

Categories Aristotle had rejected the idea that the soul is a separate substance. It could arguably be read in precisely the opposite sense, for if soul and body are not separate, where are sickness and health supposed to reside, in Aristotle's account? In both? He certainly does not say that; there is no reason to think that he means it.

II The 'Eudemian' and the 'Nicomachean Ethics'

The much debated question of the development of Aristotle's ethical writings now seems somewhat nearer to resolution, though many substantive points still remain unsettled. Kenny has proved beyond reasonable doubt that the so-called disputed books, those that have come down to us in the manuscript tradition both of the *Eudemian Ethics* (4–6) and of the *Nicomachean Ethics* (5–7), were originally composed as part of the *Eudemian Ethics*.[10] Kenny has also summed up much of the debate about the third ethical treatise, the so-called *Magna Moralia*. It is now clear that this work must have been written *after* about 335 BC,[11] that it depends primarily on the *Eudemian Ethics*, but that its author is also acquainted at least with parts of the *Nicomachean Ethics*.[12] Kenny's further claim, however – which he advances more modestly – that the *Nicomachean Ethics* is an earlier work than the *Eudemian Ethics*, is far from universally accepted; some of the considerations I advance in this and other chapters tell against that part of Kenny's proposal (see also 182–6, etc.). If it can be shown that the *Eudemian Ethics* advances an earlier version of Aristotle's theory of soul and mind, then all Kenny's other arguments can be met by the explanation we have already advanced, namely that the *Eudemian Ethics* is a product of the middle period of Aristotle's career, but that the *Nicomachean Ethics* is even later, perhaps not being 'published' until after Aristotle's death.[13] We should have evidence in favour of such a solution if it became clear that the *Nicomachean Ethics* reflects the thinking in some of Aristotle's very latest books, namely the *De Anima* and the *De Generatione Animalium*. If that could be shown, however – and we have already observed 'political' theories in favour of such a view – a substantial problem would still remain if we had to explain the genesis of radically different accounts of happiness which Kenny and others detect in the *Eudemian* and the *Nicomachean Ethics*. But it can also be shown that these differences are greatly exaggerated, and when the exaggeration is removed, the problem appears in a different light. At that point some post-Aristotelian evidence from Theophrastus, the *Magna Moralia*, and Dicaearchus of Messene, a pupil of Theophrastus, can be used to supplement the view to be taken here of Aristotle's latest developments in psychological theory.

There is no need to undertake a full-scale comparison of the *Eudemian Ethics* and the *Nicomachean Ethics*. I propose to discuss in detail a few sections only, those dealing with the nature of the function of soul (*EE* 2.1219A26–38) and of man (*NE* 1.1097B22ff), and those dealing with the nature of the happy life in the final book of each ethical treatise. First of all, then, let us turn the much-controverted section about function.

Of the two Aristotelian discussions, that in the *Eudemian Ethics* seems the more straightforward; it has certainly caused less disagreement among scholars. Aristotle's definition of happiness is as follows: it is an activity of complete life in accordance with complete virtue. The definition is offered at the end of a discussion of the function of the *soul*, and the soul is said to have as its function the achievement of the good (*spoudaia*) life. Despite the word *spoudaia* we have no reason to deny that happiness is thus again, as in the *Protrepticus*, what has been dubbed an 'inclusive' end,[14] a summation, as it were, of all the virtues in the soul, but in which contemplation (as Anaxagoras may have thought) is the most important and 'blessed' (1.1215B14, 1216A11). This is indeed borne out by Aristotle's discussion in the final book of the *Eudemian Ethics*, where the happy man is the *kalos kagathos*, the man of all round excellence, to whom we shall turn in a moment. It is characteristic of the earlier date of the *Eudemian Ethics* that *kalos* and *agathos* are united in the claim that nobility is the highest end for man; in the *Metaphysics* they are more carefully distinguished (71 above). But the *Eudemian Ethics* excludes more violent passages which contrast pleasures of soul and body, though still advocating that one should be as unconscious as possible of the irrational part of the soul (8.1249B23).

The word *nous* in Aristotle can be used in at least two importantly distinct ways: to refer to specific mental operations that men are capable of performing, such as grasping first principles, as in the *Eudemian Ethics* (5.1139A), or more generally recognizing universals as in the last chapter of the *Posterior Analytics*; or to refer to some essentially separate cause of such operations like the so-called Productive Intellect of *De Anima* 3.5. Interestingly enough book 8 of the *Eudemian Ethics* contains an important precursor of *De Anima* 3.5 – at least if we avoid unnecessary emendations to the text. At 1248A26ff Aristotle raises the question of the origin of movement in the soul. He continues with a comparison of the soul and the universe. 'Just as in the universe God moves all [I follow Jackson's probable but not *necessary* emendation of *ekeinōi* to *ekei kinei*], so somehow the divine in us moves everything [sc. in our souls]. And the origin of reasoning is not reasoning but something superior. What would one say is superior to scientific knowledge except God?'[15]

Here then we have a parallel between the soul and the universe, exactly as in the opening to *De Anima* 3.5. As God moves the universe, as an efficient cause, and, I have argued, as a World-Mind,[16] so 'the divine in us,' that is, the mind, moves everything 'in the soul'. This 'divine in us' is clearly the most important, though not the only 'part' of our soul. In fact Aristotle has nothing further to say in the *Eudemian Ethics* about the relation of this 'part' to our soul in general, and when he proceeds to talk about the best life for man, he assumes that it is integrated with our whole soul. There is no hint, as yet, of the '*nous* from outside' and its special ethical implications which we shall shortly consider. Indeed if the analogue of the 'divine within us' is a World-Mind, as our present text seems to suggest, then the ethical difficulties of Aristotle's later years have not yet appeared. The 'divine in us' of the *Eudemian Ethics*, as of the *Protrepticus*, may be the ancestor of the Productive Intellect of the *De Anima*, but it is not yet identified as ultimately and intrinsically transcendent over man. Hence the account of human virtue in the *Eudemian Ethics* can be worked out without reference to that transcendence. That is why there is not a shadow of doubt that the goal of human life in the *Eudemian Ethics* is an 'inclusive' end.

The ideal life, according to the *Eudemian Ethics*, is the life of *kalokagathia*, which we translate as 'nobility'. It is a combination of the various virtues of the soul (8.1248B8ff), all of which are to be given their due weight. It is not only complete virtue (*aretē teleios*, 8.1249A17), but also the most pleasurable, for, says Aristotle, with a clear reference to the doctrine of pleasure in *Eudemian Ethics* 6, we have shown in what sense pleasure is good.

It has sometimes been argued, for example by Dirlmeier,[17] that the pattern of psychological theory we have ascribed to Aristotle in the *Eudemian Ethics* is out of keeping with the clear sense of the last chapter of the book. Here, according to Dirlmeier, our 'theoretical' faculty is specifically labelled a god (1249B14) that must be served (1249B21). The view is untenable: Aristotle, though willing to refer to *nous* as 'the divine in us' only calls it 'god' (1248A29) by analogy with the World-Mind. The word 'god' in chapter 8 (1249B18) refers to a supra-human divinity deserving of our contemplation.[18]

We have then, in *Eudemian Ethics* 8, a 'theoretical part' of the soul which serves and contemplates God. This concern dominates the 'mix' which is the good life for man; it provides the limit or standard (*horos*) of nobility (1249B24). When we pursue 'natural goods' (health, wealth, friendship, etc.) we do so to the extent that such possessions will not impede, but rather will promote, that service of God. Clearly such service and contemplation is the most important part of the life of nobility; where possible it should be pursued, but the life of nobility is to be controlled, as in the *Protrepticus*, but not dominated, by this consideration. From the beginning of the *Eudemian Ethics* an 'inclusive' notion of virtue has been the goal. *Eudemian Ethics* 8 begins to spell out the relevant importance of the various elements in the mix, but the best element is still *in* the mix, for *nous* is still in the soul. Aristotle in the *Eudemian Ethics* never even considers that the life of *nous* will conflict with the life of the soul; indeed it could not do so while *nous* is a part of the soul, for if moral virtue were neglected in favour of the virtue of contemplation, the soul as a whole, not to speak of the body, would be adversely affected. It is inconceivable that Aristotle could have argued in the *Eudemian Ethics* that the service of God (not merely contemplation) would be advanced by a sage so wrapped up in thought that he could not make the effort to pull a drowning man out of a river, or to safeguard his own health.

But though Aristotle is safe from the danger of this kind of charge in the *Eudemian Ethics*, mines lie beneath the calm surface of the work. As we have seen, in chapter 2 of book 8 (1248A27), Aristotle indicates that there is 'something divine in us' and this something divine causes the 'motions' in our souls. Here we have an 'immortal and separable' *nous* in embryo. The role of that *nous* in *Eudemian Ethics* 8, presumably as 'part' of the soul, is to cause motions of some sort, somehow: Aristotle himself vaguely says 'somehow'. But if it is divine, what does it do when movements of the soul, presumably, are over, that is, after death? Or does 'divine' merely have the weak sense of 'better'? In a Greek context that is highly unlikely. And in the *Eudemus* the soul, including mind, survives.

The relationship between this 'something divine' and even the theoretical part of the soul is left uncertain and unprobed in the *Eudemian Ethics*. Aristotle is less tempted to develop the implications for psychology of mind (or some mind) as 'divine' or as a god, because he had no metaphysical reason to pursue the notion of a *transcendent* God as mind at the time when he composed the *Eudemian Ethics*. The problem will become much more severe when he develops that thesis in the *Metaphysics*.

III The Nature of the Prime Mover in 'Metaphysics' Λ

As is well known, Aristotle's 'mature' theory of soul, spelled out in the greatest detail in the *De Anima*, is that a soul is the form of a natural body possessed of organs and having the capacity for life. I shall argue in a later chapter that the *De Anima* itself was composed during Aristotle's last Athenian period, but it is the primary merit of the work of Lefèvre to have shown that some version of the theory underlies all Aristotle's writings except that early group,[19] such as the *Eudemus* and the *Protrepticus*, which we have already considered. According to the new theory all the activities of the soul have, as it were, a bodily aspect, just as anger can be described as blood boiling round the heart. But if all soul's activities have a bodily aspect, or can be described in physical as well as psychological terms, what about those activities which are non-bodily? Aristotle does not deny that there are non-bodily activities; nor, of course, does he wish to reduce psychosomatic activities to merely bodily ones.[20] Non-bodily activities would be those which occur without the use of organs (limbs, sense-organs) or of the mysterious *pneuma* which he employs in some of his latest works as a conveyer of the instructions of the soul. But Aristotle's mature position is that non-bodily activities in this sense cannot be viewed as activities of the *soul* either. For the notion that the soul is the form of the body must be taken seriously. What activities, then, which are not activities of the body as the material of the soul, or of the soul as the form of the body, does Aristotle identify? Clearly there are two such activities at least: the activity of the Prime Mover in the *Metaphysics* and that of *nous* or of some aspect or part of *nous* in the *De Anima* and *De Generatione Animalium* – unless these two cases can be reduced to one.

First, the Prime Mover. The notion of the Prime Mover exists, as we have seen, in some (late) sections of the early books of the *Physics* and the *De Caelo*, and in more detail and more coherent structure in book 8 of the *Physics*. From these works we can see how the doctrine developed. The Prime Mover is introduced to solve problems about the origin of motion. But we should note that neither in the *De Caelo* nor in the *Physics* is there any discussion of the nature of the activity of the Prime Mover itself, and indeed in one version of the theory Aristotle gave the Prime Mover a spatial location, at the edge of the cosmos (*Phys.* 8.267B8–9). In the *Metaphysics*, however, the Prime Mover is indubitably and totally immaterial and non-spatial. He 'moves' as a final cause, that is, as the object of desire. Furthermore, Aristotle makes his notoriously unpersuasive attempt not merely to identify him as First Cause, but to describe his nature and activity. He is, as the *Eudemian Ethics* might have led us to expect, to be identified with mind, in part presumably because Aristotle is unable to find any other kind of activity which he is satisfied to call immaterial. As for the nature of his thought, as it is worked out in chapters 7 and 9 of *Metaphysics* Λ, it is argued that he 'thinks himself,' for it would be unworthy if he thought anything less than himself (and clearly there is nothing 'more' than himself to think). This self-thinking is restricted even more than many commentators incline to admit. The possibility is raised of whether the object of his thought is 'composite' (*suntheton*). That, declares Aristotle, is impossible, for that which has no matter must be indivisible. Thus even a (possibly 'Platonic') notion that God's thought could be of his Ideas is impossible. It is nothing more than absolute and unvarying self-awareness.

Perhaps it might be argued that thinking of this sort is so unlike normal thinking that at earlier stages of his career Aristotle hesitated about explaining God's Mind in this way. Now in *Metaphysics* Λ.1075A6ff, with God clearly transcendent, he faces the problem squarely. God's thought is like the thought of human minds (or at least that of composites) in that *while* the human mind thinks X it does not think not-X. God's mind, thinking X all the time and not limited by space, therefore never thinks not-X. God's mind is envisaged as like our mind at the moment of our mind's being intent on each particular thought. Be we, unlike God, must change; and we, unlike God, find our intelligible forms in sensible forms when we start to think (*De An.* 3.432A3–14). Why this is so will become clear at a later stage. For the time being we may merely note that God's thinking is life, unchanging, but also most pleasant (1072B); God's way of life (*diagōgē*) is of a kind which *we* can enjoy briefly. (Does this mean that 'we', in a sense, *are* God?) Such, then, is the life of God: not of God as soul, for souls are matter-bound, but of God as *nous*.

Difficulties about understanding the development of Aristotle's theories of the nature of mind are increased by certain current notions about the date of *Metaphysics* Λ. Jaeger held that it is an early treatise incorporated in the largely later text of the *Metaphysics*: substantially earlier, for example, than Z, H, Θ. (*Aristotle* 219–21). According to Jaeger it is a text in which Aristotle has not yet recognized that sensible substances can be discussed within the confines of 'first philosophy.' More recent studies, particularly that of Patzig,[21] have done much to diminish the force of this argument, and I shall return to it later. A more sophisticated account of substance than that offered by Jaeger enables us to see that *Metaphysics* Λ and Z, H are much less far apart than Jaeger supposed. If immaterial substance is substance par excellence, that need not prevent us admitting sensible substances within the domain of first philosophy. In *Metaphysics* Λ itself (1069B2) Aristotle suggests that there is a common subject of study, a common principle, for both physical and non-physical substances.

Quite apart from questions of the nature of first philosophy, there are other indications within *Metaphysics* Λ which conflict with the notion that this book is an isolated and rather early treatise. First, there is little attention paid in Λ to what Aristotle often seems to consider the prime metaphysical concern of the Academy, and of himself as a former member of the Academy: the relationship between Forms, numbers, and mathematicals. Such questions are not absent from *Metaphysics* Λ, but they are little emphasized – in my view because they have already been dealt with in M and N. The same sort of point arises with the Good. In chapter 10 of *Metaphysics* Λ, after discussing the nature of God as Mind, Aristotle turns to the problem of how 'nature' contains the 'good' or the 'supreme good'. Jaeger wrongly regarded this as a purely Platonic problem, for Plato had identified the source of being and the source of goodness in his Form of the Good. And so Aristotle too, in his earlier days, might have thought of it; but not here in chapter 10. Speusippus is more in his mind than Plato. Plato's views are alluded to, but there is no direct discussion of the Form of the Good. Discussions about Plato, Speusippus, and the Academy generally are jumbled together with comment on Empedocles, Anaxagoras, and the Eleatics; the book closes with an attack not on Plato, but on Speusippus.

None of my discussion so far even raises the problem of *Metaphysics* Λ, chapter 8. It has often been observed that this section, with its introduction of fifty-four or fifty-five unmoved movers, each endowed apparently with a 'material' element in virtue of their very plurality, hardly fits comfortably into its present place between chapters 7 and 9. But from our immediate point of view that is of no great importance. All we need to argue is that *Metaphysics* Λ, not merely chapter 8, is a fairly late Aristotelian text, later than the discussion of mind in the latter sections of the *Eudemian Ethics*. Nothing in such a thesis would *prevent* chapter 8 being later than the rest of the book and indeed being an insertion. In fact, the abruptness of the insertion and the lack of any attempt to fit chapter 8 with what precedes it and follows it *might* suggest either that Aristotle died before he could sort out the apparent philosophical difficulties the chapter raises for the thesis of the rest of the book, or even that it is a separate essay from elsewhere in the *Metaphysics*, wrongly inserted by an editor into the text of Λ. Of course Aristotle had been aware that there might be a problem about the number of unmoved movers as early as the eighth book of the *Physics* (258B10), but he let it go unresolved both there and in most of *Metaphysics* Λ while developing his theory of the Prime Mover. Why Aristotle (or his editor) inserted it where he did in the middle of a discussion of the character of the Prime Mover and its identification as Mind, we have, as yet, no means of knowing. We should note, however, that the appearance of a plurality of movers is not a total novelty in chapter 8; we are prepared for the possibility in chapter 6 (1071B21).

Aristotle opens chapter 9 of *Metaphysics* Λ by observing that the identification of God as Mind involves further difficulties. Although it seems to be true that Mind is the most divine of all phenomena, it is hard to understand its nature. The problem proposed indicates a considerable advance on the position of the last book of the *Eudemian Ethics* – and there are implicit difficulties also for ethics. If our mind is really *like* God's mind in the important respect of its eternity, the psychosomatic theory of man is threatened by a return of dualism, not now of soul and body (as in the *Eudemus* and *Protrepticus*), but of mind and individual (if we may so name the psychosomatic compound). Can the 'good' of mind and the 'good' of 'person' be reconciled in the way that the *Eudemian Ethics* had been able to assume?

Put the question in another form. Thinking, as the example of God shows, can be carried on by at least one non-psychosomatic being, a separable *mind*, a separable *form*, but not, of course, a separable *soul*.[22] *Metaphysics* Λ already suggests this thinking is like our thinking in the sense that we can live briefly the kind of thought-life which God leads all the time (1072B25). And chapter 9 leaves it in no doubt that Aristotle is prepared to maintain the claim that the Divine Mind is significantly similar to the human mind (1075A6ff). Though the similarity is curiously imprecise, its ethical implications cannot be shirked for long. For some sort of thinking at least can be carried on outside the framework of ensouled material structures. It is time to turn from the *Metaphysics* to the *De Anima* and the *De Generatione Animalium*.

IV The Productive Intellect and Its Work

I shall attempt in this section a resolution in outline of the problem of the so-called productive intellect in the fifth chapter of the third book of the *De Anima*. As we have seen, that chapter is foreshadowed in the *Eudemian Ethics*. What I am primarily concerned with is confirming what is generally accepted, namely that in the latest stage of his psychological theory Aristotle believed that some sort of mind is present in human beings but is outside the soul-body structure which is identified as a man in the biological writings, and in the *De Anima* in particular. Turning first then to the *De Generatione Animalium*, we are left in no doubt that *nous* is different from the other 'faculties' a man may have in that its reappearance in one generation after another is not susceptible of the same explanation as the transmission of the other faculties. Aristotle's general account of human reproduction in the *De Generatione Animalium* is clear enough, and well known to scholars. When a woman becomes pregnant, it is because the seed supplied by the male 'sets' (2.737A12–16, 2.739A7) the menstrual blood supplied by the woman herself.[23] In this way the faculties of nutrition and reproduction, and of sensation, are passed on to a new generation. But *nous*, somehow, is different. Its situation is, in fact, what our brief discussion of *Metaphysics* Λ would have led us to expect. Mind alone comes up and into us additionally (*epeisienai*: *epi* and *eis*, not merely *eis* or *en*) from outside and alone is divine.[24] With its 'proper' activity the body has no relationship (2.736B27–9).[25] The difficulty with this claim, of course, is that although it is clear that mind does not originate with the physical mingling of generative substances from the parents, we are given nothing specific on how this essential feature of human beings comes into relationship with the growing embryo.[26] One thing at least is certain: since *nous* is immaterial, it is not supplied by the female, for although females possess something of the 'soul-bearing' *pneuma* which human beings need and which is itself connected in some way, in the *De Generatione Animalium* (2.736B30ff), with the element composing the stars, female matter is only capable of attaining the life of a plant (2.736B11ff, 2.737A29) without male assistance; and in any case *pneuma* is material, whereas *nous* is not. Nor, however, is *nous* simply part of the *form* provided by the seed, for the function of that seed is to inform the matter, that is, to constitute the soul-body phenomenon which is a human being in all respects *barring* the most important, namely the ability to think. There is, in fact, nothing to be found in the *De Generatione Animalium* about how precisely the phrase 'comes up and into us from outside' is to be interpreted.[27]

Scholars have often supposed that *nous* is somehow imported by the male,[28] but Aristotle does not say that. Rather we should recall the natural slaves (or manimals) of *Politics* 1. Biologically they are humans, but they cannot think properly. I would suggest that this is because the 'productive intellect' (that is, the *nous* from outside) cannot reach them properly; it is somehow blocked off (see n. 36 below). Although they are produced by human parents, they cannot receive the light from outside. Thus the *nous* from outside – which, according to the *De Generatione Animalium*, is the key to our ability to think – should be viewed as not supplied by *either* parent, even the male. The male's function is to prepare the ground for the reception of the productive intellect, but – for whatever reason – he may be unsuccessful. Then a defective human will be born.

As for the *De Anima* itself, to which we must return, we need only a fairly brief discussion of the relationship between the 'intellective soul' (3.429A28–9) and the 'potential *nous*' (or for that matter the so-called productive *nous* which is formally introduced in 3.5). Nevertheless, a few observations on the latter are in order: first, that Aristotle does not use the phrase 'passive' intellect (*nous pathētikos*) in his initial explanation of the generation of thoughts in 3.5; second, that Theophrastus uses it without making it entirely clear what it means;[29] third, that both of them refer to the *potential* intellect (*nous en dunamei*). Aristotle only allows himself to speak of a *passive* intellect at the end of the chapter when he has finished with the *mechanics* of thinking.

In a way there is no such thing as a potential *house*; a house either exists or it does not exist. What is casually called a 'potential house' is actually bricks and mortar. Note, of course, that to say bricks and mortar are a potential house is not the same as saying a boy is a potential man, because in the latter case a further efficient cause is not needed. If then we apply the house analogy to the problem of *De Anima* 3.5, where beyond the 'potential intellect' a further 'efficient' cause *is* also needed, we have to say that, prior to thinking, the so-called *nous en dunamei* is something else. What is it? The answer, for Aristotle, can be either the *phantasmata* (the after-images of sensation which are the necessary materials of thinking),[30] or, if we put it in a slightly different way, the 'intellectual *soul*' in which these images are housed. The advantage of this reading is that it makes sense of the passage. An implication of it is that strictly speaking *nous* can have only *two* meanings in the *De Anima*: it means either the thinking which we engage in when we are actually thinking (and not before) – Aristotle sometimes calls it the *dianoia*, or 'mediated mind'; or it means the so-called productive intellect. It does not mean the *passive* intellect, for there is no time when the *passive intellect* actually exists as an intellect. What is erroneously referred to by the commentators as a 'substantive' passive intellect is in fact, as we have said, either the *phantasmata* or the 'intellective soul'[31] (which is part of *soul*) where they are stored. Had Aristotle avoided the misleading phrase 'passive intellect' in the last sentence of the chapter, and stuck to 'potential *nous*' with which he began, his meaning would probably have been clearer. As it is, if we explain the chapter as I have suggested, many of the traditional difficulties disappear. The original players in the game of thinking are the 'images' stored in the soul and the 'productive' intellect. These images are not yet thoughts, just as the colours are not yet colours until the light shines on them, for potential colours are not some sort of colour. Almost literally, as Aristotle says, the images are the material on which the craftsman exercises his art: from images he builds thoughts.

As Lloyd has pointed out, the Greek which the 'tradition' has usually translated 'active intellect' is much better translated as 'productive intellect'.[32] This rendering helps to explain better than the traditional version what the *nous poiētikos* does: it produces things; it makes things (that is, thoughts) from the images. Yet the comparison with light suggests that its action, its being an 'efficient cause', is in a sense the result not of *doing*, but of *being* as a state (*hexis*). By being *available* to men, by being there (by coming up and into us, as the *De Generatione Animalium* has it), its effect is what we call thinking.[33] We are like a room into which the light shines, so that the productive intellect comes to be 'in our souls' and enables us to think. But, as we have noticed, if the light is blocked out, we may not be able to think. Illness (and age) can produce that effect.

The explanation of *De Anima* 3.5 which is proposed here is consistent with other Aristotelian texts. We have already read in book 1 of the *De Anima*

(408B18ff) that we have a 'mind' which seems to be independent of the soul-body complex; that mind is 'unaffected' (*apathēs*) in its nature by the vicissitudes of human life; that it is 'more divine' than the soul-body unit, the *koinon*. So it is mind as a whole which is immortal – exactly the same doctrine as we have found in the *De Generatione Animalium* in relation to the 'mind from outside'. On our reading of the *De Anima* 3.5, exactly the same doctrine is found there too; there is no conflict with *De Anima* 1 or with the *De Generatione Animalium*. The 'productive intellect' of 3.5 is identical with the *nous* of *De Anima* 1 and of the *De Generatione Animalium*. All *nous* that comes to man is productive *nous*. It is false to say that Aristotle has a new theory in 3.5, by which he divides mind into two elements, a productive *intellect* and a passive *intellect*. Rather he *describes nous* as productive, and tells us that its effects are human thinking and its products are thoughts – and that its material, the potential of thinking, is images. If only he had avoided the quite unnecessary phrase *nous pathētikos*!

The productive intellect of 3.5 is separable, immortal, eternal, and without individual memories – 'We do not remember,' says Aristotle, probably referring in a curious and distorted echo of the *Eudemus* (fr. 5 Ross) to the life of the productive intellect before (as well as after) it comes to our individual body. Be that as it may, Aristotle certainly urges, both in the *De Generatione Animalium* and in the *De Anima*, that during our mortal life we have an immortal and impersonal element. Interpreters of Aristotle have long debated whether a single impersonal mind joins with each of us mortals to enable us to think – such a single mind being probably indistinguishable from the Prime Mover – or whether our productive intellects are an indistinguishable plurality (like some of the gods of Epicurus),[34] one to each mortal. I once argued, more or less agreeing with Themistius, that the latter view is the more likely,[35] on the grounds that a single individual efficient cause is needed to produce a specific effect, namely thinking, in each different human being; thus just as Peleus, not Man, is the father of Achilles, so an individual productive intellect, not Productive Intellect in general, is the cause of our thinking. There is still some weight to be attached to this argument, but it is not compelling. It depends, with its analogue to Man and Peleus, on supposing that a single productive intellect would have to be a sort of universal; but this is not the case. Since the single productive intellect is wholly immaterial, it could be present anywhere. It would resemble a Platonic substantial Form or Aristotle's Prime Unmoved Mover rather than an Aristotelian *post rem* (or even *in re*) universal.

This claim may seem hard to swallow, but there appears to be a very strong argument against the *alternative* explanation (that there is a different productive intellect for each body-soul compound) to be drawn from Aristotle's biology. If each productive intellect is different, then it is hard to avoid the conclusion that when a new human is conceived, somehow a new productive intellect comes into existence – unless we are to offer the equally unpalatable alternative that an infinite number of productive intellects are waiting around to join each new human being at the appropriate moment. This seems impossible; impossible too is the alternative that the productive intellect in each of us is generated in any way by our parents: that Aristotle virtually explicitly denies. So at least Aristotle *should* have said that a single productive intellect is common to humanity. And despite the Platonic flavour of this proposal, there is no evidence in the text which rules out the possibility that this is what he meant.[36]

The remaining problem, that of the relationship of this productive intellect to the Prime Mover, is even more obscure. The safest course might appear to be the suspension of judgment. There is no evidence clear enough to guarantee certainty. We know, of course, that in chapter 8 of *Metaphysics* Λ Aristotle is prepared to specify a plurality of unmoved movers, but I shall argue later that these are emmattered souls, and can tell us less than we might hope about Mind or God's nature.

But whatever may be the interpretation of Unmoved Movers, there seems to be a special difficulty about following Alexander of Aphrodisias in assimilating the productive intellect to the Prime Mover. For – so it might be argued – the productive intellect, as *De Anima* 3.5 makes indubitably clear, functions somehow as an efficient cause, not a final cause, when it is tied to our soul-body compound. And we read in the *De Generatione et Corruptione* (1.324B15) that final causes are not 'productive' (*poiētikos*). But in the *De Anima* the productive intellect is, like light, a state (a *hexis*). *De Anima* 2.6 tells us what light is; it is the presence (418B20) of fire or something else 'in the transparent.' As in 3.5, then, light is the *cause* (*aition*, 418A31)[37] of seeing. True, in 3.5, the productive intellect is compared to a craft – but in a very odd way. Aristotle does not say that light does things like a craftsman, but that the productive intellect acts 'as a craft *experiences* in relation to matter'; that is, its *effect* not its *action* is like the effect of a craft on matter. Thus although the productive intellect affects its 'matter', it does not do things to matter by 'moving' it physically. Nor, of course, can it be the object of desire; if it were, it would be a *final* cause. It certainly makes things, i.e., thoughts, out of the images, but, as we suggested, solely by being there. Without art there would be no statue; without the productive intellect we would not think. Aristotle does not say that the productive intellect works as a craftsman works, but rather by shining on potential colours. Its presence *produces* the result. If this is so, then no *individual* productive intellect is needed. Mind (God) will produce effects on those animals (e.g., men) who are able to be affected in this way by its presence. Mind operates in heaven as a final cause by stimulating desire, but in man as an efficient cause by the illuminating effect of its own nature. On the principle of Ockham's razor, Alexander of Aphrodisias was probably right in thinking that the productive intellect is none other than God.[38]

What happens when we decide to think, or start thinking? Simply that we are provoked by stimuli of some sort to attend to the images before us which the ceaseless activity of the productive intellect is constantly illuminating. Not to think is a failure of the soul/body complex.

V Ethical Applications of Psychology

We have seen reason to believe that *Metaphysics* Λ, *De Generatione Animalium*, and *De Anima* propose or imply a common theory about 'our' mind as a substance separate from the soul-body complex. We must now consider whether effects of this new psychological theory are visible in ethics, and how it might be related to the problem, still unsettled amid the disagreements of scholars, about Aristotle's conception of the best life in his latest ethical text, the *Nicomachean Ethics*. After that we will glance briefly at how Aristotle's dilemma, and particularly his view of the role of the contemplative life, apparently contributed to a 'revolution'[39] in the Peripatos, a revolution which led rapidly to an emphatic affirmation by Dicaearchus of Messene of the supreme claims of 'practical virtue'. First, then, we should consider the *Nicomachean Ethics*.

But that is easier said than done. If we accept the view that the 'common books' were originally part of the *Eudemian Ethics*, then the *Nicomachean* is incomplete – and throughout this study we have accumulated further evidence which all points to the truth of this view. That means that we lack a new discussion of justice (to replace *Eudemian Ethics* 4), a discussion of *akrasia* (though the account of action in the *De Motu* could promote a clearer exposition of the topic), and a discussion of the 'intellectual' virtues, particularly of *nous*, to replace *Eudemian Ethics* book 6 (see also 186–8 below). Furthermore, there is reason to believe that books 1 and 10 of the *Nicomachean Ethics* are earlier than books 2–4, and there are problems about where to place books 8 and 9 on friendship. An interesting feature of these books is the extension of the use of 'focal meaning' in book 3 to determine different sorts of courage (related only by analogy in *Eudemian Ethics* 3.1229A12), as well as to clarify the varieties of friendship in books 8 and 9 (though friendship is already related by focal meaning in the *Eudemian* version, 7.1236A16ff).[40] Something of focal meaning, however, is already present in book 1, for as we have already noted, Owen drew attention to its usefulness there in enabling Aristotle to make general remarks about 'goodness'. The treatment of goodness in the *Eudemian Ethics* is very different. But the use of focal meaning in book 1 of the *Nicomachean Ethics* is comparatively limited: Aristotle employs it to allow a broad discussion of goodness, not to identify and discuss various 'lesser' forms, as he does later with courage and friendship. Nevertheless, we can imagine how focal meaning could have been used to arrange and justify the different forms of 'good life' in a revised book 10.

But Aristotle does not so use focal meaning in book 10. It might be argued from this that at least book 10 is *not* Aristotle's final word on the subject of goodness and the various good lives. And that conclusion may be helpful for thinking how Aristotle *does* understand the relationship between the life of contemplation and that of 'moral virtue'. We have already noticed how book 10 is incomplete in another sense too: it looks forward to a *Politics* without book 1 (see 162 above). In its final form it will have required further work on this too. Let us therefore propose the possibility that book 10 as we have it is earlier than books 2–4, and that 8–9 go with it.[41]

Now consider *Nicomachean Ethics* 1. Here we find a repetition of the rather crude description of human psychology (1.1102A26–8) 'from the circulating discussions'. The same early source was used in the *Eudemian Ethics*, where book 2 begins with a reference to the 'circulating discussions' for a distinction between goods of the soul and 'external' (i.e. bodily) goods. This seems to refer to the *Protrepticus* (frs. B2, B3 Düring), to which Aristotle refers again in *Nicomachean Ethics* 1.1099A31ff. Now it is not surprising that *Eudemian Ethics* 2 harks back to the *Protrepticus* for its psychology (2.1219B23ff); it is more striking if *Nicomachean Ethics* 1 does so – referring by name to the 'circulating discussions' – if Aristotle himself has recently disavowed such crude treatments, as he did in the *De Anima* (3.432A25ff). For in the *De Anima* Aristotle not only rejects Platonic theories of tripartition; he disowns also the distinction between that which possesses reason and the irrational – which is his own view in the *Protrepticus, Eudemian Ethics*, and *Nicomachean Ethics* 1. Commentators often gloss over this evidence, saying either that Aristotle does not need such precision in the *Nicomachean Ethics* or that the *De Anima* distinction is of no help in ethics, though why that should be so – since it has ethical implications even in the *De Anima* itself – remains quite mysterious. Surely if Aristotle had already worked out the new theory, so emphatically mentioned in the *De Anima*, he would not have totally neglected it in the *Nicomachean Ethics*.

A more plausible explanation is that our *Nicomachean Ethics* 1, like the *Eudemian Ethics* and the *Protrepticus*, precedes the *De Anima*. If that is true, then we should not expect the theory of mind developed in the *De Anima*, the *De Generatione Animalium*, and the related discussion of God in *Metaphysics* Λ, to affect the discussion of goals in *Nicomachean Ethics* 1 and 10. Thus we date *Nicomachean Ethics* 1, 8, 9, 10 as part of a joint ethico-political project (to include the freshly composed books 4–6 of the *Politics*) which Aristotle embarked on in about 328. Any further revision was delayed by Aristotle's work on books M, N, and Λ of the *Metaphysics* and on the *De Anima*. By the time Aristotle had finished all these and had time to return to ethical work again he was near the end of his life. After writing about action in the *De Motu*, he came back to ethics and politics again. *Politics* 1 and *Nicomachean Ethics* 2–4 were completed, but death cut the project short. Books 1, 8, 9, and 10 were unrevised; other parts were not written at all.

Indeed *Nicomachean Ethics* 1 and 10 are unaffected by the new psychology of the *De Anima*. Even casual inspection of these books, particularly of the sections dealing with happiness, indicates that they are heavily based on the *Protrepticus*. We have already seen how the *Protrepticus* enables us to join together the accounts of pleasure in *Eudemian Ethics* 6 and *Nicomachean Ethics* 10. The roots of both accounts can be found in the *Protrepticus* within a single sentence. We also find there the first version of the notorious problem generated by certain texts of *Nicomachean Ethics* 10, where Aristotle says we are 'mind' or 'primarily' so (1178A2), and that the life of the mind, since that is primarily us, is the happiest life. Compare this with fr. B62 (Düring) of the *Protrepticus*: 'Whatever is the excellence of this part must be the most choiceworthy generally for all beings and for us. For, I think, one would suppose that this part [mind] is either alone or primarily us.'

Aristotle does not raise the question of the relation of the contemplative life to the active life again in book 10 of the *Nicomachean Ethics* as we have it. There is no reason why he should. His basic view of the matter is still unchanged from that of the *Eudemus* and *Protrepticus* – though he may have felt better equipped to defend it – so on this point there was no need to modify his attitude as expressed in the *Eudemian Ethics*. But *Nicomachean Ethics* 10 is certainly meant to replace *Eudemian Ethics* 8, and there are differences of emphasis within a basically similar psychological framework. In fact the *Nicomachean* treatment of the good life looks in certain limited respects like a return from the *Eudemian Ethics* to the *Protrepticus*. The highest kind of happiness is now, both in *NE* 10 and in 1, referred to on several occasions as 'blessedness' (*makariotēs*). The word is not unknown in the *Eudemian Ethics*, but there the highest form of happiness is, as we have seen, nobility (*kalokagathia*), which includes, of course, contemplation of

God. *Nicomachean Ethics* 10 returns to the emphasis of the *Protrepticus*, not, we might observe, yet impelled by a new theory of mind, but almost as though in preparation for it. The psychology of *Nicomachean Ethics* 1 and 10 is identical, as has often been noticed;[42] these books talk of blessedness because they are substantially based on an as yet unrevised *Protrepticus* (and perhaps *Eudemus*). Blessedness is the perfect excellence and of our divine part. *Nicomachean Ethics* 1 and 10 have much else in common too, such as the concern with Eudoxus's theory of pleasure, which is still important but is eventually criticized more firmly (1.1101B27ff; 10,1172B9ff) than in *Eudemian Ethics* 6.

In *Nicomachean Ethics* 10, as in the *Protrepticus*, Aristotle says that contemplation is the best life; moral virtue (the 'so-called' moral virtue of the *Protrepticus*) is the second best. But he does not ask the sort of question in book 10 of the *Nicomachean Ethics* which Cooper wants him to ask:[43] shall I stop thinking to pull a drowning man out of the water? Since mind is still 'in us' in *Nicomachean Ethics* 10 we have to live a life of the soul; indeed we need (regrettably but inexorably) external goods to live, and inasmuch as the 'contemplative' is a man and lives in society, he chooses (*hairetai*) virtuous *action*. So he will need external goods to carry on as a man (1178B5–8). In other words, *if* the contemplative lived *outside* a city, he would not need to act 'virtuously'; he would not need to, if he were by himself. (This is what Aristotle means when he refuses to attribute 'virtue' to gods.) But the wise man does live in society, and hence he will fulfil his civic obligations, exactly as in the *Protrepticus*, and similar to the return of Plato's just man to the cave in the *Republic*. In a sense such obligations are regrettable, but they are right and will be done. As *Nicomachean Ethics* 1 itself points out (1097B33ff), happiness is an *ergon*, a function and a task, of man, not even of soul (as the *Eudemian Ethics* puts it);[44] a function of man, not of most of man.

Hence when Aristotle says that we must live in accordance with the best and most perfect virtue (if there is one), he cannot mean 'in accordance only, or dominantly, with the best and most perfect one.' If man was *simply* mind, it would mean that, but he is not. Mind *makes* men different from beasts; it is not identical with his nature. Since in *Nicomachean Ethics* 10, mind is still in the soul, as it is in the *Protrepticus*, it is impossible that Aristotle could mean that in accordance with a 'dominant' theory of virtue, moral virtue could be sacrificed or neglected in the interest of contemplation. If it were, the soul itself would be divided against itself, and man would act not divinely but bestially – an 'option' not available for God. Aristotle used an 'inclusive' notion of virtue in the *Protrepticus* and the *Eudemian Ethics*; he gives no indication that he has changed his mind in his 'Protreptican' *Nicomachean Ethics* 10.

One of Cooper's more interesting claims in his attempt to defend a theory of contemplation as the 'dominant end' in book 10 is the suggestion that when Aristotle contrasts the life of contemplation with the life (*bios*) of moral virtue, these two 'lives' could not exist simultaneously in the same person, or even, apparently, be possessed successively by the same person.[45] But this is incorrect. It has been rightly urged that there are passages in both Plato and Aristotle which fatally damage both versions of such a suggestion (*Pol.* 1.1256A40ff, *Laws* 5.733D7–734E2). When Greeks talk of a choice of 'lives', therefore, they can mean phases or areas of a man's life. So a man could live two lives, such as the contemplative and the 'moral', without necessary detriment to one or the other; unless, of course, one should be sacrificed to the other. But as we have seen, there is no evidence in Aristotle that the man who would 'sacrifice' his morality has any claim to be called moral at all.

At 10.1177B20ff the contemplative life is said to be complete happiness. That does not mean that we can get it by grabbing. If we were God, we would have it. As men, we can have it briefly, in so far as we have something divine about us. But the fact that we cannot have it whenever we want it does not mean that it is not the best, the most complete, and the most pleasurable end. It would be stupid not to 'choose' it (when we can) (1178A5); but similarly, at some times, or indeed perhaps usually, as we have seen, we have to *choose* the other way. We can only 'divinize' ourselves as far as we can (1177B34).

A final point: some of the texts which have been used to support the 'dominant' view of happiness are concerned with a *definition* of happiness rather than with its necessary preconditions.[46] Thus perfect happiness (attainable only by God) could indeed be defined as theoretical activity. Focal meaning could then have been invoked to make clear in what sense other beings (e.g., men) are capable of being happy. That, I suspect, would have been Aristotle's tactic if he had ever written a final and fully explicit version of book 10 of the *Nicomachean Ethics*.

VI The Composition of the 'Nicomachean Ethics'

When Aristotle had written *NE* 1, 8, 9, and 10, he had in fact the material for a revised version of the (*Eudemian*) *Ethics*. It would consist of *NE* 1, *EE* 2 (1220A4–end), *EE* 3, 4, 5, 6, *NE* 8, 9, 10; and it would be complete. It would lead on to the *Politics* (less book 1) and would pre-date the new psychology of the *De Anima*. Its approximate date would be 328/7. If this revision would soon appear untidy, that is explained by the fact that the new psychology introduced new problems. For now, for the first time, Aristotle has a theory in which mind (productive mind) comes from outside the human soul, and operates independently of it. The discussion of contemplation in *Nicomachean Ethics* 10 would need rephrasing at the very least to take account of this, for *we* would no longer be 'mind', even if still able to share from time to time in a life of God which is independent of our own.

It has puzzled scholars how in *Politics* 1 Aristotle seems to be concentrating almost entirely on man as a political and social animal. For if he lives outside society, he is a beast or a god. But it is assumed that the good man is neither a beast nor a god. Given this sort of perspective the claims of civic virtue would seem to be high. In an ideal state, presumably, arrangements would be made for 'contemplation' (but remember that if this is thought of as the life of mind itself it will continue regardless of human activity), but in an ordinary state it might even have to be still further subordinated to civic concerns, for 'we' are no longer 'mind,' but only capable of sharing in personal mental activity (even moral, let alone 'contemplative') from time to time. The so-called passive intellect is still ours; strictly speaking the productive intellect is not in us. Is there any trace of a revised theory in the *Nicomachean Ethics*? Clearly the places to look are the books which had not been written when the 'revised version' of the (*Eudemian*) *Ethics* was completed: these are *NE* 2–4, and they seem to provide some indication of what Aristotle might have done if he had had time to complete a second revision of his *Ethics*.

The opening of book 2 of the *Nicomachean Ethics* is in many respects like the opening of a treatise. Omitting Susemihl's *dē* and restoring the *de* of the manuscripts, we find that it is not necessarily tied to the previous book. Book 2 starts off by proposing not that there are two virtues (or two kinds of virtue as in *Eudemian Ethics* 2.1220A4), but that virtue is two-sided (*dittēs*), not (as in *NE* 1.1103A5) with the comment that some virtues are intellectual, some 'moral', but with a word able to suggest that there is one virtue which can be stated in its moral and intellectual aspects. This is entirely appropriate for the 'new' psychology where *nous* as a faculty is not 'part of us' any more, but something extraneous (without virtue and like God), which enables *us*, the whole of us, to think, both speculatively and deliberatively.

NE 2.1 continues with an inordinate number of references to *nature*, very like *Politics* 1, and makes remarks about the origin of the word 'ethical' which would seem more appropriate to the beginning of a work on ethics, were they not a development of the earlier *Eudemian* version. Then we have an elaborate discussion of the role of the development of potential in the history of moral growth, involving a very different and more wide-ranging treatment of potentiality than that found either in the *Eudemian Ethics* or even in the relevant sections of *Metaphysics* Θ (see ch. 12, note 9 below).

NE 2 is very systematic and well organized, as are books 3 and 4; the best comparison is with the well-organized structure of the *De Anima*. The treatment of responsibility in the opening of book 3, the elaborate and rather formal definition of virtue itself, and the systematic account of the versions of courage are evidence for this claim. It is the most carefully composed ethical material we have from Aristotle's hand. Notice the detail at 3.1115A26: the most fearful thing is death. It is the end; nothing seems good or bad to the dead man any more. Aristotle's comment is more poignant than the observation in *EE* 3.1229B8 that death is destruction. Yet the condemnation of suicide is maintained: it is not brave, but base; lack of endurance (*EE* 3.1230A2); lack of feeling and softness (*NE* 3.1116A14ff).

Books 5 is rather different. As Kenny showed, it is part of the original *Eudemian Ethics*. But it is confused; some topics are treated twice, and it almost looks as though it falls into two halves, the division coming at the end of chapter 6. Household 'justice' is discussed first at 1134Bff (where an analogue of justice is possible between master and slave) and at the end of the book, where in place of analogues we hear of metaphors and similarities (1138B5ff).[47] But the work will not divide; cross-references from the *Politics* rule that out.[48] The most likely explanation is that Aristotle was engaged on rewriting book 5 at the time of his death; our book 5 is the original *Eudemian* text with a number of unassimilated alterations. This is how far he got with the new ethics, which was to take account *inter alia* of the new psychology.

If *NE* 1 was going to reappear in the final *Ethics*, it too would have needed revision. Perhaps Aristotle intended it; but I am somewhat doubtful. After the revision of book 5 he would have had to treat *akrasia* (building on the *De Motu*), pleasure, friendship, the 'intellectual' side of virtue, and happiness. Pleasure and friendship could have been left more or less as our *NE* has them, but intellectual virtue would have needed updating, and Aristotle could hardly have avoided concentrating on the final relationship between the virtue with its two aspects and the separate life of the mind which functions within us or around us regardless of our moral being. The facts that I have presented would seem to suggest that *our* contemplation would have been *subordinated* to civic life; practical concerns would take precedence, just as in the case of the philosophers who return to the cave in Plato's *Republic*. The next step might be to remove 'contemplation' from the goals of human life altogether. Aristotle would have refused that step; not only the Stoics but some of his own school came near to taking it.

VII The Aftermath of Aristotle's Latest Work in Psychology

Aristotle's final view of soul and mind, at least its potential implications for ethics, is now clear. But the sort of difficulties scholars have raised about how to balance the claims of moral virtue, intellectual virtue, and the contemplative life are not merely modern. Aristotle's balancing-act appears to have been considered and quickly rejected by many even within the school of his pupil Theophrastus. Theophrastus himself, maintaining, as he seems to have done, much of Aristotle's latest theory of mind, probably persisted with Aristotle's solution, at least in its broad outlines, but we know that later Peripatetics, Strato above all, reduced metaphysics to a materialist physics, and rejected Aristotle's later theory of mind; this theory began its return to favour only in the second century AD.[49]

In ethics, predictably, similar developments can be found. Dicaearchus, opposing Theophrastus, was the Peripatetic who clearly de-emphasized contemplation,[50] though it is hard to see how he could have abolished it altogether from human excellence. An echo of the controversy is to be found in the ps.-Aristotelian *Magna Moralia* (1.1198B9ff),[51] itself reflecting *Eudemian Ethics* 5.1145A7; while the *Eudemian Ethics* seems to show that arguments about the respective priorities were already going on in Aristotle's lifetime. Jaeger argued that the author of the *Magna Moralia* was thinking about the opinions of a particular critic of the Aristotelian position. One of the critic's arguments is prefaced by 'he says'. 'He', Jaeger claimed, 'probably refers to Dicaearchus' (*Aristotle*, 446). That is possible – and we know Dicaearchus's view on the very limited importance of contemplation – but the author of the *Magna Moralia* may also reflect uncertainties about Aristotle's *own* revisions of his earlier theories of the best form of life. If my reconstruction is right, he would be pardonably puzzled about Aristotle's later intentions, which had not achieved overt written form.

The author of the *Magna Moralia* does not follow Dicaearchus's road; but it is interesting to note the significance of another passage where he dissents more clearly and sharply from Aristotle. In book 2 (1212B37–1213A10) Aristotle's doctrine of God thinking himself is rejected: the whole thing is bizarre (*atopon*). Now we have already observed that there is a very close link between Aristotle's theory of God's activity, his account of the productive intellect, and his view of the nature of contemplation. In fact, from an Aristotelian viewpoint, if God is not as *Metaphysics* Λ describes him, then the productive intellect cannot be as *De Anima* 3 describes it, and the nature of man – the subject of *Ethics* – must be very different from what appears to be Aristotle's latest view. The author of the *Magna Moralia* was apparently prepared to accept Aristotle's earlier thesis about contemplation and to discard the later account of mind which demanded that it be rethought.

Aristotle's account of mind is (and was) notoriously difficult to understand, but at all events the 'materialists' in the Peripatos must have rejected it. The author of the *Magna Moralia* rejects it too, preferring the theory of mind implicit in the *Eudemian Ethics* and outdated by the *De Anima*; he wants the earlier ethics, not the later theory of mind. From Aristotle's point of view Dicaearchus's theory of mind is outrageous (it had been rejected in substance as far back as the *Eudemus*), for his theory of mind must have flowed from his theory of the soul. And his view of the soul is that it is 'nothing'; nothing, that is, beyond an epiphenomenon of the bodily parts.[52]

Had Aristotle's account of the productive intellect and of its relation to the claims of the contemplative life been clearer and more fully developed, perhaps none of these disputes among his followers would have followed the path they did. The fault, it seems, lay in his death.

10

Plato's Cosmic Biology, Aristotle's *Aether* and Prime Matter

I Male and Female, God and Receptacle in the 'Timaeus'

In order to understand Aristotle's theory of a Prime Mover and of matter, and to see it as in part a critique of Plato, it is necessary to understand the Platonic background presented in the *Timaeus*. The following discussion is intended to make sense of that background and to elucidate certain aspects of the *Timaeus* most important to Aristotle; it does not purport to be anything like a complete study of the dialogue. The exact date of the dialogue, though important and briefly considered, is not the controlling factor in our present enquiry.

Half-way through chapter 6 of *Metaphysics* A, Aristotle describes Plato's account of the 'elements' of all things (987B21ff). As for the first principles of things, he says, they have the One as substance and as matter they have the 'great and the small' (or the 'Dyad'). From these principles derive the numbers (apart from one and two).[1] The One begets the numbers (*gennasthai*) as from a matrix (*ekmageion*). The nature of the model is clear: it is a model of sexual generation, with the Dyad, the matrix, as the womb. Aristotle then goes on to object: the Platonic account of sexual generation does not fit the facts. If Form generates once, it must produce one offspring out of the matter, just as we can make one table out of one piece of wood. The model is confused. Plato wants to say both that the generating Form (like the One) is like a male 'filling up' (*plēroutai*) the female, and that he is like a carpenter forming a table out of female matter. The paradox arises because in the first account the male supplies the form *and* the matter (according to Plato), in the latter the carpenter supplies only the form. The double and conflicting image of a begetter as on the one hand supplier of semen (as matter *and* form in Aristotle's terminology) and as on the other supplier of form alone (if we take the carpenter model literally) bedevilled Plato's account of the generation of the universe and of man. Eventually Aristotle resolved the problem to his own satisfaction.

Plato's account of human sexual generation in the *Timaeus* is simple. The father supplies the seed which grows in the mother's womb into a new adult (91D). The male sows his seed in the womb which is like a ploughed field; it is in the form of unmoulded (*adiaplasta*) animals which are moulded in the womb itself and are eventually born as human beings. Aristotle seems in *Metaphysics* A. 6 not to understand what Plato means, or to suggest that the sexual analogy is incoherent. He implies (in speaking of the carpenter) that the womb provides (or is) the matter; but this is not quite Plato's intention. The womb, by its own shape and (induced) movements, helps shape the matter provided. The womb, the *ekmageion*, is a mould, as Alexander of Aphrodisias saw. The seeds are 'unshaped' when they enter, as Plato puts it, using a neologism. They grow in the mould, which must therefore determine at least their basic outline by imposing limits on what shape they take; but obviously varying growths within a limited range are possible: hence monsters, and also of course inferior males, that is, females. But to understand this last point further we need to know what Plato believes females are.

A myth in the *Timaeus* supplies the answer. Originally (as in Hesiod) only males were formed. This first race, or some of it, behaved badly. They lived and died, and those who had lived badly were reincarnated next time as female (90E–91A). So that the human race could be distinguished as males and females, the gods had to construct a living creature within each male and female to enable sexual acts and reproduction to take place. Males were given genitals which could emit seed; this passed into the genitals from the head along the spine (as marrow) via the lungs. The male organ of emission is disobedient and has a lust for domination (*kratein*). In women a womb or matrix (*mētra*), desirous of child-producing, was produced.[2] It too is disobedient; it will wander all over the body if it fails to find seeds and (like Pandora's jar) will produce all kinds of sicknesses. Women, therefore, are a secondary kind of men, men reincarnated as women[3] and such punishment will continue to befall men if they fail as men (42B). Thus the superior kind of human is called a man (*anēr*, 42A). It should be noticed that a similar story of the origin of sexual difference is to be found in the *Statesman*,[4] also told in a myth. In the old days, the Eleatic Stranger tells us (271Aff), there was no sexual generation; males grew out of the earth. God looked after mankind (271E); there were no constitutions and no one had wives and children. That was the age of Cronus, and men were immeasurably happy (272C) – if they used their time properly, a matter on which doubt is cast. Eventually, however, they all died and when at some later stage of the cosmic cycle they reappeared from the earth, their method of generation was different. Now males could not be produced from the earth; as at present, a sexual partner was needed and was provided, and the relevant parts bestowed (274AB).[5]

The myth is convoluted and difficult to follow, but the similarities with the *Timaeus* are many. Males are prior; males and females are a later generation, in decadent times. But in general God is described as in the *Timaeus*; he is a Demiurge (270A, 273B) who bestows immortality on his created structures and then guides the universe from outside. He has subordinate divinities (271D); he is a father (273B) who has problems with ordering a 'bodylike' principle in the mixture (*sunkrisis*) (273B) – which is the cause of troubles that sometimes perplex even the God who has ordered the whole universe.

We began this chapter with a reference to Aristotle's *Metaphysics* A.6, where we considered not only human generation, though Aristotle suggests that topic, but primarily the generation of numbers from the One and the Dyad. That too, Aristotle thinks, is a quasi-sexual act. It is hard not to see that Aristotle has the *Timaeus* in mind when he comments thus – or something comparable with the *Timaeus*. Let us now therefore consider Plato's cosmological structure in the *Timaeus*, in the light of his remarks about human sexual generation. For although sexual imagery is not Plato's only imagery in the *Timaeus*, it is prominent, constant, and much ignored. For the relationship between the Demiurge on the one hand and necessity on the other is largely modelled on the male/female relationship. It is true that Plato does not speak of 'seeds', but he does speak of the 'sowing' of souls by the Demiurge (42D).

Plato's construction of the world of the *Timaeus* is in two sections, 'the works of reason and the works of necessity' (47E), that is, in Pythagorean language, the works of the male and the works of the female. That this is how Plato means us to understand him needs demonstration, but first we should notice that in this part of the text Plato offers only two 'causes', mind, or the craftsman (what Aristotle would call the efficient cause), and necessity which, as Aristotle frequently suggests, has some, but not sufficient, similarities with his material cause. Aristotle (in *Metaphysics* A.6) does indeed claim that Plato uses only two causes (the 'essential' or formal cause and the matter). But there are problems: Aristotle thinks that Plato uses a formal cause (as in the *Phaedo*); the *Timaeus* suggests 'matter' and an *efficient* cause. But perhaps the apparent confusion will be dissolved as we proceed, though Theophrastus already saw no confusion: for him (as reported in Simplicius's commentary on the *Physics*) Plato only had two causes, as Aristotle thought: an 'all-receiving' substrate (here we have echoes of the *Timaeus*), and a moving cause which he 'clothes' with the power of God and the Good (485, fr. 9 in Diels, *Doxographi Graeci*).

Let us consider what Plato calls 'reason'. He is, as in the *Statesman*, male, that is, he is the maker and father of the universe (28C),[6] and he has a model or paradigm which he looks at while he works. I shall return to the question of the relation of the father to his model later. First let us consider his character. He is good (29A); he is the *best* of the causes. He has no envy (29E) and desired to make all as like himself as possible, that is, good. He produced order out of chaos and discord. At this point in his narrative, I shall argue, Plato omits a stage – which has sometimes confused his readers. The sentence runs as follows: 'God, wishing all to be good and nothing to be worthless as far as was in his power, took over everything "visible": this was restless and moving in a discordant and disorderly way [cf. *De Caelo* 3.300B18]. He brought it to order from disorder.' One is tempted to assume from this that the craftsman took over pre-existing matter, but if we insist on the fact that one of Plato's models is sexual generation, this assumption must be questioned. (That there are two models, the craftsman and the begetter, is precisely what baffled Aristotle.) For in Plato's theory of conception it is the male who provides the matter itself. So when Plato says that the Demiurge 'took over' the matter, he must be referring not to the first, but to a second (non-temporal) 'stage' of conception if the Demiurge himself supplied the matter originally. In the first 'stage' of the process matter would be ejected into the (potentially) 'wandering' cosmic womb. The resulting disorderly motions need to be controlled, and in the second 'stage' the Demiurge (as male) achieves this control.[7]

That this interpretation is correct is shown by a comparison of this section with a later part of the *Timaeus* where Plato describes the 'creation' from the other end; that is, starting from the female, the element of necessity. Let us now therefore consider this element, which is essential for the propagation of the living universe. First of all it is a 'wandering cause', that is, a cause liable to erratic movement (48A), exactly like a woman's womb (91C4); then it is all-receiving (50B8); then it is a 'matrix' (*ekmageion*), a word which Aristotle (*Met* A. 988A1ff) recognizes has female connotations; then the 'images' of things (i.e., the seeds) go in and out of her and move her.[8] In her the developing being grows (*phuetai* 50D1), but she herself is 'place' (*chōra* 52A8);[9] she provides a space for generated things to reside in. As location she can be recognized 'with lack of perception' (that is, one cannot 'see' nothing, a space), but 'a bogus reason' can grasp her, despite her 'unseen and therefore shapeless' form (51A7ff, 52B2). Finally, of course, she is the mother and receptacle (51A5), a receptacle of birth like a nurse (49A6, 52B5).[10] Physical objects in the world (primarily the four elements) are begotten in her (52A5). I think we can assume that as the Demiurge is the father of the universe, 'place' is the mother.[11]

Which brings us to the question of the 'stages' of conception, of which I claimed Plato gave an abbreviated and truncated account at 30A4. Before 'conception' the *ekmageion* is liable to erratic motion. Now consider the following (52E): 'Because it is full of potencies that are neither similar nor balanced, in no part of itself is it equally balanced, but it is moving everywhere and shaken unevenly by them, and its own movement then shook them in its turn.' Remember in interpreting this that Plato is describing the generation of *bodies*; soul is not yet created, so only *disorderly* motion is to be expected. These motions, Plato says, arise from the *ekmageion*'s being made fiery and watery and receiving the shapes of earth and air. Thus the planned entry of the 'images' produces all the actual motions in the *ekmageion*,[12] for the *ekmageion*, being a 'wandering' cause like the human womb, is by itself merely capable of moving about. Its potential mobility is now realized. Clearly then the *ekmageion* is not a wax-block on which images are stamped, as Aristotle (and many recent scholars) at times seems to suggest. It is simply a receiving bowl, as Plato keeps telling us, which provides a shelter for the seed-like 'images', limits their growth in so far as it has 'walls', but no more. The effect of the 'rattling' of the images in the womb, therefore, as Plato again says, is to tend to separate them out, to tend to assemble like with like. Basically this means that heavy 'images' tend to collect at the bottom, light at the top, but in a quite unplanned way. This is the stage which Plato speaks of at the earlier section of the *Timaeus* when he talks of the Demiurge 'taking over all that is visible' but in disorderly and chaotic motion (30A). This stage is represented in the 'general' account (53AB) of the process by the discussion which follows that of the disorderly motion and deals with the 'formation of shapes' by God, who 'set' them as well as he could. Thus God's generative act has two stages which may be in fact without temporal differentiation but which can be distinguished in thought: (1) the direction of 'images' into the 'womb' of the universe, where they shake down to some extent because of their weight; (2) the encouragement of this shaking-down process by the reason principles in the images themselves – which are traces of God himself; thus their action is God's work and the result of God's will.

Two further questions about this conception of the living being (world-soul and world-body) which is the cosmos demand attention. First the *ekmageion* must provide nothing of its own except place. It is a sort of mixing-bowl of the universe (cf. 41D). Plato presumably thinks that a potential universe is spatially limited (somehow), and never asks himself *why* the cosmic womb is not spatially unlimited – for of course human wombs are not! It is spatially limited but qualitatively nothing, and yet it can 'nurse' the 'baby'. But here the image breaks down, and Plato makes no attempt to work it out. For, of course, while a womb is in a woman (though virtually an independent nature in her in the *Timaeus* [91C]), the cosmic *ekmageion* is nowhere,[13] for there is nowhere for it to *be*. It is best described as a shapeless (plastic) restrictor (50D) or 'holder'. The word *chōra* itself is connected with *chōrein*, and *chōrein* means 'to hold' or 'contain.'[14] That it can 'move' is clear from its being shaken by the seeds within it. And indeed we would expect this movement, for it is a 'wandering' cause, like a woman's wandering womb. And in mythology, at least, a womb can wander without an owner.[15] The word *ekmageion*, in fact, is ambiguous, just as the word (and act) of the Demiurge is ambiguous – and that is what puzzled Aristotle. The 'womb' both is and is not a shape – if it were 'really' a shape it would be material. Hence it can look both 'material' and 'non-material'.[16] Hence Aristotle thinks it 'must be' matter, for example at *Physics* 4.209B11–16:[17] just as the Demiurge (the sower, the father) can also be the carpenter – though, as Aristotle points out, a carpenter makes tables not of himself, but of wood.

The male (Mind, Demiurge) provides the seed, the female (Necessity) provides the place: the works of Reason and the works of Necessity. But when Plato himself sums the matter up (at 52D), he speaks not of 'mind', place, and becoming, but of *being* (*on*), place, and becoming. Why does he not say 'being' (i.e., Forms), 'mind', place, and becoming, particularly as he speaks of the Forms being recognized by 'mind' as recently as 51D, and as he says that gods (and a small class of men) 'partake' in reason (51E)? Now Aristotle persistently claims that Plato offers only two causes, form and 'matter'. Could this apparently strange claim be made because Aristotle knows that when Plato talks of 'mind,' he *really means* Forms, that somehow Mind is Forms? That view cannot be found explicitly in the *Timaeus*, but one can, I think, show that Plato comes remarkably close to it, for *both* Demiurge and Form are called 'father' (28C, 50D). Perhaps, after the *Timaeus*, Plato became more explicit. If he did, then a great deal of Aristotelian criticism of Plato's 'causes' becomes more intelligible.

In the central books of the *Republic*, the supreme cause is the Good, cause of the being and intelligibility of the Forms. Questions about the relation between the Good (and Forms in general) and Mind or God are not raised. But they *are* raised in a passage of book 10 which has always seemed rather scandalous. God, Plato tells us, 'made' (*ergasasthai*, 597Bff) the Form of 'bed,' and this Form must be unique, or an infinite regress would be generated. Thus God 'made' the unique Form of 'bed' *one* thing. And that is all in the *Republic*. Did the subject not recur elsewhere, we might be tempted (and many have been tempted) to follow the traditional approach to the text; Plato is making a clumsy analogy: as carpenter to table, so God to the Form of 'table'. But whatever he came to think about the dilemma posed in *Republic* 10, he did revert to the subject. He raised it again in the *Parmenides*.

But first the *Phaedrus*. Again the relation between gods and Forms is raised, at least by implication, in the myth. It is in virtue of knowing Forms that a god is divine; and the gods travel up to the 'place beyond the heavens' to renew their divinity, as it were, by personal acquaintance. Yet here the myth is getting thin. Do the gods maintain their divinity by *recalling* the Forms, when they come back to Hestia at home after their ride round the heavens?[18] Surely they have continual and complete awareness of them, lest they forget, as we do. The evident limitations of the myth make it not implausible to wonder whether some rethinking is the process of being formulated, or a reply to some criticism. And note that in the *Phaedrus* Plato's relationship between God and Form is *not* that of *Republic* 10. So what is the right answer?

When in doubt, try the *Parmenides*; and sure enough the problem of thinking about Forms is raised – not, notice, about *God's* thinking about Forms in the first instance (though *Parmenides* does come round to some difficulties about that in 134CD: 'If God knows Forms, how can he know particulars?'), but about thinking about Forms, and about Forms as objects of thought (*noēmata*). At 132B we read: 'But, Parmenides, perhaps each of these Ideas is a *noēma* and can come to be nowhere else than in souls.' Let us consider Parmenides' reply. If Forms are thoughts (*noēmata*), what are they thoughts of? Of what exists? And if particulars share in Forms, do they share in thoughts? So either everything is thoughts, or thoughts are 'without' thought (*anoēta*). The argumentation is shaky, but let us concentrate only on one part of it. If a Form is a thought, it is a thought *of* something, insists Parmenides. Yet it is clear that Platonic Forms cannot simply be thoughts of (in the sense of 'dependent on') some minds; that is, they cannot be concepts of something. But did Plato understand a *noēma* to be a concept? Certainly we find (in a generally dismissed passage) a certain Alcimus insisting that Plato *did* call Forms *noēmata* (D.L. 3.13). This could be folly or malice on Alcimus's part, but not necessarily, for to call X a *noēma* is *not* necessarily to call it a concept. To call X a concept is to say that it is a construct by a man or God – which Plato would never have wished of his Forms – but to say that X is thought about or is an *object* of thought (which is an acceptable meaning of *noēma*), would be philosophically acceptable to Plato. In this sense Forms *are noēmata* and God thinks about them. So if Plato was still interested in the question of the relation between Mind and Forms in the *Parmenides*, he would not have been dissuaded by mistaken attempts to read Forms as concepts (which Aristotle, of course, would prefer them to be).

That Plato really *was* worried about the relationship between Forms and

Mind which he had first raised in *Republic* 10, and that he was not put off by people misreading Forms as concepts in the *Parmenides*, are borne out by an extraordinarily difficult and much disputed section of the *Sophist*: the analysis of the theories of the 'Friends' of the Forms (248ff).[19] It seems certain that the theory of the 'Friends' is either some early theory of Plato's, or – possibly – that of some over-zealous follower of Plato. Either way Plato repudiates it. The 'Friends'' account of Forms is not compatible with a definition of being as that which can act or be acted upon, for souls act in so far as they know, and' being' is acted upon in so far as it is known. Hence the 'Friends' are wrong to deny movement (as being known), life, soul, intelligibility, to what is 'completely real', and wrong to hold that it is 'remote', 'untouchable',[20] 'mindless', 'unmoved' (i.e., unthought), and 'still'. On the contrary it is living and vital. The only reasonable conclusion from this repudiation is that 'what is comprehensively' is (or includes) knowing and being known. But that is not all. Plato seems to suggest that it is ridiculous for 'what comprehensively is' not to know. Hence somehow what comprehensively is should be (or include) both knower and known. ' What is comprehensively real' in the *Sophist* seems to suggest the universe itself (that is, the world-soul and the world-body of the *Timaeus*); hence Plato would be saying that the world-soul, which possesses a mind, affects and is affected by its body. But if Plato still recognized some kinds of Forms when he wrote the *Sophist*, perhaps they too, as the non-material paradigm of the universe, are both the knower and the 'body' of knowledge: perhaps by the time of the *Sophist* Plato is considering the possibility of real identity between Model and Mind.[21] Plato does not make such a consideration explicit in the *Sophist*; yet perhaps it underlies his remarks about the nature of the (ensouled) universe. For just as the world-soul could think (or be) the emmattered qualities, so God might think (or be) the Forms themselves. If so, then the *Sophist* would indeed represent a stage on the road from the *Republic* to the *Timaeus*. First in the *Republic* he suggests that God makes Forms; then in the *Parmenides* he floats the idea that if Forms are *noēmata*, they must be *noēmata of* (i.e., made by) a mind (perhaps again ultimately God's mind) about something. These ideas are both dropped. But the Form (at least according to Alcimus, and by implication for Aristotle) is still a *noēma* (not, as Aristotle ultimately wished, only a *noēsis*), and the problem of the relation of the Forms and God's Mind still remained. The solution of the 'Friends' of the Forms – probably, as we have noticed, that of the earlier Plato himself – is also rejected.

Let us now return to the *Timaeus*. We started by noting that Plato looks at 'creation' in two ways, as the effect of Mind and as the effect of Necessity. But he also works with another distinction, a distinction of 'kinds' (48E). The kinds are being, becoming, and the nurse-of-becoming. But interestingly here *being* is spoken of as *Form*; there is no mention of Mind at all. So if he read this page alone, Aristotle would seem justified in thinking that Plato had only two causes, namely Form and the 'matter' or 'nurse' – which is precisely his claim about the *Timaeus*. Yet this would also imply a deliberate neglect of the rest of the dialogue, and if we assume that Aristotle was not being merely obtuse, an obvious-looking explanation of his attitude can be found. Aristotle knows that Plato has not mentioned Mind because in some sense Mind is subsumed under the description of Form, or, as Theophrastus put it, because Plato has clothed the moving cause with the power of the Good. Plato's first 'kind' then would be 'Form-Mind', or Form for short.

Unfortunately, when Plato speaks of Mind and Form together at the start of the *Timaeus*, he does not explain their relationship. Hence he talks of the Demiurge looking at the eternal model (28Aff), and it is easy to assume that he never identifies Form and Mind here or anywhere else in the *Timaeus*. But as Newman might have put it: 'He never said it, did he ever mean it?' The *Timaeus* by itself gives little further help, except for Plato's apparent neglect of Mind to which I have already alluded in 52D – and Aristotle's view that Plato offers only *two* causes even in the *Timaeus*.[22] But it is possible to assemble material which supports a Platonic assimilation of Form and Mind from the *Philebus*, *Laws*, and the fragments of Xenocrates, universally acknowledged by antiquity as well as in modern scholarship as a conservative follower of Plato.

Let us first consider a notorious, but unresolved, problem about the *Timaeus* itself. At the beginning of the dialogue, Socrates, Timaeus, and three others who took part in the *Republic* (one is missing) are supposed to be meeting again, and Socrates summarizes 'yesterday's' debate. What he repeats, as is generally recognized, are the political and social regulations of the *Republic*, but no metaphysics, no discussion of Forms, no discussion of the Good. The new role of women, however, is mentioned: their natures must be 'tuned up' so that they become similar to men. The natural and correct inference has often been drawn from this: that Plato omits the metaphysics of the *Republic* because he no longer accepts it. My suggestion, of course, is that an important thesis which he no longer accepts is the separation of Forms and Mind in God. He does not spell out the new relationship in the *Timaeus*, but what he says in the *Timaeus* might assume it. It is not implausible to suggest that some of that new relationship was also to be spelled out, or had already been spelled out, in the famous lecture on the Good.

There can be no doubt that somehow or other, in his later days, Plato identified the Good and the One: ancient testimony is unanimous on the point. And in some way, as Aristotle tells us repeatedly, Plato 'generated' Forms or 'numbers' from the One.[23] If Plato really did 'generate' from the One, as Aristotle said, it is interesting to note that the One's action is comparable with that of the Demiurge. In both cases the imagery is sexual. The One 'generates' the numbers from (or in?) the Dyad; the Demiurge 'generates' the world from a sort of 'matter'. Thus both are in a sense 'efficient' causes, but the One qua Good is also a 'formal' cause. Could it be that the *two* generational processes are analogous, or somehow identical? Xenocrates, the 'conservative' Platonist, had no doubt:[24] he identified the 'Monad' (his name for Plato's One) as male and as Mind, the Mind as Good (fr. 15 Heinze). Xenocrates' principles are thus the Monad (Mind and Good) and the Dyad ('matter', the 'ever-flowing', fr. 28; cf. *Laws* 12.966E). Clearly he went beyond Plato in such identifications, since to Aristotle's continual annoyance, he defined soul (presumably the world-soul) as 'a number moving itself' (*De Anima* 1.408B32ff).[25] Interestingly, too, he *may* have thought that the Dyad, the 'matter', is a sort of soul, because it is the origin of movement. That, as we have seen, would be a travesty of the *Timaeus*, where Plato makes sure that the actual movement of the 'nurse' is originated from outside. And Xenocrates, giving the 'nurse' her own movements, would make her into an *evil* soul – if Plutarch's account of the matter is to be relied on. If it is not to be relied on, that is, if it was not Xenocrates but *Plutarch* who read the female principle as a *positive* evil principle (which Aristotle does not believe), then Xenocrates is nearer still to Plato himself. For the moment, however, let us merely observe that the testimony of Xenocrates may be taken to support our reading of the criticism of Aristotle: Plato had two 'principles': One-Mind (usually spoken of as 'One'), and place.

The *Philebus* has a little more detail. It has always been said that here, if anywhere in the dialogues, Plato's latest metaphysics is to be found – especially in the section dealing with the three 'classes' (*eidē* – note the same word as in the *Timaeus* for basic 'factors' in the production of the universe, 23cff). The three factors are limit, unlimited, and the cause of the mixing. Again it is hard not to think of the *Timaeus*: even the mixing reminds us of the mixing-bowl (not to speak of the 'mixing in love' of ordinary Greek idiom). Now consider 25C. Plato discusses the hotter and colder, wetter and drier, more and less, etc., and associates them with the 'unlimited'. Let the 'unlimited' be the womb or place (after it is first wetted, fired, etc., in the *Timaeus*). Then comes the formation stage of the *Timaeus*-theory in the *Philebus*, replete with the sexual imagery: Mix into it (i.e., into that which 'receives' [*dechomenēs*]the more and less) the *gennan* of the 'limit'. LSJ obligingly comments that *gennan* is a rare word in *prose*, and thus it is appropriate for cosmogony; it means offspring created through sexual reproduction, etc. That is, the *gennan* of the limit are the seeds of God, the father. The limit (*peras*) seems to be *not* the Form imposed by another, but the Form described itself as a begetter. For it is the son of limit which is the cosmos, what Plato later calls (27C) the 'mixed and generated being '(which is perhaps to be identified with the 'completely real' of the *Sophist*). Yet in *Philebus* 23C, and again in 27B, Plato *separates* the cause of the mixture from the limit; there are, as in parallel passages of the *Timaeus*, two causes (limit and mixer), not just one. It looks as though the *Philebus* contradicts itself, proposing now two, now three, causes of becoming. But this is *exactly* the ambiguity we found also in the *Timaeus*. Is it that Plato does not know quite whether he should 'amalgamate' Form and Mind? At least the name of Socrates' interlocutor in the *Philebus* should assure us that Plato is worrying about such things, and that Protarchus is learning about them, for the name *Protarchus* means 'man of first principles'.

Why does Plato seem to remain tentative in the *Philebus*? Why does he seem to avoid telling us outright that Form-Mind is the generator? For one thing because it is not Plato's way always to spell things out – and least of all is he likely to want to break from this practice about the highest truths of metaphysics. Remember his reticence about the Sun-Good of the *Republic*. Furthermore, the present passage of the*Philebus* (again like the *Sophist*) is primarily designed to show the contents of the present universe, not to discuss God (23C).[26] Strictly speaking, in this world, Forms are *not* present, only their images, their images in seeds provided by Mind. Hence if we are analysing the 'mixed and generated' being of the cosmos, we need to invoke (1) the unlimited (the bowl), (2) the mixture itself, (3) the 'efficient' cause, that is the active seed provided by the father as 'cause of mixture', and (4) the limit which is the Form itself, entirely outside the mixture: present only, as Proclus knew, as the 'emmattered' *form* of the seed.[27] Thus *three* 'elements' are needed to account for the condition of the mix, but only two (as Plato said earlier) to summarize (or give a 'God's-eye view' of) the process: Form-Mind as generator and limit, and Matter or the unlimited.

So once again Xenocrates and Aristotle (not to mention Proclus) have got it right. Further information may be available within the *Philebus* itself (64Eff), from the only passage in the late dialogues where Plato comes close to speaking directly about the Form of the Good: as in the *Republic* we cannot quite reach it. We have to stay in the vestibule (64C). But if we look at the cosmic mixture, we can identify a number of features which indicate goodness: measure, or proportion, beauty, truth. These three Forms (*idea* is used here) when taken as *ones* (that is as Form-Numbers indicating the Good) are best seen as the *cause* of the mixture, and *because of this*, as being good, the mixture is good. Unfortunately the text is not as clear as it might be.

But note Plato's emphasis on *one* thing. There is *one* cause of the goodness of the mixture. True, this assertion could be read as a mistake on Plato's part; he has forgotten about the 'Demiurge' figure. But it is more reasonable to assume no mere carelessness: the Demiurge *is* the limit.[28]

An extraordinary echo in *Laws* 10 supports this interpretation. In general it has been established by Hackforth that Plato, in the *Philebus*, the *Timaeus*, and the *Laws*, distinguishes between Mind and soul. The distinction is that in the begotten cosmos mind is in soul,[29] but Mind as God is separate from soul. Hence Plato could agree with Aristotle that Mind is God, or that Mind and God are good examples, indeed the best examples, of substances (see 279 below). At *Laws* 897D Plato turns to look at the 'movement of mind', and in doing so he immediately evokes the Good of the *Republic*: 'Let us not look, as it were, at the sun directly, thus bringing on night at midday, or think that we shall see Mind with mortal eyes and know it adequately. One is more sure of seeing it by looking at an *image* of it.' Commentators note the echo of *Republic* 516Aff; they fail to see that Plato is now telling us – what *Republic* 7 does not say – namely, that Mind *is* the Good.

Let us revert to the beginning of the *Timaeus*. We wondered why in the summary of the *Republic* the metaphysics is left out. Now we know. It is because a new relationship between the Form of the Good and Mind has emerged. That notion underlies *Timaeus, Philebus, Laws*. Xenocrates and Aristotle were in their different ways right, and only when we understand this shall we understand Aristotle's criticism of Plato's causes: God and the 'receptacle'. It has often been observed that in the *Timaeus* Plato only returns to the 'image-copy' notion of the relationship between Forms and particulars, and abandons participation. An explanation is now available. Mind cannot *participate* in the Good, because it *is* good; and particulars do not 'participate' in Forms, because they are created or *made* qualified. Yet the old 'objective' language about Forms is stilll retained; the Mind looks within itself for the 'patterns', still 'objects' of thought, not concepts, which it recognizes and on the basis of which it generates the universe. Yet the biological model is dominant; there are two 'causes': Form-Mind and place; Father and mother.

A few final questions related to Plato and hence to Aristotle's criticism of Plato need comment. For Plato, when did the One take on its importance (rather than the Good)? Why does Plato in the *Timaeus* speak of the 'ideal living creature', if he means the Good? What are the chronological implications for Plato's later work? What is the significance of the apparent persistence of Plato's descriptions of Forms as *noēmata* (objects of thought)? The question about the One is unanswerable precisely, but we have pointed out how the *Philebus* speaks of seeing the Forms on the threshold of the

Good 'as one', and of course back in the *Parmenides* the Forms seem to be thought of as ones or as related to some notion of unity. So we can only infer that the One did develop in importance, that though it is not explicit in these dialogues, its principles underlie them. An important result of this interpretation is that once again we avoid Cherniss's legacy: that Aristotle was either a fool who could not understand Plato (and had not the wit to ask him), or a knave who deliberately misrepresented him. In the Form-Mind analogue of *Republic* 10, *Timaeus*, *Philebus*, and *Laws* we have the One of the 'esoteric' teaching. The dialogues do *not* tell us how the Form-Mind 'causes' the 'others' – except for the biological analogy; but this is exactly the problem with the 'esoteric' doctrine too. What worried Aristotle is how the One and the Dyad 'generate the numbers', that is, the Forms, the ones. What worries the reader of the *Timaeus* is how the Father produces the product. It is a similar problem.

As for the 'ideal living creature', we have an answer here to the 'self-predication' dilemma. On the Beauty-is-beautiful principle, the 'ideal living creature', embracing the world of Forms, should be alive, and if he is alive, he should be a Mind, for life and mind are indissoluble: Mind rules the universe, as the *Philebus* has it (30D, cf. 28C). On the self-predication hypothesis the 'ideal living creature' should be alive (which has puzzled people). He looks alive, but do not be deceived; he *is* alive. He is Mind, but not merely Mind, not merely thinking, as Aristotle eventually would have liked. Not merely *noēsis*, but *noēsis* with some sort of content: not *noēsis* of itself, but *noēsis* of its Forms which *are* itself. The Middle Platonist Alcinous got this right when he said that Mind thinks itself *and* its objects, meaning (with the *kai* of added explanation) Mind thinks itself, that is, its objects.[30] Aristotle's self-thinking Prime Mover looks like a deliberate critique of this view.

The chronological implications for Plato, and hence for Aristotle, are considerable. The origins of the theory of Mind-Form go back at least to the puzzling section of *Republic* 10; the problem is somewhat clarified in the remarks about concepts in the *Parmenides*, and by the attack on the Friends of the Forms in the *Sophist*. The fully fledged debate is glimpsed in the *Statesman* and assumed in the *Timaeus*, the *Philebus*, and the *Laws*, probably in that order;[31] but minor details there cannot be worked out. There is no exotic teaching about the One, the Dyad, Number, etc., which is not more or less visible in these late dialogues. Details may differ; realities remain.

As for Aristotle, there seems to be no sign of the *Timaeus* in our fragments of the *Eudemus* or the *Protrepticus* (ca 353). This may provide evidence for dating it around 352 – not too far short of the time when Aristotle began work on his attacks on Platonic theories in *On Ideas*, *On the Good*, and *On*

Philosophy; and *On Philosophy* seems to have been particularly critical of the *Timaeus*. All these texts, I have argued, are to be dated to the period 348–346. In the *Physics* too, the attack continued, and the *Physics* seems to have used *On Philosophy*, particularly, as we shall see, in its discussions of Platonic 'matter'. The earliest parts of the *Physics* probably date from about 345, and we should notice the concern of both *Physics* 2 and the *Timaeus* with the work of Empedocles, a great source of cosmo-biological ideas.

Physics 3 and 4 make frequent reference to Plato. At 3.206B31 Aristotle calls Plato's arithmetical unit a monad, which was Xenocrates' favourite term for the One: some further indication that Xenocrates is often interesting as an interpreter of Plato. In 4.209Bff, when the *Timaeus* is first introduced by name, Aristotle comments that 'matter', 'place', and the 'receptive' (*to metalēptikon* 209B14) are 'one and the same'. He says that Plato's account of the 'receptive' differs in the *Timaeus* and the 'unwritten teachings'; yet on the identity of 'place' (*topos*) and 'room' (*chōra*) he is constant. In other words the 'unwritten teachings' are more or less identical with the *Timaeus*, though different in their account of 'reception'. The same could be said of the *Timaeus* compared with the *Philebus*. A little later (4.210A1–2) Aristotle adds that the 'receptive factor' may be 'the great and small', or 'matter', as Plato says in the *Timaeus*. But of course Plato does not say that the receptive is 'matter' in the *Timaeus*, though it is easy to see why Aristotle thought that he did, or should have done. For Aristotle, of course, he *should* have said it was matter. But without Aristotle's reformulation of the *Timaeus* on this point, the alleged differences between the *Timaeus* and the 'unwritten teachings' (represented in part by the *Philebus*), will have been even less than Aristotle thinks.

In *Physics* 4 Aristotle attacks one of the two Platonic causes, the female element or receptacle. We might well expect that eventually he would attack the other, namely Form-Mind. But in a way he has done so already. The Forms have already been questioned in *On Ideas*; and the Good itself (somehow) in *On the Good*. But the Platonic Form-Mind is in a sense a self-mover, if to be known is in some sense to be moved, and to know is to move, as the *Sophist* suggests. Hence an attack on self-movement will at the same time be an attack on the Platonic Mind and its Forms. Aristotle took longer to move against self-movement in a first principle. *Physics* 7 still tolerates it; *Physics* 8 does not. In book 8 the other Platonic 'cause' is inadequate not only as Form, but as Mind too. For a 'principle' cannot move itself; it must be unmoved. Its activity (though *Physics* 8 does not yet say it) must be thinking of thinking: what else is possible? And the way is open to the introspective nature of Mind as *energeia* of immobility which we find in *Metaphysics* Λ and which causes so much trouble in the interpretation of the

Metaphysics itself. But we have discussed some of the difficulties of *energeia* already (117–18 above).

But was the *Timaeus* a 'myth' after all? Did Plato himself think that Form-Mind generated in time (or with time), or is the biological language merely 'symbolic'? Aristotle is our primary concern now. He took it literally, so from the point of view of Aristotle's development the question is marginal. One of Aristotle's first references to the problem appears to be *De Caelo* 1.279B34ff, and *Topics* 6 (139B33ff) alludes to debate as to whether to take Plato's description of the receptacle as nurse 'metaphorically'. The context in the *De Caelo* makes clear that someone (i.e., Xenocrates) defended the *Timaeus* as symbol. It is not a literal creation story. The context also makes clear that this explanation was offered by 'certain people' trying to *defend* the *Timaeus*. Aristotle gives no indication that Plato would have endorsed their efforts. He himself thinks they are misguided; he is probably right.[32] Plato's theory of generation implies that the product of God (the cosmos) arises from God's substance, *de deo* (as Tertullian would put it). But its presence, that is, the fact of our world, is not symbolic. We really do exist and we are really not God. All that is not God comes into being, and unless it is specifically *made eternal* as such, like soul, its character changes and its individualized nature passes away. It was, of course, by no means stupid of Plato to have proposed a literal quasi-sexual creation. The mythographers had led the way, and however one explains the processes of conception, the birth of a being by sexual generation is perhaps the most unbeatable paradigm for the creation of something completely new that non-revelational religion can provide. The notion that the world is a living being was never entirely abandoned by Aristotle.[33]

II The Fifth Element 'Aether' Again

The Platonic universe, excluding the Form-God, is a self-mover, because it has a soul. In the universe there are four elements: earth, air, fire, and water. There is no hint of a fifth element. If the *Timaeus* is to be dated around 352, that probably means that any Aristotelian work written before 352 would be free of fifth elements. The *Protrepticus* was written before 352 (48–52 above). We have already assumed, on quite other grounds, that there is no fifth element in the *Physics,* though the Self-Moved Mover of *Physics* 7 (243A3ff) at the edge of the cosmos has some remarkable similarities.[34] The fifth element is introduced, with considerable energy and at considerable length, in book 1 of the *De Caelo* (1.2–6).[35] It moves naturally in a circle, yet though it moves, it is unchanging (*aidion*) and impassive (*apathes*). It is called *aether*. It is not fire – *pace* Anaxagoras (1.270B24–5).[36] It is ungenerated and indestructible. But it is, of course, natural and governed by nature. It is outside time only in the sense that its *aiōn*, its life, lasts for ever (1.279A12–B3). Such movement fits our 'premonitions' about God's nature – for the universe is a god (284B4), an ensouled being with a principle of motion. The activity (or condition) of this god (2.286A9ff) is deathlessness, that is, unending life; not, of course, that the whole universe moves: the centre remains still but the *aether* moves regularly and constantly, and on it the other movements of the universe depend (2.284A11). The *aether*, of course, has a 'purpose', for God and nature do nothing in vain (1.271A34). If we hold that all bodies move either naturally or by constraint (1.276A23), it moves naturally. It is in eternal and unchanging circular motion (1.279A30–B3). With the Good demolished in *On the Good* and the Forms in general in *On Ideas*, and with Aristotle offering bold new 'physical' theories of his own in *On Philosophy*, we can conclude that in the original unemended version of the *De Caelo*, the immanent God of *On Philosophy* has become particularly associated with the *aether* itself.[37] Problems remain about what is 'divine' apart from the *aether*; what our text of *De Caelo* means, for example, by 'the things there' (1.279A18), beyond (*exō*) the heavens. We seem to have here further interpolated material involving a transcendent mover or movers, certainly of later date.

Are there physical manifestations of the immanent divinity elsewhere in the cosmos, if the divine *aether* is restricted to the heavens? We have seen in an earlier chapter that there are, and will be (131–4 above). Their 'echoes' can eventually be found somehow in the elements, as well as in other self-moved movers such as the minds and souls of men and animals.[38] After the *De Caelo aether* disappears from the Aristotelian scene – or rather goes underground, for it re-emerges in the very late *De Generatione Animalium* where it is a 'counterpart' (*analogia*) of *pneuma* (2.736B30ff), of the 'soul-heat' in us. There it is again the 'element' of the stars and planets. 'Counterparts' are objects which perform similar functions in their respective domains, but are too divergent in their own natures to be merely categorized in terms of 'more or less'.[39] For Aristotle, therefore, feathers in birds are the counterparts of scales in fishes, while within the same species or genus we measure by the 'more or less'. So some birds have longer legs than others, and the defensive organs in males often exist 'to a greater degree than in females'; while notoriously menstrual blood in females is the counterpart of semen in males in the *De Generatione Animalium*, an example to which we shall return (*PA* 1.644A19ff, 3.661B28ff, 4.692B24; for menstrual blood, *GA*2.727A3).

We should expect, and shall indeed find, great similarities between *aether* and its counterpart. Between them they will seem to achieve the material activities of the living cosmos; while *GA* 3.762A18ff expresses the other side of the coin: 'all things in a sense are full of soul.' The composition of *aether* and *pneuma* will also be strikingly similar; in the case of *aether* it is spelled out in the *De Caelo*. Neither are the spheres fire, nor are they carried round in fire (2.289A34), though their movement produces fire in the highest sublunary level (Cf. *Mete*. 1.341A19). They do not make music, as the Pythagoreans claim (2.9),[40] though they are alive and well and at their best being supportive of the outer heaven, that of the fixed stars (2.292B15ff). There is a back reference to this discussion at *Meteorologica* 1.2.

III Prime Matter Again

Aristotle has a concept of what is called 'prime matter'; perhaps its roots lie in the Platonic 'receptacle'. This prime matter, so it is sometimes said, is not body, but it is so potentially.[41] As a notion about Aristotelian physics this may seem puzzling, for what is potentially A must be actually B. Aristotle himself denies that prime matter exists in the world *apart* from the four elements or simple bodies (*GC* 2.332A29, 332B7). But 'matter' is not a concept in Aristotelian logic; the corresponding term in logic could be 'substrate' (*hupokeimenon*), a logical core from which all predicates have been stripped away, indicating a substance without qualities. But in any case *hupokeimenon* is often better translated as 'subject', and the *Categories* already makes very clear that qualities exist only in substances, and that there is no substance without qualities. Clearly then prime matter is not qualityless substance, but perhaps it *refers* to the notion of qualityless substance (as a functional concept), just as 'privation' refers to a notion of the deprivation of quality from particular forms as such. Such a reading of the texts cannot be ruled out a priori. Perhaps it is the right answer. Are there indeed other further alternatives? We must look at the evidence again.

The phrase 'prime matter' occurs in *Metaphysics* Θ.1049A27 and in the *De Generatione et Corruptione* (2.329A24), though there it refers to Plato's 'unintelligible' receptacle or nurse (2.329A14ff), which is a substrate prior to the so-called elements. And given the phrase 'prime matter' in Aristotle, we would *appear* to be on safe ground to hold that it refers to a physical substance. But that does not necessarily mean, as Charlton assumes Aristotle could have intelligibly meant, that it is simply the four sublunary elements, each underlying one another. A major difficulty of Charlton's view as stated is that it makes Aristotle express himself bizarrely, indeed quite misleadingly ('The four elements are just *prime* matter') – and another alternative is that prime matter is *one* of the four elements. Perhaps that alternative should be considered. Scholars have often been puzzled about who it is to whom Aristotle refers when he occasionally speaks of a philosopher who argues that the basic material substance is earth; perhaps the answer – in some texts at least – is that he refers to himself.

Consider the possibility that prime matter, which in *Metaphysics* Z and H (1035B30, 1045B18) has as its opposite 'ultimate matter' (i.e., that which constitutes a formed individual like Socrates), is earth. Already in the *Topics* (6.139B33) Aristotle speaks of Plato's quasi-material nurse as 'earth' – though he claims to detect a metaphor. Thus he thinks such an identification possible when he is apparently not yet critical of the whole theory of the receptacle.[42] (If people talk metaphorically, he observes wryly, referring to the debate as to how literally the *Timaeus* should be taken, it is always possible to *pretend* [*suchophantein*] to take the words in the strict sense.)[43]

What then could 'prime' or 'first' matter be? If it is anything both specific and physical, it must at least be a substance which is totally inert, which can be acted upon, but which has no power to act in any way. It must, therefore, be matter with only 'passive' qualities. There are a few passages which indicate that this is the kind of matter Aristotle would have to have in mind.

1 *GC* 1.320A2. Matter in the strict and most authoritative sense is the substrate which is receptive of generation and destruction. Its nature is to receive; in this respect it is like Plato's receptacle.
2 *GC* 1.314B26. 'In this way it is clear that we must suppose a single matter for the contraries at any time [present in it].'
3 *GC* 1.317A34. Everything comes from *something*. This is repeated, with specific reference to the categories and the relationship between substance and the others, at 319A12ff. If we neglect the Parmenidean principle, we generate being from not-being. It is important to observe Aristotle's use of the categories at this stage of his thought.
4 *GC* 1.322A28.[44] The form (perhaps as immaterial) is some power in matter. That is, where there is matter, there must be form, and this form is a power.
5 *GC* 1.328B12. Tin almost (but not quite) disappears when it is mixed with copper. This is a model for being 'mixable'. Tin acts in a 'receptive' manner towards its form. But it is a *real* substance, not like Plato's receptacle.

Aristotle is not impressed with his predecessors' attempts at an explanation of generation and destruction. Only Democritus has made much of a success at it (1.315A35), and he attempted to explain change in terms of the rearrangement of primary figures, thus avoiding the Parmenidean trap: in an atomist's world, nothing comes from nothing, which is more than can be said, in Aristotle's view, of Plato's *Timaeus* – on which Aristotle outlines an attack to be developed in book 1 of the *Physics*. Both in this section of the *De*

Generatione et Corruptione and again near the end, Aristotle concentrates on Plato's failure in this regard: the fierce attack on 'Socrates in the *Phaedo*' (*GC* 2.335B4ff) is on the same point. The Forms are not by themselves causes.[45]

A problem with Plato is that he had no material *substance*; his receptacle can be made to do duty for matter (Cf. *Phys.* 4.209B11–13; GC 2.329A16–24), but it is not properly material. The problem with Democritus and Leucippus is that they could not explain 'alteration', change of quality. Aristotle can do better. His purely theoretical analysis of the four elements, earth, water, air, fire, is that they consist of a substrate plus primary qualities, one active, one passive: hot and cold; wet and dry. Hot and cold are active qualities (*GC* 2.329B18ff), but cold may be a deprivation (*GC* 1.318B15ff). Thus fire is hot and dry (primarily hot, 2.331A21ff). Air is hot and wet. Water is cold and wet. Earth is cold and dry (*GC* 2.331A3). Fire, as we have already seen, does not generate anything on earth: it is too hot (though heat in *aether* generates). Earth does not generate anything either: it is substrate with two qualities, both of which may in different ways be negative. And dry is less formable than wet (*GC* 2.329B31ff). That is why earth is the best individual candidate for the role of primary matter.

But to suggest that earth may be the primary element, or prime matter, cannot be simply to suggest that of itself it is the material *archē*, the complete material beginning (2.332B6). No individual element qua material is complete enough for that; they all change into one another (to use the sort of phrase which has troubled the commentators – as in *Mete.* 1.339A37–B2). No element can be an *archē*, when for X to be an *archē* means that things can be generated from X *alone*. Anaximander's *apeiron*, or Anaximenes' air are *archai*; they explain *everything*. No Aristotelian element does that. Certainly not earth, since it can *do* nothing, except (perhaps) lack; it can only *be*, and be (unlike *nous*) ineffectually. Nor, of course, would fire be an *archē*, for to turn fire into anything else, it has to be cooled: another factor is needed. In this sense the existence of earth and fire, with their '*dunameis*' of cold and dry, hot and dry, implies the other elements. But of the fire-components in these two, perhaps only the hot is positively active, and that, by itself, is *too* active for sustaining life. If we could moisten the dry in earth, then water would 'arise', and if we could moisten the dry in heat (thereby also cooling it) then air would 'arise'. To understand that no individual substance, even earth, is a self-sufficient *archē* is to see the point of Aristotle's remarks at *De Generatione et Corruptione* 1.314B23ff that water cannot be produced 'from fire' or earth 'from water'. To get these results one has to *do* things physically to fire and earth.

We have seen that all matter has some *dunamis*, such a 'capacity,' in it (*GC* 1.322A28). That *dunamis* is the ability to act or be acted upon. Clearly any substance has the capacity of being acted upon (if it is material). What, however, could the ability to act be? In other words, how does Aristotle *explain* the active power of hot and cold? Eventually the answer to this is to be found in the theory of *pneuma*, but that is not worked out in the *De Generatione et Corruptione*. *Pneuma* is the *correct* mix of air and fire; it is in fact 'hot air' (GA 2.736A1), the best combination of the hot and the wet (though there are different 'strengths' of *pneuma* itself). Its mode of operation is shown by another passage of the *De Generatione Animalium* where we see that it exists in all the elements except earth. The context is about spontaneous generation (*GA* 3.762A18ff). Animals and plants arise in earth and the wet because water subsists (*huparchei*) in earth, and *pneuma* in water, and in *pneuma* soul-(life-)heat. Note that it is in *water* (not just the wet) where the last trace of *pneuma* is to be found. If we could get earth without water, there would be no *pneuma*, no possibility of spontaneous generation. Earth would then be totally inert, though not totally without character. In the *De Caelo* too Aristotle says that water is everywhere *except* in earth (4.311B8ff), air is everywhere *except* in water and earth. We can now see one reason why Aristotle says in the *De Generatione Animalium* that only 'in a way' are all things full of soul: all but earth have 'soul-heat', and earth is constantly affected by the other elements which do have it.

Finally consider another passage from the *De Caelo*. At 1.277B15ff Aristotle interestingly talks of three (not four or five) corporeal elements. The first of these is *aether*, which revolves; the second (earth) is around the centre of the universe, which is the place for the underlying element (not *hupokeimenon* – still a logical term – but *huphistamenon*); and the third is the 'middle' body between (i.e., the other sublunary elements, water, air, and fire). *Aether* here occupies the *eschatos topos*, the last place (last is opposite to first). The same distinction is used at 3.298B6ff, where it is perhaps misread by Simplicius (and others). Aristotle says that he has discussed the first element (that is, *aether*) and that he is now going on to deal with the 'other two'. Simplicius (20.10) thinks that this refers to the two pairs (fire and air, earth and water), but in the light of the passage of book 1 (277B15ff) this may be wrong. The others could be fire, air, and water as a group, earth remaining by itself as most inert.

Charlton was right to think that there is in Aristotle nothing beyond the simple bodies, that is, the elements; but some bodies are simpler than others. Earth is the most inert; therefore at least the closest approximation to what might be called 'prime matter in the strict sense', that is, a 'prime [in the sense of "most basic"] matter' of the sublunary world as a whole. It is a prime or first element if you look at it that way round. (If you start at the top, of course, *aether* is first.) But the inertness of earth is not an absolute lack of character, and in so far as earth needs to be 'constitutively' changed if other elements are to 'arise', it cannot be prime matter in the sense of a physical substance in itself adequate to explain materiality.

Furthermore, even if earth is viewed as prime (i.e., most basic) matter in the sublunary world taken as a whole, there would also be prime matters for individual substances within that world, and some of these substances might contain no earth at all. What is 'prime matter' in any individual case would thus seem to depend above all on the nature of the substance whose matter is being discussed. Hence, it seems, prime matter cannot be any particular sort of matter, even earth; the only option seems to be that it is a functional concept after all. But note that Aristotle did not have the concept of a functional concept, even if he employed functional concepts. If he had had it, he might have thought of Plato's 'receptacle' as a functional concept too.

11

More Chronology of Aristotle's Physical and Biological Writings

I From the Beginning of the 'Historia Animalium' to the 'Meteorologica'

Aether is discussed in the *De Caelo* and mentioned in the *Meteorologica*; *pneuma* is not. *Pneuma* comes much later, and before we can proceed with it, it will be helpful to comment further on chronology. In the first chapter of *Meteorologica* 1 Aristotle tells us how far he has proceeded with his project of writing an account of nature, that nature which, as early as the *Protrepticus*, it is the task of the philosopher to watch. He began, undoubtedly, when he was convinced that Plato and many others in the Academy, by their excessive emphasis on the Forms and the One, were taking the wrong road: that is, after he had written *On Ideas*, *On the Good*, and *On Philosophy*. *Meteorologica* 1 explains the project, and gives us some idea of the sequence; and the text which provides this information is lengthy, not a mere line which may be explained away as a quick insertion. For Aristotle talks about a project which he intends to complete. He does not say, nor does he suggest, that he is merely rewriting previous work for use in a lecture-course. He appears to be engaged in the process of more or less original composition.

First, then, came the *Physics* (or its original components), then the *De Caelo*, then the *De Generatione et Corruptione*, then the *Meteorologica* itself.[1] Later, Aristotle says, he will start talking about animals. We must tidy the data up a bit more. In the *De Caelo* (2.284B14) Aristotle refers to a work on the movement of animals, which must be the *De Incessu Animalium*. Both this book and the *De Caelo* itself show an interest in such 'non-scientific,' rather Pythagorean, notions as right and left, up and down, some of which Aristotle modified later.[2] In other words Aristotle had written the

De Incessu before he set about what in *Meteorologica* 1 he calls his treatment of animals and plants. Much later, of course, he wrote *De Motu*, and although the subject-matter is not particularly similar, scholars have made too much of the insignificant differences and neglected the big one: there is *no pneuma* in the *De Incessu*. *Pneuma* is very prominent, however, in the *De Motu*. As I have already suggested, there is need for a counterpart of *aether* in the sublunary world as early as the *De Generatione et Corruptione*: that is if, as I have argued, the notion that the cosmos exhibits an overall purposiveness is to be maintained (125–9 above). But *pneuma* has not been developed by the time of the *De Incessu*, where, by later standards, it is needed.

There is a further complication. The *De Incessu* itself (704B10) refers, under the title 'Natural History,' specifically to the *Historia Animalium*,[3] the growing collection of data which were to provide the raw materials for Aristotle's major biological works. That reference suggests that as early as the *De Incessu* the collection had begun. There is no reason to assume that it was yet complete. But it may have been largely completed well before the time of *Meteorologica* 1.

It is possible, therefore, to attempt an absolute dating of this group of texts. The last chronological reference in the *Meteorologica* is to the archonship of Nicomachus (341/0). It was completed, therefore, later than that, and followed the *Analytics* and the revision of the *Topics*. The following order of composition may be regarded as highly likely:
Historia Animalium (beginning);
Physics (books 2–7);
De Incessu Animalium (after *HA* 4);
De Caelo;
De Generatione et Corruptione;
Meteorologica (ca 339). (By this time *HA* 5 is certainly complete.)

The relative dates of the *De Incessu* and the *Physics* remain uncertain (though further discussion of the relationship of the *De Incessu* and the *Historia Animalium* will clarify the situation somewhat [214–15 below]). But the order I have proposed does justice to the plausible claim that Aristotle at least began to discuss general problems of the study of nature before turning to more specific parts of the subject-matter. At the moment we cannot decide why he wrote *De Incessu* before certain other biological works (biology being, of course, a part of Aristotelian physics). We should probably persist in dating the beginning of the *Physics*, therefore, to Aristotle's period in Assos, or at the least to Mytilene (where he was assisted by his friend Theophrastus, who himself was a native of the island of Lesbos), and the *De Incessu* similarly: date ca 345. The *Historia Animalium* may have been started a little earlier and by the time of the *De Incessu* Aristotle seems to have reached at least book 4.

A radically different chronology has recently been proposed for the biological works than the one I shall argue for here. Balme agrees that the *Historia Animalium* was begun in the Academy but largely written during or after Aristotle's stay in Lesbos.[4] But he also thinks that all the other biological works (as well as *Metaphysics* Z.12) are earlier still. I argue against such a schema below: the development of theories of *pneuma* (dismissed by Balme) tells heavily against it. Balme notes that among the biological treatises, the *Historia Animalium* is 'the heavyweight', that it lists 390 of the 560 animal species discussed by Aristotle, and that such data would have taken a long time to collect. All that is true, but it provides no argument that Aristotle would have had insufficient time to compose the other treatises later than (or even in tandem with) his major collection of data. Balme also notes that at times the *Historia Animalium* offers shorter versions of what appears elsewhere in the biological writings, and thinks that in such sections it may be a summary. But the opposite conclusion is equally possible, and as for conflicts between the *Historia Animalium* and other texts, those need afford no surprise if, as I suggest, the *Historia Animalium* is an ongoing file.

II More on the 'Historia Animalium'

Before we turn to substantive questions about *pneuma*, there remain further chronological considerations in regard to Aristotle's biological works, though these too have substantive implications. I have already argued that the *De Incessu* is comparatively early – contemporary with, and possibly earlier than, some parts of the *Historia Animalium*. It apparently refers, however, to HA 4.523B21ff at 706B2 and to *HA* 2.498A31 at 714B12–13. This is not difficult to comprehend. More difficult are the last lines of the *De Incessu* (714B20–4), which seem to suggest that the *De Partibus Animalium* has already been written and that the *De Anima* is next on the list. That *De Incessu* precedes *De Anima* is readily intelligible; that it follows the *De Partibus Animalium* is not. Some have rejected the last paragraph as an addition by an editor attempting to slot *De Incessu* into a preconceived pattern of Aristotle's biology. But a better explanation is at hand: the *De Incessu* follows book 4 of the *Historia Animalium*, to which we have seen that it refers.

Book 5 of the *Historia Animalium* begins by telling us that we have now discussed *all* the parts of animals, internal and external. This is not the case *unless* we include the *De Incessu* in the *Historia Animalium* as book 4A.

Then indeed the discussion is (almost) complete; and we have already argued that the *De Incessu* is an early biological work, linked with the 'Pythagorean' concerns of the *De Caelo* and devoid of the *pneuma* material of the *De Motu*, which is largely a later replacement of it. The end of the *De Incessu* confirms this hypothesis. 'So much for the parts of animals,' says Aristotle, 'and especially those to do with progression (*poreia*).' 'Now,' continue most of the manuscripts, 'for the soul.' The last words have always puzzled the commentators, and as we noted, Brandis rejected the last paragraph. Forster, however, indicated the root of the problem, though he did not solve it. Manuscript Z originally has a blank instead of ψυχῆς; a later hand supplied ψυχῆς, while the first hand leaves the blank in the text and writes ζωῆσ in the margin. The correct reading, I would suggest, is γονῆς. Generation is in fact the subject-matter of books 5–7 of the *Historia Animalium*. Within a few lines in *HA* 5 Aristotle says he will speak *peri geneseōn*, and the word *geneseōn* is an alternative (though less likely) conjecture we might propose in the *De Incessu* itself. At any rate the meaning is right. In addition to fitting in a 'missing' section of the *Historia Animalium*, a detailed study of 'moving-parts' which is otherwise omitted, the advantage of the above explanation is that *De Partibus Animalium* can now follow *Historia Animalium* 1–7, which is a natural place for it.

The *De Partibus Animalium*, as we shall see, is introduced by an elaborate prelude urging the importance of a new project. That new project, in fact, is a second version of the biological texts. There are thus two sets of biological writings by Aristotle: the first (so far as we can see at this stage) is *Historia Animalium* 1–4, *De Incessu*, *Historia Animalium* 5–7 (on generation, culminating with the discussion of human reproduction in book 7). As we shall see, these books are a more or less 'pre-pneumatic' account of biology. Just as there is no *pneuma* in the *De Incessu* to account for movement, so there is no *pneuma* in *Historia Animalium* 1–7 to account for generation. Thus *De Motu* and *De Generatione Animalium* replace *De Incessu* and *Historia Animalium* 5–7. *Historia Animalium* 1–4, *De Incessu*, and *Historia Animalium* 5–7 are the biology of the Troad-Mytilene-Macedon period of Aristotle's life. *De Partibus Animalium*, *De Motu*, and *De Generatione Animalium* are the biology of the final Athenian stage – in that order. Naturally, in the Athenian stage, Aristotle makes use of his early work where appropriate.

It has been shown by Lee that many of the place-names in the *Historia Animalium* point to this pre-Athenian stage of Aristotle's career,[5] though they need not always be the result of Aristotle's observation; some would derive, for example, from talking to fishermen. But it is interesting to observe other 'early' features of the *Historia Animalium*. *HA* 1.488B24 provides a good example. Man is a 'dualizer' (1.488A8); he is both gregarious and a loner. He looks like a lot of social animals and yet is importantly not a social animal like a bee or wasp. Aristotle is also interested in man *vis-à-vis* other social animals in the much later *Politics* 1. But the stated *difference* between man and the other social animals is importantly distinct in *HA* 1 and *Politics* 1. In *HA* 1.488B24–6 man is different in so far as he can *deliberate* (*bouleutikon*), and in so far as he can recall past events at will. In the *Politics* the difference is defined more broadly: man is different in so far as he can identify the advantageous and disadvantageous, and hence the just and unjust. By the time of *Politics* 1 deliberation is far from being the *most* distinctive feature of man, though it is indeed distinctive and of great importance. Natural slaves, as we know, cannot deliberate. In terms of the *Historia Animalium* this would make them simply non-human. But the thesis of *Politics* 1, as we have seen (153–7 above), offers a more nuanced solution (cf. 1.1253A11–18).

In Aristotle's account of desirable reproduction arrangements there are a number of interesting parallels between *Historia Animalium* 5 and 7 and an *earlier* book of the *Politics* (book 7). According to the *Politics* (7.1335A) men are generally beyond reproduction at seventy, women at fifty. Mating too young is bad because the children are 'imperfect,' both smaller and more liable to be female.[6] Young women have more trouble in labour, and more die. Women are more self-controlled if they are married older; they seem to be more licentious if they have intercourse young. More important, male growth is affected if males have sex while 'the seed is still growing'; and seed is less plentiful later on. Hence women should marry at about eighteen, men at about thirty-seven or a little before. Then their fertility in reproduction will end at about the same time. It is better to have sex in the winter, preferably when the north wind is blowing.[7] Aristotle's discussion in *Politics* 7 ends with a promise, apparently and significantly not fulfilled, to say more about the desirable bodily constitution of the parents in a work *On Regulations for Children* (probably to be a part of the *Politics* itself and to include the best way of having them as well as how to look after them). Bearing children is a service to society (a liturgy) and should be performed by persons under fifty. After that intercourse is for health or some other reason.

Compare all this with *Historia Animalium*. Males want intercourse (5.542B1) more in winter, females in summer. As the *Politics* shows, male preference should decide the time for intercourse because the results are better in the winter. Men can sometimes generate up to seventy, women to fifty. But normally the limit is sixty-five for men, forty-five for women (5.545B28–31). Males are more likely to be born if the north wind is blowing at the time of intercourse (*HA* 6.574A1), females if the wind blows from the south. This passage explains the sentence in the *Politics* about the preferability of wind and winter, and the idea is repeated later in the *De Generatione Animalium* (4.766B34ff). Females are liable to be loose (and so are boys!) after about fourteen, the age of puberty; if they have sex, they will become more licentious. They need supervision (as do boys). Sexual experience creates physiological expectations; a memory of pleasure creates a longing for more (7.581B12–22). When semen is first produced, it is 'infertile' (5.544B15ff), or at best liable to produce small and weak offspring. This must, of course, refer to boys; men, we recall from *Politics* 7, should marry much later than women if they are to be in their prime. In *HA* 7 Aristotle makes the same point, simply saying that before twenty-one semen is 'infertile'; he clearly means not fertile enough for a good product (7.582A17). Young women have difficulties in labour, and are only fully ready at twenty-one, but men need even more development than that. (Here there is an interesting divergence form the *Politics*, where 'about eighteen' is the recommended age for women. The *Politics* discussion is probably somewhat later, and Aristotle has moved a little nearer to Plato's idea in the *Laws* that girls *can* marry as late as twenty, perhaps to allow their education to be further extended.)[8]

One of the most striking facts about the first seven books of the *Historia Animalium* is that for all the discussion of reproduction (three books altogether), not a word is said either about the role of *pneuma* or of the 'associated' importance of the menstrual blood in women. In fact it is clear that although Aristotle speaks of menstrual blood, he does not associate it with conception. Before the 330s, he thought in terms of the Platonic view that conception is a matter of sowing the male seed in the ground. The woman is the nurse, the source of nourishment, both before and after birth. The *Politics* (7.1335A17ff) specifically refers to the same theory. The people of Troezen asked why so many of their women died in childbirth. The answer of the oracle was 'Don't cut a young furrow,' according to the scholiast; that is, leave her a virgin until she is older. Women should not be sown too young. The male still provides both form and matter in the act of impregnation. As we shall see, even the *last* book of the later *De Partibus Animalium* has not entirely abandoned this view. The chronological significance of this theory for non-biological texts of Aristotle is considerable.

What about books 8–10 of the *Historia Animalium*? They are (at best) marginally Aristotelian. Book 10 (usually and rightly rejected) depends, according to Balme, on a single independent Greek manuscript (*Vat. Gr.* 262). It also contains a theory of conception which Aristotle never held, but which existed within atomist circles, possibly also, as we shall see, in the Academy, and among a number of doctors: that males and females provide different *kinds* of seeds for conception.[9] Books 8 and 9 too have long been suspect. A discussion of reproduction should *close* the strictly biological series; after that should come psychology. In Aristotle's second series we have *De Partibus Animalium, De Motu,* and *De Generatione Animalium* (with the psychological work *De Anima* and its associated *Parva Naturalia* before the *De Motu*). In fact books 8 and 9 of the *Historia Animalium* do deal with psychological matters, especially the psychology of animals, and book 9 contains a reference to the ovaries of sows which again suggests a rather sophisticated theory of conception involving two kinds of seed. For the ovary was identified as the source of female 'seed' in third-century Alexandria.

The subject-matter of *Historia Animalium* 8–9, sometimes now called an 'ethology,' is within the scope of Aristotle's original project for the *Historia Animalium* (cf. 1.487A10), but it is curiously inadequate. It cannot simply be defended as an early treatment of psychology, an early *De Anima*. Though its content is psychological, it is far from a full-scale Aristotelian treatment of the topic. Many editors have resorted to excising large chunks of the text, though it is hard to see just what to delete and what to retain. Clearly some of the material would have been acceptable to Aristotle; but that does not mean that Aristotle wrote it, or even compiled it. In view of Aristotle's specific comments on the nature of sexual differences throughout his life, for example, it is hard to see why he should have composed the unparalleled and extraordinarily chauvinistic section at the beginning of book 9. Aristotle did think that in important respects women are inferior to men, but nothing in his writings would lead us to expect what appears at 608B1–18. Even the positive qualities here offered women, that is, of having a better memory than men, lack parallels or explication in genuinely Aristotelian texts, let alone in his well-documented attitude to his wife Pythias. Book 9 is also, and unusually, full of the miraculous. Such evidently unaristotelian features may make us hesitate before saddling Aristotle with the remark that gaudy bees, like gaudy and showy women, are good for nothing (9.617A14), or with recording that dolphins frequently have a personal devotion to young boys (9.631A8–9). Books 8 and 9 of the *Historia Animalium* are curiously impressionistic; they have recently been connected, and probably rightly, with biological works of Theophrastus, though Theophrastus is not the author. They continue an Aristotelian plan, but very disappointingly.[10]

III The 'De Partibus Animalium'

1 The Relation of the *De Partibus Animalium* to the *Metaphysics*

De Partibus Animalium opens a new chapter.[11] It begins solemnly with a lengthy allocution on the primary importance of the study of final causes in nature. The final cause and the beautiful are more present in works of nature than in those of art (1.639B20); the passage recalls the *Protrepticus* of long before. The study of animals may be humble, but it is *very* rewarding (1.644B23ff). Because the subject-matter is closer to us, we can understand more than we can of the philosophy about 'divine things which we have *already* treated.' This probably refers, as Balme saw, to the *De Caelo.*[12] The heavenly bodies possess the higher value (1.644B24–5) and last for ever, but we need not behave like children who would be surly about studying the 'less honourable' animals. As Heraclitus has said when his guests found him relieving himself in the lavatory, 'there are gods here too.' So even in the lower animals there is something natural and beautiful, a work of purpose and not of chance.[13]

There is a reference at the beginning of *De Partibus Animalium* 1 (640A2) to 'theoretical sciences' distinct from physics. These theoretical sciences are concerned with what is; physics is concerned with what will be.[14] These matters, says Aristotle, have been discussed elsewhere (that is, in the *Posterior Analytics*). The modes of demonstration, the modes of necessity, are different. These theoretical sciences deal with necessary truths about form or eternal necessary movements; indeed mostly about what in the *Metaphysics* Aristotle is going to call being qua being. *PA* 1 looks forward to *Metaphysics* A.981B26,[15] where what is called 'wisdom' is concerned with first causes and principles, and where the theoretical sciences are superior to the productive. The wise man will be able to expound the causes better, that is, more basically; and Aristotle envisages a more fundamental science than physics itself. The objects of this enquiry (as *PA* 1 also suggests) are the most remote, but the most basic, and such study is for its own sake, not for anything beyond itself (*Met.* A.982A32ff). If one understands the *first* principles and causes, one will be able to understand the things which are 'from' them, that is concrete particulars and events. The highest science will know *why* each thing should be done, that is, *why* we should do anything (including, for instance, study physics and ethics). It will know *both* the good in each science (which according to the *Eudemian Ethics* is all the good there is) *and* in general the best in all nature. Metaphysics, therefore, is concerned in the first instance with identifying what is 'best' and then with understanding what is 'from it,' i.e., everything else in so far as it is. Later books are to express this as a search for first being (i.e., God) and the being of everything in so far as it is being. But we have to wait for *Metaphysics* Γ for that.

In the meantime Aristotle contents himself with discussing how 'metaphysics' arises from physics. In a sense the lover of myths is a philosopher, because myths contain wonders. The instinct to study the moon and the sun and the stars (that is, the higher subjects of physics) raises the question of the *genesis* of all – not, interestingly enough, merely of how things first *move* (which is physics) but of how they come to *be*. Thus we would expect metaphysics to be concerned not only with the *fact* of a first mover, but of the nature, the being of the first mover, and hence not only of the movement, but somehow of the 'being' of the world. Such science may be 'beyond the human' (982B29), but human nature is in many respects slavish. Now, Simonides says that higher knowledge is for God alone; but perhaps this is wrong, for it had already been taught (by Plato in the *Phaedrus* and *Timaeus*) that God is not jealous. So perhaps there is such a supreme science; if so, it will be both possessed by God and concerned with 'divine things' (983A7). Surely this means that God is a metaphysician and the objects of metaphysics are what God thinks about. Thus if, as in *Metaphysics* Λ, God is thinking about *thinking*, then thinking and the mind are the divine objects of science – and the character of such thinking is eternally the same. Thus 'to think' is to be eternally in the same state; hence there is a sense in which being qua being *is* thinking (or, as Λ puts it, the activity of thought is life); and God is 'eternal and unchanging duration' (*aiōn*: a word which the *De Caelo* [1.279A27] has already connected with everlasting *being*).[16]

But return to the *De Partibus Animalium* and notice that Aristotle not only alludes to a science of metaphysics, as we have seen; he tells us something of its content (1.641A33ff). The question is: Does natural science (physics) study all the soul or some part? If it studies all, then there is no higher science. For if it studies the intellect, it also studies the intelligibles (if they are correlative). To this dilemma Aristotle answers that not all soul is 'nature'; that is, concerned with movement and its origin. One or more parts of soul are therefore outside the scope of physics. Thus we see that the *study* of one or more parts of soul (or the study of intellect) is outside physics. Note again the correspondence of this statement with the subject-matter of metaphysics as identified in *Metaphysics* A. The belief that some aspects of the soul (qua accompanied by matter) are also part of the subject-matter of physics is repeated in *Metaphysics* E.1026A4ff. Also note that Aristotle is still not sure whether to *call* that 'part' of soul which is not 'nature' soul or intellect. The *De Anima*, of course, had not been written (nor probably the distinction between Mind as God and mind as human mental activity [*nous* = *dianoia*] clearly drawn). We may conclude from this treatment of the possibility of metaphysics that *De Partibus Animalium* 1 was written at some time not too far distant from the beginning of the *Metaphysics*. Let us therefore date it soon after the review of the *Physics* and other physical treatises, in Aristotle's last Athenian period.

The famous phrase 'being qua being' of *Metaphysics* Γ and E does not occur in *PA* with reference to the science that is beyond nature. In some ways, as we should expect, the language of *PA* is nearer to the opening book A of the *Metaphysics*: both allude to the 'absolute necessity' of what is eternal (*PA* 1.639B24ff, cf. *Met.* A.982A23), though the idea is repeated later in the *Metaphysics* itself (E.1026B27ff). *Metaphysics* A (as we shall argue in more detail) went through two versions, so there is a certain time-lag between the early chapters of *PA* and the books of *Metaphysics* beyond A: time enough to allow the development of the idea in E.1025B25 that physics itself is a *theoretical* science, though of course inferior to first philosophy. In this regard *Metaphysics* E presents a revised version of the distinction in *De Partibus Animalium* 1.

2 Cross-references in the *De Partibus Animalium* and Chronological Refinements

It is now time to turn to the cross-references in *De Partibus Animalium*, for they make chronological sense. They are as follows:

1 At 1.639A20ff Aristotle remarks that topics like sleep, respiration, growth, decay, and death are not clarified yet. Some of these *had* already been discussed in the *Historia Animalium*. Aristotle evidently means to do the work again – as he does in the *Parva Naturalia*.

2 There is a back reference to *De Generatione et Corruptione* 2.337B25ff at 1.640A8.

3 There is a probable reference to *On Philosophy* on final causes at 1.642A6–7 (or perhaps, though less certainly, to *Posterior Analytics* 2.94B36, as Balme suggested; I doubt whether this text is quite 'philosophical', however).

4 *PA* 1.642A29ff provides no reference, but an interesting comparison with *Metaphysics* A.987B1. An effect of Socrates was to improve the methodology of science (by introducing definitions) but philosophers then began to attend to 'useful goodness' and political science.

5 There is an attack on dichotomy in *De Partibus Animalium* 1.2–4; not, however, as is sometimes supposed,[17] on the whole notion of *divisions* in zoology. The *aim* of division, as Balme says,[18] is (1.643B28) to mark something off and identify its nature; all division can *do*, of course, is to list things, as parallel passages in the *Analytics* also indicate (*APr.* 1.31; *APo.* 2.5 and 13). Division is acceptable, though dichotomy is not – provided the intention is not to *prove* anything. The reference is presumably to a methodological mistake of Plato, and of Aristotle himself in some of the earlier parts of the *Topics* and the *Categories*. By now Aristotle is sure that there is a difference between identifying individuals in kinds – without necessarily doing taxonomy – and understanding their natures by a 'demonstration of the essence.'[19]

6 *PA* 1.5 starts again by distinguishing within 'nature' between the eternal and the perishable, as we have seen.

7 *PA* 2.647A27 is probably a reference to *HA* 3.515A27–B7,[20] and to other remarks on heat and blood in the *Historia Animalium* (e.g., 3.521A7–B4). The other possibility is *De Sensu* 439A2, but for reasons which will soon become apparent, this is unnecessary and false.

8 *PA* 2.649A31 is sometimes said to refer to *Mete.* 4; the correct source is *De Generatione et Corruptione* 2.329B, as was shown earlier.

9 There are references to the *Historia Animalium* (1.495B19ff, 3.514B10ff), and to the (lost) *Dissections* at 2.650A32, and to the *De Generatione et Corruptione* (again) at 2.650B10.

10 At 2.653A21 Aristotle 'refers' to material from treatises on *Sensation and Sleep*. This has often been assumed to be an allusion to two works *On Sensation* and *On Sleep* which are included in the *Parva Naturalia*. The correct reference is to *HA* 4.10, a section which comes down in the manuscripts as headed *On Sleep and Waking* but which at the end of the chapter is called *On Sensation and Sleep and Waking* – and which refers back to the *beginning* of *On the Senses* in chapter 8.

11 *PA* 2.653B18 is a forward reference to the *De Generatione Animalium* on semen and milk (not, notice, menstrual blood).[21]

12 The heart is the centre of sensations at *PA* 2.656A29, where Aristotle alludes to a work *On Sensations*. This is sometimes claimed to be *De Sensu* 438B25ff, which itself refers to the *De Anima*. The correct reference should again be in the *Historia Animalium*. This time 4.8–10 cannot be the right place: *On the Senses* is said to begin with chapter 8. Unfortunately there is no mention of the *heart* in our text: all there is is a reference to what was *later* to become the 'connate' *pneuma*. The noises of insects are caused by their 'internal *pneuma*' at 535B4 and B13. *Pneuma* in later works should be connected somehow with the heart. The explanation seems to be that there is *no* discussion of the location of the *common sense* of animals here in our *Historia Animalium*. Presumably Aristotle did discuss its location, and an obvious explanation, as we shall see, is that the end of *HA* 4 (i.e., *De Respiratione*) was 'lost' *at the time* when the *De Incessu* was also separated from *HA*. For the *De Incessu*, as we have seen, should follow *HA* 4. And the 'lost' material should deal *inter alia* with the heart.

13 There are further references to *HA* 2.504B1 and 4.536A20ff at *PA* 2.660B3; *HA* 2.507A7ff is the point of reference of *PA* 3.661B12. Notice that the author of the ps.-Aristotelian *HA* 8.597B26 gives a miraculously decorated version of the *HA* or *PA* material. Peck also cites *HA* 9.608A17, where passing of information among animals is mentioned.

This again depends on the *Historia Animalium*, and we should notice how the hand of the ps.-Aristotelian author of the passage is detected very near the 'chauvinist' material we discussed earlier (218 above).

14 There are further allusions to the lost *Dissections* and *HA* (3.511B11–515A26) at *PA* 3.668B29 (cf. *PA* 4.684B).

15 The reference to writings on the respiration of fish (*PA* 3.669A5) is probably to *De Respiratione* 476A1ff (cf. *PA* 4.697A23 referring to *De Resp.* 476B22). The treatise *De Respiratione* is probably, as we have suggested, part of the original *Historia Animalium*, again, like the *De Incessu*, dislocated. (We have already indicated another likely hole in the *Historia Animalium*.) *De Respiratione* should be at the end of book 4. It is the source of the idea that the heart is the seat of the faculties (474A25ff). It is clearly intended as a part of biology in the modern sense, rather than merely of physics in the ancient sense. It is far from limited to man, or human psychology. Its allusion to other works on smell (473B1) seems certainly to be to *HA* 4.8 (534A12ff). It refers by name to the *Historia Animalium* three times (477A6–7, 478B1, and 478A28);[22] all those references are to the first four books. It talks of *pneumatizing* at 479B31, and describes pneumatizing of the wet by heat as a pulsation of the heart (480A14–15). Thus there is 'pneumatizing' in *De Respiratione*, but there is no reason to think that *pneuma*, as distinct from hot blood, is yet connected with operations like sensing (smelling) and movement, as it is in the later *De Partibus Animalium* (2.659B18–19).[23]

My chronological conclusion from the points enumerated above would be that the order of one set of Aristotle's early writings on biology can be refined. The order would be *HA* 1–4, *De Resp.*, *De Incessu*, *HA* 5–7 (originally called *On Generation*). Let us thus proceed to the following:

16 *HA* (4.528B30ff) seems to be called Aristotle's first biological work at *PA* 4.678B23–4.[24]

17 *PA* 4 provides references to the *De Incessu* (690B16, 692A17, 696A12–13 to 708A9ff, 712A1ff, 709B7 respectively).

3 *Pneuma* and Conception

The cross-references give a consistent picture of the order of composition of a set of treatises: *HA* 1–4, *De Resp.*, *De Incessu*, *HA* 5–7, *PA* 1–4. As we have seen, the concept of *pneuma* has begun to appear; indeed it first appeared (innocuously) as far back as the *De Generatione et Corruptione* 1.321B9 (cf. 318B29), where it is called air. *De Respiratione* explains further that blood is warmed ('pneumatized') and cooled in the heart; pleasure helps to warm it, pain and fear to cool it. The *Historia Animalium* itself has already spoken of '*pneuma* inside' (4.535B4, 13) but makes little use of it as a *different substance*, even in animals, let alone in man. In the *De Respiratione* Aristotle thinks primarily, when he deals with pneumatizing, in terms of the effects of boiling the blood, that is, of *heat*, as he does even in the *De Partibus Animalium* when he comments on the effects of blood on character (2.648A2ff): the thicker and warmer the blood, the more strength; the thinner and cooler, the more sensation and intelligence. The best animals have hot, clear, thin blood. Males are said to be better equipped in these regards than females.

So in the *De Respiratione pneuma* has almost arrived; in the *De Partibus Animalium* (2.659B18–19) it is beginning to be connected with activities of the heart, with pleasures and pains and movements and sensation – even perhaps, back in *De Respiratione* (473A11ff, 474B4), with nutrition.[25] But, fascinatingly enough, it is not connected with reproduction. Aristotle does not mention it as a quality of male semen. And the reason is that even at the end of the *De Partibus Animalium* he has still not developed what I shall call his 'mature' theory of conception. He still holds to the core of the Platonic view that the male provides both form and matter for the original offspring, that the female is the source of food for growth before and after birth. This view is still unmistakable in the following texts:

1 *PA* 1.640A24. The seed which constructs must be of a similar character to the product. Man (a reference to males, not to humanity, as we shall see) begets man – note the use of this formula before the *Metaphysics* – so that *he* must be of the same kind as the child. If this looks ambiguous, a passage a few lines below clarifies it (641B31): the offspring grows *from* the seed.

2 *PA* 2.655B24–8. Seed (*gonē*) is the source of what is born; milk is the nourishment.

3 *PA* 4.689A13. This is a difficult text. Aristotle says that *semen* is a residue, as is menstrual blood. This passage is the first in which the two have been compared; but then Aristotle refers to the fact that men emit seed (*gonē*).[26] Right to the end of the *De Partibus Animalium* the old view is maintained, but the thesis that menstrual blood is a residue is a pointer to Aristotle's future theory of conception. Yet it was still to be some time before the new theory emerged. Aristotle's view of the role of menstrual blood in *PA* 4 may have been what he takes it to be in *Metaphysics* Λ.1071B31, the source of *nourishment* for sperm, as earth is for seeds.

12

The Growth of the *Metaphysics*

I The Order of the Metaphysical Writings

One of the most unexpected and delightful results of the identification of the change in Aristotle's theory of conception is that it provides a key to the old problem of the dating of the various books of the *Metaphysics*. For although there are many references to the roles of females and males in conception, only books Z and H (1044A25–35) refer unambiguously to the theory of the *De Generatione Animalium* where the menstrual blood provides the matter of the newborn: that is, the matter in its entirety, not merely nourishment, for the newborn.[1] The text of H runs: 'What is the material cause of man? The menstrual blood. What is the moving cause? The semen.'[2] Many other texts in the *Metaphysics* indicate the older view, which means that books H and Z are *later* than books I (1058B24), Θ (1049A15, 1049B21, 1050A6), Λ (1071B31ff is not incompatible with the older view), N (1092A17, 31), not to speak of A (988A6), where the female is 'filled' up with seed in coition (as Plato's Demiurge fills up the 'receptacle'). Book Δ is a little more problematic, as we shall see; book H is later than 1014B16, but not demonstrably later than 1021A23–5 or 1024A34–6. Z.1034B1 (man is produced *from* man) might seem slightly more doubtful,[3] but the *new* theory is present here. If H is the last book of the *Metaphysics*, then book Z will be readily agreed to precede it immediately. Z.1034B1 is probably to be explained by *Nicomachean Ethics* 3.1113B18ff, where Aristotle says that a man *originates* his actions; and this claim is explained by analogy with the role of the father. Thus a man is the originator of his actions as of his children. That would imply that he 'informed' his children and his actions, but that they are not a 'grown-up' bit of him; this is indeed the 'late' theory of conception. If this is right, then *Metaphysics* Z is consistently similar to book H, and these two treatises will be among the latest – in fact, as we shall see, the latest – parts of the *Metaphysics*.

What about book Θ (usually and rightly associated somehow with Z and H) and I, which is often said to be connected with Θ? Θ contains four clear references to the 'Platonic', not the late and distinctively mature Aristotelian view of conception. At 1049B21 matter (linked with a seed) and a seed and that which is capable of seeing are potentially *this* man and corn and that which sees and will (in time) become in fact what they are not *yet*. At 1049A15 (and cf. 1049A1) Aristotle says that this semen is not yet potentially a man because it must undergo change 'in another,' that is, in the womb. Then it will be potentially a man, that is, it will grow into a man. Semen in males is analogous to 'earth' where earth is not *yet* the bronze which is potentially a statue. At 1050A5 the male adult is prior to the boy, and human beings to semen – for the former already possesses the form, while the latter does not (yet). That is, boys are more 'formed' than semen but less formed than men.

At I.1058B23 the same semen becomes female and male, when it undergoes some experience. This is very similar to Θ.1049A15, but does not *necessarily* link book I to Θ. Provided there are no references in certain earlier books to these four works, therefore, it would follow (if I really does follow Θ) that the last books of the *Metaphysics* are, in this order, Θ, I, Z, H, and that Aristotle changed his mind about the processes of conception just before writing book Z. The last stage of the change was probably to move from thinking that menstrual blood 'fed' the seed (as perhaps in *PA* 4) to thinking that menstrual blood itself is the entire matter of the fetus. As the 'new' theory of conception is very much linked to developments in the concept of *pneuma*, we may also be able to conclude that no treatise which associates *pneuma* with conception, and particularly with the role of menstrual blood as matter, can be much earlier than *Metaphysics* Z.

But the question is a little more complicated. *Pneuma* can be associated with conception in two ways: in the semen and the menstrual blood. It is implicitly associated with the semen, almost certainly, as early as *De Anima* 3, where, in a much discussed passage, Aristotle connects the movement of the penis, stirred by 'the pleasant', with the movements of the heart (3.433A1). Appetition 'moves' the man and the animal (3.433B28), thus making him a self-mover reacting to pleasures and pains. Pleasure, of course, heats, while pain cools. In fact, in the *De Anima*, Aristotle is thinking primarily of *males*, of begetters (3.432B24); and it is the penis which is heated and moved (cf. *GA* 1.717B24).[4] It is the phenomena of male desire which propelled him towards his theory connecting *pneuma* with conception, and the connection between the heart and the penis enables us to understand how he worked it out. The beating of the heart and its pulsation due to pleasure generate *pneuma* (though this word does not occur in the *De Anima*); the movements of the penis are physiologically explainable in terms of the *pneuma*, and obviously the movements cease when the *pneuma* is released in semen. *De Anima* 3.9 shows how consideration of male physiology would enable Aristotle to make the connection. He has, as we have seen, spoken of *pneuma* before the *De Anima*, but not in connection with sexual desire, and certainly we know that at the end of *De Partibus Animalium* 4 Aristotle is only beginning to hesitate about the nature of menstrual blood – which for the first time he speaks of as a residue – though it is clear that he still thinks of males as providing the matter.[5]

It is a fairly short step, however, once menstrual blood is recognized as a residue, to asking what precisely is its relationship to semen. Why should Aristotle have hesitated at this point? Since as far back as the *Historia Animalium* he has commented on the phenomenon of female sexual desire, one would suppose that as soon as he connected such desire in males with *pneuma*, he would immediately find *pneuma* in female sexuality also. But we can see why he might hesitate. A *possible* deduction from the apparent facts might be that females provide equally effective *seeds*, that is, that they are equal to males in the act of conception. Such views were current among the Presocratics, especially the atomists, and with some doctors. But a double seed (double matter) theory of this sort would raise the problem of where the *form* comes from; and from Aristotle's point of view the atomist answer (that it is more or less random) would be unsatisfactory.

As we shall see, Aristotle was forced to face this dilemma between *De Partibus Animalium* 4 and *De Anima* 3; the evidence is to be found in books N and Λ of the *Metaphysics*. Before proceeding, however, we may note that the unnamed physical substance involved in male sexual desire in *De Anima* 3 is identified as *pneuma* in the nearly contemporary *De Somno* (456A1–10). Here Aristotle is again speaking of the heart as the source of sensation. It is peculiarly well located in animals with red blood, because it is half-way between the head and the 'lower hollow' area – an odd phrase, probably drawn from Plato's *Timaeus* (70Aff), and chosen deliberately to indicate not only the intestines but also the general pubic area, so that the bottom of the torso and the top of the head would be more or less equidistant from the heart. This midway place is where *pneuma* and cooling take their origin. The broad sense given to 'lower hollow' would be more appropriate to Aristotle than to Plato, because for Plato the seed (which in Plato is marrow) originates in the head. It is not entirely clear where men store semen according to Aristotle; indeed there seem to be a number of places in the torso which are filled by 'passages' leading from the heart (*GA* 1.717B1–26).[6] It is presumably to these receptacles, as well as to the intestines, that Aristotle refers in the *De Somno* by the phrase 'the lower hollow area.'

The argument that *De Anima* 3 alludes to the sexual role of *pneuma* in males is not to be read as a suggestion that Aristotle's application of *pneuma* to female sexuality is still incomplete. Such a reading would seem to be discounted by the more or less contemporary *De Somno* passage and is disproved by an earlier text of the *De Anima* itself. At 2.417B17ff Aristotle says that the first change of (or into) something sentient (i.e., an animal) is caused (or provoked) by the male parent. Note the word 'change': we have something different here from those passages in the *Metaphysics* which suggest that the male seed itself is changed when deposited in the female. The 'new theory' of conception, and of the ensuing differences between men and women, which we shall later discuss, is already available in *De Anima* 2. As we have seen, it is *not* yet quite available in *De Partibus Animalium* 4. Since it is not available in *Metaphysics* Θ (or I) either, we can do some more sequence-construction; as a result of our various comparisons we now have the following sequence: *PA* 4, *Met.* Θ (plus, perhaps, I), *De Anima* 1–3 (and presumably the *Parva Naturalia*, excluding *De Respiratione*), *Met.* Z, H. It is not inappropriate to find *De Anima* between *Metaphysics* Θ and Z, H.[7] As we shall see, Aristotle holds that the existence of simple substance (i.e., God) in *Metaphysics* Λ allows the possibility of general metaphysics. Book Θ is the bridge from pure actuality to limited actualities. *De Anima* for its part discusses human beings who both share in Mind (as pure actuality) and are composite substances. *Metaphysics* Z and H follow, in order of exposition as well as of composition – as demonstrated at least for the metaphysical books by conception-theory: they teach the metaphysics of *all* such composite substances (not just those, like men, which also share in the 'incomposite').

Before proceeding, we must clear up a remaining matter of cross-references in the *Metaphysics*. On our schema there can clearly be no non-interpolated references in books Θ and I to Z and H; scholars have sometimes claimed that the opening of Θ refers to Z.1 (though the converse could be true). In fact, the opening sentence of Θ refers to the 'focal meaning' contained in the opening sentence of Γ. Γ.1003A21 refers to 'being qua being' (i.e., substance) and things which naturally inhere in it (that is, the essential qualities). Or possibly the reference in Θ is to Γ.1003A33, where Aristotle speaks of the other senses of 'being' as referred 'to one thing or one particular nature.' We shall eventually see what the nature is. In Θ.1.1045B27 we are told that we have now dealt with 'being in the primary sense,' and that to which all other categories of being are referred; that is, we have dealt with *ousia*. And Aristotle has indeed not only written book Γ before Θ; he has also written Λ. Λ is named by Aristotle himself, in its opening words, as an enquiry 'about substance' (*ousia*), and later in the book we hear of Mind as 'simple' (1072A33) and as that 'in reference to which one thing' (*pros hen*) all else is arranged (1075A18). There are no other references in Θ.1 to Z or H.[8] The original title of books Z and H, as suggested by Z.1, would be *Peri tou ontos*, as distinct from the *Peri tēs ousias* attached to M, N, and Λ. Or perhaps it was *On the causes, principles and elements of substances* (H.1042A5–6, cf. Z.1028B4–7). I shall argue later that Λ.8 is the last chapter of this treatise.[9] The beginning of Θ, as we have seen, refers back to Γ, but more immediately also to Λ, the work on substance.

Let us then return to the *Metaphysics* as a whole. I propose to argue the following further theses:

1 That book α is an introduction to the *Physics*, written soon after Aristotle's return from Macedon to Athens, at the time when he wrote *Physics* 1 and 8 and added various material to the *De Caelo* and *De Generatione et Corruptione*.
2 That book K is an early version of B, Γ, and E, which is widely accepted. (But further development is possible).
3 That the first group of the main *Metaphysics* is A, B, Γ, and E.1.
4 That this is closely followed by Δ.1–12, I, and E.2–4.
5 That the next part of the sequence is M, N, Λ.

Thesis 1 needs little defence but can be developed; book α is clearly an opening book of encouragement. Aristotle begins with general comments on the study of truth: every thinker contributes. Truth is like the door in the proverb which no one can miss, so in a sense the job in hand is easy – something which even Aristotle would hardly say of metaphysics, particularly in view of his past dealings with the subject, but which he has already said of physics in the *Protrepticus*. And he tells us both at the beginning and the end of the treatise that he is setting forth a work *On Nature* (993B2) and that our first question is: What is nature? With what does *physics* deal (995A18)?[10]

α makes the best sense as an introduction to *Physics* 1. Both concern themselves with 'Truth', that is, as Owens points out, with Parmenides and his effects.[11] The study of nature advocated in α suits the *Physics* but not the kind of considerations we find in *Metaphysics* Λ. Book α envisages comment on the world of nature, up to and including the introduction (994A5ff) of a needed Prime Mover (which is done in *Physics* 8), but nothing in α prepares one for comment on the Prime Mover beyond that in *Physics* 8, that is, for the study of the Prime Mover as *Mind*; for the study of Mind *is* metaphysics.

Final causes are present in natural sciences, as in metaphysics (if it exists); that, as we have seen, is already Aristotle's view both in the *Protrepticus* and in *On Philosophy*; so there is nothing surprising about Aristotle discussing this in α, in an introduction to physics. Mathematical accuracy, we learn (α.995A1ff), is not to be expected of a physical science, because all nature, presumably, has a material component and its truths will not always be necessary truths. That is, the study of nature is exclusively concerned with explanations of the behaviour of 'emmattered' form, not with form as such. This kind of remark is wholly inappropriate to introduce Aristotle's *Metaphysics*, wholly appropriate to introduce his physics. Nowhere in Aristotle's discussions of *Mind* (God) in itself in the *Metaphysics* will Aristotle say that he is talking about nature. Being qua being is *not* a subject in the philosophy of nature; theology is *not* a study of nature. '*Metaphysics*' α (though admittedly in chapter 3 containing a problem faced in E.1) *is* concerned with introducing a study of nature. '*Metaphysics*' α.3 is concerned (like the *Physics*) to distinguish physics from mathematics (and thus *inter alia* free it from 'Platonism').

I would therefore propose that α was written to introduce the enlarged and corrected version of a collection of 'physical' material – now perhaps for the first time called the *Physics* and including the new book 8 on the Unmoved Mover. Aristotle completed it soon after his return to Athens from Macedon (but after he had finished the *Poetics* and *Rhetoric*). Indeed I would go further: at that time he not only wrote α and *Physics* 8 (plus the last chapter of *De Generatione et Corruptione* 2 and other tidying up on the question of the Prime Mover in physics generally), he also wrote *Physics* 1.

There is no reason why the original '*Physics*' could not have begun with book 2 and run on to book 7; indeed, as argued earlier, 7 may even precede 2–6. There are no references in the original texts of *De Generatione et Corruptione* and *De Caelo* which necessarily refer to *Physics* 1. The really informative passage in this regard is *De Generatione* 2.329A27, which is often taken to refer to *Physics* 1.6–7, but which more easily refers to *On Philosophy*, Aristotle's first attack on the *Timaeus* and its 'receptacle' or 'nurse'. *Physics* 1 does indeed deal with the same material, but the attack is more far-reaching. Plato's *Timaeus* is more squarely set against a failure to deal with Parmenides. Falling into the Eleatic trap, Plato has identified matter and privation – this indeed sums up Aristotle's problem with the 'place/nurse' of the *Timaeus* better than anything he had attempted in the *De Generatione et Corruptione*. Hence Plato makes a non-existent matter 'yearn' for existence. His biological model has in fact betrayed him. Yet he felt that he had no option: 'femaleness', the 'receptacle', the 'nurse', *must* be nothing, if the theory that females provide nothing in the act of conception is to be maintained.

And yet Parmenides is not really answered. In the *Timaeus* Plato really did make non-being (place) 'somehow exist.' None of this attack on the

Timaeus, however, means that Aristotle criticizes Plato for seeing some kind of yearning in matter. What is wrong is Plato's notion of a 'non-existent' matter. Such sharper analysis of the problem of the *Timaeus* can hardly precede the version to be found in the *De Generatione et Corruptione*. The solution is that it does not. *De Generatione* refers back to *On Philosophy* (which perhaps also contained remarks about 'prime matter'). *Physics* 1 is later; it was composed after *De Generatione* when Aristotle set about revising his physical corpus.[12] But *Physics* 1 is not very late; there are still references to Aristotle's earlier theory of conception (1.190B4, cf. 191B21), not the theory to be found in *Metaphysics* Z and H. *Physics* 1 refers to the possibility of metaphysics as 'another' science – this cannot be merely dialectic – at 185A3–4, and as 'first philosophy' (192A35ff) – which will be discussed later. The earlier parts of the *Physics*, however, were written when Aristotle still discounted the possibility of metaphysics. There could be no clearer evidence that *Physics* 1 is from the later Athenian period and that Aristotle is anticipating writing a *Metaphysics*.

Physics 1 distinguishes physics from first philosophy, a distinction largely alien to *Physics* 2–7. This is one reason why void, time, etc., are discussed in our *Physics*; there was nowhere else to put them. But mind is not discussed in the *Physics*, though *Physics* 1 envisages a forthcoming first philosophy. Of the possibility of 'first philosophy' (ruled out at the time of the *Posterior Analytics* and the *Eudemian Ethics*) Aristotle is now certain; he has changed his mind. In *Physics* 1 he distinguishes first philosophy from physics exactly as he does in '*Metaphysics*' α.

There are, as we saw, no certain references in early physical texts to *Physics* 1. '*Metaphysics*' α and *Physics* 1 are the introduction to the revised physical treatises, now composed by a man who wants to point out that there *is* a difference between physics and first philosophy. That means that 'doctrinally' book α should square with both *Physics* 1 and the rest of the *Metaphysics* itself. That its theories and ideas should be in harmony with the *Metaphysics*, and indeed helpful for our understanding of this work, is entirely proper: it was written just before the *Metaphysics*, though not *for* the *Metaphysics*. The influence of the *Protrepticus* can be seen in α, just as the *On Philosophy* is influential for *Physics* 1. But Aristotle always did regard the *Protrepticus* as important. As we have seen, he made considerable use of it in composing *Nicomachean Ethics* 1 and 10 (183–5 above) at more or less this period of his life. As for α, I am not alone in connecting it with the *Physics*;[13] it was already so connected before the time of Alexander of Aphrodisias.[14]

Regarding thesis 2, book K, it is generally agreed, is a version of B, Γ, and E, plus certain material from physics; it refers clearly to *Physics* 1 (1062B31ff). Physics, however, is not the prime concern of K, for physics has nothing to say of the good as final cause (1059A35ff).[15] It is hard to know whether metaphysical subject-matter is exclusively in sensibles or not; if not, metaphysics will have to treat of Forms and mathematicals. But Forms do not exist and the objects of mathematics do not exist apart from particulars. Nor does first philosophy deal with sensible substances in so far as they are perishable. It does, however, treat of the 'matter' of mathematical objects (which is by no means clear in *Metaphysics* Z and H). Perhaps it deals with primary genera (i.e., being and unity)? Or with universals, like 'every science' (1060B20)? But that is difficult because substance is not one of the universals. Perhaps rather it is concerned with being qua being in general and not in any particular case. It is different from physics because physics studies beings qua participants in motion, while first philosophy does not, but simply qua being (1061B5). Even the mathematician uses his common principles in individual cases (*idiōs*), so it will be the task of first philosophy to study these axioms as well.[16] In a sense physics and mathematics are parts of wisdom (that is, of first philosophy, 1061B33).

Chapter 5 deals with the law of contradiction, chapter 6 with Protagoras's saying that man is the measure of all things, and contains a cross-reference to the first book of the *Physics*, as we have seen. Chapter 7 corresponds in part to E.1, and is concerned primarily with whether the science of being qua being is part of 'natural science' or not – a matter Aristotle feels he does not need to *discuss* in E. Being qua being deals with what is separate and immovable – I repeat, he says, separate and immovable, if there really is such *a particular being*, as we shall try to show. (Notice how much more tamely this key remark appears in E.)[17] But, if there is such a being, that is the first and most authoritative principle. Chapter 8, according to Sorabji,[18] is less clear than E.3 in its discussion of coincidences.

At the beginning of chapter 9 Aristotle says that things exist either as actuality alone (like the God of Λ), or as potentiality, or as both actual and potential; or again as a substance or as one of the other kinds (that is, in one of the other categories). Clearly he means that what exists in actuality alone is God (being qua being), what exists 'in actuality and in potentiality' is other (matter-bodied) beings. These too, of course, can be studied qua being, that is, qua form. In the rest of the book, as is widely recognized, Aristotle wanders off into ways of approaching them. Some of the material is drawn from the *Physics*, as newly revised (e.g., chapter 10 on infinity), but that does not mean that Aristotle intends these chapters *simply* as physics. When he first wrote the *Physics*, he did not believe there was a science of first philosophy, as we have seen. Now he does, and he wants to select material for re-use in the new metaphysical context. In fact, some of the sections here look less like the *Physics* than like Δ of the *Metaphysics*: notice the comments on categories in K.12 and Δ.7 (though the Δ.7 account is more sophisticated in its analysis of being as having as many *senses* as there are ways of predication). Oddly enough K omits time (as does the later discussion of categories in Δ).

What conclusions can be drawn about K? Clearly that it is a *metaphysical* treatise. Its subject is the possibility of metaphysics as being qua being (not merely motion), and the search (with expected success) for an unchanging being. But it is not merely a summary of B, Γ, Δ, and E. Indeed, there is quite a lot of material to be found in K which is not presented in the other treatises. It looks like an earlier version of B, Γ, Δ, and E, written probably very soon after α. But it is not the first book of its *own* metaphysical series, as its opening makes clear. Could it not be intended to follow α as an aborted course of metaphysics, which Aristotle reworked? The answer is no, for, as we have seen, book α does not introduce metaphysics but physics. The explanation could be that book K was originally intended to follow A, or some version of A, perhaps A minus chapters 7–9. Certainly if we remove the last connecting sentence of A.6 we find that book K would follow on very satisfactorily. The end of A.6 is on principles; so is the beginning of K.

If book K can be linked to A 1–6, that reduces the likelihood of the other possible explanation, namely that K is a rather unsatisfactory student's version of the material in B, Γ, Δ, and E. But the difficulty with that, in any case, is the different material and emphasis in several parts of K itself [19] – though I suppose that, if the author of K were a student, he might have heard a somewhat different version of B, Γ, Δ, and E from ours! An interesting philological fact seems also to have been identified. According to Décarie,[20] in the early chapters of K the author almost entirely avoids hiatus; the latter sections show no such care. Perhaps the explanation is that Aristotle decided in the middle of K to abandon his tidying up of an early draft of K and to do the job again in B, Γ, Δ, and E. (The other, I think less likely, explanation is that the latter part of K is by another hand.) As for the relationship with book A, perhaps a further refinement, considered in an earlier chapter (65 above), could be added: perhaps the original version of A did not stop at 6, but included also chapter 10 – which equally could link up with K.

Yet another refinement can be added to our account of the replacement of K. Everyone agrees that book K deals with the same material as B, Γ, and E; but how much of E? Only in fact chapter 1. After that (K.8ff), there is virtually nothing of the material of E.[21] Commentators have tried to squeeze references out of E.2–4. There is no need to do that. As Owens saw long ago,[22] E.2–4 is disconnected from E.1. It is a fresh start, that is, a start on new material, not previously used (in K, perhaps), when Aristotle began working on the second project of a *Metaphysics*. E.1, in fact, is the last chapter of Γ;

thus strictly speaking K is an early version of B, Γ, and E.1, with selected useful material from the *Physics* and from what was to be Δ added on. Δ too must come later, as we shall see.

So we come to theses 3 and 4 and our 'final' version of the *Metaphysics* is growing. We have books A, B, Γ, and E.1. Γ and E.1 develop the important discussion of being qua being (originally introduced in K), and, by use of the theory of 'focal meaning' (in Owen's apt phrase), permit a study of being as such wherever it is to be found. Moreover, since other beings can be said to *be* with reference to a *primary* kind of being, first philosophy will be concerned to identify that primary kind: that will be the task of books M, N, and Λ. What then about Δ and E.2–4? The existence of K should suggest that they *follow* E.1.[23] In fact this is largely correct. The only problem is that Δ must be split into two. Only Δ.1–12 precedes E.2–4. The rest of the book is a much later addition, after Θ, near to Z and H; again biology helps us.

In Δ.28 we have a discussion of the name 'Hellenes.' It is taken from Hellen, the ancestor of the race (1024A32ff). Races are usually, says Aristotle, named from their begetter (the male ancestor), rather than from the *material*, that is, the mother. But some do get their names from the *female*, that is, we may be sure he means, from the 'matter' in the late theory of conception. The text is clear-cut. Chapter 28 of Δ is very late, as is chapter 15 (1021A25). But there are references to Δ in E.2–4 and in other texts, and Δ also contains Aristotle's *early* theory of conception (1014B16). That is true, but the relevant references are all to the early chapters of Δ. We can, in fact, almost certainly identify the end of the original Δ; it is at the end of chapter 12. After that, Aristotle begins discussing categories, but his remarks about them are not compatible with the earlier remarks in chapter 7. The most striking difference is in the discussion of 'active' and 'passive' things and why they are called 'relatives', in Δ.15, 1021A14ff. As discussed previously, these apparently 'later' developments in category theory are incompatible with the 'traditional' linking of acting and experiencing as *separate* categories, not reduced to relation, at 1017A26 (103–4 above). In fact the discussion of categories, beginning with 'quality' in chapter 13, is quite out of place; it should (if part of the original Δ) follow immediately after chapter 7. Now since we know on 'biological' grounds that Δ must be divided, it is reasonable to suppose that it is divided at the end of chapter 12. Those later texts which refer back to Δ refer back to the first twelve chapters. Thus we now have books A, B, Γ, E.1, Δ.1–12, E.2–4.

And this sequence gives us the springboard for the next leap, and for our thesis 5. E.4 ends with a mention of the next item on the agenda. We should expect that it would be a study of being qua being in its most 'authoritative' form, that is, separate substance. This is exactly what E.4 says: 'We must consider the *causes* of being and the *principles* of being in so far as they are being'; that is, not in so far as they *cause* being (which is physics), but in so far as they *are* being. The stage is set for books M, N, and Λ (or, as Aristotle calls them, *On Substance*). After that, as we should expect, will come 'incomplete' beings, or the being of physical objects.[24]

Thus we have (more or less) a complete order for the final version of the *Metaphysics*: A, B, Γ, E.1, Δ.1–12, E.2–4, M, N, Λ, Θ, Z, H. But there still seem to be further questions:

1 About the fate of Δ.13 to end.
2 About the position of I.
3 About the *relative* positions of M, N, Λ to one another.
4 About the placing of Λ.8.

To these we must now turn.

Regarding question 1, the position of Δ.13ff must remain somewhat conjectural. If it is a unit, which it probably is at least in so far as it is stuck onto Δ, then it must post-date all the books of the *Metaphysics* except Z and H. Since it is a 'floating' piece, analogous in this regard, I would suggest, to Λ.8, the most natural conjecture would be that it was affixed to Δ when the same editor affixed Λ.8 to Λ, thus completing our text of the *Metaphysics*. Hence one could *conjecture* that Δ.13 to end is the latest section of the *Metaphysics*, but more or less contemporary with H and Λ.8. It shares the 'biology' of Z and H.

Regarding question 2, book I is also somewhat problematical. It refers to Δ.6 at its opening, and probably to *Categories* 14A20 at 1055A1–2.[25] It refers to B at 1053B10 (as 'On Difficulties') and to Δ.8 (it seems) at 1053B17–18.[26] It alludes to a discussion of relatives at 1056B35. Some have taken this to be a reference to Δ.15, but 'biologically' this is impossible, and in any case the more sophisticated Δ.15 does not make the rather crude distinction of 1056B35. The reference may be to a much earlier work, perhaps again to the *Categories*,[27] but perhaps more plausibly to Γ.1004B27 with its predicate columns. Certainly *Categories* 11, 14A20ff will fill the bill as the point of reference at 1055A1–2; and indeed there is much in book I generally to remind us of the so-called *Post-Praedicamenta* (i.e., *Categories* 10–15). This is particularly true of I.4. The rather 'physical' comments on white and black as 'distinguishing' and 'merely assembling' (derived from *Timaeus* 67DE), however, seem beyond the merely descriptive concerns at least of the early parts of the *Categories*. *Metaphysics* I also refers (1055A1) to the 'columns' or 'lists' (*sustoichia*) of predicates – a tool which does not appear in our *Categories* but only in the *Analytics* (*APo.* 1.79B7, 80B27, 81A21, 87B6; *APr.* 66B27, 35) as do the connections of categorization with induction (cf. I.1058A9–13).[28]

At 1058A24 there is a reference to the clan of the Heracleidae, which might be an ancestor of Δ.28 – except that points about possible naming after the female or 'material' ancestor are not made. But interestingly enough Aristotle immediately proceeds in the next chapter to raise a question that he eventually resolves to his satisfaction only in *De Generatione Animalium*: Are males and females (who are 'contrary' biologically) different in species? This might be the opportunity (were book I late) to observe the new physiology of conception; on the contrary we find the old Platonic version (1058B22ff). The same seed 'after experiencing something' *becomes* male or female.

Assuming that book I post-dates Δ.1–12, it can hardly post-date E (2–4), since that text, as we have seen, seems to point directly to the treatise *On Substance*. And in any case a preliminary discussion of 'unity' should precede such fundamental material. The only solution – even if I is a quite separate composition simply inserted here – is to suppose that I is the last part of the original Δ. The alien material Δ.13–30 has been assembled where I should be. There is no problem about restoring I to this position, thus completing our provisional reconstruction of the final text of the *Metaphysics* as follows: A, B, Γ, E.1, Δ.1–12, I, E.2–4, M, N, Λ, Z, H, Λ.8. The chunk which got displaced in the middle was thus the whole section Δ.1–12 plus I.[29]

Regarding question 3, *Metaphysics* M begins with a reference to the *Physics*. 'We have, in the *Physics*, dealt with matter and later with activity (that is, form). Now we must enquire whether apart from sensible substances there is or is not some substance which is eternal and unchanging.' As with other topics, Aristotle thinks it is best to begin with the opinions of others. And who has talked about eternal and unchanging substances? Certainly Plato and the others associated with the Academy: Speusippus and Xenocrates. M (whatever the original reasons for its composition) can thus be used as the beginning of a treatise on substance. And I have accepted earlier the arguments of Annas that books M and N are a single, continuous treatise. After N comes Λ which begins: 'Our thinking is about substance.'

Metaphysics Λ itself leads through sensible substances to the Prime Mover who is – beyond the *Physics* – identified as God and self-thinking, hence 'unplatonic', Mind, in chapter 7. Chapter 8, as we shall see, is misplaced. Chapter 9 clears up further 'difficulties' about Mind from 7, particularly about the dignity (*to semnon*) of Mind, for God must think constantly or he will look like a mere man asleep. His mental activity is neither knowledge (of fact?) nor perception nor opinion nor intending (*dianoia*), because these activities are always of something else and only of themselves indirectly (1074B36). Chapter 10 explains how God (now called the Good and the supreme Good; cf. B.996B13, K.1059A31) is present in the universe. The universe contains goodness both in its *order* and in its 'commander', but the arrangement depends on him, not vice versa, so he is 'more' to be identified as 'the Good'. Of course, the usefulness of seeing him as a commander is limited. He causes the order (by being), but he does not give commands, since, as we have already seen, he is a final cause only. Every part depends on him, as in a household where the 'free' are the least likely to act randomly – for they will be 'organized' more or less (that is, by their rational desires). In contrast the slaves and animals (note the connection) will contribute little to the common good and act mostly at random – that is, without deliberation. For such is their nature. Nevertheless there is a *necessity* for them to come to some discrimination of roles – and there are other ways in which they all contribute to the whole. Just as in a household all contribute somehow to the common good, so it is in the entire world (*holon* here is probably to be interpreted as 'the universe').

But Aristotle does not stop here; he moves back to attacks on 'the more sophisticated thinkers', that is, the Academy, and at the end, in particular, Speusippus (1075A37). For whereas Xenocrates (who spoke of the Platonic Dyad as 'the unequal') makes 'the bad' a principle, and thus claims that everything except the One (or Monad) shares in evil, Speusippus does not make even the Good (or 'the bad') a first principle at all. Various other thinkers are then criticized for their attitude to the origin of evil: such as Empedocles for his 'strife' which is 'the nature of evil' elevated to a principle. But Anaxagoras is little better. He, as Aristotle always recognized, proposed Mind as the mover. But where does the contrary come in, if Mind is the Good? As usual, other philosophers have failed to *explain what* there is *more* than the Good, that is, why there will *always* be generation and what its cause is (1075B18). Finally, as we have noted elsewhere (73–4 above), Aristotle comes back to Speusippus again for the finale. His universe, based on the reality of mathematical number, is incoherent. Homer has said it all: many rulers are not good; let there be one king.

But why Speusippus? Because his theory of the priority of the first principles to the Good had particularly disturbed Aristotle. It was a cosmo-biological theory based on the atomist-like view that from two seeds (male and female) the universe arises. Aristotle mentions it in book Λ at an earlier stage (1071B30): matter will not move itself; we need a carpenter. And (the ambiguity of *Metaphysics* A.6 being still repeated in the next move) menstrual blood will not move itself, nor will earth. We need semen and seeds. Here finally we have the text which marks exactly when Aristotle changed his biological theory. The menstrual blood – which had begun to worry him as early as *De Partibus Animalium* 4 – is now the inert matter, and semen moves it, but *still* apparently as an efficient cause *and* a material cause. Semen is still a retained seed. We have in fact almost reached a two-seed mixture theory: the male seed moves (i.e., forms) the matter (the female, less formed, seed), but still, apparently, as a superior sown *seed*. Thus Aristotle seems to have considered the idea of a material mixing of seeds with the male being the active 'partner'. Why should he not persist with such a move? And why in book Λ should he allow a 'material' role for the female while still clinging to the sown seed theory?

Metaphysics N (also of course from *On Substance*) has a passage which may be some help. Again book N ends with an attack on Speusippus and his mathematicals. The reason, I suggest, is that the mathematicals provide the basis for Speusippus's own biology. They pre-exist the world of form. The system is basically a dualism; that is, among the mathematicals male and female are equal. The One and the Dyad (as mathematicals) are equal, neither good nor evil. They are also potentialities, as Aristotle says in *Metaphysics* Λ (1072B31ff). It is wrong to suppose, argues Aristotle, that potentialities precede actuality. A man is prior to his seed, not the man who arises from the seed (the old theory so far), but the author of the seed (i.e., the father). This passage confirms that the seed still does in some sense become the child, perhaps in a stronger sense than at 1071B31. Yet it also tells us that a very different view is at least implied (and presumably held) by Speusippus in his version of Plato's cosmo-biology. For Speusippus both females and males are providers of seed. But if that is so, says Aristotle, then where does the *form* come from?

At N.1092A12 a 'certain' philosopher (that is, Speusippus) is said to have likened his principles of the universe to those of plants and animals. But that is wrong, says Aristotle, for man begets man (yet again the echo of *De Partibus Animalium*); that is, the *father* produces the form and the father produces the seed – which grows up into the new man.[30]

Nevertheless, Speusippus's theory may have made Aristotle think again. Between N and Λ he apparently developed (or reintroduced from *PA* 4) the role of the menstrual blood (here in Λ unusually called *epimēnia*, perhaps Speusippus's term), thus allowing females some *material* role in conception. By the time he came to write Z, presumably not much later (though the *De Anima* as well as Θ came between), he was allowing females the *whole* material role. Thus male/female relations could still be understood within the general principles of the form/matter analysis of the physical cosmos. Eventually the discussion of the role of menstrual blood in *De Generatione Animalium* 1 would work the whole thesis out in detail. Aristotle had gone half-way towards the atomists' theory while his insistence on a certain male predominance seemed to prevent the atomists' 'randomness' and to provide a systematic explanation of form. Speusippus seems to have been the catalyst.

There may indeed have been a further role for Speusippus. Xenocrates certainly, and Speusippus probably, made use of the concept of *pneuma*,[31] probably deriving it, as did Aristotle, in some respects, from Plato's *Timaeus*. We do not know whether Speusippus used *pneuma* in his account of generation, whether it is the *pneuma* in the seeds which enables the basic potentialities which seeds possess to be realized in generation. If it was, then the developed Aristotelian theory of the relation of *pneuma* to semen, ultimately dependent in part on the *Timaeus*, may well have been affected by Aristotle's reflections on Speusippus's 'errors.' The Hippocratic treatise *On Seed* (which advocates a two-seed theory) speaks (ch. 4) of one or the other seed as being 'stronger.' If Speusippus understood such notions to be suggesting that 'stronger' had something to do with more (or better) *pneuma*, though not necessarily with masculinity or femininity, we would understand Aristotle's putative reaction better.

We come at last to question 4, the problem of *Metaphysics* Λ.8. This, I argue, is the last chapter of H. Λ.8 begins with the question whether there is one or more 'such substances'. Whoever put it after Λ.7 obviously thought that, because Λ.8 talks of one or more substances, Aristotle must mean one or more 'minds'. But that, as Plotinus saw (*Enn.* 5.1.9), would mean that there is a 'material' element – if we assume, as is reasonable, that all 'minds' have something in common. Hence the theory of Λ.8 has given endless trouble for commentators trying to explain this objection away. For Plotinus thought both that there is a plurality of 'minds', and that this ought to have worried Aristotle; his whole objection is that Aristotle is insufficiently concerned.

But in fact Aristotle's argument at 1073A23ff runs as follows:

1 The 'origin' and first of beings is unmoved *both intrinsically and* accidentally.

2 The Prime Mover 'moves' (i.e., causes by final causation) the first eternal and single movement: that is, of the first heaven.

3 The following explains (by alluding to *pneuma*?) how (2) occurs: since that which is moved (i.e., the *body* of the first heaven, the *aether*) must be moved by something while the Prime Mover (God) is *intrinsically* unmoved, then the eternal movement (of the first body) is moved by 'an eternal' – and each moved body is then moved by its own 'eternal'. This 'eternal' can hardly be other than the *soul* (or form) of 'bodily' *aether*, which is unmoved intrinsically but *not* accidentally unmoved. It is not God; it is not even pure form – there is only one pure form – but it is a Platonic, 'pluralist', star-soul. Aristotle then resorts to the astronomers

Eudoxus and Callippus to help explain how many such superior soul/body complexes there must be.

If we now turn to the end of book H, we may read the last sentences: 'To seek for the cause of a particular's unity is like seeking for the "cause" of there being unity [at all] ... There is no cause [of unity] except whatever has provoked movement from potentiality to actuality.' (God [Mind] of course ultimately does this.)

Aristotle next observes that 'Whatever has *no matter*, all such are simply what some one thing is' (i.e., what God is; *not* 'the *sort* of thing God is').[32] Then follows the question at the beginning of Λ.8: Well, then, how *many* ultimate substances of this kind exist? The answer is that there are as many (intrinsically *and* accidentally) unmoved substances as are required to move the fifty-four 'soul/body' complexes in the heavens – and that number is one. Aristotle eludes Plotinus after all.

Earlier sections of H lead us to expect that such subjects will be discussed somewhere in the treatise. Aristotle tells us that we must collect things together and bring the work, that is the *Metaphysics* as a whole, to a close (H.1042A3). The opening lines of H sum up the major contents of the whole *Metaphysics*, indicating indeed that this is the last book (1042A3–23). But we are then promised still more on Forms and mathematicals: this comes briefly at 1043B33ff and at more length in Λ.8, 1073A18ff, where there is a final comment on a new inadequacy of the 'theory' (*hupolēpsis*) of Forms: but 1043B33ff does not consider the *number* of heavenly soul/bodies.

At 1043B17 we are reminded that no one makes or generates the *forms* (unlike in *Republic* 10); it is the compound which is generated. But, Aristotle continues, it is *not yet* clear whether there are *some* separate substances of perishable things, that is, whether the substance of *any mortal* thing is separate. The answer, as we have seen, is that it is not. Indeed only God (Mind) as Prime Mover is absolutely separate from matter. Finally, at 1045A31, Aristotle comes to an interesting example 'among the things where there is genesis' – which in its broadest sense could mean where there is any sort of matter. He takes the example of a sphere, which might suggest analogies with the immortal sphere of the heavens. What is the reason for the potential sphere's *being* an actual (*active*) sphere? None other than its realized nature, and the realized nature of each one of them. The example of the sphere may serve to introduce the eternal movement of the heavenly spheres in Λ.8, and in Λ.8, in addition to the single spatial movement of the cosmos itself (1073A28), there are the various other revolutions, each 'naturally' dependent on its own form. So that, Aristotle concludes (1074A15), we now know the number of the *spheres* and of their movers. More powerful thinkers, he adds, can work out the details (1074A17).

But Aristotle can now go one step further. Since the soul/bodies are all subordinated necessarily to what has no body, to that which is the 'first realized nature and perfection,' the universe can be seen to be one. Not only the ancients with their plurality of worlds, but also – and finally – the 'anarchic' Speusippus, are refuted in the end. The Prime Mover is clearly distinguished from the first heaven, soul and body.

We should expect that Aristotle would end the *Metaphysics* with a flourish, just as it began with a flourish. The end of Λ.8 does not disappoint us in this expectation, thus providing the strongest evidence for its position at the end of the *Metaphysics* as a whole. An old truth, says Aristotle, has come down to us in mythical form, that the heavenly bodies are gods and that 'the divine' embraces the whole of nature. The myth has been vulgarized over the centuries, but the truth of it can be sorted out. The essence of true belief has been preserved until now as a relic of what was formerly known. Yet, Aristotle concludes, the beliefs of our ancestors and of early generations are only to a certain extent clear to us.

Metaphysics A begins with Aristotle's reflections on man's wonder at the cosmos and on his mythological attempts to find the truth (982B12–20) about the sun, the moon, the stars, and the origin of the world. Looking back at the end of the essays he has assembled in an intelligible sequence (in Λ.8), he considers that a certain amount of the ancestral wisdom – perhaps at various times past well understood by philosophers – is still unintelligible. A saying of Aristotle in his old age has come down to us, which, if not true, is *ben trovato*: the more solitary and isolated I am, the more I have come to love myths (fr. 668 Rose).

In part I of this chapter, I have attempted to reconstruct a necessary chronological order of composition for certain books of the *Metaphysics*. This order in fact also provides an intelligible sequence (though perhaps not the only possible intelligible sequence) for a course of metaphysics. I admit, of course, that while some of my arguments (such as that about conception) may help us both with an intelligible order of exposition *and* with the relative dates of composition of parts of the material, others (e.g. about I) only tell us about a reasonable date for the inclusion of material in a lengthy and intelligible *exposition* of metaphysics. None of the arguments sheds more than flickering light on how my intelligible and chronological sequence (A to Λ 8) got into the disorder of our manuscripts which start with A and end with N.

II The Programme of the 'Metaphysics'

Now that the chronology of the *Metaphysics* is somewhat clarified, it is appropriate to make a few further remarks about Aristotle's programme as it seems to emerge in the work as a whole, though I shall leave detailed discussion of the origins and achievements of his theory of substance until the last chapter. I argue that our *Metaphysics* (less α and K) can be arranged (and was indeed composed by Aristotle) in a sequence that in fact also provides an intelligible order of exposition. Now it would be bizarre to suppose that although the chronological sequence gives such an intelligible sequence (perhaps indeed the most intelligible), Aristotle did not notice and intend the fact. Book A in its revised form – with its specific movement from the old 'physicists' via the Pythagoreans to detailed comment on the Academy – introduces the topic of a science dealing with causes in a non-physical way. In particular such a science will deal with causes – if any – which are not the subject-matter of physics at all, though necessarily related to physics in so far as their analogues are to be found in physical objects, that is, as final, formal and efficient causes. Book B deals with the identification of problems and with attempts made in the Academy to pin down non-material causes. Book Γ and E.1 turn to the study of 'metaphysics' in the strict sense; they are a necessary preliminary to the study of substance. Deploying his theory of focal meaning, Aristotle argues that a science of metaphysics, denied in the *Eudemian Ethics* and in early versions of the physical treatises, is possible after all. The science of being qua being will deal with being wherever it can be found, with beings in so far as they qualify for the title 'beings'. And being is found both in pure form and in forms embodied (in varying degrees) in matter. The intelligibility of such forms is guaranteed by reference to pure form (that is, to non-sensible substance), for the definition of the focal example of being will reappear in the definitions of other 'beings'. Hence we should expect discussions of non-sensible substance (that is, for Aristotle, of Mind or God) to precede discussion of forms in matter. Indeed if there were no immaterial substance there would be no study of being qua being. *Metaphysics* in this sense would not be possible and the physics of the heavenly bodies would be the highest science. Focal meaning in Γ and E.1 allows for the possibility of metaphysics, if and only if there is at least one immaterial substance. Thus the existence of such a substance will guarantee not only the physics but also the metaphysics of sensible substances. Details of the 'mechanics' of the relation between material and immaterial substances, however, will not be matters of metaphysics, for they will involve study of the *matter* as well as the being qua being of material substances – though, as we have seen, Aristotle says a little at the end of H about the highest form of such physics.[33]

Before proceeding to consider whether or not there are immaterial substances, Aristotle offers a number of preliminary discussions, designed to clarify philosophical usage and to sharpen his tools (Δ.1–12, I). Now at last he is prepared to begin the core of the *Metaphysics*, an investigation of the possible existence of immaterial being. His approach, if our order is followed, is systematic. As book B has led us to expect, only Plato and the Academy have raised this question seriously, so it is necessary for Aristotle to examine their proposals closely: that is books M and N. Finally Λ (less chapter 8) establishes the necessity of God as Mind; God's nature, being a 'metaphysical' question in so far as he is immaterial and has no necessary relationship to matter, is here discussed for the first time. He is established as Mind and as the Good to which all else is referred (surely a reference to focal meaning, 1075A12ff), for which all else is somehow striving, and on which the intelligibility of other goodness must be based. He is himself necessarily unconcerned with the striving of the cosmos. But his mere existence is enough to allow the possibility of a metaphysics of material beings as well, for he is both a counterpart (*analogon*) and a point of reference for physical beings. Although focal meaning is not specifically applied to *being* in Λ, the Prime Unmoved Mover (which alone meets the requirements for substance laid down in Z.1028A32–B2 – for it can exist without anything else) will provide a focal point for the discussion of lesser substances.[34] This, as we have seen, is spelled out for the *goodness* of lesser substances at 1075A12–20, and the goodness of Mind (as the supreme Good) is certainly a metaphysical thesis. But it cannot be denied that, if Z.1 formed the first chapter of Λ, Aristotle would have made his point much more clearly.

Form is the analogue of God in physical objects, and is fully intelligible only with reference to him. Naturally the opposite to form will not exist in the world of metaphysics, for the 'logical' opposite to form is total formlessness, or substrate, and there is no formless substance even in physics.

Since there exists, in Λ, an immaterial being with no connection as form to a material object, Aristotle is now free to consider the counterparts of this being, namely the forms in matter. These, as the notion of focal meaning indicates, are the legitimate and intelligible objects of metaphysical study if and only if such a pure being, such a pure substance without matter, exists. Now that we know that there is such a substance, a pure substance whose immaterial activity is life, all other substances can be understood as subjects for metaphysical enquiry in so far as they can be understood as beings. *Metaphysics* Θ is the intermediate study: all 'emmattered' forms are involved with potentiality. They have limited 'actuality'; they are actual in so far as they are the result of the realization of their matter. Thus book Θ leads naturally from Λ to Z, which is the detailed metaphysics of particulars. Books Z and H conclude the metaphysical sequence. In H the ground covered so far is summarized, sometimes expanded and even varied; and Aristotle allows himself a certain amount of 'physical' material at the end: the physics of those highest beings, the heavenly bodies, whose physics is most immediately connected with metaphysics, because their *bodily* reality is the 'least material.' *Aether* is the purest body which is still a body, and thus presents a plurality of particulars. There can, in fact, be only *one* being which is totally, intrinsically, and even accidentally (as H indicates) free from direct connections with moving, hence physical and material objects. That is God or Mind. It would be wrong to say that it is even 'accidentally' moved by matter or that it is even accidentally in direct connection with the movement of matter as is the soul of the first heaven.

As we have seen, there is also a pedagogical reason for the introduction of a little 'higher' physics at the end of *Metaphysics* H, the last book of the series. *Metaphysics* A began with such questions – with wonder at the stars – and it has something to say about physical enquiries leading towards metaphysics. It is appropriate that Aristotle should recall such topics at the end of his philosophical journey. Our chronological schema demands that the *Metaphysics* was assembled in its present form roughly between 330 and 326 BC. The discussion of God as Mind in Λ will be more or less exactly contemporary with – probably slightly before – the treatment of the productive intellect (which is also God) in *De Anima* 3.5. Our *Metaphysics* is thus indeed a more or less unified series of treatises.

13

Late Biology

I The 'De Motu Animalium'

When Aristotle had finished the *Metaphysics* and the *De Anima* or perhaps while he was still completing *Metaphysics* Z and H, he was able to continue his biological sequence. This had resumed in Athens with the *De Partibus Animalium*, and the *De Anima* itself is its next step. The so-called *Parva Naturalia* (other than the long completed *De Respiratione*) followed quickly. It is no accident that *De Respiratione* immediately precedes (in the manuscripts) the obviously spurious *On Pneuma*. Like *On Pneuma* it was a floating piece stuck on to the end of what looked like similar material (the rest of the *Parva Naturalia*). If we remove *On Pneuma*, then the sequence ends (assuming we have already removed *De Respiratione*) with the *death* of the physical living organism. The last work of the genuine *Parva Naturalia* is *On Youth and Old Age*.[1]

Leaving the ethical works aside, Aristotle next turns his attention to revising his account of animal motion (*De Motu Animalium*), a work which alludes to the general theory of the origin of motion (in *Metaphysics* Λ) as now complete (1–6), and which indicates that the origin of motion in men (that is, including the productive intellect) has also been completed in the *De Anima* (700B4–6). But Aristotle's love of myths, which we noticed in the *Metaphysics*, and which is apparent in his reference to the story of Atlas (in Hesiod, *Theog*. 517) in the *very* late chapter 23 of *Metaphysics* Δ, continues into the nearly contemporary *De Motu*, where Atlas is discussed in some detail (699A27–B11); he is depicted by the myth-makers as standing whirling the heavens, which would only be possible if he had somewhere 'to stand'; that is, if the earth was outside the universe. Since it is not, of course, the origin of physical movement cannot reside within the cosmos itself, but must be outside it in the form of the Prime Mover. In a somewhat similar way Aristotle has earlier observed that the boatman in the boat cannot push the boat off unless he has something to push it against, and that must be still and stable (699A6–12).

The *De Motu* is both a continuation of Aristotle's biological sequence *and* a kind of appendix to the *Metaphysics*, to which it is quite explicitly tied in its opening chapter. As Aristotle says (698A10ff), 'We have already decided that the origin of all movements is itself unmoved' (like the wall the boatman leans on to push himself off). That being so, it is important to notice how important *pneuma* is in the *De Motu*. Certainly it is present and used already in the *Parva Naturalia*, and, as we have seen, traces of it can be found much earlier; but, as is generally agreed, its use in the *De Motu* is very extensive. Naturally it would be, for, as Aristotle says specifically in the *De Generatione Animalium* (2.736B30ff), it is the 'counterpart' of *aether*, and *aether* is necessary for the movements of the heavenly bodies in Λ.8: there could be no movement in the heavens unless there were to be the material capable of movement, and this is *aether*, the body of the heavens. So in *De Motu* there will be no motion in *animals*, unless the *pneuma* is introduced. Which it is, in great detail, in chapter 10. *De Motu* also contains a new account of the practical syllogism.[2] Similar material was probably destined also for the new version of the *Ethics* which, as has been discussed earlier, was soon to get under way (186–8 above).

II Women, 'Pneuma', and the 'De Generatione Animalium'

The final resolution of many of the problems about *pneuma* as it relates to generation is spelled out in the *De Generatione Animalium*; they had probably also been treated just before, in the lost *De Plantis*. *Pneuma* is hot air (2.736A1) which contains soul-heat (3.762A20). It is not fire (cf. *PA* 2.652B8 where soul is the hot, not fire), though fire (or the hot) is its most active element. Fire, we know already, is inadequate as a generator (*PA* 2.652B; cf. *GA* 2.737A1). To identify fire with soul would be like identifying a craftsman and his tool. *Pneuma* is present in semen (which is *pneuma* plus water), and its role (as formal, final, and efficient cause) is to set the menstrual blood (2.737A12–16, 739A7ff) as fig-juice or rennet sets milk. It is the 'tool' of generation which moulds the matter (*GA* 1.730B13–32).

In *GA* 1 Aristotle spells out his theory of menstrual blood, which he now also thinks needs detailed consideration (*GA* 2.737A28ff, 1.729A22ff). This menstrual blood is capable on its own of conveying a nutritive soul (the soul of a plant, the lowest form of life: 2.737A29, 736B11ff), but no more. Like semen (and milk) it is a residue, but insufficiently heated to be semen; the female is a less effective heater:[3] indeed femaleness is a 'natural' deformity (*GA* 4.775A16), so produced by nature as to be useful for the production of offspring. Female 'qua female' is passive (*GA* 1.729A30). It is a nature 'deviated' (like the deviant forms of political constitution) from the male, or the best kind of 'monstrosity' (4.767B6–9). When the male fails to 'master' the female (because his semen is poor as a result of his youth, old age, or some such), she will produce female offspring.[4]

Like everyone else, Aristotle knows the most obvious difference between men and women; in fact he speaks of the sexes as *opposites*, as we do (*GA* 4.766A21ff, 766B16). Like everyone else who thinks about the notion of an 'opposite sex', however, he is also puzzled by what we should call secondary sex characteristics and by the general problem of the relation of sex (understood as the difference of reproductive parts) and gender (i.e., the possible fundamental psychological differences which may or may not go with genital difference). The problem is political as well as psychological. Plato had argued in the *Timaeus* as well as in the *Republic* (and had assumed in the *Laws*)[5] that male/female differences are psychologically unimportant in the ideal society. Males and females have different reproductive roles, but otherwise can do the same work (men being, of course, stronger and generally superior [*Rep.* 4.455D]). Although it will work out that there are more 'good' men than 'good' women, there are quite enough good females to be guardians, and on the average female guardians are about as good as males.[6]

Aristotle is much more conservative and influenced by traditional opinion. He raises the question of the 'wider' implications of femininity in *GA* 1. Males and females differ in respect of their 'definition' (1.716A18), though we know of course (already in the *Metaphysics* as well as in *GA* itself [1.731B35]) that they are members of the same species. Obviously they differ in bodily parts, but how much does that involve? Aristotle denies outright (1.720A12) that the uterus 'wanders,' as in the *Timaeus*. Like the male organs it is integrated into the animal; this leads us to suspect that it will be less easy to separate its 'psychological' effects than Plato had supposed. Indeed Aristotle begins to suggest the difficulty by some physiological remarks in book 1. Light-skinned women are probably more 'female' and produce more vaginal secretion, which some mistake for seeds (*GA* 1.728A3, cf. *HA* 7.583A11). But more interesting material follows: there is some physical similarity between boys and women (1.728A18). *GA* 4.765A5ff returns to the subject: males are hotter than females (cf. 4.775A6–7), and the importance of this is that they have the power (*dunamis*) to concoct and discharge semen. Females are defective in this regard by lack of power (*adunamia*), and males in this respect are female when castrated. But castration leads to more than loss of genitalia. It affects the appearance of the body in general. The question is: Does it affect the soul? Given Aristotle's soul/body theory, it must in some way. Aristotle then continues with various gynaecological details about the effect of heat on the ability to conceive; we have found such material long ago in the *Historia Animalium*. Finally, he concludes, a proper balance of the hotter male and the colder female in coupling (4.767A23) will produce the best results; this will depend on a variety of factors such as age.

But we still have problems – aside from the special case of the 'female' eunuch – about the psychology, or at least the psychologically significant sexual characteristics, of males and females. There is discussion of milk at *GA* 4.777A3ff, but unfortunately Aristotle does not explain why eunuchs cannot produce it. Book 5 takes up the subject of secondary characteristics again. Chapter 3 on hair has some interest: children do not go bald; nor do women (782A10ff). Baldness is due to loss of hot fluid (783B18). No one is bald before he has sex; those who have a lot of sex go bald more easily (783B24–30), because sex cools a man off. Women do not go bald because their 'nature' (i.e., their impotence) is like that of children. Eunuchs do not go bald because they have 'changed into the female,' but like women they keep their pubic hair (784A10ff), which is a sign of some 'pneumatic' activity. Females generally have higher voices than males (786B18ff). Alone of animals man can make rational utterances (of which speech is the 'matter') – a view repeated in the nearly contemporary *Politics* 1 (1253A10–18) – though why male voices are deeper is not explained, except that a deep voice is a sign of a nobler nature (786B35). Here is another example of sexual difference indicating a more basic superiority of males to females (and to young males, 787A29) – and to eunuchs whose voices are also high-pitched (787B20–2). However at puberty the female voice deepens too, thus showing basic development (though less than in males, 787B34). In fact eunuchs change to the female condition both in voice and in the rest of their *shape* (788A7–8) – the formal difference between ordinary males and eunuchs is widening, for an *archē* is the 'cause of many things' (788A14–15).

Yet although we now suspect that major differences are indicated by lack of sexual 'potency', we are not told exactly what they are. But somehow it is likely that the female will be inferior to the male. Right back in *Historia Animalium* 1 (488B24) Aristotle has given us the clue. The only 'deliberative' creature is man. Hence we should suppose that maleness is believed to be associated with the power to deliberate. Certainly women are like children in some ways, and like eunuchs. But although they are like children, they are not children. Their voice has deepened at puberty; they have grown pubic hair, and they produce half-cooked semen as menstrual blood. That puts them beyond children. They should be better, therefore, at acting on the basis of deliberation than are children, but less good than men. That is exactly what the *Politics* means, as we saw in chapter 8 (152 above), when it says that they are *akuroi* (1.1260A13).[7] The comment no doubt suggests that women will be ineffective in the outside world; but it primarily means that they are ineffective within themselves. They will not be able to carry out the practical syllogism, to do what they deliberate about, to impose their will on their emotions. In a way they are like akratic men, but they are also importantly different. Akratic men are morally to be blamed; women are not – in so far as their *akrasia* is inevitable; it is a matter of nature, of insufficiently heated *pneuma*.

III Natural Slaves

The state of women is not that of natural slaves; our earlier discussion of slavery should have led us to expect that (153–7 above). Women and slaves are not to be identified, as they are among barbarians (*Pol.* 1.1252B5). Natural slaves may, of course, be male. So the fault is not in their *pneuma*, though if they are castrated they doubtless become even more inferior. But if it is not in the *pneuma* that their deficiency is located, where is it? Clearly in natural slaves *nous* itself is either lacking or significantly ineffectual.

In the *De Generatione Animalium nous*, as we have seen, comes 'from outside,' that is, it is not part of the soul/body complex. One could, therefore, be biologically a human without it. And natural slaves are biologically human. But they *totally* lack the power of deliberation; they need a master to make decisions for them. The only explanation of this is lack or ineffectiveness of mind.

An emendation in the text of *Nicomachean Ethics* 10 may provide further evidence. At 1177A9 we read that no one grants a slave (*andrapodon*) any measure of happiness *ei mē kai biou*.[8] But this makes no sense. Scholars try to avoid the problem by glossing it as 'since he does not possess any life of his own'. But that is not in the text. Had Aristotle wished to say that, he could have done so. Emend *biou* to *nou* and the point is clear. The slave cannot be happy because he has no intelligence (or mind). (Plato once made a similar remark as a debating point: a Cynic said he could see a horse but no horseness; Plato remarked that he had eyes but no mind. The Cynic would be a 'natural slave'.) As early as the *Protrepticus* (a source for the *Ethics*, as we have seen, 184–6 above), Aristotle had been thinking along these lines. 'Man deprived of sensation and mind is like a plant; deprived of reason alone he is bestialized; deprived of irrationality and abiding in reason he is like a god' (B28 Düring). In the *Politics* too a man who cannot live in a city-state is either a beast or a god (1.1253A29, cf. 1253A7–18). Whichever of the two he is, he will look like a man and be born by sexual generation. But deprived of mind, he is a beast, a cretin, a natural slave needing a natural master. Aristotle, as early as the *Eudemian Ethics*, is aware of other sorts of beasts too; we would call them psychopaths or merely retarded (*EE* 6.1–2); but, as we have seen, they may help to make the 'natural slave' more intelligible.

Why does Aristotle come up with his formal theory of natural slavery so late in life? Because he now thinks that biology enables him to *explain* the phenomenon. In his earlier days he would have thought that to be without *nous* was a kind of defect more like being mutilated, because he has not yet worked out the theory of a separate *nous* before the *De Anima*[9] – which itself depends on the theology of *Metaphysics* Λ or something like it. But now that he can imagine that *nous* comes in from outside, he can perhaps imagine that it does not come in at all, or that its light does not reach the 'images' in the memory. Hence the slave is left as a biological human, a human beast, a 'manimal' (*andrapodon*) who has the power of assenting, of being motivated, but not of motivating himself by the power of deliberation: he is thus like an animal.

Is the natural slave without an intellect at all, or is it ineffective? There is slight evidence from the *De Partibus Animalium* (4.686A29–32, cf. *De Anima* 3.429B16) in favour of the latter view, that he has a 'passive intellect' only. Being over-weight impedes the ability to think (and to use the 'common sense'). The model in Aristotle's mind, as we have already suggested, must be that something gets in the way of the light of the productive intellect, so that it does not illuminate, though it still shines. The same explanation would account for senility and other phenomena of failing mental power. In the *De Generatione Animalium*, we recall, what appears to be the productive intellect approaches us from outside; in natural slaves its 'approach' is blocked off. Our notion of a 'simpleton' seems to approach some at least of Aristotle's 'natural slaves'.

Ruling is connected with the possession of forethought, says Aristotle in a discussion of the idea that the 'higher' parts of the soul, as of the family and the *polis*, must be in some sort of commanding position. In this way, by a study of the growth of societies, we shall best obtain a 'professional' conclusion (*Pol.* 1.1252A22). The city is a natural growth, and the simplest communities are clans, extended families (1252B15–22). This should indicate the pattern for 'naturally' developed communities. Without a city, the members are like feet or bones cut off from the body (1253A21). The corollary of this, of course, is that the citizen should be prepared to give up his life for the good of his country, as in war. If a man is separated from a community, he will probably be separated from law and justice, and thus become 'lower' (morally) than the animals; he will be in the position to commit 'armed injustice'.

Some defenders of the role of nature in society will say (like Alcidamas) that slavery is contrary to nature, a mere convention (1253B22) based on force. But cities need slaves, so slaves are 'naturally' provided. Nature does nothing in vain, and supplies 'manimals' without mind for a purpose, just as the animals are for a purpose and to be used by man (1256B20–2). Humans can therefore be hunted (1256B5) and, as the *Protrepticus* suggests, perhaps bred (B25 Düring). Their purpose, though perhaps more limited than Aristotle once thought, is practical: they exist *naturally* for life, which is 'doing', 'acting', not 'production' (1254A8). Slaves can therefore, it is implied, be used 'unnaturally' in production. Their role is to promote life (in the household) and 'the good life' in the city-state. That would not include retailing and the making of goods for sale rather than for family or at least community use. For this purpose the slave is a tool, like the body. He is ruled by a master, just as the soul is the master, not the king merely, of the body (1254B4–10), for the soul is the *form* of the body. The soul's relation to body is not that of mind to desire but more authoritative. There is such a thing as the soul of a free man; it differs, as we have seen, by nature from the soul/form of a slave (1254B33–4); sometimes bodies, as we might expect, would visibly differ too. But this difference is not to be relied on.

A man is called a master not in relation to his possessing knowledge, but by being of a certain sort (1255B21); hence free men and slaves. 'Unjust' acquisition of slaves, that is, making the wrong people slaves, is not merely unjust, but unnatural; it is an act of mere brute force. There is an interesting analogy to be drawn here with the natural and unnatural arts of acquisition, to which Aristotle proceeds in *Politics* 1, because the slave is a part of one's possessions (1256A1ff). The connection is probably the result of reflection on how many slaves (or goods in general) one should acquire. Aristotle makes use of Plato's distinctions from book 9 of the *Republic* (as did Epicurus later) between natural and unnatural desires. It is natural to acquire goods (including slaves) for one's own use. And this is sometimes helped by assembling cash (currency). Such assembling is an 'artistic' extension of nature, and seems, as we should expect, more or less acceptable, provided one is not deluded into thinking that such acquisition should be unlimited. If acquisition depends merely on a desire to have, it is unnecessary (1258A1); one can live (and flourish) without it. Hence accumulation of capital (including slaves) would be excessive and unnatural.

But any accumulation even of limited capital by art can be given an 'unnatural twist'; that is, if the money is lent out at interest. This is unnatural, because it is an extreme version of acquiring the means of livelihood (and beyond), not merely from animals and fruits (that is, by farming, 1258A38), but otherwise and at other people's expense (1258B2). Aristotle does not go into the social and political problems usury will cause; but he knows Greek history well: he will not only be thinking of the 'unnaturalness' of breeding money from someone who can *afford* to pay interest, but also of breeding it from those who cannot – and thus forcing them into debt-bondage or other servile or semi-servile conditions. This is unnatural, the unnatural form of the acquisitive art (1258B7–8), an art of an art, which is not based on the 'natural' use of natural objects, and it is justly hated (1258B1–8). Thus excessive money-making, itself unnecessary, is especially unnatural if dependent on usury; and ownership of slaves, which may itself be excessive, can be unnatural too. Slaves are naturally used for 'action', and (presumably) are unnaturally used for production. That is not what they were 'grown' for. Here Aristotle appears to be correcting a view he had earlier held himself – though not necessarily that expressed in *Politics* 7 (1330A25–6). The 'productive' use treated in *Politics* 7 might still be acceptable – for it is agricultural – if the produce is not produced for retail sale or export.

It is the incompleteness of his mental activity which makes the natural slave, who can neither deliberate nor (obviously) philosophize. The inferiority of women, in constrast, lies in the fact that they cannot act on their deliberations as effectively as men do because of the impotence of their *pneuma*; but provided this impotence does not lead them into 'unnatural' social roles, there is no reason why they should not be philosophers. For Aristotle the virtues of males and females are different, but not qua the ability to philosophize. And with that our biological journey comes to an end.

14

Substance

I Theories of Substance

Traditionally there are two basic Aristotelian texts for the study of substance (*ousia*), the *Categories* (2–9) and the *Metaphysics*; there is also one subsidiary text with enough material to warrant special treatment, the *Posterior Analytics*. In this chapter I assume, of course, that the *Categories* is a genuine and early work of Aristotle's (for my argument see ch. 5 above), and I argue in more detail than hitherto that, although there are undoubtedly chronological layers beneath the surface of the *Metaphysics*, a single theory of substance can be found in the text as a whole. Thus, whatever the resolution of the problem of the genesis of the text of the *Metaphysics*, I claim that there is nothing important in the *Metaphysics* which is out of keeping with the thesis about substance outlined below. Clearly this is a considerable claim, but if it is true, or at least if no texts of the *Metaphysics* provide strong evidence against it, then solving the problem of the composition of our *Metaphysics* is of far less importance. For *within our Metaphysics* itself Aristotle's theory of substance will not vary. The possibility still remains, and will be considered, of whether (and if so, how) Aristotle's thoughts on substance developed between the *Categories* and the *Metaphysics*.

II The 'Categories'

Many scholars have claimed that the *Categories* is not a metaphysical but a logical,[1] or even a semantic, text.[2] Semantics cannot avoid the relations between words and the world, for it is a study of meaning: so for Aristotle it must have metaphysical implications. That the *Categories* is not primarily intended as a logical text, though it certainly contains logical material, is shown by nothing so clearly as the paradox that Aristotle is greatly concerned there with what he calls '*primary* substances',[3] e.g., Socrates, this pig, etc., while the propositions handled in the *Analytics* by logicians deal *especially* (though by no means exclusively) in general terms (all men, some men, no man).[4] Such premisses involve what Aristotle in the *Categories* calls secondary rather than primary substances.

Let us first identify the material relevant to the nature of substance and to a grasp of Aristotle's distinction, found spelled out in the *Categories* alone, between primary and secondary substance.[5] Aristotle's method is to start from what is known to us, so in the *Categories* he has nothing to say about possibly immortal substances; he concentrates on the here-and-now, the world we meet through the senses. Substance is the first of the categories, and when Aristotle first introduces it, he speaks ambiguously in his examples: man, horse (1B28). No distinction is made yet between Socrates and man, between man and a man. But the distinction soon follows (2A11ff). Substance in its strictest and primary sense (which is neither a predicate 'spoken of some particular subject', nor present in some particular subject)[6] can be identified thus: a particular man, a particular horse; simply individuals (*atoma* 1B6). What is meant by secondary substances, he continues, are the kinds (species, *eidē*) in which so-called primary substances are found, as well as the genera of those kinds. Man is a kind; animal is a wider kind. This passage shows beyond doubt that those scholars who identify secondary substances simply as classes are on the right lines – though there may be legitimate objections to keeping the word 'class'.[7] I have argued earlier that the *Categories* as a whole is concerned with identifying what is in the world rather than with explaining why it is as it is (54 above); so my conclusion that secondary substances are extensional will not surprise us. What does surprise us, if we think of some of Aristotle's later works, is why Aristotle in the *Categories* identifies secondary substances as substances at all.

This is a problem which Aristotle approaches in 2B7ff. Among secondary substances 'species' are more appropriately called substances than 'genera'. That is because they are 'nearer' to primary substances, that is, to the individual in the physical world. The notion of 'nearer' is explained as follows: if we want to know what a primary substance (e.g., Socrates) is, we shall give a closer (*oikeioteron*), more familiar (and therefore more intelligible, *gnōrimōteron*) answer[8] if we say that he is a man (and recognize him as a man) than if we say that he is an animal, if we speak of his 'species' rather than of his 'genus'.[9] So to name what is more intelligible is somehow to name what is more substantial. This has Platonic – and even

Parmenidean – overtones: being intelligible is connected with being substantial, being real. But Aristotle does not use the word *noēton* (object of intelligence) here or anywhere else in the *Categories*. Nor does he say that what is intelligible exists primarily or even *simpliciter*; on the contrary it is *primary* substances which exist in the most 'authoritative' sense (2B38). To say otherwise would involve a commitment to Platonism which he never made.

Aristotle offers a second argument for the priority of primary substances; they alone are *always* subjects, never predicates, whereas species are predicates as well (Socrates is a man). This relation between primary substance and 'species' (while establishing the priority of primary substance) is paralleled by the relation between 'species' and 'genus', thus also indicating the priority of 'species' to 'genus'.

But the priority of individual to kind is not merely logical; it is a priority in the order of being (2B5ff). For if there were no primary substances, there would be nothing else, neither secondary substances nor any other sort of predicates which could be grouped in non-substance categories. This aspect of the relationship between primary and secondary substance has given trouble. It has been generally agreed that Aristotle is arguing for the ontological dependence of secondary substances on primary substances,[10] and thus for a non-reciprocal relationship between primary and secondary substances, where primary substances might exist when secondary substances do not; but it has also frequently been held that Aristotle has no right to such a position. Unfortunately Aristotle does not tell us how he justifies his relationship, but a suggestion can be made on his behalf. It is a suggestion which is not in conflict with what is in the text of the *Categories*, and which is supported by what seems to be the only piece of evidence Aristotle has provided. There is, it seems, only one way in which Aristotle (or anyone) could hold that, although secondary substances depend for their existence on primary substances, primary substances do not depend on the existence of secondary substances. That would be true if secondary substances, which we have so far only been able to connect, for Aristotle, with the *intelligibility* of primary substances, exist in some way not in the world but in the mind. Thus this tree would exist whether anybody knew it or not, but the class of trees would only exist if there was a mind to identify this tree as a tree. That is, the secondary substance would be a kind viewed as some kind of universal (cf. *GA* 4.768B13), and universals would be constructs of minds. Now Aristotle does not talk of universals (or of minds) in the *Categories*; he only talks of 'species' and 'genera.' But I shall argue that in the *Metaphysics* he does regard 'species' as universals and that he at least came to believe universals to be those general constructs of the mind which are helpful in understanding the universe. He could have held this view even at the time of the *Categories*, though he may also have held a more 'realistic' view of such constructs.

For the time being we can only notice that in the much later *De Interpretatione* (17A39–40), when Aristotle speaks (once) of universals, he speaks of them in the same way as he speaks of secondary substances in the *Categories*. By universals, he says, I mean what is predicated of many individuals, by particular what is not so predicated. For example, man is a universal, Callias is an individual. In the *Categories* he presents man as a secondary substance. At any rate if being higher up the scale of secondary substances has to do with making primary substances more intelligible, then secondary substances must (even if Aristotle does not say so) exist in the man who is trying to understand the world. On this thesis secondary substances, being more or less familiar and intelligible, are also more or less informative concepts about the nature of primary substances. Thus secondary substances will be dependent on primary substances in two ways: they will be constructed within the mind of a particular primary substance, e.g., a man; but they will also be concepts of primary substances, more or less appropriate or 'like' primary substances. This would certainly give sense to Aristotle's use of the word *oikeioteron* (more related, more akin) which he says is characteristic of the species rather than the genus. It would also, interestingly, bring Aristotle close to the famous passage of Plato's *Parmenides*, where thoughts are said to be thoughts of something (*Parm.* 132B), a passage probably in Aristotle's mind at one point in *On Ideas*.[11]

Nothing in this part of the *Categories* need conflict with a section of the (probably undatable) *Post Praedicamenta* – which is sometimes said to diverge from it. It is tempting to claim that the *Post Praedicamenta* is even earlier than *Categories* 2–9 on the grounds that Aristotle, in treating of priority in chapters 12 and 13, must have written differently if he had already known the distinction between primary and secondary substance. But if that distinction itself is connected with Aristotle's view of the implications of the 'Third Man' argument, we might be forced to claim that if the *Post Praedicamenta* is even older, it goes back to Aristotle's late teens; and there are too many difficulties with a claim like that. As for 'implication of existence,' in chapter 13 Aristotle speaks of the 'priority' of 'genus' to 'species' 'in their implications of existence,' while in neither 12 nor 13 does he mention the priority of primary over secondary substance. In 13 he says that if there is a fish, there is an animal, but if there is an animal, there is not necessarily a fish. But this does not disturb our earlier passage; for although 'If there is an animal' does not imply the existence of a fish, it does imply the existence of some species; whereas to name that particular species does tell us more about the animal in the cage than merely an identification of it as an animal. There is nothing in chapter 13 that has to conflict with the claim that when Aristotle in the *Categories* speaks of secondary substances being predicated of (*kata*) a subject, he alludes, when speaking of predication, to the process of concept-formation. Thus when we predicate X (denoting a kind) of Y, we think of Y *as* an X, thus constructing secondary substances as concepts of primary substances. It is also easy to see how, basing himself on considerations of the 'degrees of substantiality' of secondary substances, Aristotle could immediately point out that primary substances are substantially equal; no primary substance is more substance than any other (2B26ff): Socrates is no more substance than this ox. The existence of neither of them depends in any way on their being more or less precisely identified as a man, an ox, or an animal.

Aristotle does not use the word 'universal' in the *Categories*; and secondary substances (even if they are [some sort of] concepts) are not simply to be identified as what he would later call universals. He makes this clear in the next section (2B29ff). If we leave primary substances aside ('after the primary substances'), he says, of all else only 'species' and 'genera' of substances are secondary *substances*. So 'man' is a secondary substance, but 'just' is not, even though later on Aristotle might call them both universals. In other words only universals in the category of substance are secondary *substances*. Other universals would presumably be secondary qualities, quantities, etc., as apparently in the later *Topics* 1.103B25.

Aristotle is particularly concerned in the *Categories* to ensure that secondary substances are distinguished from qualities, and to justify calling them substances at all. His problem seems to be that he supposes that every notion must be included in some particular category or other – a view which he later rejected, believing, not only in the *Metaphysics* but even in the *Topics*, that being and unity (and others) do not belong in any *particular* category. That being so, he *sees* a problem in the *Categories* about how to justify putting 'substance universals' in the category of substance while still distinguishing them from qualities. In terms of his own examples, he wants to distinguish propositions like 'Socrates is a man' from 'Socrates is white.' He wants to say that man is a secondary substance and white is a quality.

Aristotle starts by telling us that secondary substances 'identify' (*dēloi* 2B31) the primary substances,[12] and he suggests again that to mention the 'species' is more informative in this regard than to mention the 'genus.' On the contrary it is uninformative, alien (*allotriōs*), or, as we would say, irrelevant, to mention a quality such as white. That is, according to Aristotle, if we want to know what Socrates is, so that we may identify him, it is more informative to say that he is a man than to say that he is white (though the *Categories* does not suggest much about *why* it is more informative). But since it *is* more informative, we infer that there is an important difference between kinds and qualities. Furthermore, continues Aristotle, the relation between a primary substance and its qualities is similar to that between a secondary substance and its (presumably secondary) qualities: 'Socrates is literate' parallels 'Man is literate.' It might in some way have been a better example for Aristotle to say 'Socrates is two-footed' parallels 'Man is two-footed.' But Aristotle does not use such an example, as he shortly indicates, because he seems to want to exclude 'qualities' which might contribute to the *definition* of the subject as distinct from those which he would (elsewhere) think of as 'accidental' qualities. But in the *Categories* there is no analysis of the existential implications, if any, of a definition, no discussion of 'realized nature' (*to ti ēn einai*), only an apparent assumption that if we classify particulars, we know that they exist.

Aristotle wants us to understand that there is both a similarity and an important distinction between secondary substances and qualities: they are alike in that in some sense they both identify what sort of thing (*poion*) the individual is. Aristotle also wants to point out that to qualify as a substance of course, in the strict sense, the candidate must be a particular *this* (3B10ff). In the case of primary substances, there is no difficulty: the object identified or signalled (*dēloumenon*) by the name is 'one in number,' e.g., Socrates is one individual. Something similar *appears* to be the case with secondary substances: we speak of man or animal (as singulars); there is *one* kind called man. But words are misleading, says Aristotle; 'man' does not identify an individual but one sort of thing (*poion ti*, 3B15). A similar point is made later in the *Sophistici Elenchi*.[13] There Aristotle wants to advance such a view to avoid Platonic Forms. He rejects them precisely because being 'one over many' they *cannot* be individuals.

But the possible confusion between the secondary substance which identifies Socrates as of a certain kind (as the member of one 'species' or 'genus') and the quality which tells us something about Socrates, but not necessarily that he is a member of one species or genus (e.g., that he is white), needs to be unmasked. 'Man' and 'white' both tell us that Socrates is 'of such a kind' (*poios*). Once the problem is isolated, Aristotle has no difficulty in clarifying it. Secondary substances tell us how to *classify* the kind of substance (*peri ousian to poion*) Socrates is; qualities merely describe the particular; they may or may not be of use for classification of substances. Aristotle refers here to qualities as 'simply' (*haplōs*) 'telling us generally about a subject'; that is, they do no more than provide a descriptive epithet. Had he tried to spell out a distinction between 'essential' and 'accidental' qualification at this stage, he would have been able to make his point more clearly.

Qualities are said by Aristotle to be somehow 'in' substances; but secondary substances are said *not* to be *in* primary substances (3A14–15; cf. 1A22). So much, at least by implication, for Platonic Forms – which we have argued Aristotle never promoted. Gone too is any notion that the *eidos* (already identified as a kind) is in the particular either in the sense of supplying the nature of the particular (of existing *substantially* as what some scholastics identified as a common nature) or being understood largely intensionally, as several modern scholars have proposed.[14] All such theses introduce formally alien material into the *Categories*, as Brentano recognized long ago.[15]

Eidos in the *Categories* never means 'form';[16] it always means kind or species (though perhaps what has puzzled scholars is that Aristotle, because of the ambiguity of *eidos* in Plato, still finds it hard not to assume a certain intensionality in his notion of species itself). We should not be surprised that the *Categories* declines to discuss form; it has nothing to say either about matter, or about potentiality or actuality; nor, as we have seen, does it distinguish specifically between essential and accidental predication. All these omissions are explicable: the *Categories* has nothing to say about why things are as they are; it deals with what things there are in the world. Hence there is no discussion of causation, hence no form, no matter, no potentiality, no actuality, no 'essence' and accident, for all these notions, even if Aristotle had diagnosed them all at this stage of his writing, are the products of an enquiry not into the what is there but into the why there is what there is. Discussion of actuality and accident is for Aristotle inseparable from discussion of causation, especially of the question of what needs to be explained in terms of final causes and what does not. Thus the eyes are for seeing, but the colour of the eyes (as long as they can see) is merely an accident of matter.

The 'Platonism' of the *Categories*, therefore, is only very marginally that Aristotle is tempted to think of forms as explaining the *nature* of particulars; it appears rather in his account of secondary substances, and his apparent belief that because kinds of substances are objects of *thought* (through which we can have particular kinds of thoughts of primary substances), they therefore themselves deserve to be called 'substances' of some sort. Later, in *On Ideas*, Aristotle rejected the Platonic view that objects of thought (*noein* is the word used)[17] necessarily exist in the world. *On Ideas* does not use the language of primary and secondary. In the *Categories* itself Aristotle already denies that thoughts are independent of the thinker, but he cannot yet rid himself of the Platonic (and Parmenidean) view that at least thoughts *of substances* must be substances in some secondary sense (or at least must be *listed* as such). Even in *Metaphysics* A Aristotle is still prepared to say that if there are Platonic Forms of anything at all, there should be Forms of substances – an attitude otherwise hard to explain. It is interesting too that in this section (*Met.* A.990B22ff) he argues that on the basis of Platonic claims that Forms (*ideas*) exist, there could exist Forms not only of substances but of other things as well. Aristotle clearly thinks that the reality of *substantial* universals is a more reasonable proposition than that of others. This is more intelligible if we see that he himself, in the *Categories*, held that there are indeed *eidē* of substances, and that these *eidē* still have the right to be called 'substances'. Note also that in another version of Aristotle's later account of what is wrong with Platonic Forms (*Met.* M.1079A20ff), he specifically suggests that the Platonists move from a concept (a *noēma*), which can be 'about' non-being, to a Form. Our conclusion is that in the *Categories* Aristotle's comment on 'Platonism' is that the general concept is not in fact a Platonic Form but, in the case of so-called substance-universals, at least a secondary substance.

When Aristotle came to the Academy in 367, classification was a major concern of the philosophers he found there. Hence it is not surprising that *eidos* means 'kind/species' in the *Categories*. The evidence that has bedevilled much modern scholarship is that *eidos* might also refer to a Platonic Form. Aristotle, we would maintain, was not necessarily tempted to use it this way, but eventually had to confront a dilemma which he had not yet faced in the *Categories*. What name shall we use, if we want a name which will identify not only secondary substances, but also secondary qualities, quantities, etc., particularly if we are no longer distracted by the belief that kinds of substances have some sort of higher claim to reality than kinds of qualities or quantities? He resolves this problem by developing the use of the word 'universals'. His second problem, however, is what about the ontological status of these universals and of that to which they refer – a problem which produces 'Platonic' worries if such universals are *either in re* universals – which is not a correct description of them even in the *Categories* – or if they are concepts. For we need to determine the 'nature' of concepts. The third problem is greater for us than apparently for Aristotle: how to distinguish *eidē* as forms in the *Metaphysics* from *eidē* as kinds or species. That problem does not arise in the *Categories*, where *eidos* never means form and a form/matter distinction is not drawn. It arises in the *Metaphysics*, however, where Aristotle has no difficulty (in book Z) in distinguishing forms from kinds (or, as he there sees the problem, from universals).

It will be apparent that the *Categories* is not simply a work of logic; it is rather a work of (descriptive) metaphysics. Its aims are comparatively limited, and Aristotle makes no attempt to raise certain problems about existence and non-existence prominent in the *Metaphysics* (not to mention the *Posterior Analytics*). But to say that is not to say that the metaphysics of the *Categories* is replaced rather than developed by that of the *Metaphysics*. Replacement should not be assumed before we have considered the *Metaphysics* itself. We can certainly say that the phrase 'secondary substance' disappears after the *Categories*. We cannot yet say what happens to what Aristotle in the *Categories* calls secondary substances *after* the *Categories*; that is, whether and to what extent the status of items such as man, horse, and cabbage changes. We shall need to look, in the *Metaphysics*, at the relation between substantive and non-substantive universals, and of course between substantive universals and what Aristotle calls forms. Finally we shall need to ask whether the disappearance of the phrase 'secondary substance' reflects the disappearance of the apparently vestigially Platonic attitudes to what, in the *Categories*, we have called concepts, and whether in usually declining to call 'species' and 'genera' substances – though not in *PA* 1.644A2–9 – Aristotle also abandons the notion that an object of reference or discussion has not only to be put in one or the other of the categories but also given some kind of residually objective existence as an object of thought.

III 'De Interpretatione'

In the *De Interpretatione* (17A37–9) – a work, we have suggested, later than the *Posterior Analytics* – Aristotle uses the word 'universal' (which is absent from the *Categories*). He also uses the neutral word 'thing' (*pragma*) where in the *Categories* he would probably have said 'substance'. Of 'things', he says, some are universals (these are precisely the secondary substances of the *Categories*);[18] others are particulars. The distinction is in terms of predication: 'man' can be predicated of a plurality of subjects, 'Callias' cannot. What are we to make of the fact that the word 'substance' has gone and the vague 'thing' replaces it? Perhaps Aristotle is not yet quite clear how he wants to place what he now calls 'universals'; more likely he has not yet worked out the new notion of 'modes' of substance found in *Metaphysics* Δ.1017B23 and Z.1037A28, for a similar unclarity had appeared in the *Prior Analytics* (1.43A25). Here 'things' is not used, or 'substance' either; individuals like 'Cleon' and 'Callias' are distinguished from 'man' as different kinds of 'beings' (*onta*). Both *Prior Analytics* and *De Interpretatione* show hesitation, at least about terminology, and perhaps point to what is to come in the *Metaphysics*. But it is likely that substantial differences will appear between the *Metaphysics* and the *Posterior Analytics*, which itself appeared after the *Prior Analytics* but before *De Interpretatione*.[19]

IV Substance and Universals in the 'Posterior Analytics'

When we shift our attention from the *Categories* to the *Posterior Analytics*, we find ourselves in a world of polemic. We have already observed that Aristotle's attitude to Plato in the *Posterior Analytics* and the *Eudemian Ethics* is similar.[20] In these two works is to be found the most uncompromising rejection of a theory of transcendent Forms, or at least a rejection expressed in the most uncompromising and hostile language. Part of the explanation for this may lie in the fact that later on Aristotle's position was well known; he then did not feel he needed to be abrasive about it, merely to present arguments. Besides, in regard to the possibility of metaphysics itself, Aristotle later came to believe that he had gone too far in the *Posterior Analytics*.

In the *Posterior Analytics* it is Aristotle's repeated contention that there are no Platonic Forms 'over and above' (*para*) particulars; they are not needed for demonstration – for that universals will do (1.77A5–9); these universals are not 'something' over and above the particulars. Rather we have a belief, that is, *in our minds*, that they have a 'nature' (*phusin*) which 'subsists' (*huparchein*) 'in' things (1.85A33ff, cf. 1.73B27). This 'in' seems to be the same as 'above' (*epi*, 1.77A9), for Aristotle wants to make clear that the universal is not *merely* a common *name* (*homōnumon*); it is 'in' and 'above' particulars, but neither an additional item (*para*) in the world nor the *cause* of the particulars. It is not allowed the word *eidos*, which is here limited to Platonic Forms; nor is *eidos* used anywhere alse in the *Posterior Analytics* even to refer to the Aristotelian form as identified in the *Metaphysics*. Again Aristotle repeats (1.85B19ff) that although the universal indicates one thing about particulars, say, that Socrates is a man and that Plato is a man, this does not mean that man is an entity over and above (*para* again) the particulars. Thus man would indicate *one kind* of thing.[21] Similarly, he observes, with the other categories; that is, because this is yellow and that is yellow, it does not follow that yellow exists over and above particular yellows. If you make that sort of assumption, says Aristotle, the fault is in you, not in the argument. This side of Aristotle's attitude to Forms (*eidē*) is summed up in their rather brutal dismissal as fantasies (1.83A33). But as some of the texts we have already quoted will show, Aristotle does not entirely rid himself of these fantasies, nor does he entirely want to do so.

In the *Posterior Analytics* Aristotle has two related reasons for showing special hostility to Platonic Forms. One is that he wants to deny an overall Platonic science of dialectic, of the sort outlined in the *Republic*; the other is the corollary of this: that he wants to establish independent first principles for the separate sciences, leaving as common ground only such rules as the law of contradiction and the law of excluded middle. These, being viewed non-metaphysically and purely as matters of logic, are to have no implications for the content of the sciences or for any possible subordination of the particular sciences to metaphysics. Such 'axioms' are, of course, to be recognized intuitively (2.100B10ff, 1.72B25, cf. *EE* 5.1142A26, 5.1143A36).

In the *Posterior Analytics* Aristotle connects his two basic claims about Platonism (1.76A17ff).[22] The principles of each science cannot be demonstrated, for if they could, they would be derived from some super-science, which would be supreme over them all (*kuria pantōn*). But such a Platonic science does not exist; the principles of each science are autonomous – as the *Eudemian Ethics* repeats. If any such principles do overlap, it is only by analogy, and so far as they fall within the genus of the particular science.[23] The effect of this, of course, is not only to ban a Platonic metaphysics of Being (or Goodness), but to ban *any* such general enquiry, for any science of being as such would involve confusing the principles of the different particular sciences.

In the *Categories* it seemed as though all 'existents' should go into some category or other. The *Posterior Analytics*, with its view that some common principles 'overlap' for some reason or another, may allow the possibility of extra-categorial items. We have already found such items in the *Topics* (77 above); and the idea is confirmed by the *Eudemian Ethics*, which in its strong attack on Platonic Forms as useless recalls the tone of the *Posterior Analytics* (1.1217B22, *logikōs kai kenōs*), and which indeed quotes from the *Posterior Analytics* themselves in a nearby passage (1.1217A18). The *Eudemian Ethics* too allows that 'good' can occur in all the categories (1.1217B27ff), but that does not indicate a common science of goodness. 'Goodness' is merely an ambiguous term, as is 'being' (1.1217B34). We may observe here that the (later) *Nicomachean Ethics*, though still questioning the status of goodness, does *not* suggest that 'being' is merely ambiguous (1.1096A20ff). Rather it points to the dependence of the other categories on substance – a relationship which represents an approach to a new version of that science of metaphysics which the *Eudemian Ethics* had denied.

But this is to jump the gun. For the time being let us merely note that the *Nicomachean Ethics*, while dropping the mention of 'being' altogether, observes of 'goodness' that it is not a single and common universal term, and therefore does not fall within any one category. The effect might be the same as far as ethics goes, but note that where the *Eudemian Ethics* has no mention of universals, the *Nicomachean Ethics* denies that 'good' is a universal, while leaving as an open question whether it might still without mere ambiguity be predicable in all the categories in some other manner. Such predication in fact came to have metaphysical implications, just as it did in the case of 'being'.

There are no Platonic Forms in the *Posterior Analytics*; that is a central point. But there are universals, including substance-universals. Obvious questions therefore arise. Above all, what is the status of these universals, first in the world, then in the mind? The second question is whether there is any distinction drawn in the *Posterior Analytics* between universals and forms. This is easier to answer and may be considered first. Aristotle, as we have seen, does not use the word 'form' (*eidos*) in the *Analytics*, except when he is referring to Platonic Forms. This sets the *Analytics* alongside the *Categories* and immediately distinguishes them from the *Metaphysics*. We shall observe a little later that, in the *Posterior Analytics* (2.11), even when Aristotle wishes to list the four causes, he makes no mention of form (or matter): instead we find the notorious 'realized nature' (*to ti ēn einai*) and a reference to necessitating conditions. This is sometimes explained by reference to the 'logical' nature of the *Analytics*, but that is totally insufficient: 'realized nature' is not simply a notion in logic. But we must first consider why it becomes so important in the *Posterior Analytics*.

In order to approach this problem, we must face one of the major questions of the *Posterior Analytics* as a whole, namely the distinction that Aristotle wishes to draw between demonstrations and definitions. Merely to raise this distinction takes Aristotle far beyond the *Categories*. There, primary substances are individual members of 'genera' and 'species' – which is reasonable enough if the *Categories* is descriptive, an attempt to map out and classify the contents of the world. But as the opening of *Posterior Analytics* 2 makes clear, Aristotle has greatly widened the scope of his enquiries. Already in book 1 (chapter 27) he has tried to sort out the difference between knowledge of fact and knowledge of the explanation of fact, that is, understanding. Explanation of fact is concerned with why things are as they are, hence with explaining both the existence of *things* and the existence of *events*. Why, in Aristotle's own favourite example, is there an eclipse? The opening of book 2 of the *Posterior Analytics* elaborates on such themes, some of which we have already discussed (53–4 above).

Aristotle identifies two questions which would look for yes/no answers: 'is this happening?' – (i.e., *hoti*-questions about events); 'are there centaurs or gods?' – (i.e., *ei*-questions about the existence of substances). He then adds two further questions: *dioti*-questions about why there are eclipses (or gods); *ti*-questions (the 'what is it?' questions of the *Categories*) about what gods (or eclipses or virtues) are. Note that he does not ask what centaurs are, let alone why there are centaurs, *because there are no centaurs*. Thus the *dioti*-questions about gods and eclipses are the subject-matter for demonstrations. I do not propose to examine the interrelations between these questions at length, only to observe that Aristotle is now beyond a metaphysics of classification (*ti esti*) into a metaphysics of explanation and cause. And he generally points out that if we merely know the 'genus' and 'species' of a substance, we do not know enough about that substance to be able to comprehend its nature and its 'behaviour'. If we cannot comprehend the natures of substances, we cannot tell why substances 'do things' or why events occur.

The problem which Aristotle is facing is summed up in the possible renderings of the phrase *ti esti* (what is it?). Tredennick, typically, complains that Aristotle's use of it in *Posterior Analytics* 2 is 'tiresomely vague.'[24] He makes it approximate now *to ti ēn einai* (which he renders as 'real essence'), now to *horismos* (definition). This completely misses the point. For we must realize that whereas in the *Categories* Aristotle assumes that 'what is it?' questions about primary substances, that is, individuals, can be answered by reference to kinds, he now wants to point out that there are more important other ways of answering them. Why should he want other ways? Because only when we know that, say, a god exists, can we ask what is a god, or a man. To know 'species' and 'genera' is not enough for demonstrations. If there *are* no men, we cannot begin our argument, except perhaps for purposes of logical training, with 'All men are mortal.' Since Aristotle seems to hold that even complete understanding of 'realized natures' is not necessarily merely analytic, we must be sure of the existence of our subject-matter.[25] It is no accident that whereas the term 'realized nature' is rare in book 1 (it occurs, for example, at 82B38), it is very common in book 2. And just as in demonstrations we have to assume our first principles, so definition will not *prove* the 'what it is' either (92B37ff). Yet we know, of course, that there is a sense in which classification in terms of genus and differentiae will tell us what a thing is (1.83A20ff, 1.83B1); what Aristotle wants to say is that it will not tell us about the 'what is it?' *seen as existing*, that is, the 'realized nature' (*to ti ēn einai*).[26] Why is he now so concerned to identify this special sort of 'what it is', this 'realized nature'?[27] It is because for extra-logical purposes class-membership does not tell us enough about what the *Categories* called primary substances. It may assume the existence of primary substances, but that assumption needs to be made explicit if we are to proceed to consider *why* the primary substances exist. Now for an item to be recognizable as a primary substance, an *ousia*, in this sense, we must know not only how to classify it, but what its nature is as an existent: not just its genus and differentia but its 'realized nature'. This 'realized nature' is what Aristotle in the *Metaphysics* understandably calls form. Why does he not do so in the *Analytics*? Partly because *eidos* is constantly used there for the Platonic Forms and for 'species'. Two senses are enough for anyone, particularly for a man (sc. Aristotle) who does not wish to risk confusing his newly identified 'realized natures' with the Platonic Forms he is so vigorously rejecting. And, of course, there is nothing about *matter* in the *Analytics*.

For something to have a 'realized nature', it obviously has to exist; hence it can be used in demonstrations. We cannot *prove* its 'what it is *kat'ousian*'. Nor, of course, can we *prove* (or *disprove*) the 'realized nature' of a goat-stag (2.92B7–8); but we can deny that there are any goat-stags. Evidence of their existence is lacking. If there *were* goat-stags, we could ask what they are both in terms of their 'realized nature' and in terms of their classification (their genus and differentiae). An investigation of the 'realized nature' is necessarily an investigation of the cause (2.93A18ff). It seems, incidentally, that Aristotle in the final analysis makes little distinction (certainly not in the *Posterior Analytics*) between what we have called the investigation of events and the investigation of objects (e.g., What is a man?).[28] This, so far as it goes, is not unreasonable. To understand events we need to understand the characteristics of the objects involved in the events. To understand an eclipse, we need to know about the nature and movement of the sun and moon. For Aristotle these are questions about causes and realized natures. As to the relationships between the other 'causes' and the 'realized nature', to which Aristotle alludes in chapter 11, there is no further elucidation offered in the *Posterior Analytics*. The main function of that work, from our present point of view, is to show that 'what is it?' questions lead far beyond problems of classification; they may also concern the causes and realized nature of particulars.

Having established something of what Aristotle means by 'realized nature' in the *Posterior Analytics*, let us now return to the question of universals. Here, we recall, we wanted to answer two questions: what (if anything) is the status of universals in the world, and what (if anything) is the status of universals in the mind? But first we need some preliminary remarks about knowledge in the *Posterior Analytics*. Aristotle, as we have already seen, is far from denying knowledge of particulars in the *Posterior Analytics* or anywhere else; what he denies is understanding (*epistēmē*). The approach to understanding is by what is called induction (*epagōgē*), and induction leads us from particulars to universals. Except by induction we cannot 'see' (*theōrein*) the universal (1.81B1–3); by induction the universal, the basis for demonstration, becomes known (*gnōrimon*). It is by sense perception (*aisthēsis* in this passage) that we apprehend the particulars.[29] In contrast, we can only grasp universals by reasoning (*nous, dianoia*), since they are not particulars (but only describe them) and are not tied to a particular time (1.87B30ff). So-called abstractions, that is, the objects of mathematics, are grasped by reason in a similar way (1.81B3, cf. *De Caelo* 3.299A16–17). Necessarily some knowledge of the particular (through sense-perception) precedes knowledge of the universal (1.71A17ff); if it did not, we would be trapped in the paradox of the *Meno* (80DE): either we cannot learn anything, or we learn only what we already know (1.71A29ff).

'We have a limited knowledge (from the senses),' would be Aristotle's reply to this paradox, 'but it is neither knowledge of universals nor understanding.' Understanding is grounded on a grasp of causation and on the fact that things could not (in general) be otherwise. Finally, knowledge of the universal is 'better' than that of the particular (unless this refers to the 'species') because it is of wider scope (1.85B10–15).

Let us leave knowledge of particulars and consider the universals which, after perceiving the particulars, we see (*theōrein*) by induction. Where do we find them? In the mind or in the world? Clearly universals relate to the particulars; the word Aristotle uses for their situation 'outside' the mind is often translated as 'subsist' (*huparchein*). Thus the 'abstractions' of mathematics subsist in each genus (1.81B4); where a universal 'subsists', knowledge of it is of wider scope (1.85B15); attributes subsist in a genus (1.75A28–9). Most interesting of all, however, is the passage beginning at 85A31: 'If the universal does not exist as something apart from the particulars, and if demonstration instills [*empoiei*] a *belief* that [this universal] is something in virtue of which there is a demonstration, and that this subsists [*huparchein*] as a certain nature [*phusin*] in things, for example a triangle *apart* from particular triangles ... universal demonstration will be inferior to particular demonstration.'

The most interesting feature of this text is that it gives a meaning to the word *huparchein*. We should notice right away that Aristotle does not say that the universals exist (*einai*) in things. Had he done so, there might be a slight reason to think that he was speaking of a 'realist' doctrine of what later came to be called *in re* universals. But he does not use *einai* in this passage – though occasionally and confusingly he does so elsewhere – and the matter is quite otherwise. What he says is that demonstration makes us believe (not know) that the universal is some kind of nature 'subsisting' in things. But most interestingly our belief seems to lead us to think, rather Platonically, that the universal exists *apart* from particulars, e.g., triangles. Yet Aristotle *denies* that universals exist apart in the world!

There is nothing in what Aristotle says about 'subsistence' to contradict an explanation as follows: to speak of the 'presence of universals' in particulars is simply to allude to the common and thus classifiable structures of particular things (and to the structure of predications in propositions formed by logicians). But perhaps there is *one* small piece of counter-evidence: a passage we have already looked at where Aristotle is considering the superiority of knowledge of universals to knowledge of particulars. The section is variously rendered. Tredennick, for example, says (1.85B15ff): 'If the meaning is invariable, and the universal term is not merely equivocal, it will not be less but more really existent than some of the particulars, inasmuch as universals include imperishable things whereas particulars tend rather to be perishable.' If that is really what Aristotle says, he might seem to assert that universals are more 'existent' than some, viz. all perishable, particulars. This might seem not only to claim substantiality of some sort for universals – which many have attributed to Aristotle; it might also reverse the priority, which Aristotle has established in the *Categories*, of the primary substance, the particular, over the species and genus.[30] In that form at least the interpretation must be wrong.

The point Aristotle wants to make must be something like this: *knowledge* of universals – which is what the whole discussion is about – will be not inferior to that of some particulars; indeed it is superior, inasmuch as some universals may be imperishable (sc. genera and species); hence knowledge of them will be of necessary truths, whereas particulars are generally perishable and knowledge of them (qua particular) is contingent. This would then provide a further argument for what Aristotle indeed holds: not the existential dependence of particulars on universals but the superiority of understanding of universals and universal truths to knowledge of particulars. When Aristotle says that the universal 'exists' more than some particulars, he means that although Socrates no longer exists, man exists so long as there are any men. No conclusions need be drawn from this (despite *eiē*) as to what kind of 'existence' man (as a universal) has.

So there is nothing so far to show that universals exist as such in the world. If we turn to what Aristotle says in the *Posterior Analytics* about universals in the mind, I think it can be shown not merely that universals *may* not exist in the world, but that in fact they do not so exist. Their 'existence' (or perhaps the nature of their 'subsistence') in the world is a false inference made by Aristotle's readers; and as Aristotle himself says, that is the fault of the hearer, not of the demonstration (1.85B22).

Some universals, as we have seen, are secondary *substances* in the *Categories*; these, and probably others, are now said to 'subsist' in the *Posterior Analytics*. The term 'substance' is denied them altogether; their 'subsistence' is the projection of a unified belief that we hold about similar classifiable characteristics in particulars. We may consider how such beliefs arise in our souls. If that is clear, we shall see if universals – in the *Posterior Analytics* – can exist outside the soul as well. In the *Categories* we noticed that secondary substances seemed in part at least to acquire the title 'substances' because we think of them first and most appropriately when we begin to think about particulars. With the phrase 'secondary substance' now gone, has anything more than a name changed in the *Posterior Analytics*?

We have already observed that as a result of induction we 'see' (*theōrein*) the universal. Another term Aristotle uses in this connection is *gnōrizein*:

after 'recognizing' the universal we have the possibility of understanding (1.87B2–3). In the extended discussion of universals in *Posterior Analytics* 2.19 the same phrase occurs: we have a 'recognizing disposition' (2.99B18) for acquiring knowledge of first principles – a vague phrase which in the rest of the chapter seems to refer primarily to universals as concepts. And in 100B3–4 we read that it is by induction that we 'recognize' primary universals (*ta prōta*), for this is the way sense perception 'instils' the universal.[31] Let us consider the process in more detail, remembering that the end product is the possibility of demonstration itself. And it is demonstration, as we have seen, which instils in us 'beliefs' about the nature of universals.

Roughly speaking the process is as follows. Man, like the animals, has a faculty of sense-perception. It is an innate feature (99B35) of this faculty to be able to discriminate.[32] But while the animals can discriminate within their sensible images, man is unusual (though not necessarily unique, cf. *EE* 5.1141B1ff) in that he can retain the images in the soul in a special way. This retention offers him the possibility of knowledge beyond that of sense perception,[33] the possibility, as Kahn puts it, not merely of distinguishing a horse from a man, but of distinguishing a horse as a *horse*.[34] By itself, however, the retention of images does not give understanding, for animals, though retaining perceptions, cannot sort them out. Man is able to find order, intelligibility (*logos*), and generality in his perceptions;[35] how he does so, we are not told here, but clearly somehow by 'thinking', by making use of the mind. Aristotle calls the retention of a sense perception memory, and repeated memories of the same thing, viewed coherently, form a single 'experience'.[36] Thus experience, when it has somehow 'come to rest', seems to be the universal in the human soul; and now that we see it in the soul, Aristotle allows that it is 'over and above' the particulars; not, of course, in the traditional acceptation of that phrase, as a Platonic Form, but as something produced (by the productive intellect) in the soul. The universal then is a generalized memory of particulars known through sensation; it is not in the particulars, but in the soul. It seems clear in this passage that if there were no souls there would be no universals. Not of course that such a theory makes the structure of the world, the nature of things, dependent on the mind. The universal does not exist before sense perception, but objects of perception, similar to one another, still exist. And not only do they exist, they are structured. Their structure, which we can perceive in terms of universals, is of course dependent on their individual causes. Aristotle, in the *Posterior Analytics*, has a term to describe it. The term, however, is not 'universal'; it is 'realized nature', and 'realized nature' depends on particular causes. As he is to put it later: 'Man is the father of man (but there is no Man), but Peleus is the father of Achilles.' That is, Peleus will *in fact* hand on certain human characteristics which *he* possesses to Achilles; thus he will construct Achilles' 'realized nature'.

In the following section (2.100A15ff), where Aristotle tries to clarify his position, it is again evident that the universal appears as the result of a series of processes in the soul which began with sense perception.[37] What then are we to make of the phrase in 2.100A7, where, after calling the universal in the soul a one 'over and above [*para*] the many,'[38] Aristotle adds 'whatever is in all those things as the same single thing'? Does this not suggest that he thinks of the universal not only as in the soul, but also as in the particulars? Aristotle would certainly have been safer, if he had wished to avoid that interpretation, if he had written not 'which *is* in all particulars', but 'which "subsists" in all the particulars.' But the latter is indeed what he must mean. For when he speaks of 'one same thing' in all the particulars, he refers to the starting-point (*archē*) of art and understanding, that is, to one similar characteristic or feature (such as being feathered, or rational) in all the particulars; in other words he is referring not to one thing (*tode ti*) in particulars, but to one kind of thing (*toionde*) in the manner of the *Categories* and the *Sophistici Elenchi*. Thus the universal is *in* the soul, that is, constructed in the soul, an Aristotelian 'individual' over and above the many particulars, but an 'individual' in the sense of 'whatever is in all those things as the one similar recognized feature.' For if particulars did not have similar features, they could not be identified as belonging to *individual* 'species' and 'genera'; assemblages of particulars could only be random heaps.

Common features are only called universals when they are *identified* as such by the mind – and *inter alia* used as the subject-matter in 'scientific' enquiry. The mind creates kinds, but individuals (sometimes of the same kind) create individuals. As Aristotle puts it, sense perception *instils* (i.e., produces) (*empoiei*) the universal (2.100B5). When we speak of these universals and use them in demonstrations, we get the opinion that they *subsist* in things as some sort of nature (1.85A32). The Greek word *empoiei* occurs here too: it is demonstration which *instils* or *produces* the belief that they subsist because it uses them. But what demonstration uses, of course, are not the actual structures of things, but *concepts* of the structures of things. It is only after our senses have acted, after the images have been left in our mind, that by looking at these images, we see them (*theōrein*) and recognize (*gnōrizein*) the universal by a process called induction.

Where then are we with substances at the end of the *Posterior Analytics*? Substances are individuals and only individuals, but these individuals have a 'realized nature'. This 'realized nature' is not yet called a form; nor, of course, is it a universal. The two are kept apart. What are called in the *Categories* secondary substances ('species' and 'genera') are now not substances; substances must be unequivocally individuals (cf. 1.73B7ff), and they are recognizable (*gnōsta*) by sense perception (2.99B35) or *intelligibly* as individuals (1.82B38) – and hence universally.

It cannot be denied that Aristotle's purposes in the *Posterior Analytics* are far from transparent, but it is possible to discuss the direction of his thinking: universals in the soul, 'realized natures', and substances (the particulars themselves) can be identified and distinguished. The ambiguous status of 'substance' associated with the secondary substances of the *Categories* can be clarified.[39] But there is still no metaphysical role for what is outside the categories. 'Being', 'unity', 'good' are not in any category; but 'being' is not a genus (2.92B14), so it cannot be treated merely as a universal. What it is in the *Posterior Analytics* is uncertain. In any case no science of 'being' as such is possible, only the particular sciences and the identification of basic logical 'laws'. That 'being' is viewed as like the universals, as a concept of some sort, and as distinct from *beings* (*onta*) which exist in the world and are understood in the various categories (1.88B1ff), is likely, since there is no science of 'being' as such. But certainty on this matter cannot be found in the *Posterior Analytics*.

V Goat-stags and Other Fictions

Understandably Aristotle was worried on more than one occasion by goat-stags. The problem about goat-stags, as he observed in the *De Interpretatione* (16A16ff), is that the word 'goat-stag' looks like 'man' or 'white' in that it is 'not yet true or false', but it 'means something' – to take a safe translation of *sēmainei ti* on this occasion. (The problem about translating it as 'refers to something' [which would normally be appropriate] is that 'goat-stags' are not there to be referred to – but perhaps the normal translation can be used once the oddity has been pointed out.) Of course 'goat-stag' may refer to something in the mind, a question to which we shall have to return. At any rate, says Aristotle, 'goat-stag', like 'man' and 'white', is like a thought (*noēma*); it is neither 'combined nor separated.' Of course when such thoughts are combined, propositions with truth-value are created: 'Socrates is white' is true, 'A goat-stag is white' (for Aristotle) would be false. Why it is false is explained in another goat-stag passage: in the *Posterior Analytics*, in a text we have already considered (265–6 above), we read that we cannot know *what* a goat-stag is, because we do not know *that* it is, i.e., that there are any. We cannot know *what* non-existent things are; we only know what the name means (or 'refers' to, 2.92B7).[40] There are no *definitions* of non-existent items (2.92B30), and, of course, mere names are not definitions: if they were, then to say that this book is *The Iliad* would be to define it (2.92B32). Comparing these remarks with the claim of the *De Interpretatione* that the name 'goat-stag' is like a thought, we seem to find Aristotle saying that it is possible to speak of goat-stags and even to think of goat-stags (often mistakenly when we think) without thinking of their 'realized nature' – which, of course, is not there and does not exist. So thinking of goat-stags is thinking of non-existents as though they exist,[41] assuming their existence, and then (falsely?) imagining their 'realized nature'. We know that they do not exist, according to the *Physics* (4.208A29–31), for everyone believes that existents exist *somewhere*, since that which does not exist is nowhere. Where, adds Aristotle in what he supposed to be a rhetorical question, is a goat-stag or a sphinx? In other words, we can think of 'things', and what we think of may have a prima facie claim to exist, but that claim needs empirical confirmation.

As we shall see, that need may produce difficulties about non-sensible substances, such as the Prime Mover. Such anxieties may have affected Aristotle in the *Physics* when he wondered whether he should give the Prime Mover a spatial location. But the demand for empirical confirmation of the existence of a goat-stag has a wider importance. For 'goat-stag' could also be a sort of Aristotelian universal; we can think not only of, say, Sam the goat-stag but of goat-stags in general, though we should be out of touch with reality in doing so. For we only recognize that goat-stag is a false species when we fail to find any goat-stags. Since – before the era of genetic engineering – there never had been or would have been goat-stags (and Aristotle might, contrary to his better insights, have assumed this to follow from the fact that there were none grazing in Attica), there is no 'realized nature' of goat-stag (or a species or genus); hence goat-stag may look like a universal, but it is not a universal. The interesting thing about goat-stags, however, is that we can *think* about them as though there is a universal without knowing that there are no goat-stags. Hence goat-stag is a kind of thought but not a thought about the 'realized nature' of an animal. But if goat-stag is a thought, but not a universal, universals must be thoughts only about 'realized natures' (though not of course 'realized natures' themselves). As for 'goat-stag', let it be a pseudo-universal.

VI Substance in the 'Metaphysics'

In the *Metaphysics*, Aristotle clarifies a number of problems about universals which had troubled him in earlier days. Substance is identified with form (*eidos*) and 'realized nature' (or with the particular);[42] it is not identical with genus, universal, or matter viewed as a 'substrate'. The identification with 'realized nature' had been presented in the *Posterior Analytics*, as we have seen, but form does not occur in the *Posterior Analytics*, and we have noted the most plausible explanation (262–3 above): not so much that form is a tool to be used in physics, not in logic, for the *Posterior Analytics* goes far beyond mere logic; rather that in a strongly anti-Platonic book like the *Posterior Analytics* 'form' might suggest the false postulate of a Form over and above the particulars. That 'form' in physics could indeed have Platonic associations is borne out by a passage in the *Physics* itself (2.194B26), where in a discussion of cause form is introduced (in the manner of the later *Metaphysics*) as the explanation of 'realized nature', but also as a 'paradigm' – which should refer to the 'idea' (e.g., of a statue) in the mind of the artist. This statue in the mind would not, of course, be merely a universal, for Pheidias does not make 'any old' statue but this statue of Zeus. *That* is what Pheidias plans. But although 'paradigm' has an explanatory value, Aristotle generally avoids it (but not always – cf. *Met.* Δ.1013A27), preferring to talk in a less Platonic-sounding way simply of the form in the mind of the artist.

It is often said that in identifying substance with form or realized nature, Aristotle has both advanced and retreated philosophically: he has advanced in so far as he has distinguished forms from universals, but retreated in so far as he has abandoned the priority of the concrete particular. Often this assessment is based on a misreading of the success of the advance and a misunderstanding of the nature of the retreat. Fortunately, accounts of what seems to be the more or less correct reading of Aristotle are in print; unfortunately they are less familiar than they should be, though some of them are not new.[43] What follows will be little more than an assessment of the knowledge of Aristotle's metaphysics which is already available.

One reason why Aristotle is thought to have retreated is to be found in the false belief that Aristotle's forms are what have been traditionally called *in re* universals, that is, understood as 'common natures' which exist in the particular individuals and are responsible for their existence. According to this reading of the *Metaphysics* Aristotle (like Eudoxus) has somehow put the Platonic Form back into the particulars. An Aristotelian form thus resembles its Platonic original as some sort of causative 'one over many', but it lacks the anathematized Platonic separation from the particulars. Thus while Platonic Forms could exist in the absence of particulars, Aristotelian forms could not. Our reading of the *Posterior Analytics* should have suggested that this rendering of Aristotle is false (262–71 above).[44]

Such an 'Aristotelian' form or *in re* universal might indeed be labelled a 'common nature' and as identical with substance, but its philosophical difficulties are manifold; they include the fact that Aristotle's *own* theory of form would be damaged by the 'Third Man' and 'Sail' arguments which he held to be valid against Plato.[45] In fact Aristotle hardly uses the phrase 'common nature', and never in this sense; nor does he present the form as a reality common to all the particulars. A form is not a species, or a universal; it is the realized nature of the individual matter. That it is to be so identified as the realized nature of a *particular* body (*to ti ēn einai tōi toiōide sōmati, Met.* Z.1035B16) has been demonstrated yet again by Lloyd; and although some of his many texts are not conclusive, the case he makes is in general 'unassailable'.[46] Unfortunately a text from the *De Incessu* is too general (and perhaps too early) to be very helpful, for it actually provides us (708A11–12) with the phrase 'individual substance' (seemingly as equivalent to 'realized nature') to designate the form. But in case *idion eidos* elsewhere still seems ambiguous (*De Anima* 1.407B23–4 and *Met.* Λ.1071A14), further evidence is available in the *Metaphysics*.

Perhaps the most interesting text is in *Metaphysics* Z (1039B20ff).[47] We can speak of substance in terms both of the composite and of its formula (*logos*) (cf. Δ.1013A27). The composite can be generated and destroyed, but the formula never admits of destruction. What Aristotle means is clear: particular houses are destroyed and generated, and with them their particular 'realized natures' (that is, the 'realized nature' of *this* house), but the formula of the house neither comes to be nor perishes. Thus we can distinguish two 'phenomena': (1) the individual form whose fate is tied to the matter, for it is the form of a particular body[48] and is elsewhere called the 'last version of the matter' (H.1045B18, *eschatē hulē*); and (2) the formula of the 'realized nature', that is, the individual viewed as a universal (this house viewed as a *house*) because it has a number of features similar to those in other individuals.[49] Man and animal are the 'combination' of souls and bodies viewed universally (Z.1037A6).[50]

It should be added that despite a widely held opinion among his commentators Aristotle does not think that the formula of the 'realized nature' is recognized by 'abstraction'. We have already observed, in the *Posterior Analytics*, the process by which we come to know universals; the word 'abstraction' does not occur. It is reserved by Aristotle for describing the recognition of 'mathematical' objects, a special problem which had been highlighted by the claims made about their 'intermediate' status by Plato, and in a different way by Speusippus. Aristotle uses the word 'abstraction' to refer to the recognition of a certain kind of quantity 'abstracted' from the matter in which the quantity appears. Abstraction deals with the recognition of 'two', not just of two cows: it is the appropriate technique of what Plato in the *Philebus* called philosophical arithmetic. It deals with a special sort of concept, not just of a universal concept. When two cows have died, I can still think both of 'two' and of two cows, but of the former by abstraction.[51] In geometry I can think (*noein*) of a sizeless, but unspecified, triangle as well as of, say, the species of warning triangles at European road-accidents.

It is a pity that Aristotle does not offer a technical term for what I have called 'similar characteristics', using a phrase which might designate the characteristics in virtue of which Peleus and Achilles can both be called men, but which only exist individually as the individual forms of Peleus and Achilles; but we should not allow this to corrupt our understanding of what Aristotle says about individual forms, 'realized natures', and universals. We should not miss the wholly unplatonic nature of the doctrine of form in the *Metaphysics*, or how, since the form is the ultimate version of the particular matter (the 'realized nature' of the particular matter), there is no substantive change in the account of the metaphysical priority of the particular to the universal from the position Aristotle had already presented in the *Categories*. The difference between the *Categories* and the *Metaphysics* is that in the former Aristotle is classifying the 'contents' of the world, paying no attention to causation or to theories of 'realized nature' and of form and matter, whereas in the *Metaphysics* he is explaining the *nature* of what the *Categories* calls primary substances.

The *Metaphysics* not only offers a new account of what it is to be a *substance*; it moves beyond the *Posterior Analytics* (and the *Eudemian Ethics*) in its attitude to what it is to *be* a substance. For we have seen that the *Metaphysics* presents us with a new science of being qua being, of first philosophy and 'theology' (or what we call metaphysics), while the *Posterior Analytics* and the *Eudemian Ethics* conceive of metaphysics only in terms of a discredited Platonism. In the past (in fact, since Natorp) scholars have often found in the *Metaphysics* two conflicting notions of first philosophy: the one a science of being qua being (or sometimes of 'ontology'); the other a science of 'special metaphysics', that is, the study of separate forms (primarily in book Λ).[52] Fortunately recent scholarship has done much to resolve this problem,[53] and my treatment of the chronology of the *Metaphysics* plus attention to the central position of focal meaning clarifies the matter further (225–41, 242 above). It is clear that if any general account of being is to be allowed, Aristotle must abandon his insistence in the *Posterior Analytics* and the *Eudemian Ethics* that there is no science of 'extra-categorial' items since they are merely equivocal. Owen in particular has shown that he is able to do this by developing his notions of 'focal meaning' (and of things *pros hen kai mian tina phusin legomena* – things said with reference to one thing and one single character).[54] Being is not merely ambiguous, as the *Eudemian Ethics* seems to suggest; beings are arranged somehow hierarchically, and the science of being, if it pursues the highest being, will shed light on all beings qua being, that is, in so far as they share in the character in virtue of which the highest being is a being.

Owen has shown that in developing the notion of focal meaning Aristotle was not originally concerned with solving problems of being or with reviving the science of metaphysics. He knew of focal meaning in the *Eudemian Ethics* and used it to elucidate the notions of 'medical' and of 'friendship' (7.1236A7–33); what is new about his use of focal meaning in the *Metaphysics* is the application to being itself, which Owen seems right in finding absent in the *Organon*,[55] and in the discussion of the Good in *Eudemian Ethics* 1. Owen indeed goes further, at least by implication. He seems to suggest that the possible application of focal meaning to being had not been realized by Aristotle even when he composed the earliest parts of the *Metaphysics* itself. Our chronological organization of the *Metaphysics* makes this most unlikely. Owen is right to point out that in book A Aristotle charges the Platonists with disregarding the ambiguity of the word 'beings' (992B18–26).[56] He is right too that focal meaning is not introduced here as a way out of the problem, though he admits that what Aristotle says 'does not formally contradict the argument of the fourth book.' Certainty as to Aristotle's intent in book A is unattainable, but it should be observed that Aristotle would *not* want to save the Platonists or a Platonic account of being. Introduction of focal meaning at this point might be construed as an attempt to save the Platonic Forms.

Be that as it may, there is no doubt that focal meaning forms the basis for the science of being qua being in books Γ, E, and Z. But Owen, contrary to many of the more 'traditional' interpreters of Aristotle, finds a further tension in the *Metaphysics* itself, particularly between Γ and Λ. He claims that there is no mention of focal meaning in book Λ; instead (Λ.1071A33–5) there is a use of the concept of 'analogy'.[57] Traditional interpreters, as Owen says, have frequently referred to book Γ in terms of Λ, as advocating a theory of the 'analogy of being'. But the contrast between Γ, E, and Λ is not as sharp as Owen suggests. In book E Aristotle, who has already identified 'theology' (first philosophy) as primarily the study of separate and unchanging substances, goes on to say that if there are such substances, their study will be 'prior' to that of physics and 'universal' in the sense of primary, that is, more important (1026A27ff). In saying this, of course, he does not abolish the insights of the *Posterior Analytics* and the *Eudemian Ethics* that the principles of metaphysics cannot be used (Platonically) to control the methodology of other secondary sciences: physics still operates on physical, not metaphysical, principles. But after making clear that eternal and unchanging realities are the subject-matter of metaphysics, Aristotle continues by adding that it is the province of metaphysics to study being qua being. This, of course, is no mere later insertion into the text, for the ground for that study is prepared by the following chapters of *Metaphysics* E itself. Hencc book E argues that though in some primary sense the study of the eternal and unchanging is the nature of mataphysics, it also studies beings qua being wherever they are found. That this involves all beings (including particulars in the world around us) is the metaphysical application of the theory of focal meaning.

That being so, there is nothing *per se* alien to the project Aristotle proposes of the study of being qua being which would preclude 'theology'. Quite the contrary. 'Theology' is par excellence the study of being qua being. Why then, to revert to Owen, does Aristotle not use in book Λ that very concept of focal meaning which justifies the association of the subject-matter of Λ with that of Γ, E, and Z; indeed which subordinates the subject-matter of Γ, E, Z to that of Λ? The answer, as we saw in a previous chapter, is that he does, in 1075A18, when the order of the cosmos is said to be 'with reference to' the Prime Mover. Owen looked in the wrong part of the book, and assumed that Aristotle could not introduce 'analogy' and 'focal meaning' in the same treatise.

A false route out of the dilemma posed by Owen is to argue that focal meaning has no *metaphysical* implications at all, that Aristotle's theory would merely enable him to talk about being qua being *meaningfully* (which earlier he had denied to be possible),[58] but that such talk has nothing to do with *metaphysically* superior and inferior beings. The principal objections to this, as we have already seen, are that in book E Aristotle associates 'theology' and the study of being qua being under one heading (1026A19–32), and that in book Γ he first introduces focal meaning as a justification for a single science of being, and then observes that this science, like all others, will be chiefly concerned with what is primary and on which all its other objects depend (1003B17). Interestingly in book Λ the same word 'depends' (*ērtētai*) occurs (1072B14); after identifying the Prime Mover Aristotle argues that all the universe depends upon it. Admittedly this dependence is physical, but the character, as opposed to the existence, of the Prime Mover is not presented by physical but by metaphysical speculation. For it is perfect activity and unmoved, and the nature of such substances is not the subject-matter of physics. But apart from such considerations, to deny the relevance of focal meaning to metaphysics is unaristotelian. True propositions are about existent subjects, not merely logical subjects. Being is not, therefore, a mere concept like a goat-stag or a Platonic Form; statements about being qua being will be in some sense about sorts of beings which exist, as Aristotle often says. In book Λ Aristotle has an argument about what, if it exists, the best possible kind of being is, namely form without matter; form, we might suggest, not of nothing, but of itself, as the Prime Mover is certainly 'thinking of itself.' If there is such a form (and Aristotle in his late writings *never* denied that there is), then understanding of its nature will be relevant to grasping being qua being in whatever other beings there are. For the 'realized natures' of particulars will resemble the immaterial being of book Λ precisely in so far as they are beings.

A further minor point must be dispatched before we conclude that there is nothing in book Λ which the Aristotle who talks in books Γ, E, and Z of being qua being would have found embarrassing. In Γ.1069A30ff Aristotle speaks of three sorts of substances: eternal sensibles (i.e., heavenly bodies), perishable sensibles, and unmoved realities. The first two, he says, are the subject-matter of physics, the last of some other science. Some have said this is the special science of theology, which thus deals only with unmovable realities. But there is no need for such an interpretation, for Aristotle adds, '... *if* there is no common principle for all three sorts of realities' – which, of course, there may well be. Nothing else in the *Metaphysics* rules it out – quite to the contrary.

Hence we may conclude that there is no difference between Λ and Γ, E, and Z, about the possible subject-matter of metaphysics, namely being qua being, and that immaterial substance is the most important and 'authoritative' object of study within the discipline.

Books Γ and Λ of the *Metaphysics* are similar: they allow a metaphysics which deals both with sensible and non-sensible substances. But when book Λ uses the notion of analogy, it must be admitted that the relationship between different sorts of beings qua being is left vague; and analogy is no substitute for focal meaning in resolving the implication of earlier Aristotelian writings that a metaphysics of being qua being is impossible for the simple reason that 'being' is an ambiguous word. But in book Λ Aristotle uses analogy both to establish the primacy of substance (1071A33ff) and to explain the structure of other categories in terms of the structure of substance (1070B17–21). Analogy is vaguer and less specific than focal meaning and spells out metaphysical dependence less clearly. Yet Aristotle may not always want to say more than he has to for a particular purpose, and in book 1 of the *Nicomachean Ethics* (the revised version of the attack on the Platonic Form of the Good in the *Eudemian Ethics*), he uses an importantly strong phrase. This time, speaking of 'good', which, like being, is predicated in all the categories (being, we recall, is itself compared with 'good' in the *Eudemian Ethics*, 1.1217B27ff), he denies that it is a universal (1.1096A27–8), but implies that though predicated in all the categories, it is also prior by nature when predicated of substance and (*a fortiori*) posterior when predicated of relation. For relations are a sort of offshoot or accident of substance. The reason 'good' is not a universal is in part because good substances are not only different from good qualities; they are, as it were, the root of good qualities. Qualities, to use the language of the *Metaphysics*, depend on substance; the meaning of 'good' depends on its meaning in the category of substance. And if 'good', then why not 'being' too? Yet in neither case does book 1 of the *Nicomachean Ethics* bring in either focal meaning or analogy directly.

We should also notice that in both the *Nicomachean Ethics* (1.1096A24–5) and the *Eudemian Ethics* (1.1217B32) God and Mind are the star instances of substances. On that point Aristotle never wavered. Hence at any period between these two works or contemporaneously with them (ca 338–328 BC) it would be wholly appropriate for Aristotle to *include* theology as the most important part of metaphysics – once he has decided that metaphysics is a legitimate study. And (even if our thesis about Λ.8 be rejected) there is unlikely to have been much of the *Metaphysics* written substantially later – and here in Λ.8 gods of a sort are still under discussion. Finally, before leaving *Metaphysics* Λ, consider a text which brings 'theology' there very close to book 10 of the *Nicomachean Ethics* and to the *De Anima*. Λ.1070A, besides including a star instance of Aristotle's mature view that forms are individual, also speaks of immortality. The implications of the theory of book Z that soul is the form of the body are already clear to him: perhaps soul can exist separately, that is, after death. Or if not all of it (*mē pasa*), then mind survives, for it is presumably impossible for all of the soul to do so. Perhaps this theory is earlier than the certitude of the *De Anima* about immortality, but it is wholly appropriate to the soul/body relationship of *Metaphysics* Z and H.

Substances are individuals and their 'realized natures', but primarily where no matter is present. Forms are individual. A problem has been posed, not merely for the historical Aristotle, but for the intelligibility of the historical Aristotle.[59] Since we are aware of an *individual* form as individual only when we are *not* viewing it universally, that is, when we meet it in matter, we will recognize that such individuals qua individuals have no definition; hence they cannot be used in what the *Posterior Analytics* identifies as strict demonstrations. In what way then can the Prime Mover be recognized at all,[60] since it is neither a universal nor present in matter; and how can it be used in metaphysics if it cannot be viewed as a universal? The first question is answered in book Λ of the *Metaphysics* itself. The existence of the Prime Mover is the necessary conclusion of arguments about the eternity of motion. Although we cannot reach the Prime Mover by a mental process or processes based on direct sense perception, since it does not offer itself as a sense object, we can affirm its existence as a result of an understanding which is itself based on empirical evidence. There is every sign of its existence and the world is unintelligible without it. Since there is every reason to discover intelligibility in the world, the Prime Mover must be there as a first principle. Such is the working of our minds in recognizing or grasping first principles, as the *Posterior Analytics* explains. We would recognize the Prime Mover by *noēsis* (cf. Z.1036A5ff), but in a special way. As for the use of the Prime Mover in metaphysics, there is also no great difficulty. The Prime Mover does not need to be *viewed* 'apart from matter' in some special way, since it is of such a sort as to *be* apart from matter. Like the sun and moon, however, it could be treated, if necessary, as the unique member of a class.

Our discussion of substance has shed no further light on the development of the *Metaphysics* in the book form that we have it. Leaving aside the chronological proposals we advanced in the previous chapter, we have argued here that whatever the structure of the text of the *Metaphysics*, the structure of the thought of Aristotle in the great majority of the central themes of that book must be treated as a unity. If that is true, the philosophical necessity of dissecting the complete *Metaphysics* into earlier and later original courses is denied. Nevertheless, the attempt at dissection may help others, as it has helped me, to a more philosophical understanding. For, while our account of substance in the *Metaphysics* does not depend on the chronological reconstruction offered in the previous chapter, the two approaches can be recognized as entirely in harmony with one another.

EPILOGUE

This is not a book with a formal conclusion; indeed the conclusions were written as the opening chapter, an account of Aristotle's philosophical growth. But there are, I believe, some practical implications which should be pointed out. If I am right, there are broad and recognizable lines of development in Aristotle's thought. Aristotle does not say the same thing, and sometimes he says very different things, at different periods of his life, about major philosophical issues. Nothing is served if this point is neglected, if, for example, we take no note of the fact that Aristotle leaves no room for metaphysics when he writes the *Analytics*, or that his theory of the soul is radically different in the *Eudemus* (and even in the *Eudemian Ethics*) and the *De Anima*. To confuse such matters is to offer a synthesis to which Aristotle never subscribed, and which is on many issues almost certain to be philosophically incoherent. Few nowadays would attempt to harmonize Plato's *Protagoras* with his *Philebus*; let us hope in the future that fewer will attempt to harmonize the *Categories* with the *Metaphysics*, or the simply ambiguous 'being' of the early parts of the *Topics* with the being qua being of the *Metaphysics*. For my principal concern is with the way Aristotle is presented. His ideas should be set down in the order of their appearance. If this study does something to show him testing, moulding, developing, and rejecting philosophical suggestions, and inviting others to join him in so doing, it will have been successful. For to join the Philosopher in thinking and solving is to begin to learn to think oneself.

Chronology of Aristotle's Life and *Works*

	Relevant world events	Works of Plato and related movements	Acts and datable works of Aristotle
384			Born at Stagira
370	Death of Amyntas II		
368		*Theaetetus*	
367		Plato goes to Sicily	Comes to the Academy in Athens
364		Plato back in Athens, *Parmenides*	
ca 361		Plato's last visit to Sicily	*Gryllus*
ca 359		*Sophist*	
358–4			*Politica* (or *Statesman*) *On Poets* *Rhetoric* 1.5–15
ca 353		*Statesman*	*Categories* 2–9 *Topics* 2–4, 7.1–2 *Eudemus* *Protrepticus* (in reply to *Antidosis* of Isocrates)

	Relevant world events	Works of Plato and related movements	Acts and datable works of Aristotle
ca 352		*Timaeus*	
ca 351		*Philebus* (unpolished) *Laws* (still unfinished in 347)	
ca 349	Destruction of Stagira		*Topics* 5
348	Fall of Olynthus to Philip		
347		Death of Plato (Speusippus succeeds)	Aristotle goes to Assos with Xenocrates
ca 347			*On Ideas* *On the Good* *On Philosophy*
ca 345			*Physics* 2–7 begun; Perhaps also *De Caelo* and *Historia Animalium* Aristotle goes to Mytilene Continuation of *Physics* 2–7; *De Caelo*; *De Generatione et Corruptione*; *Historia Animalium* 1–4; *De Respiratione*; *De Incessu Animalium*; *Historia Animalium* 5–7; all finished by 339
343			Philip invites Aristotle to come to Macedonia as tutor to Alexander

	Relevant world events	Works of Plato and related movements	Acts and datable works of Aristotle
ca 343			*Topics* now revised = *Topics* 1–8.1 *Sophistici Elenchi* 3–34
341/0			*Prior Analytics* 1, 2 *Posterior Analytics* 1, 2
ca 340			Final version of *Topics* by addition of block 8.2–14 and *Sophistici Elenchi* 1–2
by 340	Report of Hermeias's death reaches Aristotle		'Ode' and dedication to Hermeias, marriage of Aristotle and Pythias
after 340			Aristotle and Callisthenes honoured at Delphi
339	Death of Speusippus, Xenocrates succeeds		*Meteorologica* 1–3
ca 338	Battle of Chaeroneia		*On Monarchy* (?) *Eudemian Ethics* (1, 2, 3, 4, 7, 5, 6, 8) begun
338–334			*Politics* 2, 3, 7, 8 (unfinished)
336	Death of Philip, succession of Alexander		
335	Destruction of Thebes by Alexander		
334			Aristotle returns to Athens *Elegy* (to Plato)

Relevant world events		Works of Plato and related movements	Acts and datable works of Aristotle
ca 333			*De Interpretatione* (*Methodics*) Revised *Poetics* Revised *Rhetoric* Original *Constitution of the Athenians*
ca 332			*Metaphysics* α *Physics* 1, 2–7, 8 Revision of *De Caelo* and *De Generatione et Corruptione*
ca 331			Beginning of *De Partibus Animalium* 1–4
ca 331			*Metaphysics* A.1–6, 10, K
by 330			Death of Pythias
ca 330 –328			*Metaphysics* A, B, Γ, E.1, Δ.1–12, I, E.2–4
ca 328			Revisions of *Constitution of the Athenians* (before 325) *Nicomachean Ethics* 1, 8, 9, 10 *Politics* 4–6 (*Ethics* = *Nicomachean Ethics* 1, *Eudemian Ethics* 2.1220A–end, 3, 4, 5, 6, *Nicomachean Ethics* 8, 9, 10) *Metaphysics* M, N, Λ (*On Substance*)
ca 327	Execution of Callisthenes		*Metaphysics* Θ, *De Anima* 1–3 *Parva Naturalia* (= *De Sensu*; *De Memoria*; *De Divinatione*; *De*

	Relevant world events	Works of Plato and related movements	Acts and datable works of Aristotle
			Longitudine Vitae; De Iuventute) *Metaphysics* Z, H (incl. Λ.8) and Δ.13–end
ca 325			*De Motu Animalium* (*De Plantis*)
ca 324	'Marriages of Susa'		*De Generatione Animalium* *Politics* 1
323	Death of Alexander (certain by September)		*Nicomachean Ethics* 2–4, 5 (revision begun) Aristotle charged with impiety; retires to his mother's estate at Chalcis
322			Aristotle dies at Chalcis
321	Nicanor in command at Munychia		
318	Execution of Nicanor		

NOTES

Chapter 2

1 For the traditional account of this see Cherniss, 'The Philosophical Economy,' 445–56.

2 As I observed in the preface, I accept the argument of Kenny in *The Aristotelian Ethics* that the 'disputed books' (*NE* 5–7 = *EE* 4–6) originally belonged to the *Eudemian Ethics*. I do not accept that *NE* is earlier than *EE* and would prefer some version of the suggestion made by Kenny (239) that *NE* in its present form was arranged after Aristotle's death. I had in fact already made this suggestion in 'Pleasure: 360–300 B.C.'; see also ch. 9, 170.

3 In *NE* 1.6 Aristotle's attitude to the Good is less bitter, and his comments are prefaced with a sort of apology for having to attack 'those who first introduced the theory.' Cf. Kenny (note 2 above), 203 and Allan, 'Quasi-mathematical Method in the *Eudemian Ethics*,' 309. Kenny seems to imply that the different attitude may suggest that *EE* is later. On the contrary, if the attack in *NE* is more perfunctory, the explanation could be that the more detailed treatment in *EE* was already available. The matter is examined further in chapter 9, 170–3. Note however that whereas in *EE* 1.1217B18ff Aristotle says that the Good is best discussed as 'logic' (implying that the problems are conceptual or linguistic), in *NE* 1.1096B31 he speaks of 'another sort of philosophy', i.e., metaphysics.

4 I take this to be the sense of *exōterikoi logoi*, though other renderings have been offered.

5 Ps.-Philop., *In Met.* f.67B (p. 120 Ross) and Ps.-Alex., *in Met.* 837.3; Syrianus, *In Met.* 195.10–14. For the views of Alexander (our primary source) and other evidence see Leszl, *Il 'De Ideis' di Aristotele*, 57–8.

6 Some of the 'epistemological' and 'ontological' points which Leszl observes (note

5 above, 320–9, *could* be *ad hominem*, and Leszl resorts to much later Aristotelian writing to support them; but see particularly Kung, 'Aristotle on Thises and Suches,' 216–20, for comment on Alex., *In Met.* 84.21ff (p. 126 Ross). Fine, 'The One over Many' and 'Aristotle and the More Accurate Arguments,' discusses universals. For anti-nominalism, *In Met.* 79.15ff (p. 122 Ross), 81.8–10, etc.

7 Ross (120ff) includes fragments dealing with the One and the Dyad in his collection, being influenced by Wilpert, 'Reste verlorener Aristotelesschriften,' esp. 378–85, and *Zwei aristotelische Frühscriften.* Cherniss objected, for inadequate reasons. For bibliography and examination of the 'Platonism' attacked in this section see Annas, 'Forms and First Principles,' 257–83. For *On Ideas* as a stage in the development of Aristotle's more general dispute with the Academy, see ch. 3, 59–62.

8 Aristoxenus, *Harm.* 2.70ff (p. 111 Ross).

9 Cic., *ND* 1.13.33 (fr. 26 Ross).

10 Syrianus, *In Met.* 159.33ff (fr. 11 Ross).

11 See, e.g., Vlastos, 'Creation in the *Timaeus*'; Whittaker, 'The Eternity of the Platonic Forms'; Robinson, 'The Argument of *Tim.* 27Dff.'

12 For unity of subject-matter in *On Philosophy* see Wilpert, in *Autour d'Aristote*, 115.

13 Simp., *In De Caelo* 288.28ff (fr. 16 Ross).

14 Cic., *ND* 1.13.33 (fr. 26 Ross). The second sentence of this fragment refers not to *On Philosophy* at all, but to *De Caelo.*

15 The essay *On Prayer* (Simp., *In De Caelo* 485.19–22 [fr. 1 Ross]) cannot be invoked; it never existed. See Rist, 'The End of Aristotle's *On Prayer*.'

16 Cic., *Lucullus* 38.119 (fr. 20 Ross). The 'golden flow' of Aristotle's prose must refer to a semi-popular work, i.e., *On Philosophy* (cf. *De Caelo* 1.279A31).

17 Influentially, Berti, *La filosofia del primo Aristotele*, 344–57; Düring, *Aristoteles*, 185–9.

18 *Phys.* 194A36 (fr. 28 of *On Philosophy*, Ross). For discussion see Graeser, 'Aristoteles' Schrift *Über die Philosophie*,' 44–61.

19 Easterling, 'The Unmoved Mover in Early Aristotle.'

20 So recently Hahm, 'The Fifth Element in Aristotle's *De Philosophia*.'

21 There is no reason to think that Aristotle regularly holds the doctrine of the Unmoved Mover *in reserve* in *De Caelo*, as was argued by von Arnim, *Die Entstehung*. The reference to 'first philosophy' at *De Caelo* 1.277B10–13 is another later addition.

22 For the phrase, cf. *De Caelo* 1.270A18, which seems to refer to *Phys.* 1.7, that is, also to a late book of the *Physics* (as I argue in ch. 12, 229–31).

23 Cf. Easterling (note 19 above) and Pötscher, *Struckturprobleme.*

24 See Ross, *Aristotle's Physics* (Oxford 1936), 2.

25 Easterling (note 19 above).

26 For a correction to Jaeger, see Gigon, 'Prolegomena to an Edition of the *Eudemus*'; Düring, *Aristoteles*, 557–8; Rees, 'Theories of the Soul.' Jaeger (*Aristotle*, 44, note 3) claims that Plotinus in *Enn.* 4.7.8 uses not the *Phaedo* but the *Eudemus*, on the grounds that Plotinus follows Aristotle in 'breaking up' Plato's proof. He 'silently' substitutes this, according to Jaeger, for the version of the *Phaedo*. In fact Plotinus follows a tradition, which may depend on the *Eudemus*, but he himself shows no awareness of that possibility – characteristically taking the traditional reading of Plato as Plato.

27 Them., *In De Anima* 106.29ff (fr. 2 Ross).

28 Elias, *In Cat.* 114.25 (fr. 3 Ross).

29 Proclus, *In Remp.* 2.349ff (fr. 5 Ross).

30 Proclus, *In Tim.* 338C (fr 4 Ross).

31 Philop., *In de An.* 144.22 (fr. 7 Ross).

32 Simp., *In de An.* 221.31 (fr. 8 Ross). Only the sentence that says that soul is a form can be claimed for the *Eudemus*. Ross's text is misleading, including as *Eudemus* what refers to the *De Anima*. See Guthrie, *HGP* 6.70.

33 Düring ('Aristotle and Plato in the Mid-Fourth Century,' 115) tries to dismiss *theamata* (despite Aristotle's inordinate use of *theōria*) as a Neoplatonic formula. This is rightly rejected by De Vogel, 'Did Aristotle Ever Accept Plato's Theory of Transcendent Forms?' 273–6. Aristotle's developed theory of induction is intended *inter alia* to avoid the necessity of 'recollection', which, as *Topics* 2.111B27 shows, was already being scrutinized in the Academy. But the *Topics* passage confuses 'recollection' with 'memory', hence seeing difficulties about how we can 'remember' future events like eclipses! Aristotle gives no indication in the *Topics* that induction, which he discusses, is to be explained as replacing 'recollection'. He does so, however, in the *Posterior Analytics*; see ch. 14, 269–70.

34 I accept (more or less) the reconstruction of Bywater ('On a Lost Dialogue of Aristotle'), as do the vast majority of scholars, except Rabinowitz, *Aristotle's Protrepticus*. A first glance at the extant fragments of the *Protrepticus* might induce the belief that it is dependent on *NE* 10; that is, the *NE* 10 was Iamblichus's source. But this is impossible, for, although it is true that *NE* 10 (not to speak of *NE* 1) is immensely indebted to the *Protrepticus*, the *differences* between the two cannot be explained as due to the hand of Iamblichus. *NE* 10 is a fresh draft, based on unfinished corrections of the *Protrepticus*. (Had Cooper taken the *Protrepticus* more seriously as a source for *NE* 10, he would have realized that many of his problems with the latter disappear. See ch. 9, 184–6, and Cooper's *Reason and Human Good*.)

35 So Einarson, 'Aristotle's *Protrepticus*,' 281–5; Düring, *Aristotle's Protrepticus*, 33–5.

36 So Jaeger, *Aristotle*, 58–9 (following Wendland); Ross, *Aristotle*, 26.

37 For the Academic distinction, perhaps due to Xenocrates, see *Top*. 1.105B20ff. For Aristotle see *Protrepticus* B32. Jaeger (*Aristotle*, 84–5) improbably reads the relevant section to refer to 'physics' and 'the rest of truth' separately. Aristotle's *te ... kai* construction suggests something else. The later part of the text makes it certain that Jaeger has misconstrued the relevant sentence.

38 Because the Good itself has 'mathematical' connotations, Jaeger seems to argue that Plato in the *Philebus* regards ethics as an exact science (*Aristotle*, 88). If Plato ever held that view it was in the *Republic*, and the *Philebus* is designed, in part, as a retractation of it – dealing as it largely does with the good for man in a way which Aristotle doubtless approved.

39 *Pol.* (i.e., *Statesman*), fr. 2 Ross. Almost all the remaining fragments of the *Statesman* tell us that the book contained an influential discussion of anger; but for a nugget of gold see ch.8, 138.

40 Cf. *Laws* 4.716C (cited and misused by Jaeger).

41 Boeth., *Cons*. 3.8 (C104.2 Düring); Boethius probably quotes Cicero's *Hortensius* quoting the *Protrepticus*.

42 Aristotle also, probably in earlier and less earnest days, wrote a *Symposium* (or *On Drunkenness*), though our fragments indicate little more than that it discussed drunkenness, connected *methuein* with *meta to thuein*, and claimed that old men get drunk most and women least. It may be connected with similar discussions in Plato's *Laws*.

43 Düring seems to mistranslate the first words, however, as 'Reason is the god *in* us' (93).

44 Some have denied that Aristotle is raising a simple question about existence here (so Owens, *The Doctrine of Being*, 289; Kahn, *The Greek Verb 'to Be'*, 245–65; Hintikka, 'On the Ingredients of an Aristotelian Science,' 67–8.) Such views are well criticized by Landor, *The Ei esti – Ti esti Distinction*, esp. 7–28. For further comment see ch. 14, 264–5.

45 Alex. Aphr., *In Met*. 97.27 (fr. 5 Ross). Leszl (*Il 'De Ideis' di Aristotele*, 335–40) tries to reject Alexander's testimony about Eudoxus. His arguments are a priori and unconvincing. They are (1) that Eudoxus's espousal of Forms does not square with his theory of the supremacy of pleasure, and (2) that there was not a 'close association' between Eudoxus and the Academy. Against (1) we should note that Eudoxus's theory of Forms was probably only a theory of *physics*; and (2) seems to be false. For fragments of Eudoxus see Lasserre, *Die Fragmente des Eudoxus von Knidos*. A similar theory is attributed to Eudoxus at *Met*. A.991A17, and, as we noted above, it is probably already the subject of *Top*. 2.113A25ff. For further discussion see especially Dancy, 'Predication and Immanence.'

Chapter 3

1 Jaeger (*Aristotle*, 111–13, 173) accepts the letter as genuine, largely on the basis of the historical reliability of its contents as demonstrated by Brinkmann, 'Ein Brief Platons.' (See also esp. Wormell, 'Hermias of Atarneus.') The strongest argument *against* its being genuine is that it is just too useful and convenient to be true. Those who find it a product of well-informed debates among Plato's successors may well be right. See Edelstein, *Plato's Seventh Letter*, 122–3.

2 For Speusippus more generally see Tarán, *Speusippus of Athens*; Dillon, *The Middle Platonists*, 11–12; Guthrie, *HGP* 5.457–69.

3 *Met.* M.1085A7ff; Dillon (note 2 above), 27.

4 The most interesting contributions are those of Robin, *La théorie platonicienne*; Cherniss, *Aristotle's Criticism*, 194–8; Annas, *Aristotle's Metaphysics Books* M *and* N, 62–73.

5 Forms are monads and numbers in *Eudemian Ethics* 1.1218A19–20, a passage which confirms the *Philebus* and will be discussed further in the present chapter.

6 Annas (note 4 above), 8–11 has other references.

7 This would seem to rule out views like that of Isnardi Parente, repeated again in 'Le ΠΕΡΙ ΙΔΕΩΝ d'Aristote.'

8 For induction see ch. 14, 267.

9 Annas (note 4 above), 84.

10 For the elegy see Düring, *Aristotle in the Ancient Biographical Tradition*, 316–17.

11 For Polemarchus, see Simp., *In De Caelo* 493, 5–8 Heiberg; Tarán, *Academica*, 107. For the dates of Eudoxus see Merlan, *Studies in Aristotle and Epicurus*, 98–104.

12 Tarán (note 11 above), passim.

13 Annas (note 4 above), 5–13. Other evidence that Plato advocated the real existence of 'mathematicals' (what Annas calls his 'Platonism in mathematics') can be found. Plato is named at *Met.* Z.1028B18–21 and referred to in many other places (note esp. A.987B29). See Annas (ibid.) and 'On the Intermediates.' Ideal 'geometricals' do not occur in chapter 6.

14 Aristotle does not claim that *Plato* denied such Forms in *Metaphysics* M either. The confusion has largely arisen because of a false interpretation of Λ.1070A18–19 and of Xenocrates' remark that Plato accepted Forms of all that exists by nature. Scholars have read into this Aristotle's own distinction between natural objects and artefacts. See for full discussion Cherniss (note 4 above), 240–57.

15 For further discussion see the present chapter, 66–9.

16 See recently Dillon (note 2 above), esp. 28; also *Met.* Z.2 (1028B24ff), with the remarks of Asclepius.

17 Plato's own difficulties with the relationship between the Good and the One as cause are highlighted by *Eudemian Ethics* 1.1218A25. See Brunschwig, 'L'Ethique à Eudème 1.8.1218A15–32,' 197–222. The passage is characteristically 'Eudemian', in that Plato is said to have made an unreasonable supposition. It is discussed further below.

18 Arist., *Elem. Harm.* 2.30–1. This *could* militate against the view that Plato's lecture on the Good is the particular target of *EE* 1218A25ff, but see the present chapter, 69. Both Aristoxenus and Aristotle mention health and strength among the ordinary 'goods' which need explanation but did not receive it. That, of course, could mean only that Aristotle is the source for Aristoxenus.

19 Annas (note 4 above), 71 and note to M.1078B22 (154). For *anagō* see LSJ II. Guthrie, *HGP* 5.436, gets it right.

20 Annas (note 4 above), 68–73.

21 Guthrie *HGP* 5.304.

22 Annas (note 4 above), esp. 81–8.

23 A marginal note in manuscript E alleges that Aristotle's previous writings and *On the Good* had dealt with the topic. This *may* in fact only refer back to *EE* 1.1218A20–3, which *may* also be alluded to in both *Met.* M.1078A32 (*en tois akinētois*) and 1078B1 (*taxis*). See Brunschwig (note 17 above), 217. Whether *EE* 1.1218A itself depends on *On the Good* is unknown, but it is certainly possible; just as *Met.* A.6 and 9 depend on *On Ideas*. According to Alexander, Aristotle discussed Plato's lack of final and efficient causes in *On the Good* (*In Met.* 59.28 Hayduck = fr. 4 Ross); see ch. 2, 39.

24 Dillon (note 2 above, 17–18) says that Speusippus had rejected the Forms. Guthrie, *HGP* 5.459, says that he had abandoned them. I have raised doubts as to whether he ever accepted them.

25 See above note 23.

26 I have sketched a solution for Aristotle, so that kingship is restored, at ch. 14, 239–40. The best introduction to Aristotle's own view of the status of 'mathematicals' is to be found in Lear, 'Aristotle's Philosophy of Mathematics'; cf. *Phys.* 2.1; *Met.* K.7, E.1, as well as M and N. It seems that if first philosophy studies substances qua being, second philosophy (physics) studies them qua movement, 'third' philosophy – not an Aristotelian phrase – qua numerable. 'Mathematics is true, not in virtue of the existence of reputed mathematical objects, to which its terms refer, but because it accurately describes the structural properties and relations which actual physical objects have' (Lear, 'Aristotle's Philosophy,' 191).

27 See Tarán (note 11 above), 107.

Chapter 4

1 Thielscher, 'Die relative Chronologie.' For an opposing view Barnes, 'Proof and the Syllogism,' 46. See my comments in the Preface.

2 Whether the wise *man* is envious is not discussed directly in the *Phaedrus* (247A), but only that God and the divine choir lack envy (cf. *Tim.* 29E).

3 For self-predication (and the *Parmenides*, perhaps) see 4.126B35ff. For Eudoxus see Owen, 'Dialectic and Eristic,' 110; cf. Alex. Aphr., *In Met.* 98.22–4. For Aristotle's attitude to Plato and to the theory of Ideas in the *Topics*, help can be found in De Vogel, 'Aristotle's Attitude,' 91–102. For speculation on Eudoxus and the *Parmenides* see Schofield, 'Eudoxus in the *Parmenides*.' Note that *Topics* 2–4 has nothing to say about the treatment of the 'friends of the Forms' at *Sophist* 248E. If we were prepared to bring the date of the *Sophist* down to about 355, this might indicate that at least parts of the *Topics* pre-date it; but perhaps this is too late for the *Sophist*. It is of course possible to claim that 4.121A22ff refers to the ideas but not the text of the *Sophist*. For unwarranted certainty on the matter see Düring, 'Aristotle's Use of Examples in the *Topics*,' 202, but Düring attempts no chronological scheme. The reference to the *Sophist* in *Topics* 5 is a simpler matter; see the present chapter, 81.

4 On indivisible lines in Plato and Xenocrates see Ross, *Aristotle's Metaphysics* 1 (Oxford 1924), 203–7. Aristotle specifically and emphatically says this was Plato's view at *Met.* A.992A20ff.

5 Plato's later argument (*Phil.* 53C4–7) that pleasure is (not a *kinēsis* but) a *genesis* (coming-to-be) is not mentioned in the *Topics*. Note that Aristippus (the younger) also called pleasure a movement (D.L. 2.85).

6 Maier, *Die Syllogistik des Aristoteles*, argued that 2–7.2 are earlier than the rest of the *Topics*. Solmsen, *Die Entwicklung der aristotelischen Logik und Rhetorik*, and Gohlke, *Die Entstehung*, lost Maier's insight about book 1 and made 1–7 as a block earlier than the rest. See also Huby, 'The Date of Aristotle's *Topics*.'

7 Barnes (note 1 above, 45), is right about the fact that *Topics* 7.153A11 and 153A24 cannot refer to the *Posterior Analytics* (where *different* positions are offered). 7.153A11 could refer to a future, yet-to-be-written *Analytics* (in which Aristotle would have had other intentions), but 153A24 could not. Both *may* refer back to *Topics* 6, or to something lost.

8 For the connection of '*peirastic*' with dialectic see *Met.* Γ.1004B25.

9 I take the sentence *peri de tōn agnōstikōn kai eristikōn nun legōmen* (at the end of *SE* 2) to be the original (and retained) link between *Topics* 8.1 and *SE* 3.

10 References of a chronologically earlier type continue: to Xenocrates (perhaps) and Plato on the soul and number (6.140B2–5), and to Xenocrates again at 7.152A7. There are new 'physical' points, as on cooling as *sterēsis* at 6.141B10ff. Individuals as *atoma* occur at 6.144B3, while in the new material we also find repeated references to the 'training' of the mind (from *Parm.* 132A2) at 1.101A27, 8.159A25; cf. 163A29, 164B1, 164B9. The problem of knowledge as perception (from the *Theaetetus*) recurs at 1.102A7, while the claim that it is a

characteristic of being to act or be acted upon (as in *Soph.* 248C) appears at 6.146A23 (cf. 5.139A5), as is noted by Düring (note 3 above), 202. Düring supplies much further material, but without sorting it.

11 On the origin in the *Phaedo* of some of the ideas underlying the 'syllogism' see Shorey, 'The Origin of the Syllogism.' See also on *endoxa*, Solmsen, 'Dialectic without the Forms.'

12 The threefold division is attributed to Xenocrates by Sextus Empiricus (*Adv. Math.* 7.17; cf. Cicero, *De Fin.* 4.5.11–13). In Aristotelian terms it denies (or circumscribes) the possibility of 'first philosophy.' For 'logical' treatment of the good see *EE* 1.1217B22. For a 'logical deduction', that is, without reference to existence, see *APo.* 2.93A15, cf. 93B16 and *APr.* 1.46A33 ('weak syllogism').

13 Cf. 5.137B3–13 (see the present chapter, 81) and De Vogel (note 3 above), 92. Also 3.119A30, 4.123A2, 6.149A35.

14 The connection with the *Sophist* is noted by De Vogel (note 3 above), 94.

15 Alex. Aphr., *In Met* 84.21ff.

16 Barnes (note 1 above), 45.

17 I adopt the translation 'understanding' from Burnyeat, 'Aristotle on Understanding Knowledge'; cf. Barnes, *Aristotle's Posterior Analytics*.

18 Cf. Sorabji, 'Definitions: Why Necessary and in What Way,' esp. 219.

19 Cf. Barnes (note 1 above). Something should be said about the relation between the *Analytics* and *Physics* 2–7. My separate arguments for the dating of the works carry the further implication that *Physics* 2–7 is earlier. This raises certain difficulties even though I admit that our *Analytics* contains much (finally undatable) earlier material. In particular *APo.* 2.11 gives an apparently different (and some would say less comprehensive) list of 'causes' than *Physics* 2.3. Thus *APo.* speaks of 'necessitating conditions' where *Physics* deals with material causes. But, as we have insisted, some parts of *APo.* contain undatably early material; and – more important – matter is not discussed at all in *APo.*, although Aristotle (on any theory) had been thinking about it for years; and *APo.* is really *not* concerned with specifically physical explanations, so we do not need to worry about the absence of references to matter.

20 Even Barnes (note 1 above), argues that our *Analytics* is a polished whole. For the unity of the *Posterior Analytics* see Brunschwig, 'L'objet et la structure des Seconds Analytiques.' The titles *Prior* and *Posterior Analytics* are not Aristotelian; see Moraux, *Les listes anciennes des ouvrages d'Aristote*, 87–9. For simultaneous development of 'syllogistic' and 'apodeictic' see Smith, 'Aristotle's Two *Analytics*' and 'The Syllogism in *Post. Anal.* 1.' For links of the *Analytics* with *EE* see ch. 14, 262. Note Aristotle's distinction in *APr.* 1.49B10ff between saying pleasure is a good and pleasure is the good: it is similar to the distinction made in *EE* 6.

21 Barnes (note 1 above), 56.

22 Cf. *Rhet.* 1.1356B24; D.L. 5.24. Cf. Düring, *Aristotle in the Ancient Biographical Tradition*, 69, 90.

23 For the date of the *Poetics* see ch. 8, 144–6. For voice see *Poetics* 1456B23, *HA* 4.535A28ff.

24 The development of Aristotle's theory of categories is discussed in chapter 5. For the more developed discussion in the *Topics* (1.9) see S. Mansion, 'Notes sur la doctrine des catégories,' 189–201.

25 For a reference to Isocrates' inexperience in pleading, see *Rhet.* 1.1368A20ff.

26 For discussion of the ode see especially Wormell, 'Hermias of Atarneus'; Düring, *Aristotle in the Ancient Biographical Tradition*; Renehan, 'Aristotle as Lyric Poet.' Problems have arisen because the English 'hymn' does not render the Greek *humnos* (see Harvey, 'The Classification of Greek Lyric Poetry').

27 Barnes (note 17 above), xvi.

28 For such matters see Patzig, *Aristotle's Theory*, 17–18.

29 *Methodos* may be significant here. As we have observed (ch. 4, 84 above), Aristotle was later to put together his *Methodics*, a work probably dealing with formal questions relevant to all kinds of reasoning (cf. *De An.* 1.402A20). If *Topics* supplies material, *Methodics* tells us how to use it strictly.

30 Cf. Mueller, 'Greek Mathematics and Greek Logic.' For non-mathematical influences on Aristotle's account of deduction see Mignucci, 'Ὡς ἐπὶ τὸ πολύ et nécessaire.'

31 For *Meno* in *Prior Analytics* see 2.67A21, in *APo.* 1.71A29. For Zeno on motion in the *Prior Analytics* see 2.65B18.

32 Sometimes called demonstration (1.81B1).

33 Cf. for *epistēmē* 71B15, 73A21, 73B16; for *haplōs* in the *Topics* see De Strycker, 'Concept-clés et terminologie dans les livres ii à vii des *Topiques*,' 160–1.

34 The *possibility* of a non-Platonic metaphysics seems canvassed at *APo.* 1.77A30.

35 For more on substance see ch. 14. Naturally there is no 'understanding' or demonstration of the chance event: it is neither 'necessary' nor 'usual' (1.87B19–23).

Chapter 5

1 For the terminology of Aristotle's discussion of 'categories' see Mansion, 'Notes sur la doctrine des catégories,' 189–92. Aristotle regularly refers to lists of virtues, vices, etc.; these are frequently said to be 'on the diagram.' For the translation of *katēgoriai* as 'kinds of predication' see Frede, 'Categories in Aristotle,' 5–9. Frede (1–24), Kahn ('Questions and Categories,' 227–78), and Malcolm ('On the Generation and Corruption of the *Categories*') prefer to start discussion of categories with the *Topics* (as of course do those who deny the authenticity of the *Categories*, such as Mansion, 'Notes'). Malcolm's discussion is badly harmed by an indiscriminate use of the word 'essence'. I have argued in the previous chapter, on grounds quite unconnected with category-theory, that *Topics* I must be dated in the late 340s, far too late, as all, I think,

would agree, to pre-date the *Categories*. Frede's chief *reason* for treating the account of categories in the *Topics* as early is that he thinks he can exclude the category of *substance* from the *Topics*. This reading of Aristotle's early philosophy is highly implausible, and if the argument I give in this chapter is on the right lines, it is false.

2 On the title of the book see the *apparatus criticus* in the text of L. Minio-Paluello (Oxford 1949), 3. Frede ('Titel, Einheit and Echtheit,' 11–18) argues strongly that the original title was 'Pre-Topics' (*Ta pro tōn topikōn*). If so, this would support our dating of *Categories* to the time immediately prior to the earlier parts of the *Topics*.

3 See Husik, 'The Categories of Aristotle.' Prominent deniers of authenticity include Dupréel, 'Aristote et le traité des *Catégories*,' and S. Mansion, 'La doctrine aristotélicienne de la substance' and 'La première doctrine de la substance.' Occasionally judgment is suspended, as by Dumoulin, 'Sur l'authenticité des *Catégories* d'Aristote,' though Dumoulin is a firmer rejecter in 'L'ousia dans les *Catégories* et dans la *Métaphysique*,' 57. The most recent defence of authenticity is that of Frede (note 2 above), 1–29.

4 Cf. Sachs, 'Does Aristotle Have a Doctrine of Secondary Substance?', Owens, *A History of Ancient Western Philosophy*, 298–9, and 'Aristotle on Categories,' 79.

5 For *katēgoria* see 3A35, 3A37, 10B19. *Genos* is used in the strange section 11B15 (which is probably not part of the original *Categories*). See below note 11.

6 Mansion (note 1 above), 191; *Top.* 1.103B22.

7 Aristotle had already made the point in *On Ideas* (Alex. Aphr., *In Met.* 82.11, 83.17).

8 On the *kath'hauto/pros ti* distinction see especially Owen, 'A Proof in the ΠΕΡΙ ΙΔΕΩΝ,' esp. 107–11. The distinction can be found in the Platonic dialogues themselves; see Annas, 'Forms and First Principles,' 266–70. Aristotle already in *On Ideas* had come to the conclusion that Plato was far from clear about the nature of relatives, in fact that when discussing Ideas he posited a non-relative class of relatives. See Owen, 'A Proof' and 'Dialectic and Eristic in the Treatment of the Forms,' 113–15; also Strang, 'Plato and the Third Man,' and (with full account of the earlier scholarly literature) Leszl, *Il 'De Ideis' di Aristotele*, 185–244. Lastly, if my approach is right, there is no reason to suppose that the items 'categorized' were originally humans and their attributes, as was proposed by Gillespie, 'The Aristotelian Categories,' 80 – followed by Kahn (note 1 above), 240.

9 Trendelenburg, *Geschichte der Kategorienlehre*. Note, however, that the priority of the kinds to the problem of the uses of the verb 'to be' seems clear from *Met.* Δ.1017A22ff.

10 Benveniste, 'Catégories de pensée et catégories de langue,' in *Problèmes*, 63–74.

But Aristotle was not compelled by the nature of the Greek language to choose the categories he offers; see Veuillemin, *De la logique à la théologie*, 76ff.

11 Minio-Pauluello (note 2 above) accepts Cook Wilson's rejection of 11B10–16.

12 *Pace*, e.g., Anscombe, in *Three Philosophers*; see the criticisms of Lloyd, 'Aristotle's Categories Today,' and Körner, 'Substance,' 79–90.

13 *Pace* Anscombe (note 12 above), 7–8.

14 So Kahn (note 1 above), 244. Kahn (at note 29) observes that the phrase *tode ti* (particular) occurs occasionally elsewhere in the *Topics* (e.g. 6.144A20) and in *SE* in this connection.

15 See Kahn (note 1 above), 252–3.

16 The critique of Owen's 'Logic and Metaphysics' by Evans (*Aristotle's Dialectic*, 46) is interesting but should not be over-valued.

17 *Met* Δ.1016B34, 1017A23, 1024B13, Z.1028A10, 1029A21, 1030B11, I.1054B29, Θ.1045B33, 1051A35, N.1089A2–15; *NE* 1.1096A24ff; *De An.* 1.402A24, 410A13ff. *Met.* K.12, though the earliest of the references in the *Metaphysics* to category-theory (see ch. 12, 233), has nothing to add of significance.

18 For the chronology of the *Metaphysics* see ch. 12, 224–41.

19 The objection is that this 'development' also occurs in *Physics* 3.200B28–32. Ross (*ad loc.*) noticed that this passage looks out of place, and it may, like Δ.13–30, be a late addition; but it could also be a foreshadowing. Certainty cannot be obtained.

20 Edel makes the interesting suggestion ('Aristotle's Categories,' 52) that 'position' and 'state' may also be related to what Aristotle later came to think of as different sorts of actualities. The connection with actuality might be right, but the distinctions *among* actualities (first and second) are harder to locate.

Chapter 6

1 Kosman, 'Aristotle's Definition of Motion,' 41; Owens, 'Aristotle – Motion as Actuality of the Imperfect,' 121–2.

2 Blair, 'The Meaning of *Energeia* and *Entelecheia* in Aristotle.' There is a table of occurrences (103).

3 De Strycker, 'Concepts-clés et terminologie,' 159; also now Hagen, 'The Energeia-Kinesis Distinction,' esp. 272. Plato, *Euthyd.* 280B8–E3.

4 Ackrill, 'Aristotle's Distinction between ENERGEIA and KINESIS,' 141. For general reaction to Ackrill see especially Penner, 'Verbs and the Identity of Actions.'

5 Owens, 'Motion as Actuality,' 121.

6 Cf. *Rhet.* 1.11.1369B33ff, and Rist, 'Pleasure: 360–300 B.C.,' 168–9.

7 The position taken in the *EE* has clear resemblances to our passage of the *Topics*, though, as we shall see, it goes further.

8 For the dependence of at least our version of the *Parva Naturalia* on the *De Anima* (which I take to be late) see Kahn, 'Sensation and Consciousness in Aristotle's Psychology.' See further ch. 13, 245.
9 For recent comment on the useful phrase 'focal meaning', see Owens, 'Is There Any Ontology in Aristotle?' 698.
10 Cf. Owens, 'The Notion of Actuality in Aquinas,' 15.
11 E.g., Ross, *Aristotle*, 181.
12 Owens (note 10 above) has some good comment on Neoplatonic and other influences (the concepts of infinite, not finite, etc.) which enabled *energeia* to be developed in Aquinas. But other developments were also possible.
13 Note the remarks of Patzig about the Prime Mover as the 'being of beings', in 'Theology and Ontology' 44–5. See further, chapter 14, 275–80.
14 On such passages, especially in *Physics* 3 (often the 'source' of *Met.* K), see the remarks of Gill, 'Aristotle's Theory of Causal Action,' esp. 130–1, and the scholarly literature cited in her note 2. But Gill does not raise the question of Aristotle's development.

Chapter 7

1 So Vlastos, 'Creation in the *Timaeus*'; and Whittaker, 'The Eternity of the Platonic Forms.'
2 Rist, 'Some Aspects of Aristotelian Teleology.' Objections to this are to be found in Skemp, 'The Activity of Immobility,' 236–7; in Sorabji, *Necessity, Cause and Blame*, 164; and in Kahn, 'The Prime Mover,' 199.
3 Furley, 'Self-Movers,' 165.
4 Sorabji (note 2 above), 164; Solmsen, 'Antecedents of Aristotle's Psychology and Scale of Beings,' 148–64; *De An.* 3.435B1; 2.424A33. The nutritive faculty has no connection with sensation or desire (*orexis*, 3.432B16), but one of these is required for spatial movement. Cf. also Skemp, 'Plants in Plato's *Timaeus*,' 53–60.
5 Ross, *Aristotle's Metaphysics* I (Oxford 1924), cxxxvii.
6 Cf. Sorabji (note 2 above), 164.
7 Rist (note 2 above).
8 For anxiety about unconscious desires, see Gotthelf, 'Aristotle's Conception of Final Causality,' 226–54. For further proposals about the late date of *Physics* 1 – after the rest of the *Physics* – see ch. 12, 229–31.
9 Sorabji (note 2 above), 167.
10 See, for example, chapter 9, 187–8.
11 Ross, *Aristotle's Physics* (Oxford 1936), 95, seems to want to dismiss the force of this by translating it as 'the world (or the *prōtos ouranos*).'
12 *De An.* 2.415A25ff, *GA* 2.731B28ff; cf. *PA* 3.665A18ff, 3.667B22–5, etc. For discussion of some of this (e.g., Aristotle's favouring the front, top, and right

parts over the rear, bottom, and left) see Cooper, 'Aristotle on Natural Teleology,' 220–1. See also Sorabji (note 2 above), 157 and 'Function,' 289–302.

13 The use of *hina* seems to exclude the possibility that Aristotle is simply saying that animals are suitable for human use, that a possible effect of their existence is their use by man seeking his own advantage. Thus the conjunction *hina* (rather than *hopōs*) rules out Kullman's denial of any universal teleology in this passage ('Different Concepts of the Final Cause in Aristotle,' 173).

14 It would seem to make no sense to interpret the *Politics* passage as meaning that the real role of, e.g., horses is to provide services for men – as the real role of the *polis* is to enable men to achieve the good life (*Pol.* 1.1252B30) – *unless* the making of the horse were somehow analogous to the making of the *polis*; that is, that both have makers in some sense independent of the thing made.

15 Ross, *Aristotle*, 126. Cf. *PA* 4.696B24 –32. Ross's comment on *Politics* 1 is singularly inappropriate. See chapter 8, 154–8. On this point, Wieland follows a line similar to Ross in 'The Problem of Teleology' in *Articles on Aristotle* 1, 158. (Originally from *Die aristotelische Physik*, 274.)

16 Cf. *De Anima* 3.5.430A10. In *EE* Aristotle says 'in the whole,' in *De Anima* 'in all nature.' The difference is because in *De Anima* Mind (e.g., God) itself is beyond nature.

17 Sorabji (note 2 above), 167. For the biology of *Politics* 1, see ch. 8, 154–8.

18 The *De Caelo* is to be dated before the *De Generatione et Corruptione* despite its use of the 'fifth element', which represents a refinement on the earlier, vaguer notions of the workings of an immanent God. But, as I have observed, the 'undifferentiated', unexplained immanent God, not yet connected with *pneuma* (*aether* would be irrelevant in 'this' world), is still deployed in the *De Generatione* (and also in *EE* 8.1248A26ff). *Pneuma* (the 'counterpart' of the fifth element) was only developed after these works; indeed it is only *clearly* visible in the *Parva Naturalia*, the *De Motu*, and *De Generatione Animalium*. *De Caelo* points forward to *De Generatione et Corruptione* at 2.286A31–2 (to *De Generatione* 2.331A1–2) and at 2.286B6–7 (to *De Generatione* 2.336A32) and has to pre-date it. It is appropriate to write of the heaven before the earth. On the revised and argumented version of *De Generatione et Corruptione* see ch. 12, 229.

19 Solmsen, 'The Vital Heat, the Inborn *Pneuma* and the Aether,' 119–23, particularly emphasizes the lateness of the crucial section 2.736B29–737A7 of *GA*. There is no reason to explain away *pneuma* (or *aether*) as merely a mixture of fire and air. Aether is a 5th element, not *merely* a combination of two of the others; and the same goes for its analogue.

20 On 'analogues' or 'counterparts' see esp. Philippe, '*Analogon* and *Analogia* in the Philosophy of Aristotle.' For further discussion of *pneuma*, see ch. 12, 226–8, and ch. 13, 246–9.

21 On strengths of *pneuma* see Peck's edition of *GA* (Loeb), 582, and more generally Preus, 'Science and Philosophy in Aristotle's *Generation of Animals*.'
22 Skemp (note 2 above), 236.
23 Trans. D'Arcy Wentworth Thompson, in *The Works of Aristotle* 4 (Oxford 1910).
24 Note Peck's comment (note 21 above), 585: 'Matter might be looked upon as considerably more than mere lifeless, inert material.'

Chapter 8

1 Some of the fragments suggest that the original title may have been *On the Republic and on the Statesman* (Ross, 63–4).
2 Cic., *De Republica* 3.8.12. Elaborate attempts have been made to reconstruct the dialogue *On Justice* from Cicero and Lactantius. I find the case unproven, but see Moraux, *À la recherche de l'Aristote perdu*, and 'From the *Protrepticus* to the Dialogue *On Justice*.'
3 Cf. von Fritz and Kapp, *Aristotle's Constitution of Athens and Related Texts*, 214–15.
4 For a survey of Isocrates' views see Kennedy, *The Art of Persuasion in Greece*, esp. 74–9, 174–203.
5 See the note of Cope, in *The Rhetoric of Aristotle*, 174–5, with Thucyd. 3.82 and Plato, *Rep.* 560E.
6 Similar points are made in *NE* 2.1107A10ff, where it is the nouns like adultery, theft, and murder which have to be erased; see also *Rhet.* 1.1374A and the observation that it is easy to praise Athenians in Athens (cf. Plato, *Menex.* 235D).
7 For discussion of the context of this see Rist, 'Pleasure: 360–300 B.C.' For the question of how seriously to take Aristotle's definitions in the *Rhetoric*, Fortenbaugh, 'Aristotle's *Rhetoric* on Emotion.'
8 Cf. H. Sauppe, *Fragmenta Oratorum Atticorum* (Zurich 1845) fr. 1, 154.
9 The speech about the Messenians is mentioned again at 2.1397A11, but not the crucial material on slavery. Since this is probably a late section of the *Rhetoric*, it may provide weak support for the view I shall argue later in the present chapter, that Aristotle's developed theory of natural slavery is very late. Note also the refinement of the definition of equity from *Rhet.* 1.1374A26ff to *EE* 4.1137B13, where Aristotle spells out that equity corrects a legally *just* enactment.
10 See recently Sorabji, *Necessity, Cause and Blame*, 295–8.
11 The secondary literature is immense, but see esp. the helpful discussion of Stinton, '*Hamartia* in Aristotle and Greek Tragedy.' Stinton seems right to insist that *hamartia may* connote culpability, wrong to claim that it cannot include mishaps.

12 That *hamartia* does not mean a flaw of character is now well established. See, e.g., Lucas, *Aristotle: Poetics,* 163–4 and 299–307. It is probably irrelevant to Aristotle's immediate concerns in the *Poetics* whether the error made by a tragic hero is culpable or not.

13 The most influential attempt to date different layers of the *Rhetoric* is that of Solmsen, *Die Entwicklung der aristotelischen Logik und Rhetorik.* My own claims (ch. 4, 85–6) are far more modest, but less unitarian than those of Grimaldi, *Studies in the Philosophy of Aristotle's Rhetoric.* Grimaldi's position seems an over-reaction.

14 Cope's notes are a rich source for such data.

15 So, rightly, Grimaldi (note 13 above).

16 See the note (*ad loc.*) of W.D. Ross, *Aristotle's Prior and Posterior Analytics* (Oxford 1949), 499ff, with discussion of the Platonic background. Cf. the remarks on signs in *Rhet.* 1.1357Bff.

17 So Cope (note 5 above), 226–7.

18 On the life and chronology of Theodectes see Kennedy (note 4 above), 80–2; Capps, 'Chronological Studies in the Greek Tragedians and Comic Poets,' 58–9; Solmsen, 'Theodektes.'

19 Aristotle also refers to the *Politics* at 1.1366A21, probably to the latter part of book 3.

20 Note the more sophisticated comment in the *Nicomachean Ethics* (8.1155B28–9).

21 See Lucas (note 12 above), 273–90. The medical notion of catharsis was first popularized by Bernays, *Zwei Abhandlungen über die aristotelische Theorie des Dramas.* Various attempts to dislodge it must be accounted failures.

22 Perhaps referred to at 1454B18. It should be recalled that Aristotle's discussion of names at *Poetics* 1457A10 reflects that of *De Interp.* 16A19.

23 According to Proclus and Iamblichus (fr. 5 Ross).

24 See Rowe, 'Aims and Methods in Aristotle's *Politics*.'

25 Kenny, *The Aristotelian Ethics,* 5–7, though Kenny does not use the references to *EE* 4–6 as part of his argument for the Eudemian origin of these books at this stage.

26 It is true but seriously misleading to cite this text for evidence that Aristotle 'is very explicit' in saying that no such friendship can exist, as (for example) does Smith, 'Aristotle's Theory of Natural Slavery,' 113. At *EE* 4.1134A29–30 Aristotle says that without law 'political justice' cannot exist, but there may be 'likeness' of justice, and at 1134B17 he adds that 'household justice' exists strictly between man and wife 'more than' towards children and possessions (i.e., slaves), but again some sort of justice (or analogue) remains for the latter groups.

27 For the proper dignified behaviour of *free* women see *Poetics,* ch. 26.

28 That the virtue of men and women is distinct is Aristotle's consistent position.

In the *Rhetoric* (1.1367A17ff) we hear that the virtues of naturally better specimens are finer and their deeds superior, as are those of a man to those of a woman. Specifically female virtues of body are said (at 1361A6) to be beauty and size, of soul moderation and an industriousness that is free from servility (see note 27 above). Spartan women are inadequate in this respect (cf. *Pol.* 2.1269B12) – a traditional accusation. In *Poetics* 15 it is argued that women should not be portrayed as courageous or clever, and that they are 'perhaps' inferior to men. The point is re-emphasized in book 7 of the *Politics* (1325B4) as well as in book 3 (1277B20ff) at length: there are different *kinds* of virtue like justice, moderation, and courage, different in men and women. (A man would be a coward if he was as brave as a woman, a woman a chatterer if she was only as decorous as a good man.) Hence spring different roles for husband and wife in the household: his job is to acquire, hers to preserve. (For the notion of traditional spheres of influence see Gould, 'Law, Custom and Myth: Aspects of the Social Position of Women.' Male dignity and courage are contrasted with female orderliness and moderation in Plato's *Laws* 7.802E; compare *Laws* 6.781C, 11.917A, etc. *Laws* 6.781 B–C is a very informative passage in which Plato comments on how difficult it would be to get women to eat in public or even to go outside.)

29 Aristotle seems to mean that the justification of a slave in nature is that he is to be a tool useful in the actions of the family. That is the original definition of the slave: he is a living chattel (*empsuchon ktēma*) 'for the maintenance of life.' But that is in the family situation; there seems no reason why in larger natural communities Aristotle would not be willing to extend his use of slaves, so that they might operate shuttles, for example, to make products for sale. We noticed that selling a shoe for wear is not the same sort of intrinsic use of a shoe as wearing it oneself (or presumably giving it to a member of the household), but there is nothing necessarily unacceptable about it, even though it is not the 'proper' use of it). Similar extended use of slaves would seem permissible, though 'unnatural' uses (e.g., as prostitutes) would presumably be outlawed. Hence when in *Pol.* 7 (1330A25–6) slaves are to be used for agriculture, Aristotle is not necessarily contradicting himself, as is suggested by Schlaifer, 'Greek Theories of Slavery from Homer to Aristotle,' 192, note 2.

30 Something which, as we have seen, the natural slave cannot do, since he lacks deliberative power (1.1260A12). This is spelled out further in an important passage of book 3 (1280A32–4), where Aristotle says that if man's good were merely living (not flourishing), a city of 'slaves and other animals' would be possible. But this is not possible because slaves do not share in happiness or a life involving choices (that is, with deliberation).

31 So recently Smith (note 26 above), reflecting the views of Schlaifer (note 29 above), and Barker, *The Political Thought of Plato and Aristotle*, 365, as well as others.

32 Fortenbaugh, 'Aristotle on Slaves and Women,' 136. This short article provides the most careful and helpful discussion of slavery in Aristotle which is currently available.

33 In *EE*, of course, *irrational* emotions are also possible, but these are precisely animal-like in that reason fails (2.1220B12ff).

34 The *comparison* with animals occurs at 1254A26 and at 1254B23, but at 1259B27–8 they are said to be human. For strong and weak senses of human (and man) see Rist, 'Aristotle on the Value of Man and the Origin of Morality,' 1–6.

35 Aristotle even suggests that it is the 'wish' of nature to distinguish the bodies of the naturally free from those of the naturally slave, but frequently the opposite turns out to be the case (1.1254B27ff). No explanation is given as to why nature is so thwarted in this regard.

36 In Aristotle's work *Alexander or On Colonies* a similar attitude is found to that of *Politics* 1. Greeks are to be treated as Greeks; they are to be led, but in the spirit of leadership, not of 'despotism'. That is to be reserved for barbarians (fr. 2 Ross).

37 It has often been observed that Aristotle's will provides for the freeing of various slaves he owned. If these slaves are natural slaves, then freeing them would presumably be wrong. If they are not natural slaves, then presumably they should not have been kept as slaves. There is no solution to this dilemma, except to say that Aristotle is well aware that many actual slaves are not natural slaves. Some of his own would seem to be within this group, and their existence marks the difference between the actual and the 'ideal' worlds. Perhaps it takes time to tell whether an actual slave is a natural slave or not. This explanation may be supported by Aristotle's remark that certain slaves will be freed *when* they grow up, if they deserve it (*en hēlikiāi … kat'axian*). For 'desert' see the present chapter, 158. For the will see D.L. 5.11–16, with various discussions in Düring, *Aristotle in the Ancient Biographical Tradition*, 35–7, 61–5.

38 Note that in the later book 5 of the *Politics* (1305A30) traditional democracy (republicanism) is said to make use of the property qualification.

39 See Gould (note 28 above).

40 For Aristotle's willingness to maintain talk of *praxis* alongside that of *energeia* see *NE* 1.1098B22–3. His idea here seems to be that *eupraxia* is nearer to ordinary Greek than *energeia*.

41 For the importance of the passage of *EE* see the present chapter, 159.

42 The text does not speak of 'the natural freeman' and 'the natural slave,' as Barker (note 31 above) suggests. It should probably also be compared with Plato, *Laws* 6.777B6, where Plato speaks of *to doulon te … kai eleutheron*.

43 Jaeger, *Aristotle* 270, note 1. That Aristotle is not (at least primarily) concerned

with taxonomy is argued by Pellegrin, see esp., on this passage, 'Aristotle: Zoology without Species,' 98, 103–4.

44 Barker (note 31 above), 193, note 1.

45 Using the new para-biological method Aristotle claims that Plato's account of the parts of the state is clear but inadequate.

46 For problems about the original version and revisions of *Ath. Pol.*, see Rhodes, *A Commentary*, 51–61. The final additions must have been made before 322 when Athenian officials ceased going to Samos; they were still going, it seems, when *Ath. Pol.* 62.16 was composed. The text was probably finalized before 325 when quinquiremes are known in the Athenian fleet; none is mentioned at 46.1. *Ath. Pol.* 8 seems to correct the statements of *Pol.* 2.1273B41 and 1274A15 about Solon's prescriptions for the appointment of Athenian magistrates, but it is impossible to sort out a chronological pattern from the conflicting evidence of differences between the *Politics* and *Ath. Pol.*

47 In Diogenes' catalogue of Aristotle's works, the words *hōs hē Theophrastou* are added before the number of books of the *Politics* (i.e., 8) is given.

Chapter 9

1 Nuyens, *L'Evolution de la psychologie d'Aristote.*

2 Block, 'The Order of Aristotle's Psychological Writings.'

3 Hardie, 'Aristotle's Treatment of the Relation between the Soul and the Body'; also Kahn, 'Sensation and Consciousness in Aristotle's Psychology', esp. 61ff.

4 Lefèvre, *Sur l'évolution d'Aristote en psychologie.*

5 For the correct interpretation of fr. 8 (in the context of the *Eudemus*) see ch. 2, 46–8.

6 Nuyens (note 1 above), 93–4, thinks that there is more emphasis on teleology in the *Protrepticus* than in the *Eudemus*, but all that we know is that teleology is a little more prominent in the fragments we have.

7 Düring, *Aristotle's Protrepticus*, 249–51.

8 Nuyens (note 1 above), 117.

9 *Cat.* 14A16; cf. Nuyens (note 1 above), 107.

10 Kenny, *The Aristotelian Ethics.*

11 Kenny (note 10 above), 216–18.

12 See especially Allan, '*Magna Moralia* and *Nicomachean Ethics.*'

13 Rist, 'Pleasure: 360–300 B.C.,' esp. 178–9. An important point about the dating of *EE* earlier than *NE* is made by Owen, 'Logic and Metaphysics,' 166 (repr. in *Articles on Aristotle* 3, 15). Owen observes that in *NE*, but not in *EE*, Aristotle holds that all uses of 'good' may be connected by 'focal meaning' (1.1096B26–9).

14 This term is originally due to Hardie, 'The Final Good in Aristotle's Ethics.' Anaxagoras is cited as an advocate of 'contemplation' in the *Protrepticus*; see ch. 2, 50.
15 The addition of *kai nou* from the Latin text *De Bona Fortuna* by Spengler is unnecessary for the sense and can be misleading. It is probably a Neoplatonic addition to the *De Bona Fortuna* (which is a Latin version of *EE* 8.2 and *MM* 2.8). For the importance of *De Bona Fortuna* in determining that Aristotle never wrote the dialogue *On Prayer* attributed to him by Diogenes Laertius (5.22) and 'quoted' by Simplicius (fr. 1 Ross) see Rist, 'The End of Aristotle's *On Prayer*.'
16 For further comment on World-Mind in *EE*, see ch. 7, 129.
17 Dirlmeier, 'Merkwürdige Zitate in der Eudemischen Ethik.' Düring, *Aristoteles*, takes the same line.
18 Dirlmeier's arguments are rejected by Kenny (note 10 above), 174–5, and by Woods, *Aristotle's Eudemian Ethics*, 197–8. The correct reading was more or less identified by Verdenius, 'Human Reason and God in the *Eudemian Ethics*,' and by Rowe, *The Eudemian and Nicomachean Ethics*, 68–9.
19 Lefèvre (note 4 above).
20 This is well described by Sorabji, 'Body and Soul in Aristotle,' 63–89, repr. in *Articles on Aristotle* 4, 42–64.
21 Patzig, 'Theology and Ontology in Aristotle's *Metaphysics*,' 44–5. Patzig destroys Jaeger's theory of the distinctness of book Λ from the first six books of the *Metaphysics*, but in his original text he seems to agree with Jaeger that Z and H still stand apart. He appears to withdraw this latter position in his additional note, 49. Kahn ('On the Intended Interpretation,' esp. 317ff) tries to combine Jaeger and Patzig. Thus while the subject-matter of Λ 1–5 and Z, H is now closely connected, Λ is still early. Thus Kahn thinks that a new version of Λ remains unwritten. My explanation of the similarities of Λ and Z, H is more economical (see ch. 12, 236, 242–3; ch. 14, 277–9).
22 Lloyd (*Form and Universal in Aristotle*, 41), following Owens, 'The Reality of the Aristotelian Separable Movers,' 319–37, suggests that God is a separate 'form' in a way comparable to that in which Aristotle holds that there are forms in matter. But if there are separate 'forms', they are minds. In fact Aristotle talks in the *Metaphysics* of separable beings, not separate forms, while calling mind a form in the *De Anima* (3.432A2).
23 For 'setting' see Preus, 'Science and Philosophy in Aristotle's *Generation of Animals*,' 27.
24 The phrase *exōthen epeisiōn* occurs similarly in Theophrastus (fr. 1.3 Barbotin).
25 For the translation see Lefèvre (note 4 above), 255. In human life, of course, the effects of the presence of 'mind' can be 'damaged' by bodily ailments, old age, etc. (cf. *De. An.* 3.429B16 and *PA* 4.686A28–32). 'Images' are made 'worse' by

disease or deformity at *EE* 2.1219B25ff. Aristotle could observe such effects whether or not he held *nous* to be 'transcendent' – which he probably did not in *PA*.

26 This problem is already recognized by Theophrastus (fr. 12).

27 In general see Barbotin, *La théorie aristotélicienne de l'intellect d'après Théophraste*.

28 So De Corte, *La doctrine de l'intelligence chez Aristote*, 288, followed by Moraux, 'À propos du νοῦς θύραθεν chez Aristote,' 269–70. Moraux's attempt (294) to solve all problems by emending the text to eliminate *nous thurathen* (*pace* the evidence of Theophrastus) is unconvincing and unnecessary.

29 Fr. IVb (Barbotin). In fr. 4 he uses the ambiguous *to hupokeimenon*.

30 See Brentano, *Die Psychologie des Aristoteles* (Mainz 1867), 208–9, whose neglected (but now translated) text points out the importance of *phantasia*. Cf. *De Mem.* 450A12, but particularly *De Anima* 3.427B27ff (where Aristotle typically fails to tell us how *hupolēpsis* takes place) and 3.433A9, where *phantasia* is a 'kind of thinking.'

31 There is no doubt that we should make as much use of Theophrastus as possible in studying *De Anima* 3.5. After all he both knew the doctrine and was in a position to discuss it with Aristotle himself. But there is a rather strange feature of his discussion. He seems to refer to mind as a 'mix' (*mikton*, fr. 12 Barbotin) 'of some sort' (*pōs*) of the productive intellect and the potential. (Note that he avoids the use of the word 'passive' at this point.) But it is an odd kind of mixing that he speaks of, if it is between the immaterial productive intellect itself and the images which are the potential intellect. But perhaps all he means is that the act of thinking in us (the Aristotelian *dianoia*) is a mix which is the *effect* of the 'impact' of the productive intellect on the images. Aristotle calls the productive intellect itself *amigēs*; that would then square with Theophrastus.

It will be evident from my discussion here that I should wish to withdraw a number of proposals I advanced in 'Notes on *De Anima* 3.5.'

32 Lloyd (note 22 above), 56.

33 For this special kind of 'efficient causation,' cf. the use of the word *poiētikos* itself at *De Anima* 2.417B20.

34 Merlan, *Studies in Epicurus and Aristotle*, 44–59.

35 Rist (note 31 above).

36 I used to think that the phrase *en tēi psychēi* (3.5.430A13) ruled out 'Averroist' interpretations. I still think that anxieties about translating this as 'in the realm of soul' or 'in the case of soul' are serious, though not serious enough to override other evidence. It is possible to translate the phrase as I did earlier, 'inside the soul,' but to take this to mean that, although during our lifetimes the productive intellect gets 'inside the soul' (as light gets into a room), it is only so

incidentally, not essentially. It is available to us, unless it is somehow blocked off.

37 The pun – *enargeia tou logou* (the light of reason) – may refer to the productive intellect.

38 So, hesitatingly, Anscombe, *Three Philosophers* 58; Clark, *Aristotle's Man*, 5.3, 174ff; Guthrie, *HGP* 6 (Cambridge 1981), 322–30; most recently, Kahn (note 21 above), 329, note 26. For Aristotle's reasonably firm grasp on the notion of identity see Matthews, 'Accidental Unities,' 230–5; and Mignucci, 'Puzzles about Identity,' 57–97.

39 The term – a very appropriate one – is Allan's (note 12 above), 7.

40 Note the five *tropoi* of courage at *NE* 3.1116A17ff, and how people 'refer' *thumos* to courage at 3.1116B23–4. *Tropoi* are the modes of the figures of the syllogism (*APr*. 1.43A6); they are thus all proved with reference to (and depend on) the first figure. Fortenbaugh ('Aristotle's Analysis of Friendship') denies that 'focal meaning' is to be found in the discussion of friendship in *NE* (though he admits it in *EE*). Perfect friendship, he thinks, becomes a kind of focus of resemblance. It has the priority of a mediator. But this kind of priority is not the priority of focal analysis. It is not the priority of a focal definition mentioned in or implied by dependent definitions. I am inclined to think that focal meaning could be (and indeed is) found in the 'Nicomachean' discussion of friendship. But even if Fortenbaugh is right my general view is not seriously affected.

41 Books 8–9 (on friendship) are more difficult to place. They are far more developed than the parallel discussion in *EE* 7, but there seems no reason not to put them with *NE* 10 as we have it. The end of book 9 (apart from the editorial link) *does* refer to the pleasure of friendship. The opening of the *Eudemian* discussion – unlike that of the *Nicomachean* version – suggests that originally Aristotle discussed friendship as a kind of justice (*EE* 7.1234B31). This *might* indicate that in the *Eudemian Ethics*, book 7 was originally placed after book 4 (on justice) and before book 5 (on intellectual virtues). This would give the additional advantage of bringing books 6 and 8 (which have much in common) together. Thus, as in *NE* 10, discussion of pleasure would immediately precede discussion of happiness.

42 See especially Ackrill, 'Aristotle on Eudaimonia'; also and more generally Keyt, 'Intellectualism in Aristotle,' 364–6. Unfortunately current discussion largely ignores the *Protrepticus*, despite the availability of Düring's edition.

43 Cooper's *Reason and Human Good in Aristotle* has done much to sharpen the discussion of Aristotle's ethical goals, since he presents the 'dominant' theory of *theōria* in its extreme, and most philosophically interesting – as well as most implausible – form. The notion is not new, of course. For earlier versions see Verbeke, 'L'idéal de la perfection humaine chez Aristote,' 84 and Hardie (note

14 above). Recently Kenny (note 10 above), 208–9 and White, 'Goodness and Human Aims in Aristotle's Ethics,' 240–1, have come out strongly in support of Cooper. On the other side, to some degree (beside Keyt [note 42 above], who is strongly opposed), is Devereux, 'Aristotle on the Active and the Contemplative Lives' and 'Aristotle on the Essence of Happiness.' My own view has similarities to Devereux's idea that in *NE* 10 the 'inclusive' end is implicit, but I invoke the *Protrepticus* as partial explanation of why Aristotle does not need to be more explicit.

44 The importance of this shift seems to be exaggerated, if not misinterpreted, by Kenny (note 10 above), 200–3.

45 Cooper (note 43 above), 159–60; for the opposing view, see Keyt (note 42 above).

46 See especially Devereux, 'The Essence of Happiness,' 256–7. It should also be noticed that Cooper (note 43 above), 169–75, is right not to involve book 9 in the discussion, for there mind includes practical reasoning in the crucial texts, i.e., Aristotle is speaking generally about thinking, not about contemplation as distinct from practical reasoning.

47 Rowe, *The Eudemian and Nicomachean Ethics*, 100–7. For the opposing view, see von Fragstein, *Studien zur Ethik des Aristoteles*, 162–214.

48 Kenny (note 10 above), 6.

49 See generally Movia, *Anima e Intelletto.*

50 Cic., *Ad Att.* 2.16 (fr. 25 Wehrli); cf. Jaeger, *Aristotle*, 451. This 'appendix' to Jaeger's *Aristotle* originally appeared as 'Ursprung und Kreislauf des philosophischen Leben,' *SB* Berlin, phil. hist. Kl. (1928).

51 Despite a continuing minority opinion (recently Cooper, 'The *Magna Moralia*'), the author of *MM* is most unlikely to be Aristotle himself (Kenny [note 10 above], 216–29). It will be suggested later in the present chapter that the author was probably a contemporary of Dicaearchus. Such an interpretation need not be too different from that of Kenny, who sees him as a rather incompetent pupil and hearer of Aristotle's. If Kenny would allow that he published his notes on Aristotle *some time* after Aristotle's death, our positions would be almost identical (Kenny's arguments against this [219] are not conclusive). The author knew the *NE* but primarily uses the *EE*. My view of the unfinished state of the *NE* need not affect the conclusions about the *MM*. The reference to Neleus of Scepsis (son of Coriscus) at *MM* 2.1205A23 suggests a date of about 300 BC or even later. Neleus, the nephew of Theophrastus, inherited his books at his death (ca 285), according to Strabo (13.608). See Kenny, 217.

52 For Dicaearchus on the soul see F. Wehrli, *Die Schule des Aristoteles: I Dikaiarchos* (Basel 1944) frs. 7–9. For denial of both *animus* and *anima*, fr. 7. For the soul's mortality, frs. 9–10. For the soul described as harmony, frs. 11–12. A similar thesis was also maintained by Dicaearchus's pupil, Aristoxenus

(frs. 118–121 Wehrli). That Dicaearchus's theory is not identical with that of Simmias in Plato's *Phaedo*, but that it is itself an epiphenomenalist theory based on Aristotle's account of the soul, is shown by Gottschalk, 'Soul as Harmonia,' esp. 182–90. Gottschalk is probably right in saying that only Aristoxenus actually used the word 'harmony'.

Chapter 10

1 Unnecessary trouble seems to have been generated by the phrase *exō tōn prōtōn*. Some think it means 'apart from prime numbers'; others, following Heinze, propose to emend the text to *perittōn* (following N.1091A23) and get the sense 'odd numbers'. Alexander of Aphrodisias tries to make *prōtōn mean* odd. But all that is required is that one and two are not generated because they exist already (i.e., as the One and the Dyad). Problems have been exaggerated by believing that one is never a number but only the source of number. So Ross, *Plato's Theory of Ideas*, 188, where fantasies can be found and the truth, spotted by Taylor, is casually rejected. The theory that one is not a number is recently corrected again by Annas, *Aristotle's Metaphysics* M *and* N, 110. See ch. 3, 61. Earlier scholars, e.g. Taylor, 'Forms and Numbers,' (1927) 22–3, often got it right.

2 Note that *Eros* is male and the female desire for child-growing is *epithumia*.

3 The importance of reincarnation is seen by Smith, 'Plato and Aristotle on the Nature of Women.' But Smith wrongly supposes that 'souls are fundamentally sexless' (472) rather than male. Bad males become females, but good females will become males later. Smith also manufactures a false contrast between the *Timaeus* and the *Republic* – which he explains by Plato's weariness in his old age.

4 It is also visible earlier in Diotima's speech in the *Symposium*. See Morrison, 'Four Notes on Plato's *Symposium*.' Socrates calls ejaculating 'sowing children' in *Phaedr.* 251A1. Note the connection with 'unnatural' homosexual acts; cf. 254B1.

5 We should notice an interesting side-effect of Plato's account of men and women. A woman is basically a man with a womb instead of a penis. If she can control it, she will be able to live like a man, and act like a man. In Plato's ideal state men and women are both to be guardians, for their sexuality is controlled. And with sexuality regulated women can live like the men they once were. Good women have male souls and will be (without doubt) reborn as men in the next life. Diotima, the good woman, is like a *man*, is an *erōtikos*. As her name suggests, she is worthy of Zeus, that is of (male) authority. She is a woman fit to rule and to instruct. Very properly, she assures Socrates in the *Symposium* that the attainment of immortality by sexual reproduction is

very much a second best (208E). She knows, though this is not said in the text of the *Symposium*, that when we were all men, we did not need that kind of immortality. She knows that all men are pregnant both in body and in mind, but the best (males and females) are pregnant in soul. Interestingly women depend for physical pregnancy on men, but not necessarily for mental pregnancy. In the mind they are *already* male (if they are good), as they will eventually also be in body.

That the Academy included female students has been recently reconfirmed by *Pap. Oxy.* 3656. Note that one of the two women known to have been taught by Plato was called Axiothea (worthy of God). Her name means the same as Diotima. Is she Diotima (or half of Diotima) or is she an invention of the tradition based on Diotima? Diotima comes from Mantinea (*Symp.* 201D). Unfortunately Axiothea, who according to Dicaearchus wore men's clothes, does not. She is from Phlius, but the other woman pupil (the other half of Diotima?) Lastheneia *is* Mantinean (D.L. 3.46; 4.2). Interestingly Diotima knows how to ward off plagues and helped Athens for years in this regard (*Symp.* 201D). The ordinary woman, according to *Timaeus* 91C, is, because of her womb, liable to all kinds of diseases (and probably to cause them, like Pandora); the wise Diotima (as spiritually ex-female) can overcome them. About the time of the *Symposium* we can observe a great interest – probably originating with Socrates – in the wise (or even political) woman (Xen. *Symp.* 2.9). Speculation often centred around Aspasia, to whom Plato has given a speech in *Menexenus*, whom Aeschines of Sphettus uses in the title role in a Socratic dialogue (cf. Cic., *De Inv.* 1.31.51), and whom Xenophon mentions twice as wise (*Mem.* 2.6.36; *Oec.* 3.14). See Field, *Plato and His Contemporaries*, 118. And there is also Aristophanes' *Ecclesiazusae*: are Socratics concealed among the women named at 11.41–51 (Gluke = Glaucon, Sostrate = Socrates, and the lady with two husbands – a wife in common – at 51–2)? Both Lastheneia and Axiothea are said also to have attended lectures by Speusippus (D.L. 4.2). Diogenes Laertius already retails alleged mocking comments of Dionysius on Lastheneia ('It is possible to learn wisdom from the Arcadian woman who is your pupil'), which doubtless spring from the same source as that of Athenaeus (7.279E) who says she was his mistress from Arcadia. But, as we shall see, Speusippus's theory of conception put a higher value on women than Plato's!

6 That the Stoics understood these parts of Plato is indicated indirectly by Hahm, *The Origins of Stoic Cosmology*, 72, but Hahm overestimates the influence of Aristotle at the expense of the *Timaeus*.

7 Notice the use of the words *sunhistēmi, sustasis*, etc. (48A), and the description of the Demiurge as *sunhistas* (32C). The verb is widely used by Aristotle to describe the male 'setting' of the female matter, but it has no such specific sense in the *Timaeus*.

8 Guthrie, puzzled as to why she is like a 'nurse' (*HGP* 5.263), misses the whole point. Females *are* 'nurses,' both before and after giving birth. The word *thēlus* (female) means 'suckler' in Greek, and breast-feeding is the continuation after birth of the fetus-feeding before birth which is the female role. Plato speaks of 'begetters' and 'nurses' at 87C.

9 *Chōrein* (LSJ II) means 'to hold.' Note Herodotus 1.51 on how much a mixing-bowl contains. *Chōrēma* later means 'space'; *chōra* in the *Timaeus* is an earlier version of this.

10 Proclus seems to have understood something of this when he referred to the qualities as 'emmattered forms' (*In Tim.* 3.357), as Cornford noted (*Plato's Cosmology*, 183).

11 As Sorabji pointed out to me, Philoponus (*In Phys.* 516, 16–19) recognized the 'parental' language: 'For he compares the separate and transcendent Form to a father, the matter to a mother, and the creative reasons to a seed. These reasons empty out into the matter. And he compares to a fetus the developing natural kinds that arise in the matter as a result of the activity of the creative reasons.' Philoponus believes, however, that the seed provides form and some matter – which is 'fed' by the matter of the menses (*De Aet. Mundi* 432, 11–16). This is not the view of the *Timaeus*; nor is it Aristotle's latest theory. It is easy to see, however, why Philoponus advocated it. It follows an intermediate Aristotelian thesis found in *PA* 4.689A13 and, more or less, still in *Met.* Λ. See ch. 12, 237–8.

In the *Timaeus* itself the cosmos is the offspring (*ekgonos*, 50D), but of an odd kind, for it will never grow up, as it were, to be like its father, but will always remain an image. The best discussion of that image is perhaps Lee's 'On the Metaphysics of the Image in Plato's *Timaeus*.'

12 Hence, as *Phaedrus* and *Laws* have it, natural motion *is* ultimately due to the *action* of mind or soul. For it is the planned act of begetting which ultimately causes all movements in the world. At 89D Plato says that the 'least good' movement is that 'which, when a body is lying quietly, moves it part by part (*kata merē*) through other things.' This is exactly the movement of the *ekmageion*. For further argument that *Tim.* 46C7–E6 and 57D7–58C4 present soul as the source of *all* motion, see Tarán, 'The Creation Myth in Plato's *Timaeus*,' esp. 384–90. I do not, however, accept Tarán's view that the *Timaeus* must be read metaphorically; nor am I the first to find Plato's account of the movements of the Receptacle (prima facie) obscure.

13 Attempts to identify the *ekmageion* as 'geometrical' lack evidence. Nor is there any text to suggest that Plato 'reduced' matter to space, or even that the 'matrix' is 'stuff without property' (as Popper, *The Open Society and Its Enemies* 1.211).

14 See the interesting discussion by Brisson, *Le même et l'autre dans la structure ontologique du Timée de Platon*, 208–20.

15 For wombs possibly in Democritus and certainly in Epicurus see Lucretius, 5.808; Censorinus, *De Die Natali* 4.9.

16 These comments on the *ekmageion* perhaps owe most to Burnet, *Greek Philosophy: Thales to Plato*, 344.

17 Hence Aristotle is not so misguided as some (e.g., Cherniss, *Aristotle's Criticism of Plato and the Academy*, 112–24) are inclined to suppose.

18 Dillon, *The Middle Platonists* 25, says that Hestia (in Xenocrates' version of the *Phaedrus*, fr. 15 Heinze) is beyond the heavens: a false correction of the text. Guthrie (*HGP* 5.474) has it right; she is below the heavens. The text of Aetius is falsely 'corrected' from the *Phaedrus*. But in fact in the *Phaedrus* Hestia does not go to the *huperouranios topos*; she stays at home. No one now seems to know why Hestia is left at home. Xenocrates did, I think. He calls the Dyad 'Mother of the Gods,' the female 'natural' principle: that is, Hestia is the *hedra* of the *Timaeus*. *Hedra* can mean 'the right place' (LSJ I.3) and a 'temple' (LSJ 2). *Aph' hestias* can mean 'from the beginning' (LSJ II). We shall notice later how much Xenocrates knew about Plato.

19 The following remarks in this chapter are in part a recantation of views I expressed on this passage in *Eros and Psyche*, 42, where I attempted to defend a 'traditional' account of the separation of Mind and Form in the version of Grube, *Plato's Thought*, 295–7. The inadequacy of my reading of the passage was first made clear to me in 1980 by Richard McKim (then an undergraduate). Guthrie (*HGP* 5.142) more or less follows the view I now question, and conveniently lists most of his supporters, but he does admit, 'I do not see how anyone can doubt that Plato is preparing the reader for a modification of his own metaphysics' (141). But his account of the modification lacks rigour. To say merely that Mind is 'real' is to say very little more than what Plato was already prepared to say in the *Phaedo* in connection with Anaxagoras.

20 Note the association of *semnos* and *hagios* in Isocrates (11.21).

21 For the standard interpretation see again Guthrie, *HGP* 5.259–62. Guthrie demolishes the (false) theory that *Republic* 6 as it stands can be used to interpret the *Timaeus*. *My* point is that *Republic* 6 is replaced.

But it would not be helpful to invoke Rich, 'The Platonic Ideas as the Thoughts of God.' Rich's excellent article shows that to think of Plato's Forms as concepts (in God's mind or anywhere else) is non-Platonic. That is right, but I am not claiming that Plato ever thought that Forms are simply concepts.

22 Guthrie, unwittingly, makes the same point: 'If the Forms made themselves sole efficient causes, Plato would be more naively susceptible to Aristotle's criticism than he was' (*HGP* 5.259, note 4). Guthrie does not face up to the problem of why Aristotle *does* think that Plato was liable to his criticism; he certainly was not naïve.

23 For the meaning of 'numbers' see chapter 3.

24 For comment see Aetius (Xen. Fr. 15 Heinze); Xenocrates adapts Plato and passes him on to the Stoics.

25 Frs. 60, 68 Heinze. Xenocrates is named by Plutarch. Xenocrates presumably argued that soul is intermediate between form and particular; mathematicals are intermediate between form-numbers and particulars; therefore soul is a mathematical.

26 Guthrie rightly draws attention to the importance of this passage (*HGP* 5.213), and concludes that it is mistaken simply to identify Form as limit. So far so good. In the cosmos itself it is the form-characters which limit, as I argued in 'The Immanence and Transcendence of the Platonic Form,' 19–32, to which Guthrie gives limited assent (214, note 1).

27 That not Forms but their embodied 'likenesses' are in particulars was probably claimed by Plato at *Politicus* 300C. Here the world's *best* written code of law is an 'instantiation of truth.' Aristotle's *Protrepticus* has a very similar passage (fr. 13 Ross), but Aristotle appeals not to Forms but to 'nature' and 'the divine'. We should also note that in the *Politicus* myth, the 'disintegration' of the world and its 'roll-back' need no 'cause of unmixing.' In this respect the dialogue resembles *Philebus* 23D, where a 'power of separation' is quietly dropped. So much for Empedocles – but if the Mixer and Form can be amalgamated, clearly an Unmixer could only 'amalgamate' with 'Matter' – which would produce an unwanted evil world-soul.

28 Gosling's note is instructive here: 'The "cause" here is clearly not the efficient cause, but the *peras* of 23 seq.' (*Plato*: *Philebus*, 135). But why 'not' and 'but'? Read (perhaps): 'The "cause" here is clearly not the efficient cause, unless, that is, it is also the *peras* of 23 seq.,' which in places it is.

29 *Phil.* 30C, *Tim.* 30B. Cf. *Soph.* 249A; Hackforth, 'Plato's Theism.' If Hackforth is right, the problem about the evil world-soul disappears.

30 Alcinous (Albinus), *Didask.*, 10. For the correct name Alcinous, see most recently Whittaker, 'Platonic Philosophy,' 83–102. For *kai* as added explanation, see rightly Dodds, in *Les sources de Plotin* 416; wrongly Rist, *Eros and Psyche* 66. Alcinous's language is Aristotelian; my claim is that his thought is Platonic.

31 If my argument is correct, it strengthens the position of traditionalists in the debate about the date of the *Timaeus*. Against the attempt of Owen to remove the *Timaeus* from the late period of Plato's philosophical activity ('The Place of the *Timaeus* in Plato's Later Dialogues'), see (originally) Cherniss, 'The Relation of the *Timaeus* to Plato's Later Dialogues,' and Rist, 'The Order of the Later Dialogues of Plato.' Very recently Fine (summing up Owen's achievement) concludes that on stylistic grounds alone the *Timaeus* must post-date the *Parmenides* and *Theaetetus*. I would go still further and put it after the *Sophist* and *Statesman*, but to go even as far as Fine is to concede that Owen

was wrong in principle about Plato's development (see Fine, 'Owen's Progress,' esp. 374–83).

32 For the 'literal' interpretation see especially Vlastos, 'Creation in the *Timaeus*.' Tarán offers a good recent statement of the opposite view (note 12 above). *Topics* 6 (139B33ff) seems to be the earliest reference to the debate as to whether Plato's *Timaeus* should be taken 'metaphorically.' Xenocrates is prominent in *Topics* 6 (e.g., 141A7).

33 See again recently Verdenius, 'Hylozoism in Aristotle,' esp. 102–4. Verdenius properly rejects attempts to demythologize the text.

34 And the effects of the 'action' of the Prime Mover of *Physics* 8 (267B18ff) are somehow felt on the outside first. Of course the mode of the action of the Prime Mover is not worked out here (nor is his 'nature'). It seems at this point that Aristotle is thinking (misleadingly) of the Prime Mover as whipping a top (the top being the outermost sphere). The lack of efficient cause is not yet spelled out.

35 We have already discussed the relationship between *De Caelo* and *Physics* 6–7 (ch. 2, 44–6). It is probably impossible to be precise about details of the chronological relationship between the *De Caelo* and *Physics* 2–7 as a whole, of which 7 was perhaps the earliest book. (Cf. 7.2, 244A5ff with 5.3 and 6.1 on *hama* – 'together'.) *De Caelo* 1 seems to refer several times to books of the *Physics*: 268A31, 268B17, 272B30, and 274A22 seem to refer to *Physics* 2, 3, and 6. But Sorabji, in *Time, Creation, and the Continuum*, 212, points out that *De Caelo* 1.12 ignores the discussion of infinity in *Physics* 3 – inexplicably if *Physics* 3 is the earlier text. The simplest explanation seems to be to maintain the usual view that *De Caelo* post-dates most of *Physics* 2–7, but not all. We do not know in what order *Physics* 2–7 were written, or rewritten, or when additions were inserted. It seems likely, however, that work on the *Physics* began in Mytilene and continued in Macedon, and that other works, including the *De Caelo*, were being composed more or less simultaneously. Cross-references to the 'Physics' in the *De Caelo* and *De Generatione et Corruptione* may suggest that at this stage 'Physics' 2–7 were not called *Physics* at all, but *On Causes* (cf. *De Caelo* 1.274A22) and *On Motion*. Similar terminology is used at *Mete.* 1.338A20, where what is certainly some version of the *Physics* is reference to as *On the First Causes of Nature* and *On All Natural Motion*.

36 Anaxagoras is mentioned again at *Mete.* 1.339B23. For the view that the sun is not fire – for fire does not generate – see *GA* 2.737A1ff, also *Mete.* 4.382A7 (though this is spurious). *Aether* however does generate life on the moon, *GA* 3.761B21; it makes fertile seeds (*gonima spermata*, 2.736B30–5). But in *HA* 5.552B10ff Aristotle thinks that fire *can* generate, and salamanders can survive fire. *HA* 5 is corrected at *GA* 3.761B13.

37 Aristotle observes (*De Caelo* 1.279A30ff) that in the 'circulating philosophical

writings,' presumably *On Philosophy* (as Simplicius says, *ad loc.*), the *highest* divinity is said to be 'immutable' (*ametablēton*), for there is nothing superior which can move it. That squares with what I claim Aristotle argued in the original version of *De Caelo* 1: the *aether* embodies the highest divinity. With the *Timaeus* 'myth' rejected and Aristotle's assertion of the eternity of the world, that is inevitable. No further principle is required. Sorabji (note 35 above), 126–7, took *De Caelo* to refer to 'either God or the outermost shell, or both.' Now, however (in correspondence), he advances what seems to be the correct interpretation of the passage – namely that Aristotle's discussion 'wobbles.' I would account for the wobbling chronologically.

38 For more on self-movers in general see Furley, 'Self-Movers.'

39 For counterparts generally in Aristotle see Philippe, '*Analogon* and *Analogia* in the Philosophy of Aristotle'; A.L. Peck, *De Generatione Animalium* (London/Cambridge, Mass. 1963), lxviii.

40 The Pythagoreans are also wrong about a 'counter-earth' and about the idea that fire is at the centre (*De Caelo* 2.293B).

41 The postion is that of Williams (*Aristotle's De Generatione et Corruptione*, 211), but it is also the traditional view. For bibliography of the problem see the end of Charlton's 'Prime Matter: A Rejoinder.' Charlton's own position derives from that of King, 'Aristotle without Materia Prima.' Also of great interest is Brunschwig's 'La Forme, prédicat de la matière.'

42 This dates at least part of *Topics* 6 to after about 351. See ch. 4, 79–81.

43 It would follow from this that the *honest* philosopher who took Plato literally must really believe that he means to be so taken. Aristotle took Plato literally.

44 There is a textual difficulty here, but it does not affect our argument.

45 I would argue that 2.9 is the last chapter of the original *De Generatione*. Chapter 10, dealing with unmoved movers, is outside the main subject. It is an amplification of the *Physics*, and refers to *Physics* 8. I have suggested that when Aristotle wrote *Physics* 8, he revised the rest of the *Physics*, *De Caelo*, and *De Generatione*, adding this chapter as well as the other references to the Unmoved Mover. One of the later sections of *De Generatione* would be 1.318A5ff, which appears to allude to *Phys.* 8 (258B10ff) as *On Motion*. Here we have a reference to a kind of first philosophy (i.e., metaphysics) which clearly Aristotle has not yet written but is thinking of writing. Such a programme would not be necessary until an Unmoved Mover, outside the *ouranos* or nature, had been introduced. If I am right about *De Generatione* 2.10, then the attack on the *Phaedo* would be the culmination of the original book 2. *GC* 2.9.335B9ff looks like what is to come in more detail in *Metaphysics* A.6. Interestingly, however, there is no mention of author or person in the later *Metaphysics*. Joachim (*Aristotle on Coming-to-be and Passing-away*) recog-

nized that chapter 10 presupposes the Eudoxan astronomy (253), and that chapter 11 'is to be regarded as an appendix' (270).

Chapter 11

1 *Mete.* 4 seems to be spurious, or at least much revised by someone other than Aristotle. It appears not to be referred to in any genuinely Aristotelian text. *GA* 2.743A7 is precisely not to be interpreted in the spirit of *Mete.* 4; *PA* 2.649A33, often said to refer to *Mete.* 4, refers to *GC* 2.329B22, etc. Furley, however, repeats the view that these texts suggest the authenticity of *Mete.* 4 ('The Mechanics of *Meteorologica* IV,' 73). Inauthenticity was originally argued (though often implausibly) by Hammer-Jensen, 'Das sogenannte IV Buch der *Meteorologica*'; Furley is the latest to reject her better instincts. That is not to say, however, that Strato was the author. For this and other matters see Gottschalk, 'The Authorship of *Meteorologica* Book IV.' For more doubt on the truth of the question see Strohm, 'Beobachtungen zum vierten Buch der Aristotelischen Meteorologica.'

Guthrie (*HGP* 6.227) was impressed by Gottschalk's negative verdict, and the majority view of the conference on what is authentically Aristotelian concurred with this (*Zweifelhaftes*, 'Vorwort'). Further arguments against authenticity have now been added by Solmsen ('Citations in Their Bearing').

2 The chronological problem is missed by Cooper, 'Aristotle on Natural Teleology,' 220 and by Byl, *Recherches sur les grands traités biologiques d'Aristote*, 210–37, whose excellent discussions would thus need some modification, and the final result might look a bit less 'pre-scientific.' At *HA* 5.552B10ff, fire-animals are engendered in fire. At *GA* 3.761B13, Aristotle says that we might expect fire-animals (since animals exist in air, plants in earth, etc.) but there are none, only *aether-animals* in the *aether* above the moon. This *correction* of *HA* 5 is also to be found in ps.-Aristotle, *Mete.* 4.382A7, but there the author makes another mistake. He claims that animals are *generated* in air (it would be true of hot air, i.e., *aether*), *contrary* to *GA* 3.761B14. Hence, we have further evidence against the authenticity of *Mete.* 4 and an indication that *HA* 5 (unless interpolated) pre-dates 339, the date of composition of *Mete* 1.

3 If *De Incessu* 706B2 refers, as some think, to *PA* 4.684B14ff, as well as to *HA* 4.523B21ff, it is an addition. But it almost certainly refers only to the original version in *HA*. If so, Aristotle had reached at least that stage of the *HA* by the time of the *De Incessu*, and *HA* began some time before.

4 Balme, 'The Place of Biology,' in *Philosophical Issues*, eds. Gotthelf and Lennox (Cambridge 1987), 16–18.

5 Lee, 'Place-names and the Date of Aristotle's Biological Works.' Lee's thesis is

overstated, in that he includes both Aristotelian and non-Aristotelian parts of the *HA* in his statements (see Solmsen, 'The Fishes of Lesbos and Their Alleged Significance for the Development of Aristotle'). The *Historia Animalium* should be thought of as an open-ended file, in which data could be added (or inserted). Lee argues, however, that *PA* is close in subject-matter to *Physics* 2.8–9: nature and art, final causes, Empedocles. He thinks that *PA* 1 was also written in Assos, where he plausibly assigns the beginning of the *Physics*. But there seems to be an important difference between the *Physics* and *PA* 1 over the question of Mind – in *PA* Mind is not part of the subject-matter of physics – which would suggest that *PA* is considerably *later* than most of the *Physics*, although they do indeed have much in common.

6 Read *thēlutoka* as in *GA* 4.766B29, where a reason is given: the heat is not perfected in the young. Better to wait until the 'prime,' as with Miss Jean Brodie. The old have the same problem; they are working off less 'natural heat.' For the temperature of blood see also the discussion of menses at *GA* 1.726B31ff, 4.766B17ff.

7 Doctors have discussed seasons, and physicists winds, says Aristotle (*Pol.* 7.1335A40). Cf. *GA* 4.766B35ff. Peck (*GA*, *ad loc.*) cites the Hippocratic *On Sacred Disease* 13 and *Airs Waters Places* 3 for the effects of the south wind. Generally, women in antiquity are said (from Hesiod on) to like it hot for sex, but men are less good in the Dog Days.

8 Plato's ages are sixteen to twenty for women, thirty to thirty-five for men (*Laws* 6.785B). Thus in Magnesia a couple might be only ten years apart (the woman twenty, the man thirty). But note that sexual activity *apart* from child-bearing is more severely treated than by Aristotle: such wrong-doing and ignorance are presumably what is referred to as controlled by the female inspectors (6.784C). A ten-year procreation period is allowed (6.784B). But *girls'* birthdays are to be recorded. This fits with Plato's general view that the 'best' women are male in soul. Aristotle's 'lower' view of women, tied to his estimate of non-reproductive gender difference, is probably at the root of his willingness to permit recreational sex between spouses. For Plato recreational sex (involving the issue of 'unfruitful seed,' *Laws* 8.841D) is shameful, and barely tolerated (840D–841E). The Magnesians may be corrupted by 'the so-called disorderly Aphrodite' (cf. the disorderly motions of the *Timaeus*) who is too popular among 'Greeks and barbarians.' Plato even apparently rules out sex with slave-women (8.841D) or other women of the household.

9 Balme allows that there is no place for *HA* 10 *after* GA ('Aristotle Historia Animalium Book Ten,' 191–206), but my discussion in the present chapter (223–4) will show that there is no room for an *Aristotelian* two-seed theory of this type at any time.

10 See Huby, 'Theophrastus in the Aristotelian Corpus,' 316–18.

11 See the excellent discussion on part of this by Balme, *Aristotle's De Partibus Animalium 1 and De Generatione Animalium 1.*
12 Balme (note 11 above), 123.
13 For Heraclitus cf. fr. B.96 (DK); Robertson, *PCPS* 169–71 (1938) 107 cited by Balme.
14 For the data (appearances) of physics, including both those from observation and those agreed by wise men, see Owen, 'Τιθέναι τὰ φαινόμενα.'
15 Note the back reference to the *Eudemian Ethics* (5.1139B14–1141B8). For *nous* in the *Posterior Analytics* see ch. 14, 266, 269–70.
16 Sorabji, *Time, Creation and the Continuum*, 127.
17 As by Lloyd, 'Aristotle's Theory of the Classification of Animals.'
18 Balme (note 11 above), 105–6. For further discussion see Balme, 'Aristotle's Use of Differentia in Zoology,' 195–212.
19 As Lloyd, (note 17 above), 67, observes. There is a different project in Aristotle's mind at a later stage, namely in *Metaphysics* Z.1038A11ff and *Pol.* 4.1290B20–38, which I have argued earlier (ch. 8, 161) to be a very late addition to the *Politics*, part of the revised final version which is introduced by the new *Pol.* 1. Aristotle's aim here is, perhaps, for a comprehensive classification of the animal kingdom; there will be as many species as there are combinations of necessary parts. The notion of combination (*suzeuxis*), absent in *Met.* Z, *may* indicate that *Pol.* 4 represents a substantial change.
20 Peck (*ad loc.*) refers to *De Somno* 455B34ff, where similar topics arise, but *there too* (456A2) they are said to be discussed in another work. In fact *De Somno* (speaking only of sensation and movement – not nutrition) probably refers to *De Anima* 3.433A1, where the effect of emotion in animals is located primarily in the heart (*and* – not *or*, as it is often translated – in the penis). The connection with nutrition, as in *PA*, is not explicit in our texts of Aristotle, but the *heart* is spoken of in general as an origin of the movement (affected by heat and cold) at *HA* 3.515A27–B7. For the heart see Tracy, *Physiological Theory and the Doctrine of the Mean in Plato and Aristotle*, 354–9.
21 Cf. *PA* 3.668A8–9 (and 4.689A21, 692A15–16, 695A28) which suggests that our *GA* is incomplete. Aristotle refers to the forthcoming work as *On Generation and Nutrition* at *PA* 3.674A20; it is certain that Aristotle would have wished to write on the other 'part' of the 'reproductive' faculty, that which nourishes.
22 I take the reference to *De Anima* at 474B11–12 to be a gloss by an editor (or copyist) who included *De Resp.* with the rest of the *Parva Naturalia*.
23 Cf. *PA* 3.669A2, where innate *pneuma* cools the body only in *bloodless* animals.
24 Further references to *HA* are as follows: *HA* 4.528B10ff at *PA* 4.680A2; *HA* 4.525A30–527B34 at *PA* 4.684B4–5; *HA* 1.493A24–B6 and 1.497A24 at *PA*

4.689A18; *HA* 2.504B28ff at *PA* 4.696B15. *HA* is referred to as the 'first writings' at *PA* 4.682A3 (*HA* 4.531B34).

25 For a succinct account of all this see Tracy (note 20 above), 354–9.

26 The passage has puzzled commentators who think that Aristotle is talking about *females* emitting seed (cf. *GA* 1.718A3ff). The interest of the passage is that for the first time Aristotle is concerned with the menstrual blood as a 'residue.' He is *almost* (but not yet) at the stage of his new view that it is unheated semen.

Chapter 12

1 The comparative novelty of the account of conception in *GA* is realized by Balme, 'Development of Biology in Aristotle and Theophrastus,' esp. 94–6, but (at this point in his text) no chronological conclusions are drawn, either for the biological writings or for the *Metaphysics*. Spontaneous generation is 'without seed' at Z.1032A31–2.

2 For the new theory that the seed is a 'mover', an active *dunamis*, see Peck (*GA* lii [Loeb ed.]).

3 Balme too (note 1 above, 95) regards this text as doubtful. But note that Aristotle says that females (as well as males) are produced by males. All human *forms*, that is, are due to males. All defective creatures (e.g., mules) cannot beget. That means that in so far as woman has form, she is formed by a man; in so far as she is defective, that is due to the matter (cf. Z.1032A25, 1033B33–5).

4 It might be supposed that Aristotle is thinking of both male and female genitals here, but that seems to be mistaken. For although *pneuma* is connected (in *GA*) with female sexuality, it is specifically associated not with arousal leading to female orgasm or vaginal secretions (*GA* 1.728A33ff; 2.739A33), but with menstrual blood. Aristotle believes the clitoris to be analogous to the penis in relation to sexual pleasure (*GA* 1.728A32), but he knows that female orgasm (or even arousal) is not, as is male orgasm, necessary for conception (*GA* 1.727B7). Presumably female arousal *is* also somehow associated with *pneuma*, but not in a manner sufficient to provoke Aristotle to comment. The star instance of 'pneumatic' arousal is male.

5 Aristotle gives a detailed analysis of the problem of the role of the female only at *GA* 1.726A28ff.

6 To ejaculate one must hold the breath (or not take in seawater if you are a fish), but concocting the *pneuma* and generation cannot occur simultaneously (*GA* 1.718A4). There are various storage areas which are softer (presumably because of the hollows) near the male and female pubic hair.

7 There is a further reason to date H later than the *De Anima*: the *De Anima* always speaks of the reception of intelligible *form*, never of intelligible matter;

but the intelligible matter of H.1045A34 should also be 'received' (cf. Z.1036A3, 10–12, 1037A5 [the matter of mathematical circles is intelligible]). Indeed Aristotle is only prepared to be specific about intelligible matter in Z and H, though he appears to allude to it at E.1026A8ff and to suggest in K that it needs study by the metaphysicians (1059B15–17). Possible development here is not considered seriously by Gaukroger, 'Aristotle on Intelligible Matter.'

There are many signs of a similarity of concern in *De Anima* 2 and *Met.* Z – not least the fact of their being rare examples of the large-scale use of *entelecheia* rather than *energeia*. Normally *entelecheia* is the less common word, but *De Anima* 2 uses it twenty-two times (as against twenty-seven for *energeia*), while *Met.* Z uses it eight times where *energeia* does not occur. Subject-matter has something to do with this, but the only more striking statistics can be found in *De Generatione et Corruptione*: four for *energeia* to eighteen, according to Blair, 'The Meaning of *Energeia*.' In particular Z is unique in the *Metaphysics* on this point; even the following H goes back to the standard pattern: eighteen for *energeia* to two for *entelecheia*. *Met.* Z.1035B14–20 and *De Anima* 2 are also both concerned (*inter alia*) with the soul as entelechy of the body, or as the 'definition in accordance with the formula.' Z and H probably follow *De Anima* 3 while looking behind the *De Anima* to Λ and Θ.

8 There is, of course, no need to refer Z.1037A11–13 to M or N (or for that matter H.1042A22); Z.14 and H.3 deal with these questions. Note also that Θ.8 refers not to Z, but, as it says, to *On Substances* (i.e., Λ.1070A36ff).

9 For the relative dating of *Met.* Θ and *NE* 2–4 see ch. 9, 187. There is not much biological (as distinct from merely physical) *dunamis* in Θ. Nor is there any use of the ethical notion, found in *NE* 2 (but not in *EE*) that we become runners by running and good men by acting well, that is, that we develop our moral capabilities which are bestowed by *nature* (1103A26) in a potential form (1103A24–1103B25). Our natural capacities (needing development) resolve the question of how we become good – the problem of Plato's *Meno* (the point is missed in Burnyeat's interesting study 'Aristotle on Learning to Be Good'). All this suggests that *NE* 2 is after Θ, and we should notice that some expansion of the traditional discussion of *dunamis* seems envisaged in Z.16 and H.5. The omission of ethical potentiality is particularly startling at Θ.1047B32ff, where the notion of exercising is used, but for learning to play the flute, not for becoming good.

10 Recent studies have shown that the alleged composition of α by Pasicles of Rhodes can be ruled out; there is no question but that the text is by Aristotle himself. See the contributions of Vuillemin-Diem, Gigon, Szlezák, and Berti in *Zweifelhäftes im Corpus Aristotelicum*. See also Owens, 'The Present Status of Alpha Elatton in the Aristotelian *Metaphysics*'; Crilly, '*The Role of Alpha Elatton in Aristotle's Metaphysics*'; Berti, 'Note sulla tradizione dei primi

due libri della *Metafisica'* (who reasonably suggests that α was inserted in the *Metaphysics* by Peripatetics in Rhodes, 37); Bernardinello, 'Gli scoli alla *Metafisica* di Aristotele.'

Connections of α with the *Protrepticus* (frs. 5, 6 Ross) are noted by Szlezák (234) and by Berti (in *Zweifelhäftes*, 279–81); Berti's acceptance of the view that the *Protrepticus* admits a 'physique au sens large' (275) is entirely in accord with my comments on the *Protrepticus* (ch. 2, 48–52), and Berti also rightly emphasizes comments linking α with the *Physics*, e.g., with 1.184A24–6 (ch. 12, 229–30).

11 See Owens (note 10 above). But Owens unnecessarily supposes this must refer to *Met.* A. But *Physics* 1 is far more concerned with Parmenides (cf. *Phys.* 1.191A24; α 993A30, 993B21).

12 Sorabji points out to me that *GC* 1.4, denying that a subject persists through a change from water to air, contradicts the (later, as I would say) *Phys.* 1.190A10–1 and *Met.* Z.1032B31.

13 There is some discussion of this connection in *Zweifelhäftes* (note 10 above).

14 Jaeger, followed by, e.g., Ross, Colle, and Oggioni, held a version of the theory in hs early *Entstehungsgeschichte*, 114–7, but gave it up. See Asclepius, *In Met.* 113.12–114.20 (Hayduck), and Alex. Aphr., *In Met.* 137.21–138.4 (Hayduck). Jaeger tried to connect α.3 with *NE* 1.1; again the *Protrepticus* is the common source, an important work for introductions to later philosophical texts.

15 This question is raised in considerably *clearer* form in B.996A22ff. Increased sophistication is noticeable in the remarks on mathematics at B.996A30ff, that it has nothing to do with good and bad.

16 Aubenque ('Sur l'inauthenticité du livre K,' 329) discusses the oddities of the notion of the matter of the mathematicians (which is replaced in Z and H).

17 E.1.1026A18–20 makes reference to visible divine things which (qua divine) are the subject of theology. No reference appears here to the *particular* divine being of K. Aristotle has long since made his point. Of course E is concerned with the 'causes' of visible divine things, but the emphasis is gone.

18 Sorabji, *Necessity, Cause and Blame*, 9–10. Madigan, '*Metaphysics* E.3,' arguing that in E.3 Aristotle defers his difficulties, thinks that he must be ignorant of *Physics* 2 (where coincidences are given sophisticated treatment). But Aristotle might decline further comment in E.3 *because* he is doing metaphysics, not physics. In K Aristotle is altogether less unwilling to ramble off into physics.

19 Oggioni (*La 'filosofia prima' di Aristotele*, 9ff) underestimated the philosophical differences between K and B, Γ, E, thus enabling himself to see K as a synopsis rather than an earlier version. As an earlier version, of course, it is much more interesting; we can see Aristotle growing.

20 Décarie, 'L'authenticité du livre K,' 297, with Couloubaritsis, 316, makes some interesting points about the use of *hōsper* instead of *kathaper*, and points to a remarkably similar performance in *Phys.* 1, *Pol.* 7, and *SE. SE* is particularly interesting in this regard; it indicates a change in Aristotle's practice. If the statistics are significant, they would bring *SE* much closer than the *Topics* (in general) to *Pol.* 7 etc. – which is what we have tended to find on other grounds. Further work would be useful.

There is no need to worry (with Couloubaritsis, 316) about Aristotle's shift in K from *energeia* (1065B5) to the use of both *energeia* and *entelecheia* at 1065B15–17. In fact the latter is a very precise instance of the *distinction* between *energeia* and *entelecheia*. I would translate: 'Since in every kind of thing we distinguish the potential from the realized potential, I call motion the behaviour [activity] of the potential qua potential.' See discussion of this text in ch. 6, 119.

The remarks of Aubenque (note 16 above), 318–44, explain many of the differences of form and content between K and B, Γ, E, but Aubenque assumes that this means that the author of K is a compiler. Aubenque's observations are usually helpful but the assumption is not necessary. K can be linked with A.1–6.

21 This is realized by Décarie (note 20 above), 314.

22 Owens, *Doctrine of Being* 86, 'With E.2 commence references back to Δ.'

23 That Δ is in the way between Γ and E is realized by Aubenque (note 16 above), 319.

24 There is an interesting analogue here with Aristotle's method of discussing the best life in the more or less contemporary *NE* 10; first the best life, then that which is second-best (and is defined with reference to the best).

25 Or possibly to Δ.10. Annas, 'Aristotle, Number and Time,' suggests that discussion of time in *Physics* 4 (e.g., 221B2ff) depends upon the analysis of number in *Met.* I. Her case seems good that the ideas in *Met.* I are assumed in *Physics* 4, but that does not mean that our *Met.* I, rather than part of its content, pre-dates *Physics* 4. In fact book I presumably took a long time growing.

26 The 'biology' of I rules out a reference to Z, which might seem to be suggested by 1053B17–18.

27 The remarks about categories in Δ.5 do not fill the bill. In the *Categories* itself 6B15ff and 6B28 are probable.

28 A possible solution is that our *Categories* is not the immediate source of I, which in fact draws on a later version of this sort of material which appeared in the lost *Methodics*. Aristotle seems to have compiled the *Methodics* at about the time of the final version of the *Topics*. See ch. 4, 84–5. *Cat.*, *Post Praedicamenta*, and *De Interpretatione* could be three parts of this text, though parts of our *Cat.* are much older.

29 If I wished to speculate, I would suggest that Θ.10 (to which E.2.1026A33 would refer) is also misplaced, lying originally between Δ.12 and I. Scholars often connect Θ and I; but I am not a speculator.

30 Cf. below N.1092B33, and, for Speusippus's cosmobiology, Dillon, *The Middle Platonists*, 12–13.

31 For Xenocrates see fr. 56 Heinze; for Speusippus, Cicero, *ND* 1.32 (fr. 39 Lang), where we hear of a *vis animalis* (*dunamis pneumatikē* or *psuchikē* – which might be identical).

32 Reading *hoper hen ti* with ms. A[b] and Alexander of Aphrodisias.

33 It is a major theme of Owens's *Doctrine of Being* that Aristotle never wrote an *integrated* metaphysics of sensible substances, and that the *Metaphysics* as we have it, however arranged, is thus still incomplete. This has never won wide support, though it is much more plausible than the view of Aubenque, *Le problème de l'être chez Aristote*, that theology and 'ontology' must be kept quite distinct. For recent criticism of Owens's view see S. Mansion, *Rev. Phil. de Louvain* 78 (1980), 138–40 and Verbeke, 'L'objet de la métaphysique selon des études récentes,' 28–30. One reason for Owens's conclusion is that he fails to see the course of progression within the *Metaphysics* itself, and thus underestimates Aristotle's thesis that general metaphysics (beyond 'physics') is impossible without 'special metaphysics.' This is also the problem with views like that of Merlan, *From Platonism to Neoplatonism*, who thinks of 'metaphysics' as the study of the supra-sensible world, but underestimates the 'presence' of this world in physical objects. But the whole thrust of Aristotle's objection to Platonic metaphysics is that it fails to account for the 'metaphysical dimension' *in sensibles* as well as in supra-sensibles.

34 For a similar view see now Owens, 'Is There Any Ontology in Aristotle?' 702. Owens's remarks might cause him to reconsider his view (note 33 above) that Aristotle has not *completed* his *Metaphysics*. Note also the remarks of Kahn, 'On the Intended Interpretation,' 325.

Chapter 13

1 *De Longitudine* 464B31 indicates that Aristotle has already dealt with sleeping and waking, and that discussion of life and death is to come. Cf. 470B, where work on a further stage of biological enquiry, namely the study of plants, may be envisaged; it had already been envisaged in the days of *Mete.* 1.339A8 and was finished before *GA* 1.731A30. The ps.-Aristotelian *De Plantis* (surviving in a Latin version of an Arabic version of the Greek) offers a *different* theory of sex in plants to that of *GA*; it is often attributed to Nicolaus of Damascus. According to *GA* 1.23 (cf. 1.715B19–21) plants are bisexual, as Empedocles held; in *De Plantis* they are not, though Empedocles' (and perhaps Aristotle's)

views are known. Nicolaus's work may, however, contain Aristotelian material (as well as some from Theophrastus); see Drossaart Lulofs, 'Aristotle's Περὶ φυτῶν.'

De Sensu 436A refers to *De Anima* and looks forward to *De Memoria* (449B1ff) – the latter being an appropriate sequel. The next work (*De Somno*) refers back to *De Anima* (455A8), which, of course, sets the stage for the whole series. Note that just as Λ (with its account of pure mind) precedes Z and H in the metaphysical series, and Z precedes H, so in the psychological series the investigation of the human soul culminates in *De Anima* 3.5; after that we return to the treatment of soul-in-body; that is, a study of potentialities. As Aristotle says in *De Sensu*, at the beginning of the *Parva Naturalia*, 'The most important characteristics of animals are those *common* to soul and body (e.g. sensation, memory, passion, desire, and the appetites generally)'; that is, what is common to form and matter. It is possible that the 'Arabic' tradition (going back to Nicolaus of Damascus) is right in suggesting that Aristotle originally intended a *De Sensu et Sensibilibus* in three books: book 1 is our *De Sensu*; book 2 is *De Memoria, De Somno, De Somniis*, and *De Divinatione*; book 3 is *De Longitudine* and *De Iuventute*. See Drossaart Lulofs, *Nicolaus Damascenus on the Philosophy of Aristotle*, 25. Note that *De Somno* itself contains one block of 'earlier' material; see Lowe, 'Aristotle's *De Somno*.'

2 For discussion recently see Nussbaum, *Aristotle's De Motu Animalium*, 201–10; cf. *De Anima* 3.11.

3 *GA* 1.716A17, 2.728A13ff, 4.766A32ff. Further general comment on *pneuma* may be found in Nussbaum (note 2 above), 143–64, Peck, *GA* (Loeb ed.), esp. 576–8; and for an earlier treatment, see Jaeger, 'Das Pneuma im Lykeion'; see also Solmsen, 'The Vital Heat, the Inborn *Pneuma* and the *Aether*'; Verbeke, *L'évolution de la doctrine du pneuma*. Menstrual blood (perhaps as *pneuma*) is present in a woman's eyes during her period (*De Somniis* 459B25–460A9). It is an old idea; possibly Aristotle would have thought that semen is in the male eyes during ejaculation.

4 Cf. generally Preus, 'Science and Philosophy in Aristotle's *Generation of Animals*' and *Science and Philosophy in Aristotle's Biological Works*; Lloyd, *Science, Folklore and Ideology*, 94–105, etc. These discussions are all impaired by failure to consider the chronology of the biological works and the variations in Aristotle's theory.

5 Smith, 'Plato and Aristotle on the Nature of Women' (cf. ch. 10, note 3).

6 Cf. Rist, *Human Value*, 27–8.

7 Fortenbaugh, 'Aristotle on Slaves and Women,' 138, and Rist (note 6 above), 166.

8 Animals are declared incapable of happiness at *EE* 1.1217A24ff; cf. children at 1219B5.

9 In addition to 3.5, see *De Anima* 2.413B24ff, 2.414B18, 3.432B27–8.

Chapter 14

1 Sachs, 'Does Aristotle Have a Doctrine of Secondary Substances?'; Owens, 'Aristotle on Categories.'

2 Düring, *Aristoteles*, 59.

3 I would prefer the term 'entity' for 'substance,' following the usage of Owens, *The Doctrine of Being*, but in this case tradition is too strong to be avoided. And substance does have the necessary ambiguity: this is an interesting substance; the substance of the thing is ...

4 Frede, 'Stoic vs. Aristotelian Syllogistic,' 24.

5 Anscombe (in *Three Philosophers*, 7–8) wants to say 'second' rather than 'secondary,' but, as we have seen, this seems to be merely a way of diminishing the obvious inferiority which Aristotle attributes to secondary substances. A *deuteros plous* is not merely an alternative route from A to B, but an inferior one. The notion of secondary substance, but not the word 'secondary', seems present in *Topics* 1.103B25, 7.153A17ff and 'ultimate species' are called 'substances' at *PA* 1.644A29. But the theory in *Met.* Δ.1017B23 and Z.1037A28 is quite different. In these passages 'first substance' is the realized nature while another 'mode' of substance is the composite (i.e., the *first substance* of the *Categories*).

6 Whether 'in' a subject refers to the presence or inherence of, for example, an individual colour in each individual or more generally colour in many individuals has been much debated since the appearance of Owen's 'Inherence,' which argued for the 'general' interpretation. Against Owen see particularly Matthews and Cohen, 'The One and the Many.' Owen is defended by Frede ('Individuen bei Aristoteles,' 16–39) and both are challenged again by Heinaman, 'Non-substantial Individuals in the *Categories*.' Owen has not established his case, and perhaps both he and his critics are right. There is also the possibility that Aristotle did not see the problem at this time. If that were true, Heinaman's good evidence from later works does not necessarily help.

7 E.g., Lloyd, 'Aristotle's *Categories* Today'; Vlastos, 'The "Two-Level Paradoxes" in Aristotle,' 333 (though Vlastos thinks Aristotle confuses class-membership and class-inclusion); Düring (note 2 above), 347. See also Dancy, 'On Some of Aristotle's First Thoughts about Substances,' 347.

8 See Burnyeat, 'Aristotle on Understanding Knowledge,' 128–9, note 53.

9 For a discussion of recognition and related matters see Anscombe (note 5 above); Körner, 'Substance'; Lloyd (note 7 above).

10 So, for example, Ackrill, *Aristotle's Categories and De Interpretatione*, 83; Moravcsik, 'Aristotle on Predication,' 95 – though he hedges his bets; Stough, 'Language and Ontology in Aristotle's *Categories*,' 263.

11 Fr. 3 Ross (Alex. Aphr., *In Met.* 81.25). For Forms as concepts see also *Met.*

A.990B22–26, M.1079A19–23. For *On Ideas* recently see Leszl, *Il 'De Ideis' di Aristotele*, esp. 173–81.

12 Lacey, '*Ousia* and Form in Aristotle,' 64, uses 'refers to.' Perhaps 'signals' (or 'tags') is more effective; see Irwin, 'Aristotle's Concept of Signification,' 253.

13 *SE* 178B36–179A10; though here Aristotle does not distinguish what in the *Categories* are secondary substances from qualities. But this *argumentum ex silentio* only tells us that Aristotle does not *choose* to distinguish, not that he could not. Cf. also *SE* 169A29–37.

14 E.g., Duerlinger, 'Predication and Inherence in Aristotle's *Categories*,' 194: 'Aristotle's discussion of predication undoubtedly presupposes a Platonically inspired doctrine about intensional relations.' But Aristotle does not even use the language of participation in the *Categories* (as he does in *Topics* 5). Duerlinger's account echoes other notions of an allegedly Aristotelian concept of the 'essence' of the species. Jones ('An Introduction to the First Five Chapters of Aristotle's *Categories*,' 163) wants both a 'property' view and an 'aggregate' view of 'species.' But Aristotle's view of a 'species' is certainly not that of a mere 'aggregate.' Harter, 'Aristotle on Primary *Ousia*,' 6, speaks more ambiguously of secondary substances as 'defining the natures' of the primary substances. Aristotle does use the phrase 'common nature' (*PA* 1.644B4), but it has no existential commitment; here it refers to the largest biological classes (e.g., birds, fish, mammals).

15 Brentano, *On the Several Senses of Being in Aristotle*, 91

16 See Driscoll, 'Εἴδη in Aristotle's Earlier and Later Theories of Substance.'

17 *De Ideis ap.* Alex. Aphr. *In Met.* 81.25 (fr. 3 Ross).

18 Cf. Hadot, 'Sur divers sens du mot PRAGMA,' 312.

19 Barnes, 'Proof and the Syllogism,' 17–59, rightly argues for the integral nature of our *Analytics*. One of the few references to 'strict' syllogistic terminology outside the *Analytics* (noted by Barnes, 57, note 65) is in the *Eudemian Ethics* (5.1142B24, 1143B3), a work which right from the beginning refers regularly to the *Analytics*. My discussion in the present chapter (and see ch. 4, 86–92) assumes that our *Analytics* pre-dates the *Metaphysics*, and appeared while Aristotle was in Macedonia.

Kenny, *The Aristotelian Ethics*, 221–4, also notes the evidence that the *Eudemian Ethics* is Macedonian but misses the significance of the *Analytics* in the matter. His arguments for a Macedonian origin for the *EE* are as follows:
1) *EE* 2.1220A19, 7.1240B25. Mentions of Coriscus probably mean that the Assos period is the earliest possible.
2) 3.1229A23. The tyrannicide at Metapontum (who killed Archelaus of Heraclea) is probably Antileon (Plut., *Mor.* 760C, cf. Jacoby, *FGrH* II 298). Unfortunately Archelaus's killing is not dated, but, as Kenny says, sometime during the campaign of Timoleon (344 BC) is the most likely.

3) 7.1243B17–25. Here we have the lovers Python and Pammenes, and the harpist who quarrelled with 'the king.' Python of Byzantium was an envoy of Philip of Macedon to Athens in 343; there is no need to identify Pammenes as the well-known Theban – if you are writing in Macedonia where Python certainly and presumably Pammenes would be well-known. The 'king,' of course, is most likely King Philip or King Alexander, probably the latter. The story is told by Plutarch (*De Alex. Fortuna* 2.1) of Dionysius of Syracuse, but finding it in a work on Alexander, we can see how Plutarch confused his source.

4) 6.1150B12 (i.e., *NE* 7.1150B12). Court gossip about Xenophantus, the musician who apparently laughed at Alexander's efforts on the flute, also suggests Macedonian times. Kenny thinks the incident probably occurred during Aristotle's final period in Athens. More probably it was when Aristotle was on hand in Macedonia. Seneca (*De Ira* 22) says Xenophantus worked for Alexander. The incident is probably from the early part of his actual reign, but the latter days of Philip would do as well.

5) 2.1226A29 (cf. *Topics* 3.116A38): 'We do not deliberate about affairs in India.' Who would, in the 340s? By the time of *NE* India is not mentioned. The Spartans do not deliberate about what is best for Scythians (3.1112A28). Kenny misses the point (225).

20 See esp. ch. 5, 102–3, and Owen, 'Logic and Metaphysics in Some Early Works of Aristotle,' 165–72.

21 See above note 13.

22 Cf. 1.75A38, 76A32ff, 76B14, 87A38ff (where the first principles of the sciences have no metaphysical significance), 1.88A36–B3; cf. *Met.* Γ.1005AB for the role of the philosopher as student of 'axioms' such as the law of contradiction. In general see Owen, 'Aristotle on the Snares of Ontology,' 84, and 'Logic and Metaphysics' (176, note 20).

23 *APo.* 1.76A39. Note that in *EE* 5.1142A15ff – assuming that experience helps and makes one *sophos* in ethics rather than in metaphysics – the basic sciences are mathematics, physics, ethics: no metaphysics.

24 *APo.* (Loeb ed.), 184, note b.

25 Cf. Sorabji's penetrating 'Definitions: Why Necessary and in What Way?' esp. 222. But Sorabji is misleading (but in good company) to talk about the 'essence of kinds' in Aristotle (223). Admittedly the text he cites is from the *Topics*, where *to ti ēn einai* can perhaps be rendered 'essence', but even there not 'essence' of *kinds*, but of individuals. In *Necessity, Cause and Blame*, 190, Sorabji urges that *APo.* 1.79A28 does suggest an essence of kinds and that Aristotle oscillates on the matter. I would dismiss 79A28 as imprecision, and, as Sorabji allows, Aristotle's normal view is otherwise. The word 'essence' should be banned from translations of Aristotle outside the *Topics*. It neither

renders *ti esti*, which comes out as 'class' (or 'substance' in the sense of individual), nor *to ti ēn einai*, for this phrase deliberately points to the *existence* of the substance (of the *ti esti* = *ousia*). Such a ban would render rather irrelevant much of the discussion in White, 'The Origins of Aristotle's Essentialism,' and Kung, 'Aristotle on Essence and Explanation.'

26 Hypotheses assume existence: 1.72A21ff, cf. 1.76B4ff.

27 For *to ti ēn einai* see Owens (note 3 above) and Arpe, *Das* τὸ τί ἦν εἶναι *bei Aristoteles.*

28 The collapsing of events into 'objects' is facilitated by Aristotle's identification of verbs as nouns (*De Int.* 16B20). 'Realized nature' makes his point intelligible whereas 'essence' does not. What is the essence of an event?

29 Cf. 1.87B28ff; so too apparently in 1.71A8 the particular is self-evident (*dēlon*). On the very general nature of Aristotle's term 'induction', see von Fritz, 'Die ἐπαγωγή bei Aristoteles,' 51. See also Hamlyn, 'Aristotelian *Epagoge*'; Burnyeat, 'Aristotle on Understanding Knowledge,' 130–1.

30 See Barnes, *Aristotle's Posterior Analytics*, 40. The passage is wrongly offered by Heinaman as evidence for *in re* universals and the identity of universals and form in a review of Lloyd's *Form and Universal in Aristotle* (*CR* 32 [1982], 44–8).

31 I render *empoiei* here as 'instils', following Barnes. Tredennick (begging the question) over-translates as 'conveys'.

32 *Kritikēn* here cannot refer to the making of judgments, for all animals have it; cf. *De Anima* 3.432A15ff (where Aristotle speaks more generally of *to kritikon* as a function of both sense-preception and of the mind [*dianoia*]) and *De Insomniis* 461A1–2 (*dianoia*).

33 Note again that sense perception gives a kind of *knowledge* (*gnōsis*) of particulars.

34 Kahn, 'The Role of *Nous* in the Cognition of First Principles in *Posterior Analytics* II 19,' 402; cf. *De Anima* 3.429B11ff.

35 Kahn (note 34 above, 402) seems to think that *logos* in the text is to be identified with man's capacity to reason, but it is hard to see how a faculty can arise 'from the persistence of images.' The correct exposition is given by Lesher, 'The Meaning of ΝΟΥΣ in the *Posterior Analytics*,' esp. 68. Lesher well explains the breadth of Aristotle's use of the word *nous*.

36 That is is a *single* experience is repeated in the similar section of *Metaphysics* A.981A1ff. Aristotle continues here by explaining how from *ennoēmata* (concepts) of experience arise universal judgments (*hupolēpsis*) about like objects. The role of images in the mind is developed further in the *De Anima*: for concepts (3.432A8–14); for judgments (3.427B16); for discursive thinking (3.431A14–17). For the Platonic background of 'coming to rest' see Verbeke, 'The Aristotelian Doctrine of Qualitative Change in *Physics* VII 3,' 558–9.

37 A similar line appears in the *Eudemian Ethics* (5.1139B28); again in this section the *Eudemian Ethics* refers to the *Posterior Analytics*.

38 Fine has recently pointed to the unusualness of this phrase when it does *not* denote separate existence in the world: 'The One over Many,' 200–1, note 6.

39 But as we note (ch. 14, 261), even in *PA* 1 (after the *Analytics*) Aristotle is still prepared to call species 'substances' (1.644A29). Presumably he no longer feared to be misunderstood.

40 Cf. Sorabji (note 25 above), 196, note 54.

41 Cf. *APr.* 1.49A24 where goat-stags are known ('scientifically') qua non-being. Perhaps Platonic Forms, another kind of fantasy-object according to the *Posterior Analytics*, are a bit like goat-stags! Parallels with dreams might also be drawn (*De Insomniis*, esp. 462A30–31); dreams are *phantasmata* derived from *disturbed* sense-impressions.

42 *Met.* Δ.1017B23 and Z.1037A28 identify substances as form and as composite; Δ speaks of the two 'modes' (*tropoi*).

43 Modern studies of this part of the subject are without limit. I have particularly benefited from Albritton, 'Forms of Particular Substances in Aristotle's *Metaphysics*'; Lloyd, *Form and Universal in Aristotle*; and above all Owens (note 3 above). It is easy to get the impression that, if Owens's book had been read more carefully, much of the secondary literature after Owens's work would not have been written. Other useful comment will include Sellars, 'Substance and Form in Aristotle'; Harter, 'Aristotle on Primary *Ousia*'; Hartman, *Substance, Body and Soul: Aristotelian Investigations*; Loux, 'Form, Species and Predication in *Metaphysics* Z, H, and Θ'; Driscoll (note 16 above) – though if my approach is on the right lines Driscoll's distinction of formal causes and particular forms is expressed misleadingly (144). Driscoll has powerful arguments against the identification of primary substance as species by Owen, 'The Platonism of Aristotle,' and by Woods, 'Problems in *Metaphysics* Z, Chapter 13.' Further light has recently been shed on the whole question by Frede, 'Substance in Aristotle's *Metaphysics*.'

44 At *APo.* 1.85B24–7 Aristotle speaks of the universal being 'causative', but this implies no existence commitment for the universal as *in re*. For, as we have observed, the universal 'man' begets man, but there is no such thing as the universal 'man' (in the world). It merely 'follows' the particular (*Top.* 4.128B4; *GA* 5.768B13).

45 Lloyd (note 43 above), 31

46 The word 'unassailable' is that of Owens (review of Lloyd, in *Review of Metaphysics* 35 (1981–2), 395). In fact Owens seems to come out more strongly in favour of Lloyd's view in his review than he would have done on the basis of his own book on the *Metaphysics* (cf. pp. 391–2). Heinaman's interesting review of Lloyd (in *CR* 32, 44–8) weakens a few arguments, but leaves the structure intact. Heinaman does *not* demolish Lloyd's use of *Met.* M.1087A19–

20 (Lloyd, 24); cf. of course the famous Peleus at Λ.1071A20–9, and for Socrates as composed of this soul and this body, Z.1037A9–10 (with Z.1036B23).

47 Cf. Lloyd (note 43 above), 25 with H1044B21ff and Λ.1070A15. Here Aristotle says that universals do not exist, that is 'in the world' as distinct from the mind.

48 On the way in which we speak of the identity of a particular and its realized nature see Z.1032A3ff, H.1043B2–5.

49 See Owens (note 3 above), 367–74. On the distinction of forms and universals see Z.1037A10–11 and especially Λ.1071A20–9. Universals are *eidē noēta,* i.e., forms identified as thoughts or concepts (*noēmata*); cf. *De Anima* 3.432A1–11, where intelligible forms are 'in' sensible forms. *Phantasmata* are the *aisthēmata* 'viewed' without the 'matter'. Cf. *De Anima* 2.417B23–4: universals are 'somehow' in the soul. Hughes ('Universals,' in *Notes on Z,* recorded by Burnyeat and others) raises the interesting question as to whether universals (e.g., 'man') are the names of potentialities. Thus the potentiality 'man' is actualized in Achilles. The objection to this would seem to be: (a) that it has to be *read* into the text rather than found in it, for Aristotle does not introduce the concept of potentiality into his comments on these questions; and (b) that whereas the 'potential house' *is* bricks and mortar, the potential Achilles is not 'man', but (perhaps) the seed of Peleus. Nevertheless there are points of contact between Hughes's view and my own.

50 Definition is not of *this* circle, but we recognize individuals by *noēsis* and *aisthēsis* (Z.1036A5ff). Z.1039B28–9 states that definition is not possible of individual substances because they contain matter which has the possibility of non-existence. We saw in the *Posterior Analytics* that definition has to be of *existents.* We must answer 'Do they exist?' questions before proceeding to definitions. Aristotle alludes to his treatment of definition in the *Analytics* at Z.1037B9. Even supposedly unique individuals (such as the sun and moon) are only 'definable' as single members of a kind (Z.1040A29ff).

51 Kahn (note 34 above), 409; cf. *De Caelo* 3.299A17; *APo.* 1.87A35; *Met.* K.1061A28. Of course the medievals who use 'abstraction' in a wider sense may not always be very different in *spirit* from Aristotle; see Leszl, 'Mathematics, Axiomatization and the Hypotheses,' 326.

52 For the history of the problem of general and special metaphysics, see the masterly survey of Owens (note 3 above), 1–68. Interestingly a total identity between the study of being qua being and a study of separate transcendent substance is discovered in the Greek commentators by Kremer, *Der Metaphysikbegriff in den Aristoteles-Kommentaren der Ammonius-Schule.* Verbeke, 'Aristotle's *Metaphysics* Viewed by the Ancient Greek Commentators,' 107–27, reads the evidence slightly differently. While agreeing that

many Greek commentators simply *identify* metaphysics (the study of being qua being) with theology, the study of the highest substance, he finds them involving 'physical things' in metaphysics indirectly. This is what we should expect, since many of the commentators were Neoplatonists, as Verbeke sees (126). But it is interesting to see 'Neoplatonizing' accounts of the relation of sensible to non-sensible substances even in Themistius and Alexander. Alexander used focal meaning (*In Met* 643.3), but 'Neoplatonically'.

53 See Owens (note 3 above); Owen, esp. 'Logic and Metaphysics'; Patzig, 'Theology and Ontology in Aristotle's *Metaphysics*.'

54 Owen (note 53 above), 17; *Met.* Γ.1003A33–4; cf. *Met.* E.1026A29ff, where we find the notion of a first philosophy which studies unmoved substance (if there is any), and being qua being and its essential attributes; cf. *Met.* K.1064B12–14, where the study prior to physics is not only of substance which is *chōristos* (separate – the adjective could refer to particulars seen as indivisible specifically), but also of unmoved substance.

55 Owen also seems correct in claiming that focal meaning was not developed – at least in Aristotle's view – effectively enough by members of the Academy to deal with problems like the 'Third Man' (note 53 above, 29–31). Berti, 'Multiplicité et unité du Bien selon *EE* 1 8,' tries to dispute Owen's claim that focal meaning is absent from the discussion of good in *EE* 1, but seems to me to provide no evidence, tending rather (at 180–1) to read the *NE* back into the *EE*.

56 Owen (note 53 above), 24–5.

57 Cf. Λ.1070B17–21. Owens (note 3 above), 125 recognizes that *pros hen* equivocals are not 'analogies', despite Scholastic assimilation, but he does not deal with Owen's substantive claims about the different books of the *Metaphysics*.

58 Hamlyn, 'Focal Meaning,' thinks of 'focal meaning' as *simply* about meaning. This is unaristotelian, as we argue below. See also Irwin, 'Homonymy in Aristotle,' 531, note 12; and Rutten, 'L'analogie chez Aristote,' on analogy and focal meaning. For analogy see especially Philippe, 'Analogon and Analogia in the Philosophy of Aristotle.' For more general problems see Matthews, 'Senses and Kinds.'

59 See Heinaman (note 46 above), 47–8.

60 Similar problems are raised by Aubenque, *Le problème de l'être*, 410.

SELECT BIBLIOGRAPHY

The bibliography contains full details of secondary literature referred to in the text and notes, as well as a selection of those other (especially more recent) writings which I have found particularly helpful in thinking about Aristotle. Normally, standard editions, commentaries, and general books on Aristotle are not included.

Collections

1 *Symposia Aristotelica*

Aristotle and Plato in the Mid-Fourth Century, edited by I. Düring and G.E.L. Owen. Göteborg 1960

Aristote et les problèmes de méthode, edited by S. Mansion. Louvain 1961

Aristotle on Dialectic: The Topics, edited by G.E.L. Owen. Oxford 1968

Naturphilosophie bei Aristoteles und Theophrast, edited by I. Düring. Heidelberg 1969

Untersuchungen zur Eudemischen Ethik, edited by P. Moraux and D. Harlfinger. Berlin 1971

Etudes sur la Métaphysique d'Aristote, edited by P. Aubenque. Paris 1979

Aristotle on Mind and the Senses, edited by G.E.R. Lloyd and G.E.L. Owen. Cambridge 1978

Aristotle on Science: 'The Posterior Analytics', edited by E. Berti. Padova 1981

Zweifelhäftes im Corpus Aristotelicum, edited by P. Moraux and J. Wiesner. Berlin/New York 1983

2 *Other Collections on Aristotle*

Aristotle, edited by J.M.E. Moravcsik. New York 1967

Aristotle on Nature and Living Things: Philosophical and Historical Studies, edited by A. Gotthelf. Pittsburgh/Bristol 1985
Aristoteles: Werk und Wirkung I, edited by J. Wiesner. Berlin/New York 1985
Articles on Aristotle, (4 vols.), edited by J. Barnes, M. Schofield, and R. Sorabji. London 1975–9
Aristotle: The Collected Papers of J. Owens, edited by J.R. Catan. Albany 1981
Autour d'Aristote: Festschrift for A. Mansion. Louvain 1955
Essays on Aristotle's Ethics, edited by A. Rorty. Berkeley/Los Angeles/London 1980
New Essays on Plato and Aristotle, edited by R. Bambrough. London 1965
Paideia: Special Aristotle Number. Brockport 1978
Philosophical Issues in Aristotle's Biology, edited by A. Gotthelf and J.G. Lennox. Cambridge 1987
Schriften zu den Politika des Aristoteles, edited by P. Steinmetz. Hildesheim 1973
Studies in Aristotle, edited by D.J. O'Meara. Washington 1981

Other Studies

Ackrill, J.L. *Aristotle's Categories and De Interpretatione*. Oxford 1963
– 'Aristotle's Distinction between ENERGEIA and KINESIS,' in *New Essays* (ed. Bambrough) 121–41
– 'Aristotle on Eudaimonia,' *PBA* 60 (1974) 339–59 (= *Essays on Aristotle's Ethics* [ed. Rorty] 15–34)
Allan, D.J. 'Aristotle's Account of the Origin of Moral Principles,' *Actes du XIe Congrès Internationale de Philosophie*, 12 (1953) 120–7 (= *Articles on Aristotle* 2 [ed. Barnes, Schofield, Sorabji] 72–8)
– '*Magna Moralia* and *Nicomachean Ethics*,' *JHS* 77 (1957) 7–11
– 'Quasi-mathematical Method in the *Eudemian Ethics*,' in *Aristote et les problèmes de méthode* (ed. Mansion) 303–18
Albritton, R. 'Forms of Particular Substances in Aristotle's *Metaphysics*,' *JP*. 54 (1957) 699–708
Allen, R.E., ed. *Studies in Plato's Metaphysics*. London 1965
Annas, J. 'Forms and First Principles,' *Phronesis* 19 (1974) 257–83
– 'On the Intermediates,' *AJP* 57 (1975) 146–66
– 'Aristotle, Number and Time,' *PQ* 25 (1975) 97–113
– *Aristotle's Metaphysics, Books* M *and* N. Oxford 1976
Anscombe, G.E.M., and P. Geach. *Three Philosophers*. Oxford 1961
Arnim, H. von. *Die Entstehung der Gotteslehre des Aristoteles*. Vienna 1931
Arpe, C. *Das τὸ τί ἦν εἶναι bei Aristoteles*. Hamburg 1937
Aubenque, P. *Le problème de l'être chez Aristote, essai sur la problématique aristotélicienne*. Paris 1962

– 'Sur l'inauthenticité du livre K de la *Métaphysique*,' in *Zweifelhäftes* (ed. Moraux and Wiesner) 318–44

Balme, D.M. 'Aristotle's Use of Differentia in Zoology,' in *Aristote et les problèmes* (ed. Mansion) 195–212

– 'Development of Biology in Aristotle and Theophrastus; Theory of Spontaneous Generation,' *Phronesis* 7 (1962) 91–104

– *Aristotle's Use of Teleological Explanation*. Inaugural Lecture, University of London 1965

– *Aristotle's De Partibus Animalium 1 and De Generatione Animalium 1*. Oxford 1972

– 'Aristotle's Biology Was Not Essentialist,' *AGP* 62 (1980) 1–12

– 'Aristotle Historia Animalium, Book Ten,' in *Aristoteles: Werk und Wirküng* (ed. Wiesner) 191–206

Barbotin, E. *La théorie aristotélicienne de l'intellect d'après Théophraste*. Louvain 1954

Barker, E. *The Political Thought of Plato and Aristotle*. London 1906

Barnes, J. 'Aristotle's Theory of Demonstration,' *Phronesis* 14 (1969) 123–52 (revised in *Articles on Aristotle* 1 [ed. Barnes, Schofield, Sorabji], 65–87)

– *Aristotle's Posterior Analytics*. Oxford 1975

– 'Proof and the Syllogism', in *Aristotle on Science* (ed. Berti) 17–59

Benveniste, E. *Problèmes de linguistique générale*. Paris 1966

Bernardinello, S. 'Gli scoli alla *Metafisica* di Aristotele nel foglio 234^r del Par. Gr. 1853 (E),' *Elenchos* 3 (1982) 39–54

Bernays, J. *Zwei Abhandlungen über die aristotelische Theorie des Dramas*. Berlin 1880

Berti, E. *La filosofia del primo Aristotele*. Padova 1962.

– 'Multiplicité et unité du Bien selon *E.E.* 1 8,' in *Untersuchungen* (ed. Moraux and Harlfinger) 157–84

– *Studi Aristotelici*. L'Aquila 1975

– 'Note sulla tradizione dei primi due libri della *Metafisica* di Aristotele,' *Elenchos* 3 (1982) 5–37

– 'La fonction de Métaph. Alpha Elatton dans la philosophie d'Aristote,' in *Zweifelhäftes* (ed. Moraux and Wiesner) 260–94

Blair, G.A. 'The Meaning of *Energeia* and *Entelecheia* in Aristotle,' *IPQ* 7 (1967) 101–17

Block, I. 'The Order of Aristotle's Psychological Writings,' *AJP* 82 (1961) 50–77

Brentano, F. *Von der mannigfachen Bedeutung des Seienden nach Aristoteles*. Mainz 1862. English trans. by R. George, *On the Several Senses of Being in Aristotle*. Berkeley 1975

– *Die Psychologie des Aristoteles inbesonders seine Lehre vom* ΝΟΥΣ ΠΟΙΗ-

ΤΙΚΟΣ. Mainz 1867. English trans. by R. George, *The Psychology of Aristotle*. Berkeley 1977)
Brinkmann, A. 'Ein Brief Platons,' *Rh. Mus.* 66 (1911) 226–30
Brisson, L. *Le même et l'autre dans la structure ontologique du Timée de Platon*. Paris 1974
Brown, T.S. 'Callisthenes and Alexander,' *AJP* 70 (1949) 225–48
Brunschwig, J. 'L'Ethique à Eudème 1.8 1218A15–32 et le ΠΕΡΙ ΤΑΓΑΘΟΥ,' in *Untersuchungen* (ed. Moraux and Harlfinger) 197–222
– 'La Forme, prédicat de la matière,' in *Etudes sur la Métaphysique* (ed. Aubenque) 131–66
– 'L'Objet et la structure des Seconds Analytiques d'après Aristote,' in *Aristotle on Science* (ed. Berti) 61–96
Burnet, J. *Greek Philosophy: Thales to Plato*. London 1924
Burnyeat, M. 'Aristotle on Learning to Be Good,' in *Essays on Aristotle's Ethics* (ed. Rorty) 69–92
– 'Aristotle on Understanding Knowledge,' in *Aristotle on Science* (ed. Berti) 97–139
Burnyeat, M., and others. *Notes on Book Z of Aristotle's Metaphysics*. Sub-faculty of Philosophy, Oxford 1979
– *Notes on Eta and Theta of Aristotle's Metaphysics*. Sub-faculty of Philosophy, Oxford 1984
Byl, S. *Recherches sur les grands traités biologiques d'Aristote*. Brussels 1975
Bywater, I. 'On a Lost Dialogue of Aristotle,' *JP* 2 (1869) 55–69
Capps, E. 'Chronological Studies in the Greek Tragedians and Comic Poets,' *AJP* 21 (1900) 38–61
Case, T. 'The Development of Aristotle,' *Mind* 34 (1925) 80–6
Charlton, W. *Aristotle's Physics, Books I and II*. Oxford 1970
– 'Prime Matter: A Rejoinder,' *Phronesis* 28 (1983) 197–211
Cherniss, H. 'The Philosophical Economy of the Theory of Forms,' *AJP* 57 (1936) 445–56
– *Aristotle's Criticism of Plato and the Academy*. Baltimore 1944
– 'The Relation of the *Timaeus* to Plato's Later Dialogues,' *AJP* 78 (1957) 225–66
Clark, S.R.L. *Aristotle's Man*. Oxford 1975
Code, A. 'The Persistence of Aristotelian Matter,' *Phil. Studies* 29 (1976) 357–67
– 'On the Origins of some Aristotelian Theses about Predication,' in *How Things Are*, ed. J. Bogen and J.E. McGuire, 101–31. Dordrecht 1985
Colli, G. *Aristotele: Organon*. Torino 1955.
Cooper, J.M. 'The *Magna Moralia* and Aristotle's Moral Philosophy,' *AJP* 94 (1973) 327–49
– *Reason and Human Good in Aristotle*. Cambridge, Mass. 1975
– 'Aristotle on the Forms of Friendship,' *Rev. Met.* 30 (1977) 619–48
– 'Aristotle on Natural Teleology,' in *Language and Logos: Studies in Ancient*

Philosophy Presented to G.E.L. Owen, ed. M. Schofield and M. Nussbaum, 197–222. Cambridge 1982

Cope, E.M. *The Rhetoric of Aristotle*. Cambridge 1877, reprint New York 1977

Cornford, F. M. *Plato's Cosmology*. London 1937.

Corte, M. de. *La doctrine de l'intelligence chez Aristote*. Paris 1934

Crilly, W.H. 'The Role of Alpha Elatton in Aristotle's Metaphysics.' Thesis, Fribourg 1962

Dancy, R. 'On Some of Aristotle's First Thoughts about Substance,' *PR* 84 (1975) 338–73

– 'On Some of Aristotle's Second Thoughts about Substance,' *PR* 87 (1978) 372–413

– 'Predication and Immanence, Anaxagoras, Plato, Eudoxus, and Aristotle' (*SAGP*. 1984) 1–44

Décarie, V. *L'objet de la métaphysique selon Aristote*. Paris 1961

– 'L'authenticité du livre K de la Métaphysique,' in *Zweifelhäftes* (ed. Moraux and Wiesner) 295–315

Devereux, D.T. 'Aristotle on the Active and Contemplative Lives,' *Phil. Research Archives* 3 (1977)

– 'Aristotle on the Essence of Happiness,' in *Studies in Aristotle* (ed. O'Meara) 247–60

Dillon, J.M. *The Middle Platonists*. London/Ithaca 1977

Dirlmeier, F. 'Merkwürdige Zitate in der Eudemischen Ethik des Aristoteles,' *SB* Heidelberg 1962

Dodds, E.R., and others. *Les sources de Plotin*. Geneva 1960.

Driscoll, J.A. 'Εἴδη in Aristotle's Earlier and Later Theories of Substance,' in *Studies in Aristotle* (ed. O'Meara) 129–59

Drossaart Lulofs, H.J. 'Aristotle's Περὶ φυτῶν,' *JHS* 77 (1957) 75–80

– *Nicolaus Damascenus on the Philosophy of Aristotle*. Leiden 1965

Duerlinger, J. 'Συλλογισμός and συλλογίζεσθαι in Aristotle's Organon,' *AJP* 90 (1969) 320–8

– 'Predication and Inherence in Aristotle's *Categories*,' *Phronesis* 15 (1970) 179–203

Dumoulin, B. 'Sur l'authenticité des *Catégories* d'Aristote,' in *Concepts et catégories chez la pensée ancienne*, ed. P. Aubenque, 23–32. Paris 1980

– 'L'ousia dans les *Catégories* et dans la *Metaphysique*,' in *Zweifelhäftes* (ed. Moraux and Wiesner) 57–72

Dupréel, E. 'Aristotle et le traité des Catégories,' *AGP* 22 (1909) 230–51

Düring, I. 'Aristotle and Plato in the Mid-Fourth Century,' *Eranos* 54 (1956) 109–20

– *Aristotle in the Ancient Biographical Tradition*. Göteborg 1957

– *Aristotle's Protrepticus: An Attempt at Reconstruction*. Göteborg 1961

– 'Did Aristotle Ever Accept Plato's Theory of Transcendent Ideas?' *AGP* 48 (1966) 312–16

– *Aristoteles*. Heidelberg 1966

– 'Aristotle's Use of Examples in the *Topics*,' in *Aristotle on Dialectic* (ed. Owen) 202–29
Easterling, H.J. 'The Unmoved Mover in Early Aristotle,' *Phronesis* 21 (1976) 252–65
Edel, A. 'Aristotle's Categories and the Nature of Categorial Theory,' *Rev. Met.* 29 (1975) 45–65
Edelstein, L. *Plato's Seventh Letter*. Leiden 1966
Einarson, B. 'Aristotle's *Protrepticus* and the Structure of the *Epinomis*,' *TAPA* 67 (1936) 261–85
Evans, J.D.G. *Aristotle's Concept of Dialectic*. Cambridge 1977
Field, G.C. *Plato and His Contemporaries*. London 1930
Fine, G. 'The One over Many,' *PR* 89 (1980) 197–240
– 'Owen, Aristotle and the Third Man,' *Phronesis* 27 (1982) 82–9
– 'Aristotle and the More Accurate Arguments,' in *Language and Logos: Studies in Ancient Greek Philosophy*, ed. M. Schofield and M. Nussbaum, 155–77. Cambridge 1982
– 'Owen's Progress: A Critical Notice of *Logic, Science and Dialectic*,' *PR* 97 (1988) 373–99
Fortenbaugh, W.W. 'Aristotle's *Rhetoric* on Emotion,' *AGP* 52 (1970) 45–53
– *Aristotle on Emotion*. London 1975
– 'Aristotle's Analysis of Friendship: Function and Analogy, Resemblance and Focal Meaning,' *Phronesis* 20 (1975) 51–62
– 'Aristotle on Slaves and Women,' in *Articles on Aristotle* 2 (ed. Barnes, Schofield, Sorabji) 135–9
Fragstein, A. von. *Studien zur Ethik des Aristoteles*. Amsterdam 1974
Frede, D. 'Theophrasts Kritik am unbewegten Beweger des Aristoteles,' *Phronesis* 16 (1971) 65–79
Frede, M. 'Stoic vs. Aristotelian Syllogistic,' *AGP* 56 (1974) 1–32
– 'Individuen bei Aristoteles,' *Antike und Abendland* 24 (1978) 16–39
– 'Titel, Einheit und Echtheit der aristotelischen Kategorienschrift,' in *Zweifelhäftes* (ed. Moraux and Wiesner) 1–29
– 'Categories in Aristotle,' in *Studies in Aristotle* (ed. O'Meara) 1–24
– 'Substance in Aristotle's *Metaphysics*,' in *Aristotle on Nature* (ed. Gotthelf) 17–26
Fritz, K. von. 'Die ἐπαγωγή bei Aristoteles,' *SB Bay. Akad.* (Munich 1964) 3
Fritz, K. von, and E. Kapp. *Aristotle's Constitution of Athens and Related Texts*. New York 1950
– 'The Development of Aristotle's Political Philosophy and the Concept of Nature,' in *Articles on Aristotle* 2 (ed. Barnes, Schofield, Sorabji) 113–34
Furley, D.J. 'Aristotle on the Voluntary,' in *Articles on Aristotle* 2 (ed. Barnes, Schofield, Sorabji) 47–60
– 'Self-Movers,' in *Aristotle on Mind* (ed. Lloyd and Owen) 165–79

– 'The Mechanics of *Meteorologica* IV: A Prolegomenon to Biology,' in *Zweifelhäftes* (ed. Moraux and Wiesner) 73–93

Gaukroger, S. 'Aristotle on Intelligible Matter,' *Phronesis* 25 (1980) 187–97

Gigon, O. 'Prolegomena to an Edition of the *Eudemus*,' in *Aristotle and Plato* (ed. Düring and Owen) 19–33

– 'Versuch einer Interpretation von *Metaphysik* Alpha Elatton,' in *Zweifelhäftes* (ed. Moraux and Wiesner) 193–220.

Gill, M.L. 'Aristotle's Theory of Causal Action in *Physics* III 3,' *Phronesis* 25 (1980) 129–47

Gillespie, C.M. 'The Aristotelian Categories,' *CQ* 19 (1925), 75–84 (= *Articles on Aristotle* 3 [ed. Barnes, Schofield, Sorabji], 1–12)

Gohlke, P. *Die Entstehung der aristotelischen Logik*. Berlin 1936

Gosling, J.C.B. *Plato: Philebus*. Oxford 1975

Gotthelf, A. 'Aristotle's Conception of Final Causality,' *Rev. Met.* 30 (1976) 226–54

Gottschalk, H.B. 'The Authorship of *Meteorologica* Book IV,' *CQ* 11 (1961) 67–79

– 'Soul as Harmonia,' *Phronesis* 16 (1971) 179–98

Gould, J. 'Laws, Custom and Myth: Aspects of the Social Position of Women,' *JHS* 100 (1980) 38–59

Graeser, A. 'Aristoteles' Schrift *Über die Philosophie* und die zweifache Bedeutung der *causa finalis*,' *Mus. Helv.* 29 (1972) 44–61

Grimaldi, W.M.A. *Studies in the Philosophy of Aristotle's Rhetoric*. Wiesbaden 1972

Grube, G.M.A. *Plato's Thought*. Boston 1958

Guthrie, W.K.C. 'The Development of Aristotle's Theology,' *CQ* 27 (1933) 162–71 and *CQ* 28 (1934) 90–9

– *A History of Greek Philosophy* (abbrev. as *HGP*), vols. 5 and 6. Cambridge 1978 and 1981

Hackforth, R. 'Plato's Theism,' *CQ* 30 (1936) 4–9 (= *Studies in Plato's Metaphysics*, ed. R.E. Allen [London 1965] 439–47)

Hadot, P. 'Sur divers sens du mot PRAGMA dans la tradition philosophique grecque,' in *Concepts et Catégories dans la pensée antique*, ed. P. Aubenque, 309–20. Paris 1980

Hagen, C.T. 'The Energeia-Kinēsis Distinction and Aristotle's Conception of Praxis,' *JHP* 22 (1984) 263–80

Hahm, D.E. *The Origins of Stoic Cosmology*. Columbus, Ohio 1977

– 'The Fifth Element in Aristotle's *De Philosophia*,' *JHS* 102 (1982) 61–74

Hamlyn, D.W. 'Aristotelian Epagōge,' *Phronesis* 21 (1976) 167–84

– 'Focal Meaning,' *PAS* 78 (1978) 1–18

Hammer-Jensen, I. 'Das sogenannte IV Buch der *Meteorologica* des Aristoteles,' *Hermes* 1 (1915) 113–36

Happ, H. *Hyle. Studien zum aristotelischen Materie-Begriff*. Berlin 1971

Hardie, W.F.R. 'Aristotle's Treatment of the Relation between the Soul and the Body,' *PQ* 14 (1964) 53–72
– 'The Final Good in Aristotle's Ethics,' *Philosophy* 40 (1965) 277–95 (= *Aristotle* [ed. Moravcsik] 297–322)
– *Aristotle's Ethical Theory*. Oxford 1968
– 'Aristotle on the Best Life for a Man,' *Philosophy* 54 (1979) 35–50
Harter, E.D. 'Aristotle on Primary *Ousia*,' *AGP* 17 (1975) 1–20
Hartman, E. *Substance, Body and Soul: Aristotelian Investigations*. Princeton 1977
Harvey, A.E. 'The Classification of Greek Lyric Poetry,' *CQ* 5 (1955) 156–75
Heinaman, R. 'Non-Substantial Individuals in the *Categories*,' *Phronesis* 26 (1981) 295–307
– Review of A.C. Lloyd, *Form and Universal* in *CR* 32 (1982) 44–8
Hintikka, J. 'On the Ingredients of an Aristotelian Science,' *Nous* 6 (1972) 55–69
– *Time and Necessity: Studies in Aristotle's Theory of Modality*. Oxford 1973
Huby, P. 'The Date of Aristotle's *Topics*, and Its Treatment of the Theory of Ideas,' *CQ* 12 (1962) 72–80
– 'Theophrastus in the Aristotelian Corpus, with Particular Reference to Biological Problems,' in *Aristotle on Nature* (ed. Gotthelf) 314–25
Hughes, G.J. 'Universals as Potential Substances,' in *Notes on Book* Z (ed. Burnyeat) 107–26
Husik, I. 'The Categories of Aristotle,' in *Philosophical Essays*, 96–112. Oxford 1952
Irwin, T.H. 'Homonymy in Aristotle,' *Rev. Met.* 34 (1980–1) 523–44
– 'Aristotle's Concept of Signification,' in *Language and Logos*, ed. M. Schofield and M. Nussbaum, 241–66. Cambridge 1982
Isnardi Parente, M. 'Le ΠΕΡΙ ΙΔΕΩΝ d'Aristote: Platon ou Xénocrate?' *Phronesis* 26 (1981) 135–52
Jaeger, W. *Entstehungsgeschichte der Metaphysik des Aristoteles*. Berlin 1912
– 'Das Pneuma im Lykeion,' *Hermes* 48 (1913) 29–74 (= *Scripta Minora* [Rome 1960] 57–102)
– *Aristoteles: Grundlegung einer Geschichte seiner Entwicklung*, Berlin 1923. English trans. by R. Robinson, *Aristotle: Fundamentals of the History of His Development*. Oxford[2] 1948. All references are to the English text.
Joachim, H.H. *Aristotle on Coming-to-be and Passing-away*. Oxford 1922
Jones, B. 'An Introduction to the First Five Chapters of Aristotle's *Categories*,' *Phronesis* 20 (1975) 146–72
Kahn, C. H. *The Greek Verb 'to Be' and the Concept of Being*. Dordrecht 1966
– 'Sensation and Consciousness in Aristotle's Psychology,' *AGP* 48 (1966) 43–81 (= *Articles on Aristotle* 4 [ed. Barnes, Schofield, Sorabji] 1–31)
– 'Questions and Categories,' in *Questions*, ed. H. Hiz, 227–78. Dordrecht 1978

– 'The Role of *Nous* in the Cognition of First Principles in *Posterior Analytics* II 19,' in *Aristotle on Science* (ed. Berti) 385–414
– 'The Place of the Prime Mover in Aristotle's Teleology,' in *Aristotle on Nature* (ed. Gotthelf) 183–205
– 'On the Intended Interpretation of Aristotle's *Metaphysics*,' in *Aristoteles: Werk und Wirkung* (ed. Wiesner) 311–38
Kennedy, G. *The Art of Persuasion in Greece*. Princeton 1963
Kenny, A. *The Aristotelian Ethics*. Oxford 1978
– *Aristotle's Theory of the Will*. London 1979
Keyt, D. 'Intellectualism in Aristotle,' in *Studies in Ancient Greek Philosophy* 2, ed. J.P. Anton and A. Preus. Albany 1983
King, H.R. 'Aristotle without Materia Prima,' *JHI* 17 (1956) 370–89
Kirwan, C. *Aristotle's Metaphysics Books* Γ, Δ, E. Oxford 1971
Kneale, W. and M. *The Development of Logic*. Oxford 1962
Körner, S. 'Substance,' *PAS* Supp. 38 (1964) 79–90
Kosman, L.A. 'Aristotle's Definition of Motion,' *Phronesis* 14 (1969) 40–62
Kremer, K. *Der Metaphysikbegriff in den Aristoteles-Kommentaren der Ammonius-Schule*. Münster 1961
Kullmann, W. 'Der Mensch als Politisches Lebewesen bei Aristoteles,' *Hermes* 108 (1980) 419–43
– 'Different Concepts of the Final Cause in Aristotle,' in *Aristotle on Nature* (ed. Gotthelf) 169–76
Kung, J. 'Aristotle on Essence and Explanation,' *Phil. Stud.* 31 (1977) 361–83
– 'Aristotle on Thises, Suches and the Third Man Argument,' *Phronesis* 26 (1981) 207–47
Lacey, A.R. '*Ousia* and Form in Aristotle,' *Phronesis* 10 (1965) 54–69
Landor, B. 'The Ei esti-Ti esti Distinction in Aristotle's Theory of Science.' PhD thesis, University of Toronto 1980
Lasserre, F. *Die Fragmente des Eudoxus von Knidos*. Berlin 1966
Lear, J. 'Aristotle's Philosophy of Mathematics,' *PR* 91 (1982) 161–92
Lee, E.N. 'On the Metaphysics of the Image in Plato's *Timaeus*,' *Monist* 50 (1966) 341–68
Lee, H.D.P. 'Place-names and the Date of Aristotle's Biological Works,' *CQ* 42 (1948) 61–7
Lefèvre, C. *Sur l'évolution d'Aristote en psychologie*. Louvain 1972
– 'Sur le statut de l'âme dans le *De Anima* et les *Parva Naturalia*,' in *Aristotle on Mind* (ed. Lloyd and Owen) 21–68
Lesher, J.H. 'Aristotle on Form, Substance and Universals: A Dilemma,' *Phronesis* 16 (1971) 169–78
– 'The Meaning of ΝΟΥΣ in the *Posterior Analytics*,' *Phronesis* 18 (1973) 44–68
Leszl, W. *Il 'De Ideis' di Aristotele e la teoria platonica delle idee*. Florence 1975

– *Aristotle's Conception of Ontology*. Padova 1975.
– 'Mathematics, Axiomatization and the Hypotheses,' in *Aristotle on Science* (ed. Berti) 271–328
Lloyd, A.C. 'Aristotle's Categories Today,' *PQ* 16 (1966) 258–67
– *Form and Universal in Aristotle*. Liverpool 1981
Lloyd, G.E.R. 'Aristotle's Theory of the Classification of Animals,' *Phronesis* 6 (1961) 59–81
– *Science, Folklore and Ideology*. Cambridge 1983
Loux, M.J. 'Form, Species and Predication in *Metaphysics* Z, H and Θ,' *Mind* 88 (1975) 1–23
Lowe, M. 'Aristotle's *De Somno* and His Theory of Causes,' *Phronesis* 23 (1978) 279–91
Lucas, D.W. *Aristotle: Poetics*. Oxford 1968
Lynch, J.P. *Aristotle's School*. Berkeley 1972
Madigan, A. '*Metaphysics* E.3: A Modest Proposal,' *Phronesis* 29 (1984) 123–36
Maier, H. *Die Syllogistik des Aristoteles*. Tübingen 1900
Malcolm, J. 'On the Generation and Corruption of the *Categories*,' *Rev. Met.* 34 (1980) 662–81
Mansion, A. *Introduction à la physique aristotélicienne*. Louvain 1945
Mansion, S. 'La première doctrine de la substance: la substance selon Aristote,' *Rev. Phil. de Louvain* 44 (1946) 349–69
– 'La doctrine aristotélicienne de la substance et le Traité des Catégories,' *Library of the Tenth International Congress of Philosophy* (Amsterdam 1949) vol. 1, 1097–1100
– 'La critique de la théorie des idées dans le περὶ ἰδεῶν d'Aristote,' *Rev. Phil. de Louvain* 47 (1949) 169–202
– 'Notes sur la doctrine des catégories dans les *Topiques*,' in *Aristotle on Dialectic* (ed. Owen) 189–201
– *Le jugement d'existence chez Aristote*.[2] (Paris 1976)
– Review of J. Owens, *The Doctrine of Being*[3] in *Rev. Phil. de Louvain* 78 (1980) 138–40
Matthews, G.B. 'Senses and Kinds,' *JP* 69 (1972) 149–57
– 'Accidental Unities,' in *Language and Logos*, ed. M. Nussbaum and M. Schofield, 223–40. Cambridge 1982
Matthews, G.B., and S.M. Cohen. 'The One and the Many,' *Rev. Met.* 21 (1967–8) 630–55
Merlan, P. 'Aristotle's Unmoved Movers,' *Traditio* 4 (1946) 1–30
– From *Platonism to Neoplatonism*.[2] The Hague 1960
– *Studies in Epicurus and Aristotle*. Wiesbaden 1960
Mignucci, M. 'Ὡς ἐπὶ τὸ πολύ et nécessaire dans la conception aristotélicienne de la science,' in *Aristotle on Science* (ed. Berti) 174–203

– 'Puzzles about Identity: Aristotle and His Greek Commentators,' in *Aristoteles: Werk und Wirkung* (ed. Wiesner) 57–97
– 'Aristotle's Arithmetic,' forthcoming in Proceedings of the Tenth Symposium Aristotelicum
Moraux, P. *Les listes anciennes des ouvrages d'Aristote*. Louvain 1951
– 'A propos du νοῦς θύραθεν chez Aristote,' in *Autour d'Aristote* 255–95
– *À la recherche de l'Aristote perdu: Sur la Justice*. Louvain 1957
– 'From the *Protrepticus* to the Dialogue *On Justice*,' in *Aristotle and Plato* (ed. Düring and Owen) 113–32
Moravcsik, J.M.E. 'Aristotle on Predication,' *PR* 76 (1967) 80–97
Morrison, J.S. 'Four Notes on Plato's *Symposium*,' *CQ* 14 (1964) 42–55
Movia, G. *Anima e Intelletto*. Padova 1968
Mueller, I. 'Greek Mathematics and Greek Logic,' in *Ancient Logic, and Its Modern Interpretation*, ed. J. Corcoran, 35–70. Dordrecht 1974
Mulgan, R.G. 'Aristotle's Doctrine That Man Is a Political Animal,' *Hermes* 102 (1974) 438–45
Mulvany, C.M. 'Notes on the Legend of Aristotle,' *CQ* 20 (1926) 155–67
Natorp, P. 'Thema und Disposition der aristotelischen Metaphysik,' *Philos. Monatsch.* 24 (1888) 37–65, 540–74
Nussbaum, M. *Aristotle's De Motu Animalium*. Princeton 1978
Nuyens, F. *L'évolution de la psychologie d'Aristote*. Louvain/Paris 1948
Oggioni, E. *La 'filosofia prima' di Aristotele*. Milan 1939
Owen, G.E.L. 'The Place of the *Timaeus* in Plato's Later Dialogues,' *CQ* 3 (1953) 79–95
– 'A Proof in the ΠΕΡΙ ΙΔΕΩΝ,' *JHS* 77 (1957) 103–11 (= *Studies in Plato's Metaphysics*, ed. R.E. Allen [London 1965] 293–312)
– 'Logic and Metaphysics in Some Early Works of Aristotle,' in *Aristotle and Plato* (ed. Düring and Owen) 163–90 (= *Articles on Aristotle* 3 [ed. Barnes, Schofield, Sorabji] 13–32)
– 'Τιθέναι τὰ φαινόμενα,' in *Aristote et les problèmes* (ed. Mansion) 83–103 (= *Aristotle* [ed. Moravcsik] 167–90 = *Articles on Aristotle* 1 [ed. Barnes, Schofield, Sorabji] 113–26
– 'Inherence,' *Phronesis* 10 (1965) 97–105
– 'The Platonism of Aristotle,' *PBA* 50 (1965) 125–50 (= *Studies in the Philosophy of Thought and Action*, ed. P.F. Strawson [London 1968] 147–74 = *Articles on Aristotle* 1 [ed. Barnes, Schofield, Sorabji] 14–34)
– 'Aristotle on the Snares of Ontology,' in *New Essays* (ed. Bambrough) 69–95
– 'Dialectic and Eristic in the Treatment of the Forms,' in *Aristotle on Dialectic* (ed. Owen) 103–25
– 'Aristotelian Pleasures,' *PAS* 72 (1971–2) 135–52 (= *Articles on Aristotle* 2 [ed. Barnes, Schofield, Sorabji] 92–103)

Owens, J. 'The Reality of the Aristotelian Separable Movers,' *Rev. Met.* 3 (1949–50) 319–37
– *A History of Ancient Western Philosophy*. New York 1959
– 'Aristotle on Categories,' *Rev. Met.* 14 (1960–1) 73–90 (= *Aristotle* [ed. Catan] 14–22)
– 'The Teleology of Nature in Aristotle,' *Monist* 52 (1968) 159–73 (= *Aristotle* [ed. Catan] 136–47)
– *The Doctrine of Being in the Aristotelian Metaphysics*.[3] Toronto 1978
– 'Aristotle – Motion as Actuality of the Imperfect,' in *Paideia* (1978) 120–32
– 'The Notion of Actuality in Aquinas.' General Address to the 4th Mid-Atlantic States Conference, Villanova University 1979
– 'The Present Status of Alpha Elatton in the Aristotelian *Metaphysics*,' *AGP* 66 (1984) 148–69
– 'Is There Any Ontology in Aristotle?' *Dialogue* 25 (1986) 697–707
Patzig, G. *Aristotle's Theory of the Syllogism*. Dordrecht 1968
– 'Theology and Ontology in Aristotle's *Metaphysics*,' in *Articles on Aristotle* 3 (ed. Barnes, Schofield, Sorabji) 33–49
Peck, A.L. 'The Connate Pneuma: An Essential Factor in Aristotle's Solutions to the Problems of Reproduction and Sensation,' in *Science, Medicine and History: Essays in Honour of C. Singer*, ed. E.A. Underwood, 111–21. Oxford 1953
Pellegrin, P. *La Classification des animaux chez Aristote, Statut de la biologie et unité de l'Aristotelisme*. Paris 1982
– 'Les fonctions explicatives de l'Histoire des Animaux d'Aristote,' *Phronesis* 31 (1986) 148–66
– 'Aristotle: Zoology without Species,' in *Aristotle on Nature* (ed. Gotthelf) 95–115
Penner, T. 'Verbs and the Identity of Actions: A Philosophical Exercise in the Interpretation of Aristotle,' in *Ryle*, ed. O.P. Wood and G. Pitcher, 393–460. London 1971
Philippe, M.-D. '*Analogon* and *Analogia* in the Philosophy of Aristotle,' *The Thomist* 33 (1969) 1–74
Popper, K. *The Open Society and Its Enemies*.[5] London 1966
Pötscher, W. *Struckturprobleme der Aristotelischen und Theophrastischen Gottesvorstellung*. Leiden 1970
Preus, A. 'Science and Philosophy in Aristotle's *Generation of Animals*,' *JHBiol.* 3 (1970) 1–52
– *Science and Philosophy in Aristotle's Biological Works*. Hildesheim/New York 1975
Rabinowitz, W.S. *Aristotle's Protrepticus*. Berkeley 1957
Reale, G. *The Concept of First Philosophy and the Unity of the Metaphysics of Aristotle* (English trans. J. Catan). Albany 1980

Rees, D.A. 'Theories of the Soul in the Early Aristotle,' in *Aristotle and Plato* (ed. Düring and Owen) 191–200

Renehan, R. 'Aristotle as Lyric Poet,' *GRBS* 23 (1982) 251–74

Rhodes, P.J. *A Commentary on the Aristotelean Athēnaiōn Politeia*. Oxford 1981

Rich, A. 'The Platonic Ideas as the Thoughts of God,' *Mnem.* 4.7 (1954) 123–33

Rist, J.M. 'The Order of the Later Dialogues of Plato,' *Phoenix* 14 (1960) 207–21

– 'The Immanence and Transcendence of the Platonic Form,' *Philologus* 108 (1964) 19–32

– *Eros and Psyche*. Toronto 1964

– 'Some Aspects of Aristotelian Teleology,' *TAPA* 96 (1965) 337–49

– 'Notes on Aristotle *De Anima* 3.5,' *CP* 61 (1966) 8–20 (= *Essays in Ancient Greek Philosophy* 1, ed. J.P. Anton and G.L. Kustas [Albany 1971] 505–21)

– 'Aristotle on the Value of Man and the Origin of Morality,' *CJPhil.* 4 (1974) 1–21

– 'Pleasure: 360–300 B.C.,' *Phoenix* 28 (1974) 167–79

– *Human Value*. Leiden 1982

– 'The End of Aristotle's *On Prayer*,' *AJP* 106 (1985) 110–13

Robertson, D.S. 'Aristotle's Story of Heraclitus,' *PCPS* 169–71 (1938) 10

Robin, L. *La théorie platonicienne des Idées et des Nombres d'après Aristote*. Paris 1908

Robinson, H.M. 'Prime Matter in Aristotle,' *Phronesis* 19 (1974) 168–88

Ross, W.D. *Aristotle*. London 1949

Routila, L. *Die aristotelische Idee der ersten Philosophie*. Amsterdam 1969

Rowe, C.J. *The Eudemian and Nicomachean Ethics in the Development of Aristotle's Thought*. Cambridge 1971

– 'Aims and Methods in Aristotle's *Politics*,' *CQ* 27 (1977) 159–72

– 'The Proof from Relatives in the *Peri Ideōn*: Further Reconsiderations,' *Phronesis* 24 (1979) 270–81

Rutten, C. 'L'analogie chez Aristote,' *Rev. Anc. de Phil.* 1 (1983) 31–48

Sachs, D. 'Does Aristotle Have a Doctrine of Secondary Substance?' *Mind* 57 (1948) 221–5

Schlaifer, R.O. 'Greek Theories of Slavery from Homer to Aristotle,' *HSCP* 47 (1936) 165–204 (= *Slavery in Classical Antiquity*, ed. M.I. Finley [Cambridge 1960] 93–132)

Schofield, M. 'Eudoxus in the *Parmenides*,' *Mus. Helv.* 30 (1973) 1–9

Sellars, W. 'Substance and Form in Aristotle,' *JP.* 54 (1957) 688–99

Shorey, P. 'The Origin of the Syllogism,' *CP* 19 (1924) 1–19

Skemp, J.B. 'Plants in Plato's *Timaeus*,' *CQ* 41 (1967) 53–60

– 'The Activity of Immobility,' in *Etudes sur la Métaphysique* (ed. Aubenque) 229–41

Smith, N.D. 'Aristotle's Theory of Natural Slavery,' *Phoenix* 37 (1983) 109–22

– 'Plato and Aristotle on the Nature of Women,' *JHP* 21 (1983) 467–78

Smith, R. 'Aristotle's Two *Analytics*,' *CQ* 32 (1982) 327–35
– 'The Syllogism in *Post. Anal.* 1,' *AGP* 64 (1982) 113–35
Solmsen, F. *Die Entwicklung der Aristotelischen Logik und Rhetorik*. Berlin 1929
– 'Theodektes,' *RE* Band VA, cols. 1722–34
– 'Antecedents of Aristotle's Psychology and Scale of Beings,' *AJP* 76 (1955) 148–64
– 'The Vital Heat, the Inborn *Pneuma* and the *Aether*,' *JHS* 77 (1957) 119–23
– *Aristotle's System of the Physical World*. New York 1960
– 'Dialectic without the Forms,' in *Aristotle on Dialectic* (ed. Owen) 49–68
– 'The Fishes of Lesbos and Their Alleged Significance for the Development of Aristotle,' *Hermes* 106 (1978) 467–84
– 'Citations in Their Bearing on the Origin of "Aristotle" *Meteorologica IV*,' *Hermes* 113 (1985) 448–59
Sorabji, R. 'Function,' *PQ* 14 (1964) 289–302
– 'Body and Soul in Aristotle,' *Philosophy* 49 (1974) 63–89 (= *Articles on Aristotle* 4 [ed. Barnes, Schofield, Sorabji] 42–64)
– *Necessity, Cause and Blame*. London 1980
– 'Definitions: Why Necessary and in What Way?' in *Aristotle on Science* (ed. Berti) 205–44
– *Time, Creation and the Continuum*. London 1983
Stinton, J.C.W. '*Hamartia* in Aristotle and Greek Tragedy,' *CQ* 25 (1975) 221–54
Stough, C. 'Language and Ontology in Aristotle's *Categories*,' *JHP* 10 (1972) 261–72
Strang, C. 'Plato and the Third Man,' *PAS Supp.* 37 (1963) 158–62
Strohm, H. 'Beobachtungen zum vierten Buch der Aristotelischen *Meteorologica*,' in *Zweifelhäftes* (ed. Moraux and Wiesner) 94–115
Strycker, E. de. 'Concepts-clés et terminologie dans les livres ii à vii des *Topiques*,' in *Aristotle on Dialectic* (ed. Owen) 141–63
Szlezák, T.A. 'Alpha Elatton: Einheit und Einordnung in die *Metaphysik*,' in *Zweifelhäftes* (ed. Moraux and Wiesner) 221–59.
Tarán, L. 'The Creation Myth in Plato's *Timaeus*,' in *Essays in Ancient Greek Philosophy* I, ed. J.P. Anton and G.L. Kustas, 372–407. Albany 1971
– *Academica: Plato, Philip of Opus and the Pseudo-Platonic Epinomis*. Leiden 1975
– *Speusippus of Athens*. Leiden 1981
Taylor, A.E. 'Forms and Numbers: A Study in Platonic Metaphysics,' *Mind* 35 (1926) 419–40, and 36 (1927) 12–33 (= *Platonic Studies* [London 1934] 91–150)
Thielscher, P. 'Die relative Chronologie der erhaltenen Schriften des Aristoteles nach den bestimmten Selbstzitaten,' *Philologus* 97 (1948) 229–65
Tracy, T.J. *Physiological Theory and the Doctrine of the Mean in Plato and Aristotle*. The Hague/Paris 1969.

Trendelenburg, F.A. *Geschichte der Kategorienlehre*. Berlin 1846
Verbeke, G. *L'Evolution de la doctrine du pneuma du stoicisme à S. Augustin*. Paris/Louvain 1945
– 'L'idéal de la perfection humaine chez Aristote et l'évolution de sa noétique,' *Fontes Ambrosiani* 25 (1951) 79–95.
– 'The Aristotelian Doctrine of Qualitative Change in Physics VII 3,' in *Essays in Ancient Greek Philosophy* I, ed. J.P. Anton and G.L. Kustas, 546–65. Albany 1971
– 'Aristotle's *Metaphysics* viewed by the Ancient Greek Commentators,' in *Studies in Aristotle* (ed. O'Meara) 107–27
– 'L'objet de la métaphysique selon des études récentes,' *Rev. de Phil. Anc.* 1 (1983) 5–30
Verdenius, W.J. 'Traditional and Personal Elements in Aristotle's Religion,' *Phronesis* 5 (1960) 56–70
– 'Human Reason and God in the *Eudemian Ethics*,' in *Untersuchungen* (ed. Moraux and Harlfinger) 285–97
– 'Hylozoism in Aristotle,' in *Graceful Reason*, ed. L.P. Gerson, 101–14. Toronto 1983
Veuillemin, S. *De la logique à la théologie: Cinque études sur Aristote*. Paris 1967
Veuillemin-Diem, G. 'Anmerkungen zum Pasikles-Bericht und zu Echtheitszweifeln am grösseren und kleineren Alpha in Handschriften und Kommentaren,' in *Zweifelhäftes* (ed. Moraux and Wiesner) 157–92
Vlastos, G. 'Creation in the *Timaeus*: Is It a Fiction?' in *Studies in Plato's Metaphysics*, ed. R.E. Allen, 401–19. London 1965
– 'The "Two-Level Paradoxes" in Aristotle,' in *Platonic Studies*, 323–34. Princeton 1973
Vogel, C.J. de. 'The Legend of the Platonizing Aristotle,' in *Aristotle and Plato* (ed. Düring and Owen) 248–56
– 'Did Aristotle ever Accept Plato's Theory of Transcendent Forms?' *AGP* 47 (1965) 261–98
– 'Aristotle's Attitude to Plato and the Theory of Ideas in the *Topics*,' in *Aristotle on Dialectic* (ed. Owen) 91–102
Waterlow, S. *Nature, Change and Agency in Aristotle's Physics*. Oxford 1982
White, N.P. 'The Origins of Aristotle's Essentialism,' *Rev. Met.* 26 (1972) 57–65
– 'Goodness and Human Aims in Aristotle's Ethics,' in *Studies in Aristotle* (ed. O'Meara) 225–46
Whittaker, J. 'The Eternity of the Platonic Forms,' *Phronesis* 13 (1968) 131–44
– 'Platonic Philosophy in the Early Centuries of the Empire,' in *Aufstieg und Niedergang*, II.36.1, ed. W. Haase and H. Temporini, 81–123. Berlin/New York 1987
Wieland, W. *Die aristotelische Physik*². Göttingen 1970. Chapter 2 is translated into English and printed in *Articles on Aristotle* 1 (ed. Barnes, Schofield, Sorabji), 141–60.

Williams, C.C.P. *Aristotle's De Generatione et Corruptione*. Oxford 1982
Wilpert, P., 'Reste verlorener Aristotelesschriften bei Alexander von Aphrodisias,' *Hermes* 75 (1940) 369–96
– *Zwei aristotelische Frühschriften über die Ideenlehre*. Regensburg 1949
– 'Die aristotelische Schrift *Uber die Philosophie*,' in *Autour d'Aristote* 99–116
Woods, M.J. 'Problems in *Metaphysics* Z, Chapter 13,' in *Aristotle* (ed. Moravcsik) 215–38
– *Aristotle's Eudemian Ethics, Books I, II, and VIII*. Oxford 1982
Wormell, D.E.W. 'The Literary Tradition concerning Hermias of Atarneus,' *YCS* 5 (1935) 57–92

INDEX OF PASSAGES IN ARISTOTLE

GENERAL INDEX

Phoenix Supplementary Volumes Series

1 *Studies in Honour of Gilbert Norwood* edited by Mary E. White
2 *Arbiter of Elegance: A Study of the Life and Works of C. Petronius* Gilbert Bagnani
3 *Sophocles the Playwright* S.M. Adams
4 *A Greek Critic: Demetrius on Style* G.M.A. Grube
5 *The Coastal Demes of Attika: A Study of the Policy of Kleisthenes* C.W.J. Eliot
6 *Eros and Psyche: Studies in Plato, Plotinus, and Origen* John M. Rist
7 *Pythagoras and Early Pythagoreanism* J.A. Philip
8 *Plato's Psychology* T.M. Robinson
9 *Greek Fortifications* F.E. Winter
10 *Comparative Studies in Republican Latin Imagery* Elaine Fantham
11 *Oratory in Cicero's Brutus: Prosopography and Chronology* G.V. Sumner
12 *Caput and Colonate: Towards a History of Late Roman Taxation* Walter Goffart
13 *A Concordance to the Works of Ammianus Marcellinus* Geoffrey Archbold
14 *Fallax opus: Poet and Reader in the Elegies of Propertius* John Warden
15 *Pindar's 'Olympian One': A Commentary* Douglas E. Gerber
16 *Greek and Roman Mechanical Water-Lifting Devices: The History of a Technology* John Peter Oleson
17 *The Manuscript Tradition of Propertius* James L. Butrica
18 Parmenides of Elea *Fragments: A Text and Translation with Introduction* edited by David Gallop
19 *The Phonological Interpretation of Ancient Greek: A Pandialectal Analysis* Vit Bubenik
20 *Studies in the Textual Tradition of Terence* John N. Grant
21 *The Nature of Early Greek Lyric: Three Preliminary Studies* R.L. Fowler
22 Heraclitus *Fragments: A Text and Translation with a Commentary* T.M. Robinson
23 *The Historical Method of Herodotus* Donald Lateiner
24 *Near Eastern Royalty and Rome, 100–30 BC* Richard D. Sullivan
25 *The Mind of Aristotle: A Study in Philosophical Growth* John M. Rist
26 *Trials in the Late Roman Republic, 149 BC to 50 BC* Michael C. Alexander